Jesus in History

An Approach to the Study of the Gospels

Jesus in History

An Approach to the Study of the Gospels

THIRD EDITION

Howard Clark Kee

William Goodwin Aurelio Professor of Biblical Studies, Emeritus
Boston University

Harcourt Brace College Publishers
Fort Worth Philadelphia San Diego New York Orlando Austin San Antonio
Toronto Montreal London Sydney Tokyo

Publisher	TED BUCHHOLZ
Editor in Chief	CHRISTOPHER P. KLEIN
Senior Acquisitions Editor	DAVID TATOM
Developmental Editor	J. CLAIRE BRANTLEY
Project Editor	LOUISE SLOMINSKY
Production Manager	MELINDA ESCO
Art Director	BURL DEAN SLOAN
Electronic Publishing Coordinator	JILL PETERSON

Address for Editorial Correspondence:
Harcourt Brace College Publishers
301 Commerce Street, Suite 3700
Fort Worth, TX 76102

Address for Orders:
Harcourt Brace & Company
6277 Sea Harbor Drive
Orlando, FL 32887-6777
1-800-782-4479, or 1-800-433-0001 (in Florida)

Library of Congress Catalog Card Number: 95-76768

Printed in the United States of America

ISBN: 0-15-501125-1

5 6 7 8 9 0 1 2 3 4   066   9 8 7 6 5 4 3 2 1

PREFACE

As we move toward the two thousandth year since the birth of Jesus, there has been a surge of interest in him and in efforts to reconstruct or redefine what can be known about him. Some of the more radical new portraits of Jesus drawn by certain groups of scholars have attracted the attention of popular media, from newspapers and news magazines to television talk shows. On the other hand, those churches and religious groups that accept only traditional images of Jesus have been growing in membership, not only in America but around the world. Debate in both scholarly circles and among lay people has been spurred by the discovery and growing popular awareness of recently found documents: Jewish, such as the Dead Sea Scrolls; and Christian, such as other Gospels. These may provide new information and insights about the origins of Christianity.

It seems especially important therefore to offer a third edition of *Jesus in History: An Approach to the Study of the Gospels* at this time. This edition aims to provide earnest seekers, in both academic and informal settings, with fresh analysis of the evidence for our knowledge of Jesus. This includes detailed examination of the ancient sources, together with scholarly reconstructions of the figure of Jesus that have been offered over the years. Special attention is given to some of the more recent proposals that claim to alter radically our understanding of who Jesus really was. The method employed here, as in the previous editions, has as its aim to reconstruct and assess the ways in which the figure of Jesus has been perceived from the perspectives of his earliest followers. To understand this evidence one must employ analytical insights from social, cultural, literary, and historical perspectives. It is essential to note the differences within

Judaism and among various first-century religious and philosophical movements about the divine element in human experience and the defining of those communities that claim to have a special relationship with God.

Following the Introduction, which sets the book in the context of current debate about Jesus, Chapter 1 discusses historical methods for knowledge of Jesus, Chapter 2 analyzes Jesus in extrabiblical sources, Chapter 3 seeks to reconstruct and analyze the oldest source underlying the Gospels (the so-called Q source), and then proceeds with detailed examinations of each of the four Gospels in the New Testament (Chapters 4–7). Chapter 8 examines the ways in which the gospel traditions were understood and adapted in the early centuries of the church. Following a concluding statement about the results of our study of the information about Jesus, the Appendix analytically classifies the material incorporated in the first three Gospels.

The process of preparing this third edition has been helped enormously by input from writings by, and scholarly discussions with, colleagues across the country and around the world. I have indicated in footnotes my indebtedness to insights derived from such interchange. Of special help were the perceptive comments of the reviewers who examined drafts of this edition. My thanks go to S. Scott Bartchy, University of California, Los Angeles; Judy D. Saltzman, California Polytechnic State University, San Luis Obispo; and Dana Andrew Thomason, Hendrix College. Of essential importance for me has been access to the Van Pelt Library at the University of Pennsylvania, where I have been designated a Research Fellow since my retirement from the faculty of Boston University. Finally, George Schneider provided invaluable computer assistance for me in the revision process.

CONTENTS

LIST OF ABBREVIATIONS

Biblical Books, Old Testament

Gen.	Genesis	Prov.	Proverbs
Exod.	Exodus	Isa.	Isaiah
Lev.	Leviticus	Ezek.	Ezekiel
Num.	Numbers	Jer.	Jeremiah
Deut.	Deuteronomy	Dan.	Daniel
1 Sam.	First Samuel	Mic.	Micah
Ps.	Psalms	Mal.	Malachi

Biblical Books, New Testament

Matt.   Matthew, Gospel of

Pauline Letters

Rom.	Romans	Gal.	Galatians
1 Cor.	First Corinthians	Phil.	Philippians

Books Outside the Hebrew Canon

Bar.	Baruch
2 Bar.	Second Baruch
1 En.	First Enoch
Sir.	Sirach; also known as Ben Sira, Wisdom of Sirach
Wisd. of Sol.	Wisdom of Solomon

Dead Sea Writings

1QS	Manual of Discipline, or Scroll of the Rule
1QSa	Annexe, or Appendix to the Scroll of the Rule
1QH	Hodayoth, or Thanksgiving Hymns
1QpHab	Commentary (pesher) on the Book of Habakkuk
4QFlorilegium	A collection of prophetic texts found in Dead Sea Cave 4

Noncanonical Early Christian Writings

Inf. Thos.	The Infancy Gospel of Thomas
Prot. of Jas.	Protevangelium of James
Thos.	The Gospel of Thomas
1Qap Gen.	Genesis Apocryphon
11Qtg Job	Targum of Job

Other Terms

ANRW	Aufftieg und Niedergang der Römischen Welt
LXX	The Septaugint, an ancient translation of the Jewish Scriptures into Greek
NRSV	The New Revised Standard Version of the Bible, published in 1989
Oxy.	Oxyrhyuchus Papyr
RSV	The Revised Standard Version of the Bible, first published in 1952
SBLSP	Society of Biblical Literature Seminar Papers
SNTSMS	Society for New Testament Study Monograph Series

INTRODUCTION

Even though nearly 2000 years have passed since Jesus was born, interest in him and the traditions about what he said and did continues to be high in the popular media as well as in scholarly circles, not only in Western countries but also around the world. In China, for example, where the Marxist leadership has no respect for religion—including Christianity—a press in Nanjing is now producing millions of copies of the Bible each year, but is unable to keep pace with the popular demand. When trucks loaded with thousands of Bibles arrived outside the Russian parliament a few years ago, the members rushed out of the building in order to obtain copies for themselves and their friends.

In America and in England during the past two decades, the pop musical *Jesus Christ, Superstar!* has enjoyed long and repeated runs. Nikos Kazantzakis' book *The Last Temptation of Christ*[1] has been widely read and vehemently debated over a period of years. Currently, the opinions of a group calling itself the Jesus Seminar, which claims to be reaching definitive scholarly decisions about what Jesus really said,[2] is receiving wide publicity in the popular press and on television. Other groups of scholars are promoting the thesis that the real Jesus behind the New Testament writings was a kind of itinerant philosopher, on the Cynic-Stoic model, who wandered about Galilee and Judea uttering timeless truths in the form of clever sayings and brief stories.[3] Still others now insist that the historical person commonly known as Jesus was a woman, whose name was Sophia,[4] and that it was ancient male chauvinists who transformed this wise and insightful human into the male figure who has been venerated in the mainstream Christian tradition. A life of Jesus by a prominent English literary figure A.N. Wilson—titled simply, *Jesus*[5]—asserts that Christianity started life as a Jewish heresy, and

1

that its proponents invented the notions of the emergence of a distinct community and of its persecution by the Jewish religious authorities. Others have claimed that the so-called historical Jesus was invented by Christians around the beginning of the second century, including the story of his having been crucified under Pontius Pilate. G.A. Wells is the most persistent and voluble champion of this theory.[6]

The basic sources for our knowledge of Jesus, of course, are the four Gospels included in the New Testament. The English word *gospel* derives from the old English word *godspel*, which meant "good news," and was an obvious translation for the term *euangelion*, which is used in the Greek New Testament for the proclamation by Jesus and then by the apostles about what God was doing and communicating to his people. Later the word served as a designation for the writings in which the career and message of Jesus were conveyed, which came to be known as the four Gospels: Matthew, Mark, Luke, and John. Other Gospels were produced in the early centuries, usually in the name of one of the original followers of Jesus, and these will be discussed later. In recent decades, a group of scholars has proposed that these other Gospels which are not included in the New Testament are antecedents of and sources for the four that are in the New Testament.[7] The evidence concerning Jesus from outside the New Testament is examined in Chapter 2, "Jesus in Extrabiblical Sources."

The question that is obviously important for a whole range of our contemporaries—both scholars and inquiring nonspecialists—is, What can we know about Jesus, this enigmatic figure whose life, death, and continuing influence evoke such interest two millennia after his execution by the Romans?

What Is Meant by "History"?

Before we explore the evidence for the history of Jesus, however, we must raise a more fundamental question: What do we mean when we speak of "history"? The title of this study, *Jesus in History*, intentionally carries multiple meanings. The phrase "in history" can be understood in at least four different ways. These are not mutually exclusive categories, but facets of each have importance for modern undertanding of this ancient figure who evokes such enduring interest and continues to have a significant impact, not only in religious circles but also in the popular culture.

1. One approach to Jesus in history is to examine how historians in the past two-and-one-half centuries have used the historical methods developed during the eighteenth-century Enlightenment, and subsequently refined, in order to reconstruct what has come to be widely known as "the historical Jesus." This line of inquiry has involved not only assessment of historical evidence from the centuries just before and after the birth of Jesus but also the formulation of rational, critical methods by which that evidence could be evaluated and used in historical reconstruction of the life and teachings of Jesus. Major features of this strategy are sketched in Chapter 1.

2. To speak of Jesus in history in the late twentieth century requires one to take account of the radical changes that have occurred in the past few decades as to what is now understood to have been the historical world in which Jesus lived. The new perspectives on Jesus' historical situation have developed in large measure because of newly discovered evidence, as well as from the emergence of fresh understanding of long-known Jewish and early Christian writings and of the context in which they were produced. The new evidence consists of documents discovered in the past fifty years which derive from the period approximately 150 B.C.E. to 150 C.E.[8] These include the Jewish writings commonly known as the Dead Sea Scrolls,[9] which shed new light on the options open to faithful Jews at the time of Jesus, as well as early Christian writings produced by a group (the Gnostics)[10] which split away from the mainstream of the church in the early second century.[11] The discovery of this ancient material has not only provoked fresh appraisals of the Gospels in the New Testament but has also provided new insights concerning the diversity within Judaism in this period. Both Jewish and Christian apocryphal writings[12] have also been reexamined in light of these finds, and new understandings have been achieved about the world of Jesus and about the subsequent development of the Jesus tradition.

Similarly, archaeological explorations in biblical sites, particularly in Galilee, have shown the inadequacy and inappropriateness of the assumptions of many scholars about Palestinian Judaism in the time of Jesus. The traditional image of Galilee as a predominantly rural backwater, where the kind of Judaism which is represented in the Talmud and the Mishnah was dominant, has been shown to be a wholly unwarranted scholarly construct. The diversity among Jews in this region, and the range and depth of their social, cultural, and even linguistic involvement in the Greco-Roman world, have been demonstrated by extensive architectural and inscriptional finds.[13]

3. How we are to understand "history" has also undergone radical change from the post-Enlightenment theory which dominated scholarly investigation of Jesus in history down to the middle of the present century and which still has its champions. The former way of viewing "history" was to assume that the historian simply assembled objective evidence about the past which was then arranged by detached scholarly observation into an historical reconstruction dictated by that evidence. Instead, it is now widely acknowledged that both what the historian finds and how it is interpreted are profoundly influenced by the social and cultural values of the context in which that material originated as well as those of the setting in which the historian carries out the interpretive task.[14]

It is essential to take into account in our investigation the radical changes that came in the current century as to what constitutes human knowledge and what is involved in what is called scientific investigation. In *The Structure of Scientific Revolutions* Thomas S. Kuhn showed that the natural scientists do not carry on their investigations by means of language and questions which are purely neutral, but that their choice of an interpretive paradigm determines large areas of experience. He illustrated this by noting that with the development of atomic theory, chemical reactions "behaved quite differently from the way they had before," the data themselves had changed, and the scientists were now working "in a different world." As a result of the shift in space concepts from those of Euclid to those of Einstein, "the whole conceptual web has to be shifted and relaid; a whole new way of regarding the problems and the factors in their solution emerges."

Similar insights developed in the social sciences, beginning with the work of Alfred Schütz and Thomas Luckmann, who observed that human beings always find themselves in a world that is taken for granted: "It is the unexamined ground of everything given in my experience, as it were, the taken-for-granted frame in which all the problems which I must overcome are placed." For this they coined the term "the structure of the life-world." It is shaped by the social world and expressed in language which simply attributes the factors experienced in life to nature or to society. Peter Berger has described the congenital compulsion of humans "to impose a meaningful order upon reality.... Every human society is an edifice of externalized and objectivated meaning, always intending a meaningful totality."[15]

Historical analysis, therefore, requires the investigator to reconstruct as precisely as possible what the world was within which the writer and his community understood themselves to be living. It is essential to identify not only the explicit conceptual details of the documents under examination but also to seek to understand the assumptions about reality which underlie and contribute to the shaping of the material under investigation. One must take into account both the basis upon which the data were selected for inclusion and the larger framework of meaning in which they have been placed by the historian. The component features that have been chosen for inclusion in the historical reconstruction and the overall framework in which the details are examined involve awareness of the literary and rhetorical forms in which the ancient evidence has been transmitted, the social patterns of life of the people involved, and the unspoken but powerful assumptions that are operative in the thinking of the ancient speakers or writers, as well as of the ancient reporters who have preserved the records. Items that must be recognized in historical analysis include

> How arguments were developed in written and oral debate on common issues.

> What the effect of certain literary styles was on the historical reports.

> What beliefs about the world, its origins, and its operation were shared by ancient writers and readers, and hence are simply taken for granted in historical documents.

Examples of this sort of tacit, basic assumption include the following: In what ways the group, by and for whom the document was produced, believed that God—or the gods—work in the realms of nature and human history? Is there a divine purpose operative, and if so, how is it to be known? What are the objectives of the divine activities in human experience, individually and in wider society? Do the gods also act directly in human life in ways which are contrary to normal expectations? In short, do miracles occur?[16] Do the powers of evil work in the universe and in human experience, and if so, by what means? How is evil to be understood, and how can it be combated? Is evil the result of demonic activities or simply the product of wicked human schemes? What is the basis of identity for members of this community who believe that God or the gods has/have a special purpose for them? How are they to live in order to participate in the fulfillment of that purpose?

4. The historical investigation must take into account the range of meanings and connotations that many of the basic terms have in

the Jewish and early Christian writings. Careful research in the Jewish sources—written and archaeological—from the two centuries before and after the time of Jesus has shown that many of these terms within Judaism shifted meaning significantly over this span of time. Such evolving terms include *synagogue*, *council* (or *Sanhedrin*, as many modern scholars render it), *rabbi*, *Pharisee*. The same shifts and variants in meaning are evident also in relation to such basic Jewish concepts as Messiah, covenant, and even what being a Jew involves. Similarly, among Christians there is a range of understandings of such terms as *Christ*, *church* (or in Greek, *ekklesia*), *covenant*, *Kingdom of God*, and what is required for participation in this new community. These same terms are used in Jewish and early Christian sources with a wide range of meanings. With regard to the promise of entering the Kingdom of God in the New Testament writings, the phrase at times points to a future age on earth in which the powers of evil will be defeated and the purpose of God, in and through his people, will triumph. But a profoundly different set of assumptions is evident, for example, in the Letter to the Hebrews, which is powerfully influenced by a Platonic view of the world, and therefore makes distinctions between the transitory, ephemeral realm of space and time, and the changeless, eternal sphere of being, where the hope of the community is to focus. Analogous distinctions in fundamental views of the world and of ultimate reality significantly influenced the writers who tell the story of Jesus, his life, death, and resurrection. When an early Christian writer uses a term like *Kingdom of God*, one must ask what is the larger perspective on reality that is operative for the writer of the passage under scrutiny and for that segment of the Jewish or early Christian community that is being addressed. Historical investigation of Jesus and his impact on his contemporaries must be based on sensitivity to the perspectives, assumptions, and values of those who preserved and transmitted the traditions about him.

Prime Examples of Different Frameworks of Meaning in the Early Reports About Jesus

The Gospels serve as clear examples of the diversity of perspectives in which human beings think and act as they assess the past and understand the present and the future. We shall trace in detail the differences in historical outlook and evidence concerning Jesus adduced by the early Christian writers, but it may be useful to sketch briefly what some of the distinctions are that can be discerned in the primary sources for our knowledge of Jesus.

In the Gospel of Mark and in the Sayings source known by scholars as Q (used by the writers of Matthew and Luke)[17] Jesus is pictured as messenger and active agent of the coming era when God's purpose will rule the world (Kingdom of God), the powers of evil will be defeated, and his faithful people will be vindicated. The perspective on the world and the style of communication are akin to those of Jewish apocalyptic: God has revealed to his chosen people his purpose for them and his plan for the triumph of his will in the world.

In the Gospel of Matthew, the End of the Age is still expected, but the community that is addressed is offered detailed guidelines for the moral behavior of its members, for their relationships with their Jewish contemporaries, for leadership and decision making in the interim before the New Age comes. And Jesus is depicted as a new Moses, bringing God's message to his people from the mountain and setting up the norms by which they are to live.

In the Gospel of Luke—which unlike the other Gospels has a second volume, the Book of Acts—we have a work which combines literary and conceptual features from the Jewish Scriptures with modes of communication widely used in the Greco-Roman world. Here there is heavy emphasis on the role of Jesus as seeking to achieve the establishment of a new community which will bring together people from a wide range of social, cultural, and linguistic origins to constitute the newly defined people of God. This cross-cultural outreach which (according to the Gospel of Luke) Jesus initially launches in Galilee, Paul (in the Book of Acts) expands symbolically in the wider Roman world, culminating in his activity in Rome itself.

In the Gospel of John, the story of Jesus is told in a manner which is not only different from the other Gospels in style and at most points in content, but keeps moving the reader beyond the realm of information about Jesus' career and teaching to the mystical realm of present participation in eternal life. The hope of a new era has not disappeared, but there is a recurrent emphasis on the new life in which the followers of Jesus now share: They *have* life (John 5:24); they *have* been given eternal life and shall *never* die (John 10:28).

Other Gospels, such as the Gospel of Thomas, have no interest in Jesus' activities: his healings, his sufferings and death, his resurrection. Instead, they concentrate on and rework the traditions of his teachings in such a way as to present him as one who transcends space-time limitations and whose aim is to free human beings from all such distinctive human characteristics as sexuality and bodily functions (eyes, hands, feet).[18] Jesus is portrayed as a divine being who merely masquerades in human form, and whose goal is to liberate humans from all bodily identity and limitations.

In each of these presentations of Jesus, here sketched briefly and analyzed in detail later, there are not only differences in content, but also fundamental divergences as to views of the world, of God, of divine purpose, and of human destiny. Each of these accounts of Jesus rests on a different set of assumptions about reality, although these distinctions are largely implicit in each of the writings rather than being explicitly indicated. Responsible historical analysis must be concerned, however, not only for what these writers state directly, but also for what they take for granted—the assumptions about reality and about Jesus that are shared with their respective communities and are largely implicit in what they wrote. This mode of analysis enables us to understand Jesus "in history" in all four of the ways sketched previously:

1. Examining the modes of inquiry and alleged historical results of post-Enlightenment inquiries and reconstructions of Jesus, his teachings, and his career.

2. Fresh investigation of the time of Jesus in light of newly found documents and other ancient evidence—archaeological and literary—which provides new information and insights concerning the Roman world in the time of Jesus.

3. Careful attention to new perceptions about the proper role of historical inquiry, including how to use the ancient evidence and what the changing social settings were that produced this material.

4. The cautions and encouragements which derive from these lines of investigation must be brought to bear on the specifics of the context in which Jesus lived—in its Jewish as well as its Greco-Roman dimensions—and the range of ways in which his life and work were responded to in the first two centuries of the Common Era.

Before addressing these issues in detail, it is important to trace the rise of the historical methods and quests during the past two centuries that have posed these questions about historical investigation and have produced the historical constructs which purport to describe for us the historical Jesus.

NOTES

[1] Translated from the Modern Greek; first English ed., New York: Simon & Schuster, 1960; 9th printing, 1968.

[2] The Jesus Seminar and other comparable groups reassessing the Jesus tradition are analyzed later, pp. 33–34.

[3] Various individuals and scholarly coteries are promoting these images of Jesus. Helmut Koester, in his *Ancient Christian Gospels: Their History and Development* (Philadelphia: Trinity Press International, 1990), pp. 149–50, develops the thesis that the original edition of the sayings source (known as Q; see Chapter 3, "Jesus as God's Eschatological Messenger: The Q Document") was a collection of wisdom sayings, devoid of accounts of healings and exorcisms, of the other activities of Jesus, and of his death and resurrection. He subscribes to the hypothesis of John Kloppenburg (in *The Formation of Q* [Philadelphia: Fortress Press, 1987]) that all the apocalyptic features in the Q tradition were added and interfere with the original purely wisdom material. By combining this reconstructed version of Q with the Gospel of Thomas (see Chapter 8, pp. 247–50), Koester composes an image of Jesus as purely a purveyor of wisdom. Burton L. Mack comes up with a similar reconstruction of Jesus in *A Myth of Innocence: Mark and Christian Origins* (Philadelphia: Fortress Press, 1988) and in his reconstruction of what he considers to have been the earliest gospel in *The Lost Gospel* (San Francisco: HarperCollins, 1993). For Mack, all the canonical Gospels are later developments, in contrast to which he offers his own reconstruction of what the earliest gospel contained. These and related works are discussed in detail in Chapter 3, on the Q source.

[4] Susan Cady, *Sophia: The Future of Feminist Spirituality* (San Francisco: HarperCollins, 1986).

[5] New York and London: W.W. Norton, 1992, p. xi.

[6] G.A. Wells, *The Jesus of the Early Christians* (London: Pemberton, 1971); *Did Jesus Exist?* (London: Pemberton, 1975); *The Historical Evidence for Jesus* (New York: Prometheus, 1982).

[7] A prime example of this kind of proposal is that of John Dominic Crossan, in *Four Other Gospels: Shadows on the Contours of Canon* (Minneapolis and New York: Seabury, 1985). Crossan's candidates for earlier Gospels (or traditions) are the Gospel of Thomas, a fragmentary work known as Egerton Papyrus 2; the Secret Gospel of Mark (of which only a fragment is available); and the Gospel of Peter. These will be discussed in Chapter 2, where we examine extrabiblical sources, and in Chapter 8, in connection with the Gospels in the early church.

[8] In recent years the discussion about Jesus in history has had major contributions from scholars not committed to Christian faith, so instead of making the familiar chronological distinction of Before Christ (B.C.) and *Anno Domini* (A.D.—in the year of Our Lord), a common practice has been to refer to the change in chronology as Before the Common Era and the Common Era (B.C.E. and C.E.).

[9]A comprehensive translation of the Dead Sea material, with brief useful introductions, is that of Geza Vermes, *The Dead Sea Scrolls in English*, 3d ed. (London and New York: Penguin Books, 1987).

[10]Found in the 1940s at Nag Hammadi, a monastic site in Egypt, these Gnostic writings have evoked claims made by some scholars as to their historical value which are discussed in Chapters 2 and 8. An English translation of the basic documents from this collection is available in *The Nag Hammadi Library in English*, ed. James M. Robinson (San Francisco: Harper & Row, 1977).

[11]A perceptive analysis of this material against the background of early Christianity is that of Edwin Yamauchi in his *Pre-Christian Gnosticism: A Survey of the Proposed Evidences* (Grand Rapids, MI: Eerdmans, 1973).

[12]The Jewish apocryphal writings are available in fresh English translations in the New Revised Standard Version of the Bible, which appeared in 1989. The writings which were never included in the Jewish or Christian Scriptures have been published in *The Old Testament Apocrypha*, ed. James H. Charlesworth, vol. 1, 1983; vol. 2, 1985 (Garden City, NY: Doubleday). The New Testament noncanonical writings were published in translation in *New Testament Apocrypha*, ed. Edgar Hennecke, a new edition of which has recently been prepared by R. McL. Wilson, vol. 1, *Gospels and Related Writings*, 1991; vol. 2, *Writings Related to the Apostles; Apocalypses and Related Writings*, 1992. (Louisville, KY: Westminster/John Knox Press).

[13]Eric M. Meyers and James F. Strange, *Archaeology, the Rabbis, and Early Christianity* (Nashville: Abingdon Press, 1981).

[14]Here is sketched briefly the methodological task involved in historical interpretation, as illumined by insights from the sciences and sociology; a fuller analysis is offered in my book, *Knowing the Truth: A Sociological Approach to New Testament Interpretation* (Minneapolis: Fortress Press, 1989; rev. ed. forthcoming from Trinity Press International).

[15]Alfred Schütz and Thomas Luckmann, *The Structures of the Life-World* (trans. Richard Zaner and Tristram Engelhardt, Jr.; Evanston, IL: Northwestern University Press, 1973), p. 4; Peter Berger, *The Sacred Canopy* (Garden City, NY: Doubleday, 1967), pp. 22–28.

[16]Investigation of the range and significance of miracles in the Greco-Roman period, before and after the turn of the eras, is offered in my book, *Miracle in the Early Christian World: A Study in Sociohistorical Method* (New Haven: Yale University Press, 1983), and in *Medicine, Miracle and Magic in New Testament Times* (Cambridge: Cambridge University Press, 1986; reprint, 1990).

[17]Q, which probably derives from the German word *Quelle*, meaning "source," does not exist as an ancient document, but can be inferred from the many passages where Matthew and Luke are in basic agreement while departing from their common basic source, Mark. Detailed analysis of this source is offered in Chapter 3.

[18]The Gospel of Thomas is discussed in detail along with the other Gnostic Gospels in Chapter 8.

CHAPTER 1

The Rise of Historical Methods for Analysis of the Evidence Concerning Jesus

Historical inquiry about Jesus and the debate over the results are almost as old as the Jesus tradition itself. In the first half of the second century C.E. Papias, bishop of Hierapolis, reported that Mark wrote down from memory, presumably after the death of Peter, what he had learned from that apostle. Later in the second century Clement of Alexandria describes how Peter's many hearers prevailed on Mark to write down what Peter had preached about the message and activities of Jesus, adding that Peter merely acquiesced in the proposal. Recently a dubious document was discovered not far from Jerusalem which reports that when Mark moved to Alexandria after Peter was martyred, he took with him his own notes and those of Peter, on the basis of which he composed both the Gospel of Mark and a "more spiritual gospel" to bring out the mystical meaning of Jesus for those who had gained special access to divine truth.[1] In the eighteenth century, however, what is now called critical historical method began to be articulated and employed in the analysis of these ancient documents. Yet from the outset, the resulting critical essays investigating the historical Jesus have differed in the results which were produced. By an examination of the underlying assumptions of some major representative philosophers and historians of the past three centuries who have dealt with this question, light can be shed in two directions: (1) to increase our awareness of the presuppositions about the nature of reality as they affect the investigator's view of historical problems and the solutions that are offered; (2) to invite scrutiny through and behind the words of the ancient gospel writers (and others who have dealt with the Jesus tradition) with the aim of discerning how differences among the basic assumptions of these writers affected the ways

11

in which their evidence is presented. Useful surveys of critical biblical scholarship, including discussions of the historical Jesus question, are available[2] and will not be undertaken here. Our aim will be to focus on specific thinkers and issues that illustrate how the historical questions about Jesus were posed by these pioneers in critical analysis and how, as a result, they are posed for those investigating the subject today.

Faith Challenged by Reason: Miracles and the Belief in Special Revelation to a Chosen People

John Locke (1632–1704) and his contemporaries were the first to raise these questions about the Bible: Can we believe that miracles happen? Can we accept the notion that God would reveal himself to a particular segment of humanity? So long as the Bible as a whole and the Gospels in particular were considered to be sacred books containing divine truth, it was possible to treat any seeming discrepancy as only an apparent difficulty. Any report that strained the credulity of the reader—such as Jesus walking on the water of the Lake of Galilee (Mark 6:45–52)—was treated as a summons to faith rather than as an occasion for doubt. If John's gospel reports that Jesus cleansed the Temple at the beginning of his public career but the other Gospels say that he did so at the end, the explanation is either that he did it twice or that John wrote a spiritual gospel[3] that has no interest in chronological sequence. The first serious challenge to the truth of the Gospels came with the resurgence in the seventeenth and early eighteenth centuries of a version of the originally Stoic belief in natural law. Miracles came to be regarded as violations of natural law. How could anyone whose reason led him or her to discern the operation of universal natural laws assert the truth of documents that purported to be revealed but that, especially in the accounts of miracles, were in direct conflict with natural law? In a little book called *The Reasonableness of Christianity As Delivered in the Scriptures* (1695), Locke appealed to his readers to meet on the common ground provided by reason and to work together for interpretations of Scripture and religious traditions that, he believed, when properly understood would contain nothing that was in conflict with reason. The implications of his book for orthodox faith were thought to be so radical that Locke published it anonymously, but his identity as author soon became known, and he was subjected to bitter personal attack.

Locke sought to demonstrate the reasonableness of Christianity in two main ways: (1) by showing that certain passages in the Gospels, though outwardly puzzling, actually related wise actions by Jesus or at least sensible precautions; and (2) by maintaining that belief in the possiblity of knowledge of God through natural law and belief in a special revelation of God through Christ were not intellectually incompatible. Specifically, Locke dealt at length with the fact that in the Gospels Jesus seems to want to conceal his messiahship,[4] even though he also affirmed that confession of Jesus' messiahship was essential to human salvation. The explanation that Locke offered was that if Jesus had publicly announced his messiahship, his Jewish contemporaries would have understood him to be laying claim to political, nationalistic leadership which would have obscured Jesus' intention to reach out to all humanity through his gospel. Jesus showed wisdom in selecting as disciples those who were not intellectually aggressive, since at the initial stages they might have propagandized too militantly and in too limited ways for what was only later to be disclosed as a universal faith. When that time arrived, God had ready the brilliant and more cosmopolitan Paul to launch that demanding enterprise.

In attempting to demonstrate the compatibility of belief in revelation and in reason, Locke stated that the truth of natural law had been attained by others than Christians, since much of Judaism and Platonic thought were compatible with Christianity as reasonable people understood it. What was the need for God's special revelation in Christ? According to Locke, it was essential that divine truth would be expressed concretely in the authoritative words and acts of a human being, Jesus, since otherwise most of humanity in its cultural and intellectual limitations could never have laid hold on the truth by concepts alone. Even Plato, whose rationality taught him that there was only one god, went along with the popular polytheism of his day. How much more, then, do lesser individuals need the commanding word of Christ to bring them to recognize the truth!

Equally problematical in the minds of Locke and his contemporaries was the claim of Christians that the New Testament and the events and teachings which it documented were in some sense the revelation of God. How could anyone defend God's justice if his self-disclosure was made to only a tiny segment of the human race and in a special set of historical circumstances? This issue struck at the heart of the Christian claim that God had revealed himself definitively in the history of Jesus of Nazareth. Addressing himself to this problem, Matthew Tindal (1653?–1733) wrote a book whose title reveals its central thesis: *Christianity As Old As the Creation; Or, The Gospel, a Republication of the Religion of Nature* (1730). Tindal maintained that what was true in Christianity was not peculiar to it and what was particularistic in it was not to be regarded as true. The effect of Tindal's thesis was to encourage an atmosphere of free thinking, in which attacks were made on the moral lapses in the lives of biblical characters and in which fraud was attributed to Jesus' disciples. We shall see that both these themes have recurred in present-day analysis of the Gospels.

A German Semitic scholar, Hermann Samuel Reimarus (1694–1768), was strongly influenced by such English writers as Locke and Tindal but did not limit his criticism of the Gospels to the rejection of miracles or to the limitation of Jesus' activities to Jews. Once the image of the Gospels as infallible records had been shattered, he went so far as to write a treatise (published anonymously and only after his death)[5] in which he challenged the integrity of the disciples, declaring that Jesus had preached a this-worldly kingdom along the political lines of Jewish nationalistic hopes, and that disappointed disciples had created a system of thought in which Jesus was pictured as a universal, spiritual Savior. They reworked the whole story of his ministry to conform to their new system.[6]

The reactions to this kind of radical criticism of the gospel accounts were largely of a predictable sort. The orthodox responded by reaffirming the truth of the tradition and by calling on the faithful to reject the attacks of the enemies of the faith. Others, however, in response to the growing mood of disbelief in miracles, reassessed the gospel evidence while seeking to affirm the basic truth of the biblical record of Jesus. Rightly understood, their argument ran, there is nothing incredible in the miracle stories. The seeming difficulties arose from the naive way in which the gospel writers reported everyday occurrences. Typical of this effort to mediate between orthodoxy and rationalism was the proposal by Heinrich Eberhard Gottlob Paulus (1761–1851) that the story of the transfiguration of Jesus was a pious reaction to a purely natural occurrence: the play of lights and mist on the mountaintop as a storm passed over. The report of the angels at Jesus' tomb developed from a superstitious interpretation of the winding sheets that were lying about outside the tomb. There are other examples of scholars' efforts to furnish rational explanations for miracle stories: When Jesus appeared to walk on the water, he was actually in the shallows, and a mist covering the surface added to the illusion that he was walking on the surface; at the Feeding of the Five Thousand, most of the people had their own food but kept it hidden until a little boy set a good example by offering to share his lunch.

These attempts to "explain" the miracles were a tribute to the ingenuity of the interpreters, but were no credit to the gospel writers, who appeared at best as dupes and at worst as frauds. Moreover, the narratives were no longer useful testimonies for faith. Since the miracle stories had been offered as signs of Jesus' extraordinary powers (for example, John 2:11; Luke 11:20), they were now rendered irrelevant for faith and for the history of Jesus. Reason was of no help in guaranteeing the revelatory nature of the gospel records about Jesus. On the contrary, rationalistic interpretations of the miracle stories seemed to transform the gospel accounts from "good news" into gross misunderstanding.

The problem posed by the New Testament's locating God's special revelation in a specific time (the first few decades C.E.) and a single setting (Palestine) has never been resolved, but in the nineteenth century it failed to hold a place of importance equivalent to the problems of historical knowledge about Jesus and what to believe about the miracles attributed to him. For the orthodox, special revelation was no difficulty, since they believed in divine sovereignty and could simply assign such problems to the category of an inscrutable mystery, known only to God. Meanwhile, many rationalist thinkers thought they could extract from the historical reports and tales about Jesus certain timeless, universal truths. Some philosophically inclined historians considered Jesus to be a manifestation of the universal divine spirit, so that while he was historically unique, he was only the highest and best manifestation of divine self-disclosure which has been going on throughout human history by means of other individuals and movements, and in other cultures than that of first-century Judaism. The critics who concentrated on the teachings of Jesus found their principle of universality in his ethics, which they believed were aimed at achieving the highest good for the whole of humanity and were compatible with the best ethical ideals the world around. The philosophies of Immanuel Kant (1724–1804) and Georg Wilhelm Friedrich Hegel (1770–1831) fostered these interpretations of Jesus as the ideal god-man and as the teacher of humanity's loftiest moral principles.

The Reconciliation of Faith and Reason in Myth

By the early part of the nineteenth century, the search for universal principles opened up a new strategy for dealing with the problem of faith
and history in the gospel narratives. The new method held out the hope
that the Gospels could be analyzed in a rational way. In the late eighteenth
century the emergent scholarly attention to the literatures and cultures
of other peoples had created an awareness that those who lived in other
cultural settings thought about and reacted to the world around them in
ways quite different from those that prevailed in Western Europe in
1800. At the same time, scholars assumed—as they had in the past—
that external features may differ, but that the underlying humanity is one.
Thus a kernel of universal truth awaits discovery behind and beneath
the merely accidental cultural differences that are evident in documents.
Accordingly, it was considered important for scholars to seek the universal, timeless meaning in the words of ancient and alien literatures
and to probe the writer's intent in order to discern the underlying timeless truth, of which the author may have been only dimly aware, if at all.

Applied to the study of the Gospels, this approach opened the way
for a fresh look at the history of Jesus and especially the miracle stories.
The concept that was supposed to make possible a gospel analysis that
avoided both the credulousness of the supernaturalistic approach and
the extreme rationalism of the dominant historical approach was that
of *myth*. The man who first employed the mythical approach to the
Gospels was David Friedrich Strauss (1808–1874), who as a young
instructor at Tübingen University published a massive two-volume
work, *Das Leben Jesu* [The Life of Jesus] (1835–1836). He simultaneously achieved enduring renown and ruined his chances for a profes-
sorial post by reason of the radical conclusions he reached concerning
the historical reliability of the gospel accounts.

Strauss did not regard myth as fraudulent fiction, invented by a
writer consciously bent on deception of his readers.[7] Rather, he
understood myth to be "the representation of an event or an idea in
a form which is historical, but which is determined by sensual, fantasy-
laden modes of thought and speech from antiquity."[8] The stress in
this definition should fall on "event or idea"—that which has the
appearance of history, but which is not in fact historical record.
According to Strauss, there are three main types of myths: (1) *historical myths*, which originate as stories of actual happenings, but which
blend the human with the divine and are thus colored by ancient
modes of thought; (2) *philosophical myths*, which clothe in historical

garb a thought, speculation, or idea; and (3) *poetic myths,* in which the imagery of fantasy has all but swallowed up the original fact or idea behind the mythical garb, but not the historical fact behind the description. Strauss wanted to show that the historical form of the narrative was only an appearance; the essential element was the *idea* veiled by the mythic form. There was, of course, a core of historical evidence that could be recovered about the career of Jesus, but it was not those events that gave continuing meaning to the figure of Jesus in the church's faith, nor was this historical account anything more than a framework on which the enduring mythical meaning of Jesus was hung. The mythicizing process, Strauss explained, can take place quickly. In the case of Jesus, it began among his followers immediately following his death. The objection is therefore groundless that there was not sufficient time between the Crucifixion and the rise of the gospel tradition for mythmaking to have occurred. Strauss explained that the conditions for instant mythmaking were present in the minds of the disciples:

> Around a great individual, especially one with whom is connected a profound revolution in the life of men, there soon crystallizes an unhistorical cycle of saga-like glorification, even in the most barren of historical epochs. Only think about a young community, which honors its founder with an enthusiasm that is all the greater because he had been snatched out of their lives in such an unexpected and tragic way, a community impregnated with a mass of new ideas which gave promise of reshaping the world; a community of orientals, for the most part uneducated men who were disposed to appropriate and express those ideas, not in the abstract form of comprehension and concept, but solely in the concrete manner of imagination—that is, as picture and story. It will become apparent that what did come into being under these circumstances was bound to happen: a series of sacred narratives through which the whole complex of ideas—both new ones originated by Jesus and old ones taken over and attached to him—was given concrete form in a series of single moments in his life. The simple historical framework of Jesus' life—that he grew up in Nazareth, had himself baptized by John, gathered disciples, wandered about the land of the Jews teaching, that in every situation he set himself against the Pharisees and invited men to share in the messianic kingdom, that at the end he was killed by the hatred of the Pharisaic party and died on the cross—this framework was embellished with the most richly diverse and meaningful network of pious

reflections and imaginings, in which all the ideas of early Christianity concerning the master, seemingly snatched away from them but actually transformed, were woven into the whole course of his life.[9]

Strauss had no interest in differentiating between those gospel traditions that were historically reliable and those that were not, as the rationalists had tried to do. Rather, he sought to show, mostly by comparison with Old Testament miracle stories, that the historylike narratives in the gospel were mythical, and that as such they were not objective history but ancient vehicles for conveying eternal religious truth. Accordingly, Strauss' work had no positive historical contribution to make to the study of Jesus, just as the dogmatic recontruction with which he ended his *Life of Jesus* found few takers in the academic marketplace. But what Strauss sought to do—and in this respect the aims and strategy of his work are very much with us today—was to demonstrate that the Gospels are not straightforward accounts of miraculous happenings or of actual occurrences falsely interpreted as miracles that must be "explained away." For example, the story of the transfiguration of Jesus, which believers in the miraculous accepted without question as having occurred and which (as noted earlier) rationalists explained away as the illusion produced by a storm passing overhead while Jesus stood on the mountaintop, Strauss interpreted in this way:

> The mythic tale of the transfiguration of Jesus has for historical foundation the extraordinary impression made by Jesus upon his contemporaries and upon the following generations; the ideal part, or if it be wished, the philosophical part, is that the Messiah was expected to resemble Moses and Elijah, and as a consequence, the illumination of his face is a mythical motif based on the Old Testament narratives, themselves partly mythical and partly historical.[10]

Thus for Strauss it was the faith discerned by reason behind the biblical record that was to be affirmed, not the outward form of the revelatory writings.

Reactions Against Mythical Interpretation of the Gospels

The reaction provoked by Strauss' mythical life of Jesus was violent in his own time, and its effects continue to be evident in studies of the historical Jesus today, both among orthodox writers, who in some cases show little firsthand knowledge of Strauss or the issues he raised, and among those who are as skeptical as Strauss was about the possibility of historical knowledge of Jesus, but who propose instead a conceptual reconstruction of Jesus. Although interpreters of the Jesus tradition since Strauss continue to be interested in the mythopoetic interpretation of the Gospels, the more powerful impact of his work concerns the problem he posed: Is it possible by critical methods to achieve a historical reconstruction of the life and teachings of Jesus?

Attempts at Historical Reconstruction of the Life of Jesus

There are two men who, more than any others, represent the attempt in the nineteenth century to develop a purely historical approach to the question of the history of Jesus: Ferdinand Christian Baur (1792–1860) and Heinrich Julius Holtzmann (1832–1910). Their work may be said to mark, respectively, the beginning and the culmination of what was considered to be the consistently historical view of the New Testament. Both these scholars sought to answer the question, What can be known historically about the origins of Christianity in general and about the life and teachings of Jesus in particular?

Baur's great contribution was to develop what he regarded as a thoroughly historical method for assessing the evidence about Jesus. His chief concern was to show the importance of investigating the rise of Christianity by the same methods and approach as would be used in any secular historical inquiry. His method, however, was powerfully influenced by the philosophy of Hegel, who depicted history as developing through interaction between opposing forces (thesis and antithesis) which moves to higher levels of spiritual achievement (synthesis). Baur found this pattern of development in the conflict between the Jewish and Gentile parties in the first-century Jerusalem church, which accounted for the tensions and dynamics of the church's subsequent growth, and also provided the seeds for the theological differences represented by the various books of the New Testament. Baur's entire procedure was based on the conviction that history is a network of cause and effect, and that the task of the historian is to rediscover the links that formed and shaped the historical patterns of development. Having accepted these assumptions about historical method, he sought to develop a unified approach to the history of Christian beginnings by means of what he considered to be a position of pure objectivity:

> My standpoint is in one word the purely historical one; namely, that the one thing to be aimed at is to place before ourselves the materials given in the history [of the New Testament] as they are objectively, and not otherwise, so far as that is possible. How far I have succeeded in this is not for me to say; but I am not conscious of having followed any other aim.[11]

The influence of Hegel can also be seen in Baur's notion that the moral and spiritual ideal, which is the essence of Christianity, is able to permeate civilization and to claim and hold human allegiance only because it was clothed historically in concrete human form. The Jewish national consciousness was transformed by Jesus into a radical and absolute inward moral consciousness, and thus became a universal consciousness for the world.[12] The continuity of Jesus' teaching with Judaism, as well as his important advances over Judaism (which were quantitatively so great as to be qualitatively different),[13] Baur documented by concentrating on the *synoptics*, the first three Gospels of the New Testament, which have similarities of substance and arrangement not found in John, and particularly on the Sermon on the Mount and the parables.[14] He did not dismiss the Gospel of John altogether but considered it to be of theological rather than historical value.[15]

On the question of miracle, Baur displayed relatively little concern as compared with Strauss. He declared at the outset that the appeal to miracles has no place in the work of the historian, since "miracle is an absolute beginning" and therefore by definition severs the links that bind together historical events. Even if we think of only one miracle, the "miracle of the absolute beginning" of Christianity, we have still to ask why it took place at one particular point in time—and then we are in the midst of questions that can be answered only on the basis of historical investigation. As for the miracle of the Resurrection, it did not matter for Baur whether it was an observable, objective, miraculous event or an inward, subjective, psychological experience:

> What history requires as the necessary antecedent of all that is to follow, is not so much the fact of the resurrection as the belief that it was a fact.... The important "historical fact" is the consciousness of the disciples that Jesus had risen from the dead. As a fact of their consciousness, it was as real to them as any historical event.[16]

The stage was now set and the main procedures outlined for what was announced as a purely historical analysis of the New Testament. But in spite of the avowed "objectivity," the investigators had actually determined beforehand—largely from the philosophies of Kant and Hegel—what the enduring elements of Christianity were, and were therefore preconditioned to find them at the end of their avowedly historical research. We shall see that this kind of circular reasoning is still dominant in the work of current scholars.[17] It is easy enough to adopt a patronizing attitude toward the naivete with which this "presuppositionless" investigation was begun, yet one must admire not only the grand manner in which the comprehensive research into Christian beginnings was launched, but also the genuine and enduring merit of the scholarly recognition of some sort of interdependence among the synoptic Gospels, as an important part of the attempt to reconstruct the complicated development of historical Christianity, for which the scattered writings of the New Testament provide primary but incomplete evidence.

The attitude of confidence in the possiblities of historical reconstruction reached a climax in the synoptic studies of H.J. Holtzmann.[18] From early times, questions had been raised in the church about the order of composition of the Gospels. It was widely believed, for example, that Mark was an abridgment of Matthew—a theory which still has vigorous defenders.[19] By the second half of the nineteenth century, however, it was widely acknowledged that Mark was the first of the three Gospels and that John represented a quite independent tradition. Holtzmann's investigation noted that where Mark and Matthew report the same incident, it is told in shorter form by Matthew, even though his gospel as a whole is far longer than Mark's. The same is true of parallel accounts of miracle stories in Mark and Luke. A clear instance of this is the story of the healing of the daughter of Jairus (Mark 5:21–43; Matt. 9:18–26; Luke 8:40–56). What is told by Matthew in nine verses and by Luke in seventeen takes twenty-three in Mark. And the crudity of Mark's language shows that he is not expanding either of the more polished versions found in Matthew and Luke.

Building on the work which had demonstrated Mark to be the earliest of the synoptics,[20] Holtzmann went on to show that Matthew and Luke had used a common sayings source in their Gospels but had relied on Mark for the basic framework and sequence, as well as the major narrative content. The large body of material reporting the teachings of Jesus in Matthew and Luke— of which the Sermon on the Mount is a prime example—has no parallel in Mark, and yet in many passages Matthew and Luke exhibit such close verbal similarity that their use of a common sayings source is the most plausible explanation. Scholars have come to identify this sayings source used by Matthew and Luke as Q (as noted on pp. 33–35). Chapter Three of this work offers a reconstruction and analysis of this source. These two critical conclusions—that Mark was the earliest gospel and that Q was used by Matthew and Luke to supplement Mark—are widely accepted down to the present as the best basic source theory to account for the similarities and differences in structure and content among the synoptic Gospels. Less widely accepted is the assumption that Matthew and Luke each had access to special written sources. An important possibility is that the Jesus tradition was handed down for many decades orally rather than in written form, as the early second century C.E. writer, Papias, claimed.[21] The rise of other analytical methods has lessened the importance of the purely literary analysis of the gospel tradition, but Holtzmann's argument for the priority of Mark and for the sayings source used by Matthew and Luke made a lasting contribution to the study of the Jesus tradition.[22]

Holtzmann also concluded from his demonstration of the Markan priority that the sequence of events in Mark's gospel was therefore historically reliable. But this assumption has been challenged on the ground that the greater antiquity of a source does not guarantee its historical reliability. More importantly, Holtzmann ignored the strong likelihood that Mark—like any writer—selected material (isolated sayings and narratives) from a variety of sources and arranged it in a way that would serve his own distinctive ends. We shall examine in Chapters 3 to 7 how in each case the writers of the Gospels have chosen and adapted the Jesus tradition in fulfillment of a special overall set of aims which reflect the needs and concerns of the community for which each particular gospel was prepared.

Limiting the Search to the Recovery of Authentic Teachings of Jesus

Another way of dealing with the problem of divergences among the Gospels, as to the order of events in the career of Jesus and with the lack of evidence for tracing a pattern of development in the life and consciousness of Jesus, is simply to dismiss all biographical features

and to concentrate solely on his teachings. Miracles, journeys, Crucifixion, and Resurrection are simply brushed aside. This decision is a
value judgment: that the enduring significance of Jesus does not lie
in the activities and events of his life, but exclusively in the contents
of his teachings. But even in this more limited field of investigation,
certain choices must be made as to which among the array of sayings attributed to Jesus are to be regarded as authentic and which as
later accretions—what is primary and what is peripheral. Once certain criteria for authenticity have been adopted, an impressive case
can be made for reconstructing what Jesus "really" taught. But the
reader must be willing to accept the scholarly presuppositions, which
are usually unacknowledged by the one who is creating the "historical" picture of Jesus. As we shall note, this circular procedure in
the guise of historical inquiry continues to be operative down to the
present day.

The classic instance of such an approach to the historical Jesus
is that of Adolf von Harnack (1851–1930), whose popular lectures,
What Is Christianity? (1900), were quickly translated into English and
widely read in England and America.[23] Many scholars had recognized
that the message and aims of Jesus were expressed in terms akin to
Jewish apocalypticism. Apocalyptic is a scholarly designation for a
type of literature and a worldview characterized by the claim that
God has revealed (the Greek word for which is *apokalyptein*) to the
faithful elect community his plan for history. It is characterized by the
expectation of a cosmic battle at the end of the present age between
God and the hosts of evil, ending in a cataclysmic judgment on the
wicked and a glorious vindication of the righteous. The elect community must be prepared to suffer, since cosmic conflict is a necessary
stage in the preparation of God's people and of the creation as a
whole for the coming age in which God's purpose will finally triumph.[24] This essential factor in the Jesus tradition will be discussed
later, especially in the analyses of the Q source and of the Gospel of
Mark (Chapters 3 and 4). A related but broader term is *eschatological*,
which means literally "the study of the last things." It has come to
be used by scholars with reference to those aspects of human thought
which assume a divine purpose at work in history, signs of which are
pointed to by those claiming visionary or prophetic insights. An
important type of eschatological perception is apocalyptic. Harnack,
while recognizing apocalyptic elements in Jesus' message, dismissed
apocalypticism as "a miserabilism which clings to the expectation of a
miraculous interference on God's part, and in the meantime, as it

were, wallows in wretchedness."[25] His preference was for "something inward, something which is already present and making its entrance at the moment."[26] The true essence of Jesus' message, according to Harnack, was the inward rule of God and the infinite worth of the human soul, the higher righteousness and the command of love.[27]

In spite of his deserved reputation as one of the greatest historians of early Christianity and as a master of the literature of the early centuries of the church's existence, what Harnack did with the Jesus tradition was to adopt a reductionist method of interpretation, by which he was able to brush aside those aspects of the Gospels that he found intellectually distasteful and which he therefore dismissed as unworthy of Jesus. The ostensibly historical core of the message of Jesus which Harnack set forth was in fact the embodiment of his own ethical and religious ideas. While claiming to interpret the Jesus tradition against its cultural and historical background, he in fact selected those parts of the record that he found compatible with his own views and then pronounced them to be authentic and historical. This unacknowledged principle of selection was imposed on the first-century documents based on his commitment to the early twentieth-century liberal humanitarian system of values. As we shall note later, this same strategy continues to be operative among scholars of the late twentieth century, who also claim to have discovered the essence of the message of Jesus.

Treatment of the Gospels As Historical Documents: Comparison with Non-Christian Writings

One of the constructive by-products of the critical scrutiny of the Gospels during the nineteenth century was the articulation of the principle that they should be looked at like any other human literary product, and therefore subjected to comparison with other comparable writings of their time. With regard to the analysis of what were thought to be Jewish writings contemporary with the writing of the Gospels, two important changes have occurred in the second half of the twentieth century. The first was the discovery of the Dead Sea Scrolls, which provided documentation for lively developments in first century C.E. Judaism in southern Palestine and which showed the urgency of many of the issues that the Jesus tradition reports him as dealing with, in relation to the definition of the people of God and the expectation of a new age. The second was the growing conviction that the rabbinic materials included in the Mishnah and Talmud reflect developments in Judaism after the time of Jesus (post-70 C.E.) and therefore cannot be used as contemporary parallels for the older layers of the gospel tradition.[28] Fortunately, the recognition that rabbinic Judaism cannot serve as an antecedent for the rise of Christianity has not left a contextual vacuum. Supplementing the reassessment of formative Judaism has been the publication of extensive Jewish literature dating from the post-exilic period down to the early second century C.E. Much of this is now available in English translation, with scholarly introductions and notes, in the two-volume *Old Testament Pseudepigrapha*, edited by J.H. Charlesworth.[29] From these new sources and methods light is shed on the range of understandings operative in Judaism at the turn of the eras concerning the coming of God's kingdom, the role of Messiah, the rules of life for God's people, and identity of the hostile forces that must be overcome if God's purpose is to triumph. It is precisely in the context of such hopes and expectations that Christianity arose, and so it is to these sources that one must look in order to understand the meaning and dynamic of the role and message of Jesus.

Long before these discoveries were made and the pseudepigraphic Jewish writings were generally available for study, two major scholars, working independently of each other, reached the conclusion that apocalypticism was the primary conceptual and literary basis for understanding the activity and message of Jesus: Johannes Weiss (1827–1918) and Albert Schweitzer (1875–1965). They perceived that Jesus had taken over not only the terminology and concepts of apocalypticism but also its sense of imminent fulfillment and that this provided the basis for the urgency that characterized his message and his activity. Schweitzer's reconstruction of Jesus' message was in part flawed because he used Matthew uncritically as an historical source, overlooking the distinctive features and special agenda which subsequent scholarship has detected in this gospel.[30] As a result, Schweitzer depicted Jesus as a fanatic who thought he could force the hand of God to bring in the Kingdom by confronting the religious authorities in Jerusalem, but whose precipitous action resulted in his own death. Students of the Gospels were repelled by these features of Schweitzer's construction, and as a result many ignored his valid point about the basic apocalyptic orientation of Jesus. Careful analysis of the Q material and the Gospel of Mark show that the apocalyptic orientation is constitutive in both these early sources for the Jesus tradition, as we shall seek to show in Chapters 3 and 4. Schweitzer, having reached the scholarly conclusion that Jesus was an apocalypticist, abandoned the realm of biblical studies, turned instead to the study of medicine, and spent the rest of his life as a medical missionary in central Africa. We shall show how other scholars exploring the Jesus tradition have also taken flight—conceptually, rather than geographically or professionally.[31]

Another basic approach to the study of the Jesus tradition in the early decades of the present century stressed the parallels which were perceived between Jesus and redemptive figures from the Hellenistic religions, especially the mystery religions with their divine saviors who offered the secret knowledge and sacraments by which a mortal could participate in immortality. In Chapter 8 we shall observe how these perceptions of, and communion with, the divine were indeed adopted and adapted by some early Christian groups, as is evident concretely, especially in the Gnostic writings discovered in Egypt in 1945, just before the Dead Sea Scrolls were found in Palestine. A great benefit that has come from the availability of new evidence for the comparative study of nascent Christianity and Judaism in relation to the late Hellenistic and early Roman literature has been to shed light on the language and literary forms in which religious propagandizing was carried on in the early Roman world. Insights have also been provided by archaeological discoveries in the present century of private and official letters and records that show in astonishing detail how people in this period lived and how they expressed themselves in unpretentious forms of communication. Although no literary forms have been found which are exactly analogous to the Gospels, there are certain features of the early Christian writings—especially in Acts, the Letters of Paul, the Letter of James, and the Letter to the Hebrews—which display kinship with other writings from the Greco-Roman period.[32]

Form Criticism: The Tradition-Historical Method

Especially helpful for literary analysis of the Gospels has been the recognition of patterns of thought and expression in the components which make up the Gospels. In the nineteenth century, scholars thought they could discern several literary strands that had been woven into the Gospels as we have them, on analogy with the literary elements understood to lie behind the Pentateuch (Genesis through Deuteronomy) in the Jewish Scriptures. The limits of this purely literary-component approach to Old Testament studies were reached when scholars recognized that woven into the documents as we have them were smaller units of what were likely oral tradi-tion: stories, legends, poems, legal formulations. Hermann Gunkel pioneered in developing this method of biblical scholarship, which shed light not only on the literary traditions, but more importantly, also on the social and cultural setting in which these component features originated. The question was not merely what was reported, but also how (what literary mode) and why (with what social assump-tions and aims).[33]

An analogous enterprise among New Testament scholars began in the second decade of the present century. In addition to identifying the literary sources which are discernible in the Gospels, questions began to be raised about the components of the gospel tradition. The effort was made to identify and classify the earlier component elements which may be discerned as they have been incorporated into the writ-ten Gospels as we have them. What was attempted—with impressive results—was to trace the history of the traditions which lie behind the Gospels. This enterprise came to be called *Formgeschichte*—literally, "form history," although regrettably it has been commonly known as "form criticism." The original setting in which a tradition originated and the purpose it was intended to serve were designated by the German scholars who refined this method as *Sitz-im-Leben*—liter-ally, "setting in life." The *Sitz* could shift, however: The original set-ting of the unit of tradition might have been the actual situation in the time of Jesus, but then the tradition became modified when it was preserved by, and in the interests of, a particular early Christian com-munity. And it may have undergone further change when it was incor-porated into one of the Gospels.

This approach to the recovery of the historical evolution of the gospel tradition was undertaken independently by three scholars whose methods turned out to be quite similar and whose publications appeared within a space of three years. Karl Ludwig Schmidt of Basel (1891–1956) published in 1919 a seminal essay in which he showed (1) that the Gospels had been compiled from units of tradition pre-served by a church in the service of its specific needs, and (2) that as a literary genre the gospel had no real parallel in the literature of that period.[34] In 1919, Martin Dibelius (1883–1947) of Heidelberg traced the similarities between gospel tradition (the oral units) and the various forms of folk literature, centering attention on the two chief functions of the tradition in the life of the church: preaching and moral instruction.[35] In 1921 Rudolf Bultmann (1884–1976) pub-lished his monumental *History of the Synoptic Tradition*.[36] It consisted of an exhaustive analysis of the gospel tradition, classifying the components by type, showing how it was modified in the process of transmission, and how each of the evangelists brought it together in a distinctive way in order to make it serve his own special aims.

Both Dibelius and Bultmann commented on the sociocultural settings in which the oral tradition had been preserved and in the interests of which it had been put in written form.[37] Neither one, however, proceeded to define the social setting in anything more than vague, general terms. In the intervening years the "setting" has come to be understood as involving not merely such broad distinctions as these early form critics made—"Jewish," "Hellenistic," "Palestinian," sayings, narratives, speeches, parables—but more importantly, the questions as to what were the specific values and modes of identity that were operative when a tradition was produced and when it was reshaped in the process of transmission. For example, when one can discern that a parable has been converted into an allegory (as in the Matthew's adaptation of the Markan Parable of the Wicked Tenants [Mark 12:1–12; Matt. 21:33–46]; see pp. 142–43, 170 for details), what is important is not merely the formal difference but also the important ways in which the parable has been applied to the specific circumstances of the community in and for which Matthew is reworking the gospel tradition.

Even more important has been the growing recognition of the degree to which Jews in Palestine as well as in the wider Roman world were deeply influenced by Hellenistic culture—linguistically, literarily, conceptually, and religiously. This cultural penetration has become evident through fresh, perceptive analyses of the wider Jewish literature of the Greco-Roman period and from archaeological discoveries in Palestine, including Galilee. The widespread use of Greek language and Greek iconography among Palestinian Jews is unmistakable. Sepphoris, the large city and capital of Galilee located only a few miles from the village of Nazareth where Jesus grew up, was a thoroughly Hellenized city, with a typical *agora* (the expansive central area for marketing and public gatherings, as in Athens), a theater and other buildings in Greco-Roman architectural style and with inscriptions in Greek. Galilee was crossed by major interregional trade routes, with extensive building in the Hellenistic style, including a Greco-Roman city built by Herod Antipas in honor of the emperor Tiberius and named for him, Tiberias. It is most revealing that in the second century when Bar Kochba, the leader of the Jewish nationalist revolt in 130–135 C.E., wanted to communicate quickly and unambiguously with his fellow revolutionaries, he wrote to them in Greek.[38] When by the later second century C.E. the synagogue had evolved from an informal meeting based in houses or public halls to an institution with formal organization and procedures, the architectural styles resembled Greco-Roman temples, inscriptions were in Greek and the favorite mode of decoration was the signs of the zodiac.[39] In Jerusalem during the first century, public inscriptions—including those in the temple itself—were in Greek.

To treat "Palestinian" and "Hellenistic" as two distinctly different forms of Judaism, as the form critics did, may now be seen as contrary to the mounting evidence for the penetration of Judaism by Hellenistic culture.[40] Further complicating the form-critical process is the fact that the distinctions that Dibelius and Bultmann respectively made in the literary forms of the gospel tradition cannot be harmonized. What Bultmann called a type of sayings material—a brief narrative that culminates in a saying—is treated by Dibelius as a narrative type. The story of Jesus' passion has no literary counterpart in ancient religious literature, Jewish or Hellenistic, and instead may constitute a mixture of historical recollections with adaptations of Jewish Scriptures which the early Christians believed Jesus' death had fulfilled—an enterpise which was based on the Greek version of the Jewish Scriptures.[41]

What was called for but never adequately addressed by the form critics was the issue of the particular nature of the several Christian communities that preserved and adapted the Jesus tradition to produce the documents that we now know as the Gospels. What sociocultural models were available in this period that would have influenced the shaping of these communities? What social functions did this material serve in the life of the community that preserved it? It is this kind of question that will occupy us in the analyses of the gospel traditions in Chapters 3 to 8.

The Gospel Writers As Creative Interpreters of Jesus

An important step in the direction of offering answers to these contextual questions was the effort by Bultmann and others to show how the individual gospel writers, by their selection, arrangement, and modification of the gospel tradition, presented an image of Jesus that was intended to convey their own (or their community's) understanding of him. The dynamic Jesus tradition, which the gospel writers felt free to adapt and to shape in order to serve their communities' own distinctive needs, has accordingly been preserved in the diverse forms which comprise our Gospels.

Among the first to discern and describe the shaping of the tradition by the evangelists was William Wrede (1859–1906), whose pioneering work on Mark was published in 1901, the same year that Schweitzer's basic study of the life of Jesus appeared.[42] Wrede sought to show that the idea of Jesus' having kept his messiahship a secret (as in Mark 8:30) was introduced into the material by Mark, but that it was handled in an inconsistent way so that the astute critic can detect without difficulty the evangelist's modification of the tradition. Wrede's enduring contribution was to call attention to the early church's shaping the tradition in order to support its own theological and apologetic aims.

In 1927 the American scholar, Henry Joel Cadbury (1883–1975) employed an analytical method similar to that of Wrede (although with more attention to strictly literary issues) in a superb and enduringly useful study of the Gospel of Luke and its companion volume, Acts.[43] In the period following World War II, this mode of analyzing the Jesus tradition by the individual evangelists was dubbed "redaction criticism" by Willi Marxsen, whose work on Mark helped stimulate the surge of interest in the special theological views of each of the evangelists.[44] Presupposing Cadbury's study, but concentrating almost solely on theological matters, was Hans Conzelmann's *The Theology of St. Luke*.[45] Similar work was done by Gunther Bornkamm on the aims of Matthew as evidenced by his reshaping the Jesus tradition.

With the exception of Cadbury, in his work on Luke–Acts, most of these scholars concentrated on the theological interests of the gospel writers. What did not receive adequate attention from most of them was that behind each writer and tradition (such as Q) was a community which shared certain perspectives on the world— a life-world which influenced the social outlook, the norms for community participation, the ethical demands, and the expectations about the future—which shaped each particular reworking of the Jesus tradition.

Reactions to the Critical Dilemma

The uncertain and conflicting results produced by generations of biblical scholars, all of them claiming to be working by scientific historical methods, has created in the minds of many a mood of disillusionment with the critical undertaking as a whole. Systematic theologians, whose task was to expound Christian faith in an orderly and internally consistent manner, became impatient with the unsettled and unsettling outcome of the wide range of critical analyses of the gospel traditions. They felt that they could not wait until a consensus had been reached as to who Jesus was and what he really said and did before they must formulate for the church what should be affirmed concerning him.

The Reality of Jesus Is the Preached Word

One solution to this problem was offered by what is an essential feature of Protestant theology: the emphasis is placed on the proclamation of the Word of God through preaching. It is through preaching about the meaning of Jesus Christ that human lives are changed, and it is through the preached word that the reality of Christ is to be sought, rather than in the historian's reconstruction of who he was.

This point of view was given eloquent expression long ago by Martin Kähler (1835–1912) in some addresses published in 1892 as *Der sogenannte historisch Jesus und der geschichtliche biblische Christus* [The so-called historical Jesus and the historic biblical Christ]. In the opinion of Kähler, the sources for reconstructing the life of Jesus are not sufficiently complete or reliable to give assured historical results, and the evidence that they do provide is inadequate for tracing any development in Jesus' thought or his consciousness of a messianic role. But his most serious objection to efforts to reconstruct the historical Jesus was that critics engaged in this task supposed that if they could just get behind the church tradition, behind the picture of Jesus offered in the New Testament, there they would find the real Jesus as he actually and bodily lived. The critic wants to ferret him out and exhibit him in all his old relationships, all of which will appear as desirable and delightful. But that charming person, Kähler insisted, is not the real Christ:

> The real, that is the actual Christ, who strides through the history of his people, with whom millions have had communion in childlike faith, with whom the great witnesses of faith have communed as they struggled, accepted, conquered and surrendered—the real Christ is the preached Christ.[46]

Kähler went on to assert that the effort to look behind the biblical record at "what really happened" was not only unwarranted by the nature of the evidence but was idle, since all the features of miracle and divine activity come from beyond the world that can be known and analyzed by humans.[47] Kähler's harshest words were reserved for those historical critics who assumed that faith is somehow dependent on the outcome of their work. In rebuttal to such a claim, he asserted that faith does not derive from an understanding of the relationship of the human and divine natures of Jesus as conceived in "a head schooled in philosophy."[48] Faith dare not make itself dependent on the uncertain results of a picture that is only ostensibly reliable—a picture of Jesus that has been tortuously carved out by using methods of historical research that arose only relatively recently and that are as devoid of prospects for achieving results as is any shadow picture sketched by dogma and formed out of simple concepts:

> In relation to Christ, whom we should trust and whom we dare to trust, the learned theologian must be no better off and no worse off than the simplest Christian: no better off, since he comes no closer to the living Savior than anyone else; no worse off, since he too must overcome the obstacles to faith. To overcome these, there is only a single royal way: Repent and believe the Good News.[49]

A similar sharp distinction between what historical research can recover about Jesus and what the believer affirms about him was offered by Rudolf Bultmann in the post–World War II period, and continued to exert a powerful influence until recently. For Bultmann, the essence of the Christian faith was to be found in God's addressing humanity through the cross of Jesus. The cross confronts human beings with a decision: One must choose between God and the world, between (1) trying to live on the basis of one's own resources and by the values that the world provides, and (2) opening oneself to the will of God. Those who thus live out of faith die to the demands of the present world and receive new life as a gift from God. To receive this word of the cross in faith is to enter the resurrection life.[50] But Bultmann's critical analyses of the gospel tradition led him to conclude that Jesus did not speak in this way about his own death; the early church attributed such thoughts to him as one finds in the gospel tradition, but that is not so much a record of Jesus as a creation by the gospel writers and the church for which they wrote. He assumes that Jesus' own historical ministry and message remain within the thought world of Judaism, constituting some of the presuppositions of Christian faith, but that they are not part of that faith. Historical critical methods can recover the message of Jesus, but it is an antecedent of the Christian message, rather than identical with it.[51] The Gospels are primarily testimonies of faith, though they contain some vestigial historical evidence. Though Bultmann did not acknowledge it, his approach differentiates completely between two Jesuses: the historical figure and the Christ of faith. No effort was made to demonstrate a link between the two.

The Historical Jesus As Wisdom Teacher

In recent years some scholars have placed their focus on the historical Jesus, seeking to reconstruct him and his teachings in such a way as to designate as late and regrettable the adaptation of the images of Jesus as the Christ that one encounters in the Gospels in their traditional forms. The strategy recalls that of von Harnack, although the image of Jesus which emerges is significantly different from his. Three such undertakings may be sketched here, with more detailed implications of these agendas spelled out in later chapters, especially in relation to Q, Mark, and the noncanonical Gospels. Unacknowledged in these proposals is that the determinative factor in every case is a prior judgment about how to make Jesus acceptable to late twentieth-century intellectuals. All of these hypotheses concentrate exclusively on the sayings traditions and on the whole dismiss as late and unhistorical the narrative material included in the Gospels.

The first such group of historical reconstructions of the historical Jesus focuses on Q. Representative of this trend to give priority in the Jesus tradition to an abridged version of Q is the work of John Kloppenburg, in *The Formation of Q*.[52] After differentiating strands of tradition in what is currently designated as Q (non-Markan material common to Matthew and Luke), he dismisses as later developments the narrative and apocalyptic features, concluding that the wisdom speeches and admonitions were the formative element in Q to which the motif of judgment was a later addition.[53] Not surprisingly, one of Kloppenburg's mentors, Burton L. Mack, asserts that the wisdom material is the oldest layer of the Q tradition, and he dismisses as later development any elements that do not fit that model.[54] He concludes that the narrative Gospels should no longer be read as reports of historical events that generated Christianity. The mythic figure depicted in these documents was the creation of Christian groups in northern Syria, particularly in the churches of Pauline origin. Indeed, the first followers of Jesus knew nothing about and could not have imagined such events as Jesus' baptism, his conflict with the Jewish authorities, a plot to kill him, Jesus' instructions to his disciples, his transfiguration, his march to Jerusalem, the last supper, the trial, his crucifixion as king of the Jews, and what is reported in the resurrection and empty tomb stories. All these are the product of mythmaking in Jesus movements.[55]

A group calling itself the International Q Seminar has been organized under the leadership of Helmut Koester, which has announced as its agenda the historical and literary exploration of the Q tradition, although there are indications that the conclusions have already been reached and formulated before the investigation is fully launched. This is evident in the hypothesis offered by Koester in his recent study, *Ancient Christian Gospels: Their History and Development*, that the Gospel of Thomas (found in a library of Gnostic documents in Egypt in 1945),[56] which has only sayings material and lacks any mention of Jesus' miracles or of the cross and resurrection of Jesus, preserves the Jesus tradition in a more original form than any of the canonical Gospels and indeed predates them all.[57] Koester acknowledges that he has adopted Kloppenburg's theories about Q and bases his arguments primarily on it.[58] He also accepts the theory of the authenticity of the fragment of a Secret Gospel of Mark allegedly found by Morton Smith. He attempts to explain the relationship of this fragment to the canonical Gospel of Mark by asserting that the latter "is not the original Mark used by Matthew and Luke, but an abbreviated version of the *Secret Gospel of Mark*," which was all that survived. Features from the allegedly original secret version of Mark (such as the private initiation in the nude) were removed in the canonical edition.[59]

The model that has been chosen for these recent reconstructions of Jesus and his message is that of the itinerant Cynic-Stoic philosophers of the first century. Mack asserts that the Cynics' proverbial and parabolic language, with their demeaning of contemporary social values and call to an unconventional life of total freedom from the patterns and values of mainstream culture,[60] corresponds nicely with the Jesus who emerges in what this group of scholars proposes to have been the original stratum of the Q tradition. This image of Jesus as a proverb-spouting critic of contemporary society has been seized upon by other scholars who likewise build the case for their reconstructions of him by appeal to noncanonical Gospels.[61]

Ironically, the alleged historical norm to which these reappraisals of the Jesus tradition appeal—the Cynic-Stoic itinerant philosophers—does not correspond to what a careful reading of the literature of this movement shows the Cynic-Stoic aims and message to have been. A major element in the Cynic and Stoic philosophies of the Roman period, as is evident in the preserved writings of men of this persuasion who served as advisors to the Roman rulers—especially Cicero and Seneca—was the belief in the moral responsibility of all humanity, who would be called to account by the divinities. Following rewards for the morally responsible and punishment for the wicked, there would be a new era for the creation. The analogy of this worldview with that of Jewish and Christian apocalyptic is obvious and has been discussed and demonstrated by a number of classical scholars, but has been apparently ignored by the biblical scholars whose focus is chiefly on the aphoristic mode of communication used by these philosophers.[62] Some of the scholars in the Jesus Seminar have begun to examine the narrative Jesus traditions as well as those of the sayings, but the major focus remains on Jesus as one who pronounced wisdom.[63]

Although the ideological base chosen by this group is very different from that of the liberal, moralistic Protestantism of von Harnack, the approaches are very similar, and the results are as dubious in terms of sound historical method. We shall consider details of these more recent hypotheses about the evolution of the Jesus tradition, especially in our analyses of the Q and Markan traditions (Chapters 3 and 4). The method of analysis that will be employed here is not to decide antecedently on what is credible and relevant for thoughtful people at the end of the twentieth century, but to try to enter into the diverse models of thought, value, anxiety, and aspiration that are evident in and behind the documents in which the Jesus tradition has been preserved. We must try to elicit from the evidence not only the norms and expectations that are explicit in the documents, but also the assumptions and presuppositions that lie behind but have had shaping influence on the written records and that gave rise to the diverse ways in which the Jesus tradition was transmitted and understood as we have it in the canonical Gospels as well as the apocryphal Gospels.

Before examining the tradition in detail, however, we must face the prior question: Was there an historical person, Jesus, behind the evidence that reports his life, aims, and impact?

Suggestions for Further Reading

The classic studies of form criticism of the Gospels are those of Rudolf Bultmann, *History of the Synoptic Tradition* (New York: Harper & Row, 1963) and Martin Dibelius, *From Tradition to Gospel* (New York: Scribner's, 1935). Useful analyses of form and redaction criticism are found in *New Testament Interpretation*, ed. I.H. Marshall (Exeter: Paternoster, 1977). The historical method issues are discussed perceptively by A.E. Harvey in *Jesus and the Constraints of History* (London: Duckworth, 1982). John Riches' *Jesus and the Transformation of Judaism* (London: Darton, Longman, and Todd, 1980) contains a fine analysis of Jesus in the setting of first-century Judaism.

The importance of sociological analysis for understanding the New Testament in general is set out in my *Knowing the Truth: A Sociological Approach to New Testament Interpretation* (forthcoming revised edition, Trinity Press International). A fresh analysis of the sources can be found in Ben Witherington III, *Jesus the Sage: The Pilgrimage of Wisdom* (Minneapolis: Fortress Press, 1994).

NOTES

[1] Clement of Alexandria in the late second century reported Mark as having written down what he recalled Peter to have preached, with Peter's subsequent approval. In the present century the claim arose that Clement had described Mark's writing of a secret gospel, which antedated the Gospel of Mark as it is now known. Supposed documentation for this appears in a fragment of Clement's *Stromateis* (Miscellanies) which Morton Smith claimed to have found in 1958 inserted in the binding of a fifteenth-century manuscript in a Greek Orthodox monastery south of Jerusalem.

[2] A masterful analysis of the development of the critical approach to the New Testament is that of W.G. Kümmel, *The New Testament: The History of the Investigation of Its Problems*, (trans. S.M. Gilmour and H.C. Kee; Nashville: Abingdon, 1972). Useful surveys of the historical Jesus question may be found in Graham N. Stanton, *The Gospels and Jesus* (New York: Oxford University Press, 1989) and A.E. Harvey, *Jesus and the Constraints of History* (The Bampton Lectures) (Philadelphia: Westminster Press, 1982).

[3] A term used by Clement of Alexandria with reference to the Gospel of John. Reported by Eusebius in his *Ecclesiastical History* 6.14.7. Loeb Classical Library, vol. 2 (trans. J.E.L. Oulton; Cambridge, MA: Harvard University Press, 1953).

[4] For example, following Peter's affirmation that Jesus is the Messiah, he "sternly ordered them not to tell anyone about him" (Mark 8:27–30).

[5] Parts of it appeared posthumously in 1778, edited by G.E. Lessing, under the title *Wolfenbüttel Fragmenten.* Other parts were published under different pseudonyms, such as Schmidt.

[6] Ibid., pp. 54–55.

[7] *Das Leben Jesu,* vol. 1 (Tübingen: C.F. Osiander, 1835–1836), p. 69. An English translation of the third edition of this work by George Eliot was published, with an introduction by Peter C. Hodgson: *The Life of Jesus Critically Examined* (Philadelphia: Fortress, 1975), pp. 52, 81–82.

[8] Ibid., pp. 38–41, 67–68 ("The Life of Jesus Critically Examined," pp. 53–54).

[9] Ibid., pp. 71–72.

[10] Ibid., pp. 75–76.

[11] *The Church History of the First Three Centuries* 3d ed., vol. 1, (trans. Allan Menzies; London: Williams and Norgate, 1878), p. x. For an illuminating analysis of Baur's historical method and results, see P.C. Hodgson, *The Formation of Historical Theology: A Study of Ferdinand Christian Baur* (New York: Harper & Row, 1966).

[12] Baur, *Church History,* pp. 38–39.

[13] Ibid., p. 30.

[14] Ibid., pp. 24, 29.

[15] Ibid., p. 24, n. 2.

[16] Ibid., pp. 42–43.

[17] Notable examples of circular reasoning are found in the work of the Jesus Seminar and the Q Seminar, discussed later, pp. 78–80.

[18] *Die synoptischen Evangelien: Ihr Ursprung und ihr geschichtlicher Charakter* [The synoptic Gospels: Their origin and historical character] (Leipzig: Wilhelm Engelmann, 1863).

[19] In modern times, perhaps the most persistent champion of the priority of Matthew among the Gospels has been William R. Farmer, whose initial critical study, *The Synoptic Problem* (New York: Macmillan), appeared in 1964. A group of his supporters continues to promote this hypothesis down to the present day. See the comprehensive discussion and bibliography on this issue in W.G. Kümmel, *Introduction to the New Testament* (trans. H.C. Kee; Nashville: Abingdon, 1975), pp. 38–80.

[20] A prime and comprehensive analysis demonstrating the priority of Mark was that of C.H. Weisse, *Die evangelische Geschichte kritisch und philosophisch bearbeitet* [The gospel history critically and philosophically examined], 2 vols. (Leipzig: Breitkopf & Härtel, 1838).

[21] Reported by Eusebius, *Ecclesiastical History* III.39.3f.

[22] A thorough analysis of the synoptics from the standpoint of literary dependence was that of J.C. Hawkins, *Horae Synopticae* (Oxford: Clarendon, 1909). B.H. Streeter, *The Four Gospels* (New York: Macmillan, 1925), built on the work of Hawkins and others, and in addition investigated the various types of gospel tradition represented by groups of ancient manuscripts. He attempted to assign both the manuscript traditions and the Gospels to specific centers of the early church.

[23] Adolf von Harnack, *What Is Christianity?* (trans. T.B. Saunders) which continued to be published for more than half a century (1900; New York: Harper & Row, 1957).

[24]An enduringly important and informative study of apocalyptic is Paul D. Hanson, *The Dawn of Apocalyptic* (Philadelphia: Fortress, 1974). A fine analysis of the nature of apocalyptic thought and documents is that of Christopher Rowland, *The Open Heaven: A Study of Apocalyptic in Judaism and Early Christianity* (New York: Crossroad, 1982). Essays from an international colloquium on the subject were published under the title *Apocalypticism in the Mediterranean World and the Near East*, ed. David Hellholm (Tübingen: J.C.B. Mohr [Paul Siebeck], 1983).

[25]Harnack, *What Is Christianity?* p. 22.

[26]Ibid., p. 44.

[27]Ibid., pp. 51–74.

[28]Here the preeminent and enormous contribution of Jacob Neusner in his hundreds of publications has forced historians to rethink the rise of rabbinic Judaism and to see it as primarily a development following the failure of the two Jewish revolts and the disappearance of the temple and its priesthood as a major focus for religious identity and leadership among Jews. Neusner's early study, *The Rabbinic Tradition About the Pharisees Before 70* (Leiden: Brill, 1971) has been followed by a rich stream of works analyzing the emergence of rabbinic Judaism and the context in which it and early Christianity took shape. In contrast to the term "normative Judaism," coined by George Foote Moore in his widely influential work, *Judaism in the First Centuries of the Christian Era*, vol. 1 (Cambridge: Harvard University Press, 1927), posited a uniform Jewish orthodoxy which emerged in the postexilic world of Judaism and came to normative expression in the Mishnah and Talmud, Neusner discerned a complex process of experimentation and adaptation among Jews in this period as their cultural and political circumstances were constantly changing, which he described as "formative" Judaism. A comprehensive setting out of this historical development is offered in Neusner's three volumes, *The Foundations of Judaism: Method, Teleology, Doctrine*. The first volume was *Midrash in Context* (Atlanta, GA: Scholars Press, 1988); the second, *Messiah in Context: Israel's History and Destiny in Formative Judaism* (Philadelphia: Fortress, 1984); and the third, *Torah: From Scroll to Symbol in Formative Judaism* (Atlanta, GA: Scholars Press, 1988). The interplay between formative Judaism and formative Christianity is set forth in *Judaism in the Matrix of Christianity* (South Florida Studies in the History of Judaism 8; Atlanta, GA: Scholars Press, 1991).

[29]Garden City, NY: Doubleday, 1983, 1985. The translations and notes are by an international group of scholars, Jewish and Christian.

[30]See detailed analysis of Matthew in Chapter 5.

[31]For example, instead of abandoning the field of biblical studies, as Schweitzer did, Burton L. Mack has simply sought to eliminate the apocalyptic and miracle-working features of the Jesus tradition in his studies of Mark, *The Myth of Innocence: Mark and Christian Origins* (Philadelphia: Fortress Press, 1988); and of Q, in *The Lost Gospel: The Book of Q and Christian Origins* (San Francisco: HarperCollins, 1993).

[32]These literary and conceptual analogies are analyzed in my *Who Are the People of God?* (New Haven: Yale University Press, 1995).

[33]Hermann Gunkel, *The Legends of Genesis: The Biblical Saga and History* (New York: Schocken, 1964). The implications of this attention to the sociocultural background of the New Testament writings I have sought to develop throughout this volume: They are summarized in the Conclusion, pp. 283–92.

[34]*Der Rahmen der Geschichte Jesu* [The framework of the history of Jesus] (Berlin: Trowitsch & Sohn, 1919).

[35]*Die Formgeschichte der Evangelien* [Form criticism of the Gospels], ed. Günther Bornkamm, with a supplement by Gerhard Iber (Tübingen: Siebeck, 1919; 3d ed. 1959; English trans. B.L. Woolf); *From Tradition to Gospel* (New York: Scribner's, n.d.).

[36]Third German edition (trans. John Marsh; New York: Harper & Row, 1963).

[37]Dibelius, *From Tradition*, p. 7; Bultmann, *History*, p. 5.

[38]Writing to his fellow revolutionaries, the leader of the movement for Jewish independence, known as Shimon Bar Kochba, identified himself by the Greek equivalent of his name (Soumaios), wrote in Greek literary style, and apologized that he had to write in Greek because "no one was found to write in Hebrew" (from the translation by Michael O. Wise in the article on Bar Kochba in the *Anchor Bible Dictionary*, vol. 1 (New York: Doubleday, 1992), p. 604.

[39]Useful summaries of the features of the evolving synagogue as building include *Ancient Synagogues Revealed*, ed. Lee J. Levine (Jerusalem: Israel Exploration Society, 1981); and Marilyn S. Chiat, *Handbook of Synagogue Architecture* (Brown University Judaic Studies; Chico, CA: Scholars Press, 1982).

[40]This has been powerfully demonstrated by Martin Hengel in *Judaism and Hellenism*, 2 vols. (Philadelphia: Fortress, 1974).

[41]This hypothesis is set out in my essay, "The Function of Scriptural Quotations and Allusions in Mark 11–16," in *Jesus und Paulus*, ed. E.E. Ellis and E. Grasser (Göttingen: Vandenhoeck & Ruprecht, 1975).

[42]*Das Messiasgeheimnis in den Evangelien* (Göttingen: Vandenhoeck & Ruprecht, 1901; English trans. J.C.G. Grieg); *The Messianic Secret* (Greenwood, SC: Attic Press, 1971).

[43]*The Making of Luke–Acts* (New York: Macmillan, 1927; reprint, London: SPCK, 1961).

[44]*Mark the Evangelist* (trans. R. Harrisville; Nashville: Abingdon, 1969). The original edition was published in 1954. Among the many works of this type produced in the 1960 period was Norman Perrin's useful survey called *Rediscovering the Teachings of the Evangelists* (New York: Harper & Row, 1967).

[45]*The Theology of St. Luke* (New York: Harper & Row, 1961). The original work (4th ed., Tübingen: J.C.B. Mohr [Siebeck], 1962) had the revealing title *Die Mitte der Zeit* [The midpoint of Time], which indicates Conzelmann's basic idea that Luke–Acts has revised the primitive Christian eschatological expectation of a soon and sudden end, replacing it by the model of the present age as an ongoing period of worldwide evangelistic activity.

[46]P. 44 (p. 66). Originally published in 1892, the first and second edition of Kähler's essays were edited and published in combined form by E. Wolf under the original title (Munich: Kaiser Verlag, 1953). Page number refers to Wolf's edition; that in parentheses refers to the English

edition, translated and edited by C.E. Braaten (Philadelphia: Fortress, 1964).

[47]Ibid., p. 74 (p. 91).

[48]Ibid., p. 49 (p. 72).

[49]Ibid., pp. 49–50 (p. 73).

[50]From an earlier essay by Bultmann in *Kerygma and Myth* (trans. Reginald Fuller), ed. H.W. Bartsch (London: SPCK, 1953), pp. 41–43.

[51]*Jesus and the Word* (trans. E.H. Lantero and L.P. Smith; New York: Scribner's, 1934).

[52]Philadelphia: Fortress Press, 1987.

[53]Ibid., p. 244.

[54]Burton L. Mack, *The Lost Gospel: The Book of Q and Christian Origins* (San Francisco: Harper & Row, 1993), pp. 41–49.

[55]Ibid., p. 247. Mack deals with the Gospel of Mark along comparable lines, as is evident from the title of his monograph on Mark, *The Myth of Innocence.*

[56]There is a group of scholars who insist that the Gospel of Thomas contains material older than that found in any of the other Gospels, but detailed analysis of parallel versions of Jesus' sayings in Thomas and the New Testament Gospels shows clearly that the former represents a later adaptation of the Jesus tradition. This is discussed with other later Gospels in Chapter 8.

[57]Koester, *Ancient Christian Gospels*, p. 85.

[58]Ibid., p. 134, n. 3.

[59]Ibid., p. 302.

[60]Burton L. Mack, *The Lost Gospel*, pp. 41–49.

[61]For example, John Dominic Crossan, *In Fragments: The Aphorisms of Jesus* (San Francisco: Harper & Row, 1983) and in his *Four Other Gospels: Shadows on the Contours of the Canon* (Minneapolis: Winston Press, 1985); similarly, Ron Cameron, *The Other Gospels* (Philadelphia: Westminster, 1982). The same dogmatic assumption which treats only aphorisms as the authentic words of Jesus and dismisses all the narrative material has been adopted by the Jesus Seminar, the results of whose work have been made available in Robert Funk, *The Five Gospels: The Search for the Authentic Words of Jesus* (New York: Macmillan, 1993). The specifics of the conclusions reached by Crossan and Funk are discussed on p. 9, n. 3.

[62]I began exploration of this phenomenon in "Pauline Eschatology: Relationships with Apocalyptic and Stoic Thought," for the Festschrift for W.G. Kümmel, in *Glaube und Eschatologie*, ed. Erich Grasser and Otto Merk (Tübingen: J.C.B. Mohr [Paul Siebeck], 1985), pp. 135–158. A summary of my conclusions is offered in *Who Are the People of God: Early Christian Models of Community* (New Haven: Yale University Press, 1995).

[63]For example, Marcus J. Borg considers the Jesus tradition concerning his healing, in *Jesus: A New Vision* (Valley Forge, PA: Trinity Press International, 1994); and J.D. Crossan discusses Jesus as a magician in *The Historical Jesus: The Life of a Mediterranean Jewish Peasant* (San Francisco: HarperCollins, 1991).

CHAPTER 2
Jesus in Extrabiblical Sources

Is it possible that Jesus never existed? A half-century ago doubts about the historical existence of Jesus were earnestly voiced by certain historians and theologians,[1] most notably by Arthur Drews (1865–1935)[2] in Germany and by his disciple, William Benjamin Smith (1850–1934),[3] in America. These men claimed that Jesus was a mythical figure invented by propagandists for the developing Christian faith, who built on the strand in the Jewish tradition (especially after the time of the Maccabees) that sought to bring the Gentiles as proselytes into the community of Israel.[4] According to Smith, the effort to achieve universal salvation was the essence of nascent Christianity, but the Old Testament prophecies and conceptions were not sufficiently concrete to appeal as widely as was necessary to accomplish Gentile conversion:

> There was one and only one device that could meet the demand of the situation and at the same time lay close at hand: and that was to follow the precedent of Isaiah, so native and familiar to the Hebrew mind, so appealing to the oriental fancy, and to present the Righteous Servant, the Torch-Bearer, the Light for the Gentiles, as a Man, a suffering son of the earth, "tempted in all points in our likeness without sin."[5]

The process of creating the Gospels began with the story of the passion, to which were added the accounts of the ministry and later of the prehistory of Jesus. Smith reported:

> The final product, the symbolic quasi-biography which the world knows as the Gospels, we have found was the literary precipitate of a long-continued pictorial teaching that stretched all round the

41

Mediterranean. These writings become self-luminous when and only when we *abandon the baseless assumption* of historical documents.... The story of Jesus is, therefore, an idealization of the destiny of the nation Israel in its universal inclusiveness.[6]

Smith's contemporaries did not dismiss his work as nonsense, nor should we today. He had far too many accurate insights and far too firm a grasp of historical facts about Christian origins to be labeled a crank. His intuition that some of the gospel narratives were created, or at least modified, in order to demonstrate the fulfillment of the Old Testament was propounded by David Friedrich Strauss in the nineteenth century in *Das Leben Jesu* (The Life of Jesus), a book that has continued to cast its sober influence over gospel studies down to the present day. Smith's awareness of the Hebrew practice of depicting a group under the figure of an individual, a corporate personality, is an insight that, developed by others, has been of fundamental importance for Old Testament studies in the present century.[7]

The two major flaws in Smith's thesis result from (1) his assumption that, since some materials included in the Gospels were shaped by the claim that Jesus was the fulfillment of Old Testament prophecy, the whole of the Gospels must be so regarded;[8] and (2) his neglect of the evidence pointing to Jesus' historicity in the form of allusions to him in Jewish and pagan sources.[9]

Evidence in Non-Christian Historical Writing

Historians, including Christian historians, would surely welcome direct mention of Jesus in some Roman legal documents of his day. Lacking authentic reports, early Christian imagination produced the Acts of Pilate, an apocryphal narrative that built on the brief mention of that Roman procurator in the Gospels, in an attempt to depict his reaction to Jesus and to reproduce the content of his official report on the execution. But most of the references to Jesus in the Greek and Latin writings of the first and the early second centuries are no more than brief allusions to the movement that began in his name—so brief that we can reproduce most of them in their entirety (except for those appearing in the letters of Pliny) in this chapter.

The Jewish Historian Josephus

In his *Antiquities of the Jews* (written in Greek) the Jewish historian Josephus (37–100? C.E.), who turned collaborationist at the time of the Roman invasion of Palestine 67–70 C.E., refers to Jesus twice: once in a list of notorious Jewish nationalists and other troublemakers, and again in connection with the execution of James, a leader of the Jerusalem church, who is identified as the brother of Jesus. The first of these passages has almost certainly been worked over by the Christians, who tried to make Josephus bear Christian witness to Jesus:

> About this time [that is, during the procuratorship of Pilate, 26–36 C.E., although Josephus here refers to the early phase of his rule] there lived Jesus, a wise man, if indeed one ought to call him a man. For he was one who wrought surprising feats and was a teacher of such people as accept the truth gladly. He won over many Jews and many of the Greeks. He was the Messiah. When Pilate, upon hearing him accused by men of the highest standing among us, had condemned him to be crucified, those who had in the first place come to love him did not give up their affection for him. On the third day he appeared to them restored to life, for the prophets of God had prophesied these and countless other marvellous things about him. And the tribe of the Christians, so called after him, has still to this day not disappeared.[10]

It is incredible that Josephus could have written this account of Jesus exactly as it stands, since he would have had to be a Christian believer to have affirmed unequivocally that Jesus was the Messiah. The recognition of Jesus as the Messiah is doubtless a Christian interpolation. However, in his translation of the *Antiquities*, L.H. Feldman suggests that the rest of the account that has come down to us may not be essentially different from what Josephus wrote. In its present form the passage is ambiguous and lends itself to Christian interpretation. The ambiguity may have originated with Josephus, and if so, the Christians may have found it necessary to change only a few phrases in order to make the account serve their propaganda aims. The Christian reader of Josephus, for example, interprets "if indeed one ought to call him a man" as a suggestion of Jesus' divinity. But if the emphasis falls on the "surprising feats" mentioned in the next sentence, then the inappropriateness of calling Jesus merely a man may have meant, not that Jesus was divine, but that he was a magician under demonic control. As we shall see, this was precisely the charge most commonly leveled against Jesus in the rabbinic sources. If we assume that in making explicit statements about Jesus as Messiah and about the Resurrection, Josephus is simply conveying what Jesus' followers claim in his behalf, then there would be no reason to deny that he wrote them nearly as they stand.[11] It seems very unlikely that the passage in its entirety is a Christian interpolation; thus it can serve as evidence outside Christian writing for the existence of Jesus.

Even if we assume that the passage has come down to us almost as Josephus wrote it, however, it still provides us only limited information about Jesus. It presupposes that he lived and attests that he conducted a ministry that attracted considerable attention, even among those who thought him to be a wizard, that the Romans condemned him—presumably as a threat to the peace and therefore probably as an insurrectionist—and that the belief in his resurrection developed soon after his death. The information from Josephus confirms the main points in the gospel account, but it in no way supplements it, since even in the Gospels Jesus' opponents accuse him of performing his exorcisms by being in league with the prince of demons (Mark 3:22). It is also obvious that, although Josephus thought mention of Jesus worthwhile, he gave it no more place in his narrative than his accounts of other conflicts between the Jews and their Roman overlords, and far less space than his spicy story of the goings-on in the temple of Isis in Rome.[12]

The second of Josephus' references to Jesus[13] occurs in a section dealing with the struggles for power that characterized life in Judea in the years prior to the Jewish Revolt of 66–70 C.E. Jesus' brother, James, had succeeded to the leadership of the church in Jerusalem and was apparently highly regarded by the majority of the Jewish community as well. No information whatsoever about Jesus is provided by this passage in Josephus, but it does confirm the general picture presented in the Gospels that Jesus was a well-known figure in first-century Judaism, who could be identified in a passing reference as the Jesus who was called the Messiah by his followers. There is no hint here of a Christian interpolation, which adds more weight to this as an important historical allusion and renders untenable the allegation that Jesus was a fictional figure invented by the Christians. Since mention of Jesus at this point in his narrative serves only to identify James and contributes nothing substantial to his account, Josephus certainly leaves his readers with the impression that Jesus is a historical person like any other of whom he writes.

The Roman Historians: Pliny, Suetonius, and Tacitus

Among Roman writers, the oldest reference to Jesus that has survived is found in one of the letters that Pliny the Younger (62–113 C.E.) wrote to Emperor Trajan. Around 110 C.E., writing from the seat of his governorship in Bithynia, a Roman province on the Black Sea coast in Asia Minor, Pliny asked for guidance in dealing with Christians, whose numbers and influence seem to have been on the rise in the area at this time. So greatly had the impact of the Christian faith been felt throughout the Black Sea provinces that the temples of the officially sanctioned gods were nearly deserted.[14] Christ was worshipped "as a god" and both the Eucharist and the love feast, the joyous fellowship meal that preceded it, were being celebrated by adherents of the new faith. Pliny's evidence shows us, therefore, that Christianity had a strong foothold on the Black Sea coast about eighty years after the Crucifixion, although his description of Christian practices adds nothing to our knowledge of the life of Jesus.

The Roman historian Suetonius, a contemporary of Pliny, mentions in his *Lives of the Twelve Caesars* that under the reign of Claudius (41–54 C.E.), there was a disturbance among the Jews in Rome that reached such a peak of intensity that they had to be expelled from the city. The instigator of this internal struggle was someone named Chrestos. Suetonius reports, "Since the Jews constantly made disturbances at the instigation of Chrestos, he [Claudius] expelled them from Rome."[15]

It is generally acknowledged that Chrestos, a common name, was used by Suetonius instead of Christos, which would not have been at all familiar to most Latin-speaking people. Perhaps the cause of the disturbance among the Jewish community in Rome was the coming, not of Chrestos, but of Christian preachers with their message that Jesus was the Christ(os). Although it is possible that Suetonius had his date confused and that the disturbance actually occurred during the reign of Tiberius (14–37 C.E.), it is more likely that the expulsion of the Jews from Rome was the occasion for the migration from Rome to Corinth of Priscilla and Aquila, the Christian couple who aided Paul in founding and building up the Corinthian church (Acts 18:2–26; Rom. 16:3; 1 Cor. 16:19). As in the case of the evidence from Pliny, all that we learn from Suetonius is that there was a Christian community in Rome as early as 49–50 C.E.[16]

In his *Annals*, Tacitus (55?–117? C.E.), a third Roman writing early in the second century, describes in vivid detail the fire that destroyed much of Rome during the reign of Nero (54–68 C.E.). In order to divert suspicion from himself as the one who had ordered the city set afire, Nero placed the blame on the Christians, of whom a "multitude" were convicted.

> Neither human help, nor imperial munificence, nor all the modes of placating heaven, could stifle scandal or dispel the belief that the fire had taken place by order, i.e., of Nero. Therefore, to scotch the rumor, Nero substituted as culprits and punished with utmost refinements of cruelty, a class of men, loathed for their vices, whom the crowd styled Christians. Christus, the founder of the name, had undergone the death penalty in the reign of Tiberius, by sentence of procurator Pontius Pilate, and the pernicious superstition was checked for a moment, only to break out once more, not merely in Judea, the home of the disease, but in the capital itself, where all things horrible or shameful in the world collect and find a vogue. First, then, the confessed members of the sect were arrested; next, on their disclosures, vast numbers were convicted, not so much on the count of arson as for the hatred of the human race. And derision accompanied their end: they were covered with wild beasts' skins and torn to death by dogs; or they were fastened on crosses, and when daylight failed were burned to serve as lamps by night. Nero had offered his gardens for the spectacle, and gave an exhibition in his Circus, mixing with the crowd in the habit of a charioteer, or mounted on his car.[17]

Allowing for exaggeration, we can still infer that the Christian community was at least large enough in Rome to attract public notice and aggressive enough to invite the hatred of the masses. In identifying the Christians among the many religious sects he scorned, Tacitus mentions that "Christus" was executed during the reign of Tiberius, probably about 29, having been sentenced by the procurator Pontius Pilate. Tacitus' account is the most precise and extensive information that the pagan authors provide about Jesus. Although his details match exactly what is known from Christian accounts, Tacitus, like Pliny and Suetonius, provides us with nothing that supplements what we know of Jesus from the Gospels. The writings of the Roman historians are, however, important evidence for Jesus' existence as a historical person: They show that non-Christian historical writers, and by inference their audiences, believed Jesus to have existed, and that they considered his death and his continuing influence after death to be significant enough to rate a few brief references.

Evidence in Jewish Religious Sources

The Hebrew sources in which Jesus is mentioned or alluded to have been thoroughly analyzed by both Jewish and Christian scholars.[18] The main sources are the oral interpretations and exposition of the Law attributed to the authoritative rabbis of the first two centuries C.E., but which were codified as the Mishnah only in the third century and, with additional commentary, as the Talmud in Jerusalem in the fourth century and in Babylon in the fifth. The interpretations attributed to the rabbis of the third to the fifth centuries are also included in the Talmud, and this rabbinic material, which was written down later, may incorporate older, possibly reliable material; but only the interpretations of the Tannaim, the rabbis of the first two centuries C.E., which are included in the Mishnah, are potentially of value for a Jewish historical perspective on Jesus. Even the tannaitic sources are suspect, however, since there is a clear tendency in the development of the talmudic traditions to lend weight to a polemical view by assigning it to one of the early (tannaitic) teachers.[19] Nonetheless, scholars early in this century sought to demonstrate similarities and contrasts between the teaching of Jesus and that of the rabbis by developing a series of commentaries based on the Talmud and Midrash.[20] To compare this material with the New Testament is largely anachronistic, since the Jewish sources were not given final form until the period between the third and sixth centuries. There are, however, certain historical inferences that can be made through examination of some of this rabbinic material.

Interpretations of the Tannaim

Chief among the tannaitic scholars who reputedly provide information about Jesus is Rabbi Eliezer, whose teacher, Rabbi Johanan ben Zakkai, was a contemporary of Jesus and could have heard him. However, for a figure who assumes for Christians an overwhelmingly significant place in the history of the first century, surprisingly little attention is paid to Jesus by Jewish writers in general, and most references are of a polemical or at least derogatory nature. Such references as there are are obscured by the fact that in the Talmud Jesus is not mentioned by name. Rather, in some texts he is referred to as "a certain person"; in others he is called "Balaam." (In the Old Testament, Balaam was a non-Israelite prophet whose services were available on a fee basis and who was so obstinate that God on one occasion rebuked him through the mouth of his faithful jackass

[Num. 22:21–35].) In still other early talmudic passages, Jesus is called "Ben Stada" or "Ben Pandira" (a variant is "Panthera"); in each case "Ben" means "son of," and the clear implication is that Jesus was an illegitimate child. According to one passage from the Talmud (partly from Rabbi Eliezer and partly from the later Rabbi Hisda):

> It is tradition that Rabbi Eliezer said to the wise, "Did not Ben Stada bring spells from Egypt in a cut which was upon his flesh?" They said to him, "He was a fool, and they do bring a proof from a fool." [Ben Stada is Ben Pandira.] Rabbi Hisda said, "The husband was Stada, the paramour was Pandira." The husband was Pappos ben Jehudah, the father was Stada. The mother was Miriam the dresser of women's hair; as we say in Pumbeditha [a center of rabbinical learning in Babylon], "Such a one has been false to her husband."[21]

It is not known what is implied by the cut in the flesh, except that it has to do with magical practices. The tactic of the rabbinic tradition was not to deny Jesus' existence, but to discredit both him and his mother as unworthy to be considered as participants in a divine purpose.

By contrast, Rabbi Eliezer appears in another passage to have been attracted by Christianity to such an extent that he was seized by the Roman governor on suspicion of being a Christian, perhaps during a pogrom under Emperor Trajan aimed at destroying the leadership of the early church (about 110 C.E.):

> Rabbi Eliezer ... was arrested for Minuth [holding Christian beliefs], and they brought him to the tribunal for judgment. The governor said to him, "Doth an old man like thee occupy himself with such things?" He said to him, "Faithful is the judge concerning me." The governor supposed that he only said this of him, but he was not thinking of any but his Father who is in heaven. [The governor] said to him, "Since I am trusted concerning thyself, thus also will I be. I said, perhaps these societies [the Christian churches] err concerning these things. Dimissus, Behold thou art released." And when he had been released from the tribunal, he was troubled because he had been arrested for Minuth. His disciples came to him to console him, but he would not take comfort. Rabbi Aqiba [early second century] came in and said to him, "Rabbi, shall I say to thee why thou art grieving?" He said to him, "Say on." He said to him, "Perhaps one of the Minim [Christians] has said to thee a word of Minuth and it has pleased thee." He said, "By heaven, thou hast reminded me! Once I was walking along the streets of Sepphoris, and I met Jacob of Chephar

Sichnin, and he said to me a word of Minuth in the name of Jesus Ben Pantiri, and it pleased me. And I was arrested for words of Minuth because I transgressed the words of Torah, "Keep thy way far from her, and come not nigh the door of her house, for she hath cast down many wounded [Prov. 5:8]."[22]

The chief significance of this rabbinical tradition is that it indicates how seriously both Roman and rabbinical authorities regarded the teachings of Jesus and how eager they were to suppress the movement that his followers carried on in his name. Although there is no direct historical evidence about Jesus in these traditions, it is noteworthy that the passage above attacks Christianity by classifying it as a heresy to be shunned, not by denying the existence of its founder or declaring it to be a fraud perpetrated by the disciples. The passage also implies that Christianity is a highly visible movement in Sepphoris, the chief city of central Galilee, only a few miles from Nazareth, Jesus' home town. Recent archaeological excavations in Sepphoris have shown how thoroughly Hellenized this city was, with public baths, expansive public market space, a theater, inscriptions in Greek and Hellenistic mosaic installations.[23]

Personal non-Christian recollections of him could well have survived in this region. In any case, the rabbinic sources presuppose Jesus' actual existence, but they offer little historical information about him. Rather, they are a polemic directed against the people who were wandering about the land spreading the message of Jesus and against the memory of Jesus, a man of dubious family connections, who led the itinerant preachers and teachers of error. The Talmud contains many statements that are wholly polemical—for example, that Jesus was the illegitimate son of an adulteress by a Roman soldier named Pandira or Panthera and that for forty days before his execution a herald went about announcing what was to happen and pleading in vain for someone to rise to Jesus' defense.[24]

In the following lines Joseph Klausner summarizes the extent of the objective historical information about Jesus that can be drawn from the tannaitic strata of the Talmud:

There are reliable statements to the effect that his name was Yeshu'a of Nazareth; that he "practiced sorcery" (i.e., performed miracles, as was usual in those days) and beguiled and led Israel astray; that he mocked at the words of the Wise [the officially sanctioned interpreters of the Law]; that he expounded scripture in the same manner as the Pharisees; that he had five disciples; that he said he was not come to take aught away from the Law or to add to it; that he was hanged (crucified) as a false teacher and beguiler on the eve of the Passover which happened on a sabbath; and that his disciples healed the sick in his name.[25]

Later Interpretations from the Talmud and the Midrash

If the range of inquiry about Jesus in the Talmud and the Midrash (rabbinic commentary on the Scriptures) is extended down to the fourth century, the information is somewhat more extensive but at the same time so late and so obviously polemical as to be valueless as historical evidence. It is summarized by R.T. Herford as follows:

> Jesus, called a Notzri [the Nazarene], Ben Stada, or Ben Pandira, was born out of wedlock. His mother was called Miriam, and was a dresser of women's hair. Her husband was Pappos ben Jehudah. Her paramour was Pandira. She is also said to have descended from princes and rulers, and to have played the harlot with a carpenter.
>
> Jesus had been in Egypt and brought magic thence. He was a magician, and led astray and deceived Israel. He sinned and caused the multitude to sin. He mocked at the words of the wise and was excommunicated. He was tainted with heresy. He called himself God, also "the son of man" and said that he would go up to heaven. He made himself to live by the name of God.
>
> He was tried in Lud as a deceiver and as a teacher of apostasy. [Lud is Lydda, which lies inland from modern Tel Aviv.] Witnesses were concealed so as to hear his statements, and a lamp was lighted over him, that his face might be seen. He was brought to the Beth Din [literally, the House of Justice; that is, the Jewish court].
>
> He was tried in Lud on the eve of Pesah [that is, the Passover], which was also the eve of the Sabbath. He was stoned and hung, or crucified.... Under the name of Balaam, he was put to death by Pinhas the robber (Pontius Pilate) and at the time of his death was thirty-three years old. He was punished in Gehinnom [the valley of Hinnom, which runs southwest of Jerusalem and was used as a place for dumping refuse in ancient times] by means of boiling filth.
>
> He was a revolutionary. He was near to the kingdom. He had five disciples. Under the name of Balaam [a notorious hireling prophet who caused the death of many in Israel; Josh. 13:22] he is excluded from the world to come.[26]

Later on, Jewish polemic went to even greater lengths to discredit Jesus, but it never denied his existence or the basic facts of a ministry of teaching and healing and of his execution.

Later still, probably in the tenth century, there appeared a novelistic work in Hebrew known as Toledoth Yeshua, which recounted the story of Jesus' life, drawing mostly on the gospel accounts but embellishing them with legendary features and casting the whole in a mold shaped by polemics and ridicule. The narrative is filled with racy details, such as the trickery by which the handsome Pandira (or Panthera) seduced the unsuspecting Miriam (Mary), and with such legendary elements as the report of Jesus' having written the Ineffable Name of God on a piece of leather and sewn it to his thigh so that he would not forget it. But it also contains gross errors and anachronisms—for example, Helen of Adiabene (middle of the first century) is confused with Helen the mother of Emperor Constantine (fourth century), and a rabbi who actually lived four centuries later is credited with having found the body of Jesus. Klausner is correct, therefore, when he asserts that the Toledoth Yeshua is "nothing beyond a piece of folklore," woven out of late legends and sayings from the Talmud and Midrash and combining perverted versions of the gospel accounts.[27]

There is probably some historical fact at the basis of several of these calumnies against Jesus, but others seem to represent a confusion of Jesus with some other man of the same name who was sentenced as a criminal. Of the latter type is the repeated statement that he was put to death in Lud, an area that according to the Gospels he never visited. On the other hand, the identification of the day of his execution as the eve of the Passover, which was also a Sabbath eve, fits with the chronology of the Gospel of John, although it conflicts with the chronology of the other three Gospels, according to which Jesus celebrated the Passover with his disciples the night before his execution. Designation of the valley of Hinnom as the place of his death may be merely symbolic—that is, his rejection by the nation of Israel is linked with the city refuse dump—but it could also recall the historical detail of his having been crucified on a hill that overlooked the upper part of this very valley.

The phrase "near to the kingdom" probably means that Jesus was known by friend and foe as one who announced the coming of the New Age, the eschatological Rule or Kingdom of God. For his enemies to describe him as a revolutionary is not farfetched, since he was actually almost certainly put to death by the Romans on precisely this charge: that he was the leader of an insurrectionist movement whose "kingdom" was a threat to Roman rule. Mention of boiling filth is, of course, no more than an indication of the hostility evoked by the very name of Jesus among those opposed to the Christian movement.

Other elements in the charges brought against Jesus among the talmudic traditions are clearly reflections of the gospel accounts, and as such they lack independent historical value. Of this type are the declarations that he called himself God and that he said he would go up to heaven. The report that he was brought to the Jewish court of justice may be either an independent tradition of Jewish origin or an allusion to the gospel reports of his hearing before the council, a regional assembly of Jewish leaders, including priests, set up by the Romans (Mark 14:53–72; Matt. 26:57–75; Luke 22:54–71).[28]

The Bearing of the Dead Sea Scrolls on Understanding Jesus

In 1947 (or possibly as early as 1945), Arabs living in the Judean desert of Jordan near the northwest shore of the Dead Sea found the first of a number of ancient scrolls hidden in caves in the cliffs just west of the marl terrace that overlooks the sea. Excavations by archeologists in the early 1950s and explorations of caves in the vicinity brought to light thousands of fragments of manuscripts, most of which have since been published for scholarly investigation and translated into several languages for interested nonspecialists.[29] Some of the recovered documents are commentaries—some complete and some preserved only in fragments—on books of the Hebrew Bible; some claim to be revelations of coming events in the history of the Jewish people; some are books of regulations for the life of the community that produced or preserved the writings. This community had its headquarters in a monasterylike settlement nearby, the ruins of which were uncovered by archeologists beginning in 1955 and known locally as Khirbet Qumran.[30]

Since as early as the second century C.E. there have been reports of occasional finds of ancient scrolls in caves near the Dead Sea, but until the most recent discoveries were made, there was no way to specify and identify the contents of these writings. In several well-known ancient sources, however, there are accounts of a communal settlement on the shores of the Dead Sea, whose members were called Essenes. A comparison between the picture of the community that can be drawn from the scrolls and the descriptions of the Jewish sect offered by Josephus, Pliny, and Philo of Alexandria leaves little doubt that it was the Essenes who produced the documents we now know as the Dead Sea, or Qumran, Scrolls.

Nearly fifty years earlier, at the turn of the present century, another piece in the puzzle was discovered, although its significance was not immediately recognized. Some sectarian Jewish documents were found in a storeroom of an old synagogue in Cairo. At the time of their publication it was not clear whether they were of medieval or more ancient origin. A link with the Essenes was conjectured, but the evidence was insufficient to draw a firm conclusion. The fact that copies of the same writings—otherwise unknown—have since been found at Qumran shows that they originated with the same Jewish sect. In all likelihood, the scrolls discovered in Cairo were written by the community at Qumran and taken in the ninth century to Egypt by Jewish sectaries.[31]

In the eighteenth century it was proposed that Jesus had been an Essene and that his call to the renunciation of riches and to a life of devotion to the will of God was based on Essene ethics. Also noted was the similarity between the pooling of resources called for in Acts 4:32–37 and the communal life of the Essenes. In the nineteenth century Ernest Renan called Jesus a "brother" of the Essenes and spoke of Christianity as an Essenism that largely succeeded, but he stopped short of making Jesus out to have been a member of the sect. The discovery of the Dead Sea Scrolls and the clear evidence of their link with the Essenes have revived the theory of an Essene origin of Christianity. With the added details from the Dead Sea Scrolls, the hypothesis has now been made more precise.

Some journalists, noting certain possible connections between the Qumran documents and early Christianity, have leaped to the conclusion that the Dead Sea Scrolls show that the Christian account of Jesus is almost wholly fictional, that he was in fact an Essene from Qumran, whose followers invented the stories about him that we have in the Gospels.[32] The pattern used by these allegedly pious fictionalizers was that of the founder of the Qumran community, the

Teacher of Righteousness, who, it is asserted, was crucified and reportedly rose from the dead. The Christian account of Jesus' death and resurrection was an effort to top the Essene stories.

Scholars have long recognized that there are similarities in the organization, practices, and beliefs of the Essenes and the early Christian community.[33] The Dead Sea Scrolls have provided details of three principal areas of similarity:[34] the role of the Teacher and that of Jesus, the Qumran communal meal and the Eucharist, and the Essene and early Christian radical interpretations of the Law. Although similarities can be shown, the practices and beliefs of the two communities are clearly not congruent, and claims for the direct dependence of Jesus or his followers on the Essenes—for the Christian conception of Jesus' redemptive role, for example—cannot be demonstrated persuasively.

The most telling feature against any simple identification of the Qumran community and early Christianity is the sharp difference in their respective attitudes toward the wider world. The Qumran group despaired of official Jewish institutions and of the low level of seriousness about obedience to the Law. Accordingly, they withdrew completely from society in order to live the pure life at their own retreat in the desert. Members of the group who failed to conform to the rigid standards were required to leave. Would-be members had to undergo an extended probationary period in order to demonstrate the discipline that was essential to their full participation in the community life. In the *Temple Scroll*, the description of the city and temple of Jerusalem as they will be rebuilt in the new age, there is a direct decree that those who may not enter the new city of God are the tax collectors, the blind and lame, women with a menstrual flow—precisely those to whom Jesus reached out and invited to share in the community of God's new people. Hence, Jesus and his followers were denounced by their contemporaries as friends of "publicans and sinners" (Matt. 11:19; Luke 7:34; cf. Mark 2:15–16; Matt. 15:1; Luke 18:10). Further, Jesus is reported as going outside the limits of Jewish territory in his preaching tours, and his followers spread over the Roman world inviting any who would give heed to become members of his New Covenant community. Sociologically speaking, the Qumran type of sectarianism and the Christian "sect" are categorically different in their stance toward the world, even though their respective claims to have been the recipients of divine secrets and their celebration of their unity and their hopes are formally similar. There is no basis, therefore, for the claims that have been made that

Christianity is an Essenism that succeeded or that Essene views provided the basis for some Christians' understanding of Jesus' redemptive role.

Parallels Between the Teacher of Righteousness and Jesus

Suffering and death. In one of the fragmentary texts from Qumran there is mention of the cruelty of the Lion of Wrath, who "hung men alive."[35] This archenemy is probably the same man who is elsewhere called the Wicked Priest and who appears in the Habakkuk Commentary as the persecutor of the Teacher of Righteousness (or the One Who Teaches Rightly). After quoting a passage from Habakkuk which speaks of bloodshed and violence, the Qumran Commentary offers the following interpretation:

> This refers to the wicked priest. Because of the mischief which he had done to him who taught the Law aright and to the men associated with him, God delivered him into the hands of his enemies, that they might torture him with scourging and wear him out with bitterness of spirit for acting unrighteously against His elect.[36]

The passage from the Habakkuk Commentary that immediately precedes this one actually describes in detail the horrible fate suffered by the Wicked Priest for having persecuted the Righteous Teacher. But the words of the commentary have been interpreted by some scholars to mean that what is being described is the suffering of the Teacher himself at the hands of the Wicked Priest. For example, in the translation of André Dupont-Sommer we read:

> [The explanation of this word con]cerns the Wicked Priest who rebelled [and viola]ted the precepts [of God and persecuted the teacher of righteousness. And they s]et upon him in virtue of the wicked judgments, and evil profaners committed horrors upon him and vengeance upon his flesh.[37]

Dupont-Sommer explains that the "wicked judgments" are those made by the Wicked Priest and his officials against the Teacher of Righteousness, although the identity of the victim of persecution is missing from the text. This interpretation, presenting the Teacher as the one persecuted, in combination with the Qumran text that describes those who were "hung alive," points to the conclusion that the Teacher of Righteousness was crucified.

A psalmlike collection found at Qumran has been given the title Hymns of Thanksgiving. There is a strong possibility that the

Hymns are biographical, or even autobiographical, in which case it would be plausible to assume that the Teacher was crucified.

> *I was as a man forsaken ...*
> *no refuge had I.*
> *For that which I had planted*
> *was turned into wormwood.*
> *Grievous was my pain, and could not be stayed.*
> *My soul was overwhelmed,*
> *like them that go down to Sheol,*
> *and my spirit was sunken low among the dead.*
> *My life had reached the Pit,*
> *and my soul waxed faint day and night without rest.*
> *There burst forth, as it were, a blazing fire,*
> *held in my bones,*
> *the flame whereof devoured unto the nethermost seas*
> *exhausting my strength every minute.*
> *Disasters hovered about me,*
> *and my soul was utterly bowed down.*
> *For all my strength had ceased from my body,*
> *and my heart was poured out like water,*
> *and my flesh melted like wax,*
> *and the strength of my loins was turned to confusion,*
> *and my arm was wrenched from the shoulder.*
> *I could not move my hand,*
> *and my foot was caught in a shackle,*
> *and my knees were dissolved like water.*
> *I could take neither pace nor step; heaviness replaced*
> *my fleetness of foot;*
> *my steps were trammeled.*
> *My tongue was tied and protruded;*
> *I could not lift my voice*
> *in any articulate speech,*
> *to revive the spirit of stumbling,*
> *or encourage the faint with a word.*
> *My lips were dumb altogether.*[38]

There is an obvious similarity between this poignant portrayal of suffering and the allusions to the psalms of lament in the gospel accounts of Jesus on the cross, where Jesus' cry "My God, my God ..." is a free quotation from Psalm 22. One could develop a case for the appropriateness of the anguished lyrical outcry in the Hymns of

Thanksgiving for a victim of crucifixion. All that one could conclude, however, is that it is possible to link together these Qumran texts—the historical references to the persecution of the Teacher and the poetry of suffering—and to infer from them that the Teacher was crucified. But even if the Teacher was crucified, his crucifixion would not make him specifically a forerunner of Jesus. We know from the writings of Josephus and from other historical sources that many people considered enemies of the state—or of the religious status quo—were crucified during the first century B.C.E. Martyrdom had become so widespread that in Judaism a cult of the martyrs arose (Matt. 23:29–31). It was believed that the death of the martyrs had redemptive significance for the faithful,[39] so the death of the Teacher of Righteousness—whether by crucifixion or by another form of execution—could have been understood as the vicarious suffering of one martyr among many rather than as a precise anticipation of the meaning discerned by Christians in the death of Jesus.

Object of faith. Some scholars go beyond the attempt to point out parallels between the death of the Teacher and the death of Jesus to advance the claim that the Qumran community had a doctrine of faith in the Teacher and a belief in his resurrection that directly influenced the rise of these beliefs in Christianity. The text that is usually pointed to in support of this claim is one from the Habakkuk Commentary that applies to faith in the Teacher of Righteousness the familiar phrase "The just shall live by Faith," a concept central for Paul.[40] But in the Qumran context faith means fidelity to his teachings,[41] rather than belief in his redemptive death. Indeed, there is no redemptive role assigned by the Qumran documents to the Teacher of Righteousness or to any other messianic figure. The community is called to obey faithfully the instructions of the Teacher in order to preserve their purity as the true people of God while they await the overthrow of their enemies by direct divine intervention and the establishment of the pure worship of God by the Messiah (or Messiahs) yet to come.

The closest analogy to the Qumran community's view of the Teacher is the image of Jesus in one segment of the early church as primarily a source of divine wisdom. This interpretation of Jesus is represented in the Q document, the hypothetical common source behind the Gospels of Matthew and Luke. In Q there is no explicit theological meaning attached to Jesus' suffering and death, as there is in the other gospel traditions. There is, however, a clear indication in

the Q tradition that Jesus expected to be put to death by the authorities on a charge of having violated God's covenant with his people.
Because Jesus has befriended "tax collectors and sinners," he is being
denounced as "a glutton and drunkard" (Luke 7:34), which are the
terms assigned in Deuteronomy 21:20–21 to the rebellious son who
is to to be executed (stoned to death) by the community. It is not
surprising, therefore, that the Q document was combined by Luke
and Matthew with the Markan gospel tradition, where the meaning
of the suffering and death of Jesus was an explicit and important item
of faith. Similarly, in Paul's Letter to the Corinthians, Christ is portrayed as the Wisdom of God (1 Cor. 1:18–24), but Paul hastens to
explain that it is in the cross of Christ that the divine wisdom is disclosed. For Qumran, however, it was not the death of the Teacher
but the wisdom of the divine secrets he disclosed in his teachings
that made him an object of veneration.

Dupont-Sommer tried to show that the Teacher of Righteousness
was an *eschatological* figure who corresponded to the glorified Christ of
the New Testament—a figure whose coming marked the start of God's
victory over evil.

> *And Thou, O God, has succoured my soul*
> *And lifted my horn on high.*
> *And I will shine with a sevenfold light*
> *in the Eden which Thou hast made unto Thy glory.*
> *For Thou are an everlasting light unto me.*[42]

But the translation of this passage from the Thanksgiving Hymns
that is adopted by most scholars shows that the exaltation had already
occurred in God's preservation of the Teacher (or the hymn writer)
in the face of fierce opposition. Beginning the quotation several lines
earlier brings this out more clearly:

> *Thou has raised high my horn*
> *over all that reviled me,*
> *and all who wage battle against me*
> *are routed without remnant,*
> *and all that contend with me*
> *are as chaff before the wind;*
> *and all impiety bows to my sway.*
> *For Thou, O my God, has holpen my soul*
> *and raised high my horn.*
>
> *I am lit with a light sevenfold.*
> *and with that same lustre of glory*

which Thou didst create for Thyself.
For Thou are unto me as a light eternal
keeping my feet upon the way.[43]

From the closing lines it is evident that the light is not a halo of eschatological glory but the eternal illumination by which God guides his
people into the path of obedience. The special light the Teacher
receives is granted in order that he might guide others in "the way."
No hint is really present in this or any other passage that men are to
have faith in him as a crucified, resurrected, and exalted redemptive
figure. If such details were present in the Dead Sea Scrolls, they would
go a long way toward explaining how such theological views came to be
associated with Jesus of Nazareth. But it is only after one has familiar-
ized oneself with the New Testament understanding of Jesus that one
can go to the Scrolls and read into them these essentially alien ideas.
The single link between the death of the Teacher and the death of
Jesus is the Jewish cult of the martyrs, which may have influenced the
way these deaths were interpreted by the Essene and early Christian
communities. No direct influence of the Qumran documents or the
Essene ideas on the Christian interpretation of the cross can be shown.

Qumran Rites and Christian Sacraments

Since the discovery of the Qumran documents, scholars have also
attempted to establish connections between the practices of the
Qumran community and Christian sacraments, specifically Baptism
and the Eucharist.

Baptism. Some scholars have theorized that John the Baptist either
was an Essene or was under Essene influence; the connection, they find,
is indicated particularly by the significance baptism had for him. The
argument runs that since many cisterns were found among the ruins at
Qumran, and since they had steps for easy ascent and descent, they
must have been used as baptisteries. Since John the Baptist was carrying on baptismal activity nearby in the Jordan Valley, it is likely that
he was originally associated with the Essenes and shared their understanding of baptism. Furthermore, the argument continues, at Qumran
a baptism of fire was expected to cover the earth (as in the Iranian eschatology alluded to by C.H. Kraeling in his study of John the Baptist):[44]

When the hour of judgment strikes,
when the lot of God's anger is cast
upon the abandoned,

when his fury is poured forth upon dissemblers,
when the doom of his final rage
falls on all worthless things;
when the torrents of death do swirl,
and there is none to escape;
when the rivers of Belial
burst their high banks
—rivers that are like fire
devouring all that draw their waters,
rivers whose runnels destroy
green tree and dry tree alike,[45]
rivers that are like fire
which sweeps the flaming sparks
devouring all that drink their water
—a fire which consumes
all foundations of clay,
every solid bedrock;
when the foundations of the mountains become a raging blaze,
when granite rocks are turned
to streams of pitch,
when the flame devours
down to the Great Abyss,
when all the floods of Belial burst forth
unto hell itself;
when the depths of the abyss are in turmoil,
when the earth cries out in anguish
for all the havoc wrought in the world,
when all its depths are aquake,
and all that is on it quails
and quivers in mighty havoc;
when with His mighty roar
God thunders forth.[46]

As Kraeling points out, in the Iranian eschatological scheme those
who had been purified in anticipation of the river of fiery judgment—
presumably made pure by baptism with water—would pass unharmed
through the baptism of fire. There can be no doubt that the Qumran
community parallels the Iranian view in expecting a baptism of fire to
sweep over the earth. What is not so clear is whether at Qumran
members were required to be baptized in preparation for the fires of
judgment. Indeed, the link between the cisterns at Qumran and the

Essene belief in a baptism of fire can hardly be justified, since there is no unequivocal evidence that the cisterns were used for other purposes than furnishing a water supply, or that an initiatory rite of baptism was required of those who became members of the community, although the possibility remains that entering or renewing the covenant may have involved a public immersion ceremony.[47] Josephus does report that the Essenes bathed daily before eating,[48] but such lustrations were in keeping with Old Testament ritual requirements and were widely practiced by other Jewish sects of the period in Palestine and Syria.[49] There is thus no absolutely firm basis for supposing that John's baptism was a variant of an eschatological baptism at Qumran by which one prepared oneself to pass undefiled and unharmed through the river of fire;[50] it remains a historical possibility. Since we can establish no definite historical link between the Essenes' lustration ceremonies and the baptism practiced by John, the Qumran documents are at best of only indirect importance for increasing our understanding of Jesus' baptism or of the adoption of baptism by the early church. It is highly plausible that the Iranian notion of the river of fire did help to shape John's view of baptism as a divinely sanctioned safeguard against the horrors of the eschatological judgment, but whether that influence was mediated by the Qumran community remains uncertain.

Eucharist. Another aspect of the community life at Qumran, thought by some scholars to shed light on the practices instituted by Jesus and developed in the early church, is the ceremony accompanying the eating of the common meal. It has long been recognized that there are two different traditions in the New Testament and in the early church about the meaning of the Lord's Supper:[51] One tradition is reflected in Acts, where the Christians gather daily in a meal of joyous fellowship;[52] the other tradition may be seen in the gospel accounts and in Paul (1 Cor. 10), where the meal is a memorial of Jesus' death, performed "in remembrance."[53] There is no need to look outside the rabbinic sources, in which the Passover is a family act of remembrance, to discover the material that, by similarity and contrast, furnished the background for the Christian development of the Lord's Supper as a kind of Christian Passover.[54] But for the joyous meal we must think of some tradition, presumably Jewish in origin, in which the meal was eaten in expectation of the coming of the community's deliverer. Qumran provides us with the precise archetype. In describing the obligation of members of the community to observe its rules and respect its leaders, the Manual of Discipline declares:

> Wherever there be ten men who have been formally enrolled in the community, one who is a priest is not to depart from them. When they sit in his presence, they are to take their places according to their respective ranks; and the same order is to obtain when they meet for common counsel.
>
> When they set the table for a meal or prepare wine to drink, the priest is first to put forth his hand to invoke a blessing on the first portion of the bread or wine.[55]

By itself, the instruction about the blessing on the bread and wine seems to refer only to a prayer spoken at an ordinary meal. But in another Qumran document, which declares itself to be the Rule for the Congregation in the End Time, when the members' eschatological hope is fulfilled and the Messiah is in their midst, similar instructions are given:

> If they happen to be foregathering for a common meal or to drink wine together, when the common board has been spread or the wine mixed for drinking, no one is to stretch out his hand prior to the priest. It is he who is to pronounce the blessing over the first portion of the bread or wine, and it is he who is first to stretch out his hand to the bread. After that, the anointed king, a layman, is to stretch out his hand to the bread; and after that the members of the community in general are to pronounce the blessing, in order of rank.[56]

It is not yet clear whether the Qumran community awaited only a kingly messiah (the "anointed king" of the text just quoted) or a priestly messiah as well.[57] But it is clear that the scene depicted in the ritual passage just quoted is not that of an ordinary meal; it is the procedure ordained for the End Time, when Belial and the enemies of God will be overthrown and his righteous rule established. It would seem justified, therefore, to conclude that the blessing spoken at the communal meal was an anticipation of the presence of the Messiah (or Messiahs) in the New Age, when God's will would be effected through the anointed king and anointed priest. If this is a correct interpretation of the Qumran documents, then the communal meals at Qumran seem to resemble the fellowship meals that Jesus ate with his disciples and that they continued to celebrate after his death. The disciples were convinced that Jesus would appear once more in their midst in triumph as God's anointed king the Messiah— or perhaps as king-priest, as the Letter to the Hebrews implies.[58]

Even if a case could not be made for considering the Qumran communal meal an eschatological anticipation, and therefore a forerunner of the Last Supper,[59] there is other evidence for a close connection between the meaning attached by Jesus to his final meal with his disciples and Jewish eschatological hopes of his day.[60] The crucial passage is Luke 22:15–16:

> I have eagerly desired to eat this passover with you before I suffer; for I tell you I shall not eat it until it is fulfilled in the kingdom of God.

Joachim Jeremias has paraphrased Jesus' words in such a way as to bring out their meaning against the background of Jewish liturgical usage of the period:

> I would very much have liked to eat this passover lamb with you before my death. (But I must deny myself this wish.) For I tell you I do not intend to eat of it again until God fulfills (his promises) in the kingdom of God.... Take (this cup) and divide (it) among you; for I tell you I do not intend from now on to drink of the fruit of the vine until God establishes his kingdom.[61]

Without going into the complex question of the original form and earliest version of the words spoken by Jesus at the Last Supper, we can say that Jesus is here depicted—and probably with historical accuracy—as envisioning a direct link between his final meal with his disciples and the coming of God's Kingdom in the End Time. The great difference between Jesus' practice and that of the Jews of his day is that they ate the Passover meal while he pointedly abstained. Due attention has not always been given to the fact that at least some Jews seem to have celebrated the Passover not only as a memorial of and renewal of God's covenant with Israel at the time of the deliverance from slavery in Egypt but also as a joyous anticipation of the coming of the Messiah in the last days. Accordingly, the Jews recited antiphonally Psalm 118—a psalm that was a favorite of the early Christians and was understood to predict the coming of Jesus. It was reportedly quoted at the time of his final entry into Jerusalem (Mark 11:9 and parallels) and is mentioned in connection with Jesus' Parable of the Rejection of the Vineyard-Owner's Son (Mark 12:1–11). As the climax of Matthew's account of Jesus' rejection by the leaders of Judaism, Psalm 118 is explicitly quoted:

> For I tell you, you will not see me again, until you say "Blessed is he who comes in the name of the Lord." (Matthew 23:39)

It is obvious, therefore, that the early church, and probably Jesus himself, expected him to be vindicated by God at the last day in fulfillment of Psalm 118, which was sung by Jews of this period in connection with the Passover celebration as an expresssion of their hope in the coming of God's Messiah.

> *This is the day that the Lord has made;*
> *let us rejoice and be glad in it.*
> *Save us, we beseech you, O Lord!*
> *O Lord, we beseech you, give us success!*
>
> *Blessed is the one who comes in the name of the Lord!*
> *We bless you from the house of the Lord.*
> *The Lord is God,*
> *and he has given us light.*
> *Bind the festal procession with branches,*
> *up to the horns of the altar!*
> *You are my God, and I will give thanks to you;*
> *you are my God, I will extol you.*
> *O give thanks to the Lord, for he is good;*
> *for his steadfast love endures forever!*
>
> (Ps. 118:24–29)

But the text from Psalm 118 most frequently quoted by the early Christians was verse 22.[62]

> *The stone which the builders rejected*
> *has become the chief cornerstone.*

The rejection of Jesus was therefore understood as the necessary first step toward the fulfillment of Israel's hope of the establishment of the Kingdom of God. Whether Jesus regarded his own death in the light of the prophetic saying in Psalm 118:22 cannot be determined with certainty, but there is no reason to doubt that he saw a link between the ministry he had begun and the promised day of triumph to which the Passover celebration pointed. It is not of paramount importance whether the shaping of this thought came from Qumran or from the rabbinic interpretation of the ancient Passover ceremony attested in the Midrash on the Psalms. What seems clear is that the earliest Christians were persuaded that the rejection of Jesus, to which Jesus alluded in his word about suffering (Luke 22:15), was the divinely ordained prerequisite to the fulfillment of God's promised Kingdom. The presence of this motif in the meals at Qumran as well as in the ordinary Passover is a clear indication of the fervency of eschatological hope in Jesus' day.

Radical Interpretation of the Law at Qumran and in the Gospel Tradition

Another area of alleged contact between Jesus and Qumran has to do with the interpretation of God's demand in the Jewish Law. Although the strictness of interpretation of the Law among the better-known Jewish sect, the Pharisees, has become proverbial, the latter were in fact seeking to make the Law relevant to daily life and to interpret its precepts in such a way as to take into account the changes that had occurred between Moses' day and their own. It is an unfair caricature to picture the Pharisees as heartless pedants. Indeed, the gospel tradition calls upon the followers of Jesus to surpass the Pharisees in their standards of righteousness (Matt. 5:20).[63] Apparently, the Essenes also thought that the rest of the Jews, including the Pharisees, were not sufficiently strict in preserving legal purity in their observances of the Law. Accordingly, they withdrew to the monastic life of their communal center at Qumran in order to fulfill the Law's demand for holiness. Thus the Essenes and the Christians can both be characterized as radical reinterpreters of the Law, but their perpectives are in many ways diametrically opposed. The Qumran group insisted on strict rules for admission to the community and for expulsion of violators. They also disagreed with the Christians on the question of attitude toward one's enemies, with the emphasis in the Gospels on love and forgiveness, but in the Qumran texts on punishment and destruction. Jewish scholars have often asserted that there is no passage in the Jewish Scriptures—or in the rabbinic tradition—that summons Israel to hate its enemies, as Jesus declares (Matt. 5:42). But one could infer such an attitude from such utterances as Psalm 137:9 ("Happy shall he be who takes your little ones and dashes them against the rock!") and Psalm 139:21–22:

> *Do I not hate those that hate you, O Lord?*
> *And do I not loathe them that rise up against thee?*
> *I hate them with perfect hatred:*
> *I count them my enemies.*

A feeling of hatred for one's enemies does not prevail in the Old Testament, however; consider, for example, the exhortations of Proverbs 25:21–22:

If your enemy is hungry, give him bread to eat;
and if he is thirsty, give him water to drink;
for you will heap coals of fire on his head,
and the Lord will reward you.

This compassionate attitude is quoted with approval in the New Testament (Rom. 12:20) and is wholly consonant with the message and response of Jesus to his antagonists. On the contrary, members of the community at Qumran are specifically directed to hate their enemies. In the *War Rule* there are detailed instructions for organizing the members of the community as an army whose task is to achieve the destruction of their enemies, to which they will be called by "trumpets of massacre," all to be carried out by the "Divisions of God for the Vengeance of His Wrath on the Sons of Darkness."[64] Thus, on the question of attitude toward one's enemies, the Christian and Qumran communities sharply disagree.

Finally, there are important similarities and differences between early Christian and Qumranian attitudes toward that central religious institution of Judaism: the Temple. The Essenes were waiting at Qumran until God intervened in their behalf, vindicated them, and enabled them to take over the operation of the temple cultus in what they believed to be the pure and proper manner, in keeping with their interpretation of the legal prescriptions contained in the Law of Moses. By contrast, Jesus' aggressive action in cleansing the temple (Mark 11 and parallels) is matched by his reported prediction—without regret—of its destruction (Mark 13:2 and parallels). The clear implication is that the temple is not an essential feature for the worship of God. That viewpoint is made explicit in the Johannine form of the tradition that true worship of God will not be localized in Jerusalem or any other sacred place (John 4:21–23). The "raising up" of the temple linked in John 2:19 with its announced destruction is directly asserted in John 2:21–22 to mean the raising up of his body—but that is probably also a metaphorical reference to the raising up of the church as the new place where the worship of God is to be carried on. Both in the Markan and the Johannine versions of the Jesus tradition, therefore, no positive place is given to the temple of Jerusalem. On this issue, the Christian and the Qumran traditions are diametrically opposed. The potentially universalistic outreach of the early Christian community is antithetical to the rigid exclusivism of Qumran.

Some Conclusions About the Historical Value of the Extrabiblical Sources

The limitations of the extrabiblical sources for our knowledge of Jesus are obvious. They provide us with no significant information about him that we do not have access to in the gospel accounts. But they are important in two ways. First, the Qumran materials particularly suggest the range of viewpoints among Jews at Jesus' time and the depth of their dissatisfaction with the religious establishment in Jerusalem. Even though there were many differences in detail between the Essenes and the early Christians, the community of vigorous dissenters in the Dead Sea community, who fervently awaited the coming of the New Age in which God would vindicate them, make John the Baptist and Jesus more vividly discernible against the background of contemporary Jewish life and thought. Second, these extrabiblical sources render extremely improbable the claim that Jesus is a pious fiction rather than a historical character. It is scarcely credible that Roman and Jewish writers of the first and second centuries would have perpetuated as historical record stories about an unhistorical figure whom they so patently despised. They treat him as a historical, though regrettable, personage. However much they might have wished him out of existence, they did not and could not deny his historicity.

A pressing question remains: What kind of person was he who evoked such strong and enduring reactions, both favorable and hostile? There is not sufficient evidence to write a biography of Jesus in the modern sense, not even of a segment of his public life. Of his inner psychological motivations, of the personal forces that molded his childhood and therefore shaped his adult life, we know nothing. It would be possible, of course, to extrapolate from what we know of the upbringing of Jewish boys of his epoch, but the fallacy is obvious: No one else grew up to be like him. Recognizing that, like any other historical documents, the Gospels have unacknowledged assumptions and certain special interests, we must nevertheless turn to them and the traditions preserved in them for detailed knowledge of Jesus.

Suggestions for Further Reading

Translations of primary historical materials for studying the background of the New Testament and of Judaism in that period are given in H.C. Kee, *The New Testament in Context: Sources and*

Documents (Englewood Cliffs, NJ: Prentice-Hall, 1984). The Jewish documents bearing on Jesus and early Christianity are presented and analyzed by R.T. Herford on the basis of earlier scholarly assumptions in *Christianity in Talmud and Midrash* (Clifton, NJ: Reference Library, 1966). Of fundamental value for the Jewish background of Christianity are Flavius Josephus, *Antiquities of the Jews*, especially vols. 6–8 of the Loeb edition, translated by Ralph Marcus, Allen Wikgren, and L.H. Feldman (Cambridge, MA: Harvard University Press), and the collections of deutero-canonical or noncanonical Jewish materials in *The Cambridge Annotated Study Apocrypha*, ed. H.C. Kee (Cambridge: Cambridge University Press, 1994) and *The Old Testament Pseudepigrapha*, ed. J.H. Charlesworth (Garden City, NY: Doubleday, vol. 1, 1983; vol. 2, 1985). The major documents from the Dead Sea community are available in English translation by Geza Vermes, *The Dead Sea Scrolls in English*, 3d ed.* (Harmondsworth and New York: Penguin, 1987). Earlier perceptive assessments of the Scrolls have been written by F.M. Cross, Jr. (*The Ancient Library of Qumran*,* 2d ed. [New York: Doubleday, 1958]), and Matthew Black (*The Scrolls and Christian Origins* [New York: Scribner's, 1961]). For more recent perspectives on the scrolls, see *Jesus and the Dead Sea Scrolls*, ed. J.H. Charlesworth (New York: Doubleday, 1992), and *Understanding the Dead Sea Scrolls*, ed. Hershel Shanks (New York: Random House, 1992).

*Available in a paperback edition.

NOTES

[1] See the discussion in Maurice Goguel, *Jésus de Nazareth: mythe où histoire?* [Jesus of Nazareth: Myth or History?] (Paris: Payot, 1925).

[2] *Die Christusmythe* [The Christ myth], 2 vols. (Jena: Diederichs, 1909–1911).

[3] *The Birth of the Gospel: A Study of the Origin and Purport of the Primitive Allegory of the Jews* (New York: 1927; reprint, New York: Philosophical Library, 1957).

[4] We have noted that this theory has been revived by some scholars recently; it is discussed in our analysis of the Mark and Q traditions (Chapters 3 and 4).

[5] Ibid., p. 651.

[6] Ibid., pp. 141–42 (Smith's italics).

[7] The classic study of corporate personality is by H.W. Robinson, *Corporate Personality in Ancient Israel* (Philadelphia: Fortress, 1964); see also his *Inspiration and Revelation in the Old Testament* (New York: Oxford University Press, 1946), pp. 69–74. There are important discussions in Johannes Pedersen, *Israel: Its Life and Culture*, 4 vols. (New York: Oxford University Press, 1926, 1940; vols. 1 and 2 rep., 1964; vols. 3 and 4 reprint with additions, 1959).

[8]On the effects of Old Testament prophecy on the gospel narrative, see Chapter 5. Also Barnabas Lindars, *New Testament Apolog ic* (Philadelphia: Westminster, 1962).

[9]For older assessments of some of these sources, see Maurice Goguel, *Life of Jesus* (trans. Olive Wyon; New York: Macmillan, 1946), pp. 70–104; and Joseph Klausner, *Jesus of Nazareth* (trans. Herbert Danby; New York: Macmillan, 1926), pp. 17–62. My own analysis of them is offered in *What Can We Know About Jesus?* (Cambridge: Cambridge University Press, 1992).

[10]Josephus *Antiquities of the Jews* 18, 63, vol. 9 (trans. L.H. Feldman) Loeb Classical Library (Cambridge, MA: Harvard University Press, 1965).

[11]See the discussion of the authenticity of this passage in vol. 9 of L.H. Feldman's translation of Josephus' *Antiquities*, pp. 48–51, and notes on pp. 48 and 49. Feldman reproduces and evaluates an attempt by Robert Eisler to restore the passage to its original form. See also the essay on this material by Paul Winter in E. Schürer and G. Vermes, *History of the Jewish People in the Time of Jesus Christ* (Edinburgh: T. & T. Clark, 1973), pp. 428–41.

[12]Josephus, *Antiquities*, 18, pp. 65–80.

[13]Ibid., 20, p. 200.

[14]Pliny, *Letters* 10.94. The full text in English, with ample commentary, is in A.N. Sherwin-White, *Fifty Letters of Pliny* (New York: Oxford University Press, 1967).

[15]Suetonius *Lives of the Twelve Caesars* 25. 4 (trans. Joseph Gavorse; New York: Modern Library, 1931; reprint, 1959), p. 226. "Chrestos" would be the Greek form, "Chrestus" the Latinized form.

[16]A discussion of the date of Claudius' decree concerning the Jewish disturbance in given in F.J. Foakes-Jackson and Kirsopp Lake, *The Beginnings of Christianity*, vol. 5 (New York: Macmillan, 1933), pp. 459–60. For a different interpretation of the evidence, see John Knox, *Chapters in a Life of Paul* (Nashville: Abingdon, 1950), pp. 81–83.

[17]Tacitus *Annals* 15. 44, vol. 4 (trans. J. Jackson) Loeb Classical Library (Cambridge, MA: Harvard University Press, 1931).

[18]For a succinct summary, see Klausner, *Jesus of Nazareth*, pp. 17–54. See also R.T. Herford, *Christianity in Talmud and Midrash* (London, 1903; reprint., Clifton, NJ: Reference Book Publishers, 1966). The entire book is devoted to a sifting of late Jewish sources relating both to Jesus and to early Christianity.

[19]Important methodological considerations about the trustworthiness of rabbinic material as sources for the first century C.E. were offered early on by Jacob Neusner in his pioneering study, *From Politics to Piety: The Emergence of Pharisaic Judaism* (Englewood Cliffs, NJ: Prentice-Hall, 1973), pp. 81–96, and have been supplemented over the years by his hundreds of scholarly works, including analyses of Judaism in the context of emergent rabbinic Judaism. In *Jews and Christians: The Myth of a Common Tradition* (Philadelphia: Trinity Press International, 1991) Neusner shows how, following the destruction of the temple in 70 C.E. and the replacement of the priests by the rabbis as leaders, the two movements that we now call Judaism and Christianity became sharply differentiated, although

both made claims on their common heritage as foundational for their respective developments.

[20]H.L. Strack and Paul Billerbeck, *Kommentar zum Neuen Testament aus dem Talmud und Midrasch* (Munich: Beck, 1922–1961).

[21]b Shabbath 104[b]. Quoted from Herford, *Christianity in Talmud and Midrash*, p. 35.

[22]Ibid., pp. 137–38.

[23]See reports on these excavations by Eric Meyers and James Strange in *Archaeology, the Rabbis and Early Christianity* (Nashville: Abingdon, 1981) and an analysis of the cultural and historical implications of the finds at Sepphoris for the setting of Jesus' life and early ministry by Richard Batey, *Jesus and the Forgotten City* (Grand Rapids, MI: Baker, 1991).

[24]Klausner, *Jesus of Nazareth*, p. 46.

[25]Ibid. Apart from obviously polemical traditions, the only early information about Jesus that is in direct conflict with the gospel narrative concerns his disciples. Although the tradition is not explicit, it implies that Jesus had only five disciples and that all were executed. A plausible explanation for this tradition was offered by R.T. Herford in *Christianity in Talmud and Midrash*, pp. 90–95: (1) that the names given for the disciples are actually those of early Christians, but the event referred to occurred at a later time, perhaps during the brief period of Jewish persecution of Christians under Bar Kochbah in the third decade of the second century C.E. Whatever the basis and credibility of this talmudic tradition, it would add little to our knowledge or understanding of Jesus.

[26]Herford, *Christianity in Talmud and Midrash*, pp. 348–49.

[27]Klausner, *Jesus of Nazareth*, p. 57.

[28]Many scholars refer to this council as Sanhedrin—a term which is a transliteration of the actual Greek term, *synedrion*, which was used in Hellenistic and Roman times for these regional councils which had provided a measure of local autonomy, but which were subject to the imperial authorities. Later the term was translitered into Hebrew, Sanhedrin, and used by Jews for their religious council which supervised Jewish norms and worship as the Mishnah and Talmud were taking shape. It is anachronistic to attribute this function to the Roman-appointed council in the early first century C.E.

[29]All the complete or longer fragmentary documents have long been published. The charges that scholars feared the implications of the contents of some of the scrolls for the history of Judaism or the origins of Christianity are wholly unfounded: The delays in publication were due to a mixture of lethargy and undue scholarly caution about accuracy of transcription and interpretation of the writings. Of the many English translations of these writings, there is none better than that of Geza Vermes, *The Dead Sea Scrolls in English*, 3d ed. (Harmondsworth and New York: Penguin, 1987).

[30]A brief account of the excavations at the community center in Qumran is given by J.T. Milik in *Ten Years of Discovery in the Wilderness of Judaea* (trans. John Strugnell; Naperville, IL: Allenson, 1959).

[31]Paul Kahle, in *The Cairo Genizah* (Oxford: Blackwell, 1957), pp. 1–28, gives a full description of the probable series of circumstances that brought the scrolls from Qumran to Cairo.

[32]Hugh Schonfield, in *The Secrets of the Dead Sea Scrolls* (Cranbury, NJ: A.S. Barnes, 1957), hints broadly at a link between the later phase of the

Qumran "new covenant" community and the Christian portrait of Jesus. The most elaborate and bizarre construct along these lines is that by Barbara Thiering in *Jesus and the Riddle of the Dead Sea Scrolls* (San Francisco: HarperCollins, 1992). She correlates the Gospels and Acts with the Dead Sea Scrolls, using an elaborate allegorical method according to which the stories and sayings of Jesus are interpreted as evidence of the efforts of Joseph, John the Baptist, and Jesus to reshape the Dead Sea community and its principles in preparation for a new Israel. John the Baptist was the Teacher of Righteousness mentioned in the Scrolls; Jesus was born there (the manger in Bethlehem is a symbol pointing to the Dead Sea community). In this fantastic construction, Herod comes across as the one who established the priestly and royal offices which became the popes and patriarchs of the Christian church. Thiering's allegorical method enables her to find historical events behind such sayings of Jesus as the Parable of the Good Samaritan and stories such as the miraculous feedings. By this strategy she discovers in the Gospels and Acts an accurate chronology for every important event in the rise of Christianity from 9 B.C.E. to 63 C.E.

[33] An older discussion, which is still valuable, is found in an appendix to J.B. Lightfoot, *Commentary on St. Paul's Epistle to the Colossians* (London: Macmillan, 1876). More recent comparative analyses include that of Sherman E. Johnson, "The Dead Sea Manual and the Jerusalem Church of Acts," in Krister Stendahl, ed., *The Scrolls and the New Testament* (New York: Harper & Row, 1957), pp. 129–42, and a collection of essays on the subject has been edited by J.H. Charlesworth (*Jesus and the Dead Sea Scrolls* [Garden City, NY: Doubleday, 1992]).

[34] See, for example, H.H. Rowley, "The Qumran Sect and Christian Origins," in *From Moses to Qumran* (New York: Association Press, 1963), pp. 239–79.

[35] J.M. Allegro, "Further Light on the History of the Qumran Sect," in *Journal of Biblical Literature* 75 (1956): 89–95. See also "Further Messianic References in Qumran Literature," in ibid., pp. 174–87. Allegro's interpretation of the evidence is rejected by H.H. Rowley, "4 Qp Nahum and the Teacher of Righteousness," in ibid., pp. 188–93.

[36] Translation from T.H. Gaster, ed., *Dead Sea Scriptures* (New York: Doubleday Anchor Books, 1964), pp. 249–50.

[37] *The Essene Writings from Qumran* (trans. Geza Vermes; Cleveland: Meridian, 1962), p. 264, n. 7. The brackets indicate restorations of the text by Dupont-Sommer.

[38] Gaster, *Dead Sea Scriptures*, pp. 169–70.

[39] Edward Lohse, in *Martyrer und Gottesknecht* [Martyr and servant of God] (Göttingen: Vandenhoek & Ruprecht, 1955), has made a careful study of this theme.

[40] See the interpretation by Dupont-Sommer, *Essene Writings*, p. 263, esp. n. 4.

[41] Habakkuk Commentary 2:4, in Gaster, *Dead Sea Scriptures*, p. 248.

[42] *Essene Writings*, p. 365.

[43] Gaster, *Dead Sea Scriptures*, p. 165.

[44] *John the Baptist* (New York: Scribner's, 1951), p. 117.

[45] The same image is used to depict the destruction wrought through God's judgment in Ezekiel 20:47 and is attributed to Jesus in Luke 23:31.

[46]From the Hymns of Thanksgiving (identified in the scholarly code as 1QH), col. 3; here quoted from Gaster, *Dead Sea Scriptures*, pp. 145–46.

[47]A good case for an initiatory immersion rite at Qumran is presented by Matthew Black in the *The Scrolls and Christian Origins* (New York: Scribner's, 1961), pp. 91–101.

[48]Josephus, *Jewish Wars*, vol. 2 (trans. H. St. J. Thackeray), Loeb Classical Library (Cambridge: Harvard University Press, 1927), p. 129.

[49]Details about the baptizing sects are found in Joseph Thomas, *Le mouvement baptiste en Palestine et Syrie* [The baptizing movement in Palestine and Syria] (Louvain: Duclot, 1935).

[50]Rowley, *From Moses to Qumran*, p. 230, n. 1.

[51]The classic exposition of this thesis of two eucharistic traditions is found in Hans Lietzmann, *Mass and Lord's Supper: A Study in the History of the Liturgy* (trans. D.H.G. Reeve; Leiden: E.J. Brill, 1953–1958). A concise but thorough discussion of New Testament eucharistic traditions is given in Eduard Schweizer, *The Lord's Supper According to the New Testament* (trans. J.M. Davis; Philadelphia: Fortress, 1967).

[52]A quite different view is presented in another detailed study of eucharistic origins by Joachim Jeremias, *The Eucharistic Words of Jesus*, 2d ed. (trans. Norman Perrin; New York: Scribner's, 1966), esp. pp. 31–36. Additional support for the existence of the joyous eschatological meal is given by Luke's special tradition concerning the Last Supper, particularly if one omits Luke 20:19b–20, as the textual tradition of the so-called Western text does. On this question, see Jeremias, *Eucharistic Words*, pp. 138–73.

[53]Jeremias attaches a special significance to this phrase: It is Jesus' petition to his followers to remember him before God rather than an instruction to consider the Eucharist as a memorial ceremony. See *Eucharistic Words*, pp. 237–55.

[54]A technical study of the relationship of Passover to Eucharist is given in Edward Lohse, *History of the Suffering and Death of Jesus Christ* (trans. M.O. Dietrich; Philadelphia: Fortress, 1967), pp. 35–54.

[55]Translation from Gaster, *Dead Sea Scriptures*, p. 330.

[56]Ibid., p. 310.

[57]The linking of kingly and priestly roles goes back into the Israelite tradition even before the time of David, as is evident in the description of Melchizedek, ancient king of [Jeru]Salem and "priest of the Most High God" (Gen. 14:18) and in the priestly assignment for the sons of David (2 Sam 8:15–18). See K.G. Kuhn, "The Two Messiahs of Aaron and Israel," in Stendahl, ed., *The Scrolls and the New Testament*, pp. 54–64. A critique of this position can be found in Rowley, *From Moses to Qumran*, pp. 266–68. In the Stendahl volume, Kuhn also discusses the relationship of the Qumran eschatological meal to the early Christian Eucharist in the essay "The Lord's Supper and the Communal Meal at Qumran," pp. 65–93.

[58]The portrayal of Jesus as king and priest in Hebrews 7 has itself been pointed out as showing parallels with Qumran; see Yigael Yadin, "The Dead Sea Scrolls and the Epistle to the Hebrews," in Chaim Rabin and Yigael Yadin, eds., *Aspects of the Dead Scrolls* (Scripta Hierosolymitana), vol. 4 (Jerusalem: Hebrew University Press, 1958), pp. 36–55. On the importance of the temple imagery for that segment of early Christianity which

produced the Letter to the Hebrews, see my *Who Are the People of God?* (New Haven: Yale University Press, 1995), Ch. 5.

[59]Jeremias rejects this interpretation of the Qumran scrolls and denies any link between Qumran and early Christianity on this point. See *Eucharistic Words*, pp. 31–36.

[60]Ibid., pp. 207–11, 256–62.

[61]Ibid., p. 211.

[62]On the frequency of use of this text and its importance as a theological presupposition in the early church, see C.H. Dodd, *According to the Scriptures: The Sub-Structure of New Testament Theology* (New York: Harper Brothers, 1953), pp. 35–36, 99–100, and passim; and Barnabas Lindars, *New Testament Apologetic* (Philadelphia: Westminster, 1962), pp. 45–51. Ben Witherington in *Jesus the Sage* (Minneapolis: Fortress Press, 1994) notes the importance of the psalms, especially of Psalm 118 in the Gospels' portrayal of Jesus, and suggests that this understanding of Jesus as the embodiment of wisdom may go back to Jesus himself (p. 154).

[63]On the distinctive emphases of Matthew's gospel, see Chapter 5 and the works cited there.

[64]*The War Rule*, II, III.

CHAPTER 3

Jesus As God's Eschatological Messenger
The Q Document

Probably the first written record concerning Jesus was a collection of his sayings known to modern scholars as Q. Apparently, some unknown Christian or group of Christians brought together traditions concerning Jesus, consisting mostly of his sayings. The order in which these traditions were arranged was topical rather than chronological, except that the traditions about the baptism came at the beginning and the clearest predictions of the End of the Age came at the conclusion. In this source there seems to have been only one narrative account of the miracle story type—a healing—and no explicit mention of the Crucifixion. Not only are we in the dark about the identity of the author or authors of this document, but we are not even sure about the precise extent of the work, since we do not have a single copy. Some scholars deny that it ever existed.[1] However, the weight of evidence points to the existence of such a writing; this theory accounts most plausibly for the fact that Matthew and Luke have common material, which seems to have been drawn from a single written source, since the common passages are often verbatim, or nearly so, and are frequently presented in the same sequence. Called Q probably from the German word for "source," *Quelle*,[2] this document, a collection of sayings or perhaps a strand of gospel tradition preserved in a series of short writings, is sufficiently different from Mark and so influential on the content of Matthew and Luke that it deserves to be given detailed treatment as a major factor in preserving traditions about Jesus and in shaping some of the images of him that are found in the New Testament. The source has its own distinctive themes and emphases which are analyzed below.

The Sayings Source Behind Matthew and Luke

Until Johann Gottfried Eichhorn[3] hypothesized at the beginning of the nineteenth century that Matthew and Luke had utilized a common source, many scholars had assumed that the Gospel of Mark was an abridgment of Matthew and that Matthew was the oldest of the Gospels. Eichhorn's hypothesis changed their thinking, although his theory that Matthew and Luke used multiple Aramaic sources never gained wide acceptance.[4] Recent attempts to prove that Mark and Luke were dependent on Matthew fail to convince the majority of biblical scholars.[5] The evidence points rather to the priority of Mark, as a detailed comparison of Mark with Matthew and Luke shows. In many instances Matthew and Luke smooth out the grammar or substitute more felicitous terms for awkward expressions in Mark. Examples are Mark 1:12 = Luke 4:1 and Mark 2:1–12 = Matthew 9:1–8. In the first of these passages Jesus is "led" into the wilderness by the Spirit (Luke) rather than "cast out" or "hurled" there (Mark). In the second passage Mark tells a story, filled with authentic Palestinian local color, about four friends digging through the earthen roof of a village house in order to lower their friend down in front of Jesus. Mark's version is recounted as follows:

> And when he [Jesus] returned to Capernaum after some days, it was reported that he was at home. And many were gathered together, so that there was no longer room for them, not even about the door.... And they came, bringing to him a paralytic carried by four men. And when they could not get near him because of the crowd, they removed the roof above him; and when they had dug through, they let down the pallet on which the paralytic lay. (Mark 2:1–4)

All the details of a small Palestinian village are taken for granted in the narrative: Roofs are made of beaten earth and can be dug through in an emergency; people sleep on pallets, which are as portable and as flexible as quilts; houses have a single entrance and are so small that even a modest gathering in and around the house would make access impossible for four men carrying another on a pallet. Luke, who may be unfamiliar with earthen-roofed houses, describes the removal of the roof tiles (5:19). Since he assumes that people sleep on beds, he reports the awkward process of lowering a bed through an opening made in the tiled roof. Matthew (9:2) omits all the details, relating prosaically that "they" brought a paralytic to Jesus, lying on a "bed."

It is scarcely conceivable that an early Christian writer, whose aim would be to give his gospel as wide an appeal as possible, would embellish a smooth narrative to make it sound more primitive and Palestinian; on the contrary, it is much more likely that he would even out awkward turns of speech and eliminate local references. Although we may thus assume that Matthew and Luke used Mark as a basic source—between them they reproduce nearly all of Mark, and they almost always follow Mark's sequence[6]—Mark does not account for all the material in Matthew and Luke. There is considerable material that is peculiar to one or the other of the Gospels,[7] but more than one-third of Matthew and one-fourth of Luke consist of common material that is not found in Mark. This common material is characterized by a high degree of verbal similarity and by a close correspondence in order, from the baptismal sayings through the Beatitudes to the final eschatological sayings. Remembering that the preliterary language of the tradition would have been Aramaic rather than the Greek of the Gospels, we can best account for the verbal similarity by postulating Matthew's and Luke's use of a single Greek source. And both the verbal similarity and the similarity in the order of the sayings suggest that the source was written. It seems unlikely that Matthew and Luke would overlap so much, or that they would contain so much non-Markan material, if Q were only an oral tradition that served as the main source for all the sayings materials found in Matthew and Luke, or if, as others proposed, Q contained the sayings materials found in Mark as well as in Matthew and Luke.[8]

The Nature and Original Extent of Q

Apart from two brief narrative sections (4:2b–12; 7:2–3, 6–10), Q seems to have consisted almost entirely of sayings of Jesus (and John the Baptist). There is no evidence that it included a narrative of Jesus' trial and execution. That is to say, there are no non-Markan materials common to Matthew and Luke that offer information concerning Jesus' trial and crucifixion. Rather, when Matthew or Luke chooses to supplement the Markan account of the Passion, each does so independently and then returns to the Markan order and substance. Neither are there any explicit allusions to the Passion of Jesus in the Q material; the predictions of the Passion in Matthew and Luke are either taken over from Mark or are peculiar to one or the other gospel.

Thus, nothing points to there having been a passion story in Q. But since we know that our oldest gospel, Mark, has a passion narrative as a central feature, is it conceivable that the early church had a document from which this element was missing? The question leads directly to another: Are there documents of first-century Judaism or earlier that consist entirely of sayings and that might have served as models or as precedents for Q?

The theory has been advanced that there was such a literary type, called by the proponents of the hypothesis "Sayings of a Wise Man."[9] But in the extensive wisdom literature of Judaism there is nothing that really resembles the Q material as a whole. Analogies have been drawn with such documents from the later Jewish wisdom writings as the Wisdom of Solomon and with Sirach (or Ben Sira; also known as Ecclesiasticus). There are some points of similarity—such as that Wisdom is pictured as seeking lodging (Sir. 24:7) and as demanding discipline from those who follow her (Sir. 2:5; 6:20–21)—but the entire outlook of these wisdom books is sharply different from that of Q. For these Jewish writings, wisdom is a matter of obedience to the Law of Moses (Sir. 6:30) and is to be acquired by those who seek out good teachers (Sir. 6:36). Ben Sira focuses on making the most of life, avoiding excess, eschewing pride or dishonesty. Some of the exhortations are as trivial as the contemporary cliché "Have a good day!" (Sir. 14:14). By contrast, in the Q material the response to Jesus is determinative of one's eternal destiny. Judgment turns on one's allegiance and fidelity to the words and works that Jesus has commissioned his followers to fulfill. Far from telling them to set their sights low, as Ben Sira does (11:10), or to avoid doing good deeds to strangers or sinners (Sir. 11:29, 34; 12:4), Jesus is quoted in Q as urging his followers to give up every human tie and obligation in devotion to the announcement of the Kingdom (Luke 9:59–61; 12:22–31). And in Luke 7:34 he is described as "a glutton and a drunkard, a friend of tax collectors and sinners"[10]—scarcely an abstemious life-style of the kind enjoined in Sirach. Instead, Jesus is welcoming into the new community he is shaping those "tax collectors and sinners" whose occupation and behavior violate the qualifications for covenantal participation set forth in the Law of Moses. Both Sirach, with its description of the cosmos as constructed from pairs of opposites (42:24), and Wisdom of Solomon, with its depiction of Wisdom as an emanation from God (7:25) in abstract terms drawn from Hellenistic philosophy (7:22–23), move in an atmosphere of theoretical ontological speculation that bespeaks an intellectual climate wholly other than that of Q.

It is true that elements of the late Jewish wisdom tradition have influenced Q: That is explicit in Luke 11:49[11] and 7:35. What has no counterpart in the Jewish wisdom tradition, however, is the warning here that the messengers of wisdom should expect persecution and even martyrdom. Wisdom was not the monopoly of a single group in Judaism in the time of Jesus. The close link between wisdom and the role of the prophets in Q is an important indicator that what is being disclosed is not timeless wisdom but eschatological wisdom of an apocalyptic type. Fundamental to all apocalypticism is the self-consciousness of a community that is experiencing rejection and persecution from its contemporaries, but is sustained by its sense of God's favor, both now and in the age to come, when he will act in their behalf to judge the wicked and vindicate them. It is precisely this view of life that is embodied in the Q tradition. It has its closest approximation in a Jewish setting in the group or groups that lie behind Daniel, Jubilees, and the Enoch literature, which expect divine intervention in human history and the transformation of the social and political order.[12] But the Q group's point of view is contrary to those expressed in some of these apocalyptic writings (such as the Dead Sea Scrolls), where membership in the community is restricted to those who obey the Law more rigorously than their other Jewish contemporaries. For the Q community, participation in the New Age is open to all—Jews and Gentiles—who recognize in Jesus God's final agent for historical and cosmic renewal and who discern in his words, in his works, and in the community which he has convened the in-breaking of the Rule of God (Luke 11:20, 29–32). They are the ones whose fortunes will be reversed in the Age to Come and who will share the rule with God's Agent in the New Age (Luke 22:28–30). It is this knowledge of God's purpose, esoteric in essence and yet evangelistic in thrust, that constitutes the wisdom set forth in Q (Luke 10:21–22).

   Some recent proposals for the reconstruction of Q handle this feature of a mixture of apocalyptic and proverbial wisdom features in the Q source by assigning all the former material to a late adaptation of an original Q which consisted solely of timeless truths. The model for this hypothesis derives from these scholars' construct of Cynic-Stoic philosophers who are described by these theorizers as speaking in proverbs and aphorisms.[13] To the contrary, careful study of writers in the early Roman world whose thinking was shaped by a blend of Cynic and Stoic philosophy—most notably Cicero and Seneca—shows that a major theme in their view of the world was moral accountability, which was expected to take the form of a future divine day of reckoning, followed by banishment of the wicked to the realm of darkness and vindication of the righteous, who would enter a new age of peace and justice.[14] A central theme among the

Cynics of this period was the divine rule that was to be established in this world, and the moral accountability of all humanity in preparation for that new age.[15] Cicero discusses at length, and positively, the widespread Roman phenomenon of augury, especially the important role of the Sibylline Oracles in helping Roman leaders make crucial decisions, and the role of cosmic signs as portents of the future, while scorning the doubts of some of his contemporaries that there is divine advance disclosure of the course of human history.[16] Clearly, the apocalyptic themes in the Q source would be heard as variants of the claims concerning the future being made in the early empire by proponents of Stoic philosophy.

Old Testament scholars have rightly drawn attention to the continuity between the later prophetic tradition (Daniel, Enoch, and Jubilees, for example) and apocalyptic portraits of the End of the Age.[17] Yet Gerhard von Rad is nevertheless accurate in his assertion that the apocalyptic worldview is most closely akin to the wisdom tradition. More specifically, Martin Hengel has shown that such apocalyptic features and doctrines as the successive ages of the world, the portrayal of empires as giant statues, the influence of astrology and star speculation, are all akin to Hellenistic thinking. Ironically, apocalypticism gives direct evidence of the impact of Hellenism on Judaism, even though the conscious aim of the apocalyptists was to defend the true People of God against enforced Hellenization.[18] What differentiates the apocalyptic outlook from that of Jewish wisdom in its speculative and legal forms is not that one is influenced by Hellenism and the other is not, but that the apocalyptist has given up on this world and looks beyond present suffering and persecution to vindication in the near future. The mainstream of Jewish wisdom literature wants to encourage obedience to the Law so that life will be as full and rewarding as possible; beyond that there is expectation either of no survival after death (Sir. 17:27–28) or of the escape from this world of a disembodied soul (Wisdom of Sol. 3:1–4). Imbued with the apocalyptic worldview, the members of the community of Q believe they have been summoned and commissioned to carry forward Jesus' ministry (Luke 7:22–23; 10:1–16, 21–22); meanwhile they can expect the same mixed reception accorded him (10:16). Rejection and martyrdom are the fate suffered by God's prophets and emissaries down through history (Luke 13:34–35).

The kinship of the Q tradition with aspects of Jewish wisdom and apocalyptic has been effectively demonstrated by Ronald A. Piper and especially by Ben Witherington in their perceptive analyses of the Q source.[19] Piper notes that the succinct sayings (aphorisms) of Jesus in Q are by no means witty, timeless truths (as suggested by those scholars who want to portray Jesus as a Cynic-type, counter-culture itinerant), but instead they involve a radical call to obedience in light of impending conflict. In the Q source it is a prophetic call that is central, not clever wit and wisdom. Further, the death of Jesus in fulfillment of his call to radical obedience and to redefinition of the people of God is explicit in Q.[20] Witherington shows that in Q, Jesus "reverses conventional wisdom in light of the inbreaking eschatological dominion of God."[21] He joins Richard A. Horsley in seeing the apocalyptic features of Q as basic in the source, not as secondary additions.[22]

The closest historical analogy we have for the itinerant charismatic preachers pictured in Q (Luke 10:1–20) is that of the prophetic-revolutionary leaders whom Josephus describes as rousing the people in the years just before the Jewish revolt of 66–70 C.E.[23] As we have noted, there are some similarities to the strategies of the Cynic-Stoic traveling teacher-preachers of the Hellenistic world, as well. Yet Q pictures Jesus as different from either of these groups, in that there is no nationalism in his message and the charisma he possesses and conveys to his followers does not point to the inner divine moral capacity (conscience) as central in Stoic thought, but to the imminent manifestation of God's judgment of the wicked and the vindication of his own people, which in some ways is analogous to Stoic cosmology. According to the Q source, in the service of the Son of Man and the Kingdom of God, Jesus' messengers have abandoned home, family, and every human security. That they have done so is an indicator—not of legal or practical wisdom, nor of an inevitable process of cosmic change—but of God's revelation of his eschatological purpose.

The Date of Q

The date of Q can no more be fixed precisely than can its extent, but a likely date is about 50. That would be long before Matthew (which is usually dated about 80), or Luke (which may be as late as the turn of the second century), and before Mark (probably just before 70), since Q seems to know nothing of the more nearly sequential account of Jesus' career as found in that earliest gospel. In any case, Q's independence from Mark in both form and content means that there is no certain way for determining the relative dates of these two documents. Clearly, however, the Gospels of Matthew and Luke were constructed on the basis of Mark as well as Q, and hence were written later than Mark.

A Formal Classification of Q Material

The material included in Q can be classified by form. Assuming that it was preserved originally—or created—in compact units (called *pericopes* by the form critics), Q must have been merely a loosely arranged series of these units. No scheme of classification can be discerned, since much of the tradition could be placed under two or more categories, but the following set of formal distinctions may be useful:

Narratives	Na
Parables	Pa
Oracles	Or
Beatitudes	Be
Prophetic Pronouncements	PP
Wisdom Words	WW
Exhortations	Ex

Included under the category of "prophetic pronouncements" are eschatological promises, eschatological correlatives ("as it was ... so shall it be"),[24] and the formalized pronouncements ("if anyone ..."; or "whoever does ...").[25] The remarkable feature of this material is that even those traditions classified as wisdom words and exhortations are strongly eschatological in intention and bear on the responsibilities of those who take part in the ministry of the kingdom launched by Jesus and about to be culminated. The Q material is therefore permeated by eschatological concerns and outlook.

Although any reconstruction of Q is hypothetical, the following material may be assigned to it on the theory of its having been drawn from a sayings source common to Matthew and Luke (references are to the Lukan version).

PP	3:7–9, 16b–17	John's Eschatological Preaching
Na	4:2b–12	Jesus' Struggle with Satan
Be	6:20–23	Beatitudes: The Poor, the Hungry, the Hated
WW	6:27–36	Promised Reward for Love and Forgiveness

WW	6:37–42	Rewards of Discipleship
Pa	6:43–46	Parables of Moral Productivity
Pa	6:47–49	Discipleship Must Survive Testing: Parable of the House with and without Foundation
Na	7:2–3, 6–10	Healing of the Centurion's Slave
PP	7:18–23	Response to John the Baptist's Question
PP	7:24–35	John's Place in God's Plan
PP	9:57–58 (–62?)	Leave Behind Home and Family
PP	10:2–12	Disciples Commissioned to Extend Jesus' Work
Or	10:13–15	Doom on Unrepentant Cities
PP	10:16	Disciples Share in Jesus' Rejection
PP	10:21–22	God's Gift of Wisdom to His Own
Be	10:23–24	Beatitude: Those to Whom Wisdom Is Granted
Ex	11:2-4	Prayer for the Coming of God's Kingdom
WW	11:9–13	God Answers the Prayers of His Own
PP	11:14–23	Jesus' Defeat of Demons As a Sign of the Kingdom
Or	11:24–26	The Return of the Unclean Spirit
PP	11:29b–32	The Sign of Jonah and the One Greater Than Jonah: Jesus As Prophet and Wise Man
Pa	11:33–36	Parabolic Words of Light and Darkness
Or	11:39–40, 42–43	Woes to the Pharisees
Or	11:46–48, 52	Woes to the Lawyers
PP	11:49–51	Wisdom Predicts the Martyrdom of Prophets and Apostles
PP	12:2–3	What Is Hidden Will Be Revealed
Or	12:4–5	Do Not Fear Martyrdom
Pa	12:6–7	Parable of God's Care
PP	12:8–10	Confirmation of the Confession/Denial of Son of Man
PP	12:11–12	God's Support of the Persecuted
Pa	12:22–31	Freedom from Anxiety about Earthly Needs
Pa	12:33–34	Freedom from Possessions

Pa	12:35–40	Parable of Preparedness: The Returning Householder
Pa	12:42–46	Parable of the Faithful Steward
PP	12:51–53	Jesus As the Agent of Crises
Pa	12:54–56	Signs of the Impending End of the Age
Pa	12:57–59	Parable of Preparedness for the Judgment
Pa	13:20–21	Parable of the Leaven
WW	13:24	Difficulty in Entering the Kingdom
Pa	13:25–29	Parable of Exclusion from the Kingdom
PP	13:34–35	The Rejection of the Prophets and the Vindication of God's Agent
Pa	14:16–23	Parable of the Eschatological Banquet
PP	14:26–27	Jesus Shatters Domestic Ties, Summons Disciples to Bear the Cross
Pa	15:4–7	The Joyous Shepherd
WW	16:13	Inevitable Choice Between Masters
PP	16:16	The End of the Old Era and the New Age Proclaimed
WW	16:17	Confidence in God's Promise
Ex	16:18	Prohibition of Divorce and Remarriage
Ex	17:3–4	Forgiveness Within the Community
Ex	17:5–6	Faith Within the Community
Or	17:23–37	Sudden Judgment to Fall
Pa	19:12–13, 15–26	Parable of the Returning Nobleman and Rewards for Fidelity
PP	22:28–30	The Promise to the Faithful of Sharing in the Rule of God

The Thematic Interests of Q

If we attempt to classify the Q pericopes according to their central interests, rather than their formal characteristics, the results serve only to confirm the picture of this tradition as thoroughly eschatological. Even material that is hortatory in form is set in the context of eschatological expectation or judgment. There are four main emphases in Q; we shall see how the units of tradition incorporated in the document fit into these categories. Again, all references are to Luke.

1. Discipleship: Its Privileges and Trials

6:20–23, 27–36, 37–49	The Blessedness and Obligations of Discipleship
9:57–58 (–62?)	Break with Home and Family for the Sake of the Kingdom
10:2–12, 13–15	Participation in Proclaiming the Kingdom in Word and Act
10:21–23	God's Special Revelation of his Purpose
11:2–4, 9–13	God Will Sustain His People and Give Them the Kingdom
11:24–32	Return of the Unclean Spirit
12:51–53	Jesus the Divider of Households
14:16–23	Those Included and Those Excluded from the Messianic Banquet
14:26–27	Discipleship Shatters Ordinary Human Relationships
16:13	The Demands of Discipleship
16:18	Divorce and Remarriage
17:3–6	Forgiveness and Faith: Essentials for Community Life

2. The Prophet As God's Messenger

3:7–9, 17–18	John the Baptist As Forerunner of Jesus and Prophet of Doom
11:49–51	The Fate of the Prophet and of His Emissaries
12:2–3	The Promise of Revelation of God's Purpose
12:4–10, 11–12, 42–46	God's Care for and Vindication of His Messengers
13:34–35	Jerusalem's Rejection and Martyrdom of the Prophets
16:16–17	John As Boundary of the Old Age; God's Word Is Sure

3. Repentance or Judgment

11:33–34	Warning About Darkness and Light
11:35–40, 42–43, 46–48, 52	Woes Against the Religious Leaders of Judaism
12:35–40	The Returning Householder
12:54–59	Prepare for the Impending Judgment

13:25–29	Exclusion from God's Kingdom
17:23–27, 33, 35–37	Judgment Will Be Inescapable When It Falls
19:12–13, 15–26	Reward for the Faithful, but Punishment for Those Lacking Ambition or Perseverance

4. Jesus As Revealer and Agent of God's Rule

4:2b–12	Jesus' Successful Struggle with the Devil
7:2–10	Jesus Heals the Centurion's Servant
7:18–35	Jesus As Agent of Liberation; Greater Than John
10:21–22	Jesus As Son, Agent of Revelation
11:14–23	Jesus As Agent of God's Kingdom
13:20–21	Leaven at Work Now
15:4–7	God's Joy at Reconciliation of a Sinner
22:28–30	God Grants the Share in the Kingdom to Those for Whom It Has Been Covenanted and Who Have Endured the Trials

It is obvious that one significant element is missing from this list: The passion story plays no role at all. (See pp. 76, 99.) The focus falls instead on Jesus' signs, although only one is actually described; indeed, Q makes even clearer than Mark how the healings and exorcisms are related to the coming of the Kingdom of God. There are no predictions of the suffering of the Son of Man,[26] as there are in Mark; "Son of Man" is prominent as a self-designation for Jesus in his earthly ministry (for example, in Luke 9:57–58) and as the title for the One whose coming is awaited at the End of the Age (Luke 17:22–37).

Q's Narrative Material

When we organize the Q material according to thematic interests, only the story of the Centurion's Servant fails to fit under any category. If it is regarded as a kind of symbolic tale, then the faith of the Gentile and the resultant healing are a paradigm of the faith of other Gentiles who find in Jesus the liberating, restoring powers of the New Age. That is the main point of this particular healing story: Jesus found in a Gentile faith such as he had not encountered "in Israel"

(Matt. 8:5 = Luke 7:9). Similar interest in the Gentiles is expressed in the Q version of the preaching of John the Baptist: John is reported to have rejected the notion that Jews have some special claim to be children of God by virtue of their descent from Abraham, saying God is able to raise up "from these stones [the Gentiles]" a new posterity for Abraham—that is, a true community of the faithful (Matt. 3:9 = Luke 3:8). Still another indication of the special interest of Q in the outreach of Jesus to Gentiles is given in the Parable of the Great Supper, which is apparently preserved in something closer to its original form in Luke's version (14:16–23). This parable suggests that the gospel invitation first went out to Israel, which rejected it. Now it is extended to the Gentiles—that is to those "out in the highways and the hedges" (Luke 14:23).

The healing story is the only passage in Q that contains geographical or sequential hints, with the possible exception of two other pericopes. One of these is the pericope of the lament over Jerusalem (Luke 13:34–35 = Matt. 23:37–39), but even in this case Q obviously does not preserve an exact recollection of the time and location of this saying, since Matthew locates it in Jerusalem just prior to the apocalyptic discourse, whereas Luke places it immediately after Jesus' announcement in Galilee of his intention to go to Jerusalem (Luke 13:31–33). The other inference about the locale of Jesus' ministry can be drawn from Luke 10:13–15 (= Matt. 11:21–23), where the cities of Chorazin and Bethsaida, in addition to Capernaum, are mentioned as the scene of Jesus' miracles. Valuable as these place names are, they tell us nothing about the sequence of events in Jesus' public ministry.

There seems to be complete justification, therefore, for taking up the Q material by topics rather than trying to impose a logical or chronological sequence upon it. The topical arrangement of Q material implies a quite different understanding of Jesus' place in history from that found in Mark, where the "necessary" sequence of events unfolds according to an apocalyptic scheme. For Q, it is sufficient to contrast the present as the hour of decision concerning Jesus with the future as the hour of God's vindication of Jesus and his people.

Q's Ethical Material

The saying about serving two masters (Luke 16:13 = Matt. 6:24) belongs to the specifically ethical tradition preserved in Q. The saying turns on the idea of true dedication: One cannot devote oneself wholly to the pursuit of wealth (mammon) and at the same time to the service of God. (An interesting variant of this teaching is found in the Gospel of Thomas 47 a–b, where there are two sets of comparisons: with the impossibility of stretching two bows or mounting two horses, but the saying has been given the form of a general proverb.) The force of the Q pericope is identical with that of many other sayings of Jesus, with their demand for unconditional devotion to doing God's work. The question of the disciple's eschatological destiny is not even hinted at here, as it is in most Q pericopes.

In Luke 11:34–35 there is a pair of sayings about light, preserved in a longer series of sayings that have in common the image of light (11:33–36). The intent of the Q pericope seems to be to warn the disciple to take care that his or her eye be sound—that is, that one be able to discern the truth accurately. Otherwise, those who think that they "see" the truth, will find their whole being ("body") filled with darkness. Again, there is only a solemn reminder about the present obligation, rather than any promise or prediction about the future. The same is true for the sayings on forgiveness and faith (Luke 17:3–6) that Luke linked or found linked in the Q source (Matthew distributed them in three different contexts: 18:15; 18:21–22; 17:20). An appeal to be willing to forgive repeatedly is followed by a challenge to have unlimited faith, which means "trust" rather than "belief." In Matthew's version great faith can move mountains; in Luke's it can transplant trees into the sea. Both forms of the saying are hyperbole to emphasize that true faith is not limited to what might ordinarily be expected to occur. Other variants of this saying on faith are found in Matthew 21:21 and Mark 11:22–23. In this cluster of sayings there is no explicit expectation of eschatological divine dramatic action in the near future. In all the other Q material, however, such an eschatological dimension is central.

Q's Eschatological Material

In Q, form and function converge on eschatological concerns, as becomes even more evident when the texts are analyzed in some detail. In the following survey, the material is grouped according to subject matter.

Eschatological Warning

The theme of eschatological warning is heard in what was probably the opening passage of Q, the preaching of John the Baptist as reported in the non-Markan version. In contrast to Mark, where the stress falls on the activity and appearance of John (1:4–6), Q presents a summary of the content of John's preaching. Its theme is primarily that of judgment. John denounces his hearers as a "brood of vipers,"—or in modern terms, "bunch of snakes"—whose eagerness to escape the divine judgment must be matched by a willingness (1) to change their minds and direction ("repent"); and (2) to demonstrate their repentant attitude by appropriate works. Their prideful boast in Abraham as their progenitor is based solely on their claimed ancestry, but God is creating a new covenant people, who—unlike the disobedient descendants of Abraham—will commit themselves fully to God's purpose in the world. There is not a moment to spare, John warns: God's axe is on the point of cutting down all the unfruitful trees. Only those men whose good works reveal a firm commitment will be spared when the wrath of God falls on the world, or to use the figure of Luke 3:16, when the baptism of fire occurs. The useful grain (the truly faithful people) will be gathered, but the chaff will be consumed in the fiery judgment. On this solemn note, the Q document begins its portrayal of Jesus' ministry, explaining only at a later point (Luke 7:24–35) the relationship between Jesus and John.

The theme of judgment continues in Luke 6:37–42 (= Matt. 7:1–5; 10:24–25; 15:14). The first of the sayings included in this grouping might seem initially to be a general statement advising people not to judge one another: "Judge not, and you will not be judged." But it has been widely recognized by biblical scholars that in rabbinic Judaism a verb in the passive voice ("be judged") with no agent expressed implies a reference to God,[27] so the meaning intended is: "Do not judge others and God will not judge you." What at first glance might seem to be the simple turnabout-is-fair-play principle is actually a major theme of the teaching of Jesus as presented in the gospel tradition: Unless one is prepared to forgive others, God will not be forgiving on the Day of Judgment. The positive side of this view is set forth in Luke 6:38, where the promise is given that those who live with generosity toward others will be rewarded generously by God in the day of divine reckoning, as is promised in indirect speech in the phrase "it will be given to you" (that is, by God).

The saying about the blind leading the blind (Luke 6:39) could be understood as an allusion to one's eschatological fate based on the image of falling into a pit, but the remaining sayings of this group from Q are more general in their moral appeal for humility in the relationship of disciple to teacher and of brother or sister to one another. As is characteristic of the teaching of Jesus in the synoptic tradition, humility is not an abstract quality to be emulated but a concrete way of acting in relation to others. The fact that Q places these sayings in conjunction with the eschatological warning about judgment gives them an urgency that a string of general moral appeals would lack.

A more distinctive emphasis in Q is evident in the pericope announcing judgment on the cities of Galilee that have failed to repent even though Jesus has performed "mighty works" in them (Luke 10:13–15 = Matt. 11:21–23). A contrast is offered between them and Tyre and Sidon, pagan cities from which repentance would surely have come had they been allowed to witness God's mighty acts performed through Jesus. The miracles of Jesus, described here as "powers," are understood to be eschatological signs that attest to the crucial role of Jesus in God's preparing men and women for the consummation of the present age and the coming of God's Kingdom. The saying in Luke 10:15 addressed to Capernaum, which seems to have served Jesus as a base of operations after his rejection in Nazareth, recalls the oracle in Isaiah 14, in which the doom of Satan (God's adversary) is foretold. The title Day Star, Son of Dawn, originally used for a Canaanite deity, is used in Isaiah 14:12 for the king of Babylon, who with the king of Tyre was understood in later Judaism to represent Satan. In this oracle Satan is reminded that although he aspired to set his throne above that of God and to make himself like the Most High, he will be brought down "to the depths of the Pit" (Isa. 14:15). By implication, the indifference and self-satisfaction that the cities of Galilee showed Jesus are for the Q tradition signs of satanic opposition, not merely of human negligence. The conflict in which Jesus is engaged, therefore, is cosmic and not merely human in origin. God will vindicate Jesus' works on the Judgment Day, when those who refused to be moved by his appeal will be doomed.

The woes on the Pharisees (Luke 11:39–52 = Matt. 23:25–36, with some additions and shifts in order) begin with an attack on the hypocrisy with which some Jews observe their laws of cleanliness. The reader senses that by the time Q recorded these sayings they were already being interpreted in an allegorical way to refer to the necessity of a clean heart as contrasted with a mere appearance of piety. Equally hypocritical is the Pharisees' preoccupation with the minutiae of religion, such as tithing herbs, which has crowded out concern for such fundamental matters as love and justice. After exposing the discrepancy between the Pharisees' outer show of piety and their inner lack of devotion, Jesus attacks directly those who have not only failed to hear God's message through the prophets but also shared in murdering these who were sent by God.

The two specific murders mentioned in Luke 11:51, those of Abel and Zechariah, are probably intended to encompass the whole span of the history of Israel, from the first murder recorded in the first book of the Hebrew Bible, Genesis, to the last murder in the last book of the Hebrew canon, 2 Chronicles.[28] That is, the Q tradition affirms that throughout their history those who have called themselves God's people have consistently rejected God's messengers. This and the reference to the "glutton and drunkard" in Luke 7:34 (whose violation of the covenant was to result in his being stoned to death; Deut. 21:18–21) are as close as Q comes to allusions to the Passion of Jesus, which is apparently to be understood as the ultimate rejection of God's final messenger, and therefore as the occasion for the outpouring of God's judgment on his unrepentant people. If we take Matthew's version of this passage to preserve more faithfully the original form of Q, the picture is even clearer:

> Therefore I send you prophets and wise men and scribes[29] some of whom you will kill and crucify, and some you will scourge in your synagogues and persecute from town to town, that upon you may come all the righteous blood shed on earth, from the blood of innocent Abel to the blood of Zechariah the son of Barachiah, whom you murdered between the sanctuary and the altar. Truly, I say to you, all this will come upon this generation. (Matt. 23:34–36)

Jesus has come as a prophet and wise man,[30] and his followers carry on the ministry that he launched to announce and to achieve God's purpose. But he and they are subject to martyrdom. Their vindication will come in the divine judgment that is to fall "upon this generation."

Three vivid images of conflict are brought together in Luke's version of a Q saying about the fulfillment of Jesus' mission: fire, baptism, and sword (Luke 12:49–53). The fire is the symbol of God's final judgment on an evil world and his disobedient people, to which Jesus' words point explicitly throughout Q in non-metaphorical language. The baptism is an apparent allusion to his suffering and death, as it is in the Markan saying (10:39), where in a mixed metaphor Jesus is said to have pointed to his own impending passion under the figures of "drinking the cup" of divinely ordained suffering and undergoing the "baptism" of woes that will accompany the accomplishment of his role as Messiah. The division that Jesus' ministry effects among his hearers will cause rifts in families, setting parents against children and vice versa. Given the fact that in Jewish households the solidarity of the family was the foundation of psychological and sociological stability, the familial disruptions predicted here are catastrophic, though they might not be so perceived in our day of fluid sex relationships and the widespread breakup of the family. The conflict foreseen here is an inevitable, even necessary, stage in the final, wrenching struggle that will bring to an end the old age and inaugurate the new.

The obtuseness of Jesus' generation is indicated in his scathing observation that they can predict the next day's weather, but they cannot discern the infinitely more significant change that is taking place through Jesus: the inbreaking of the Kingdom of God (Luke 12: 54–56). Preoccupied with workaday affairs, they are more concerned about the rain clouds blowing in off the Mediterranean and the searing winds from the desert to the southeast than they are about the breakup of the present order implicit in the words and works of Jesus.

The advice about bribing your accuser before he can take you to court (Luke 12:57–59) is intended not as moral counsel but as a parabolic warning to Jesus' hearers that they are about to stand before God's judgment throne. The point is this: If an admittedly guilty person being dragged to justice by his victim has the foresight to meet the crisis situation by means of a bribe, how much more should Jesus' hearers prepare themselves for the eschatological crisis that is about to befall them.[31]

A series of sayings that have in common the figure of "entering in"—that is, into the Kingdom of God—is included by Luke in what is probably the Q form and order (Luke 13:24–29), although the sayings have been scattered by Matthew (7:14; 25:10–12; 7:22–23; 8:11). Matthew's version of the first of these has been accommodated to the familiar Jewish teaching about the two ways, and therefore has taken on the character of a general moral injunction to seek the less-traveled way of righteousness. But Luke preserves the saying with an eschatological force that is more likely original: Engage in the struggle that enables you to enter into the life of the Age to Come. Not many will be able to enter. Immediately following (Luke 13:25–29) is the short parable of the householder who has closed the door and will allow no one else to enter, which suggests that the time when one may enter the New Age will soon pass; thereafter no second chance exists, even though many may try to appeal to previous pleasant associations with Jesus ("We ate and drank in your presence"). Their pleas will be without avail once the time of decision has passed. Their anguish will be made the greater by the sight of men "from east and west"—presumably Gentiles from other lands—who will have a share in the eschatological fellowship when God gathers his people in the New Age.

The familiar lament over Jerusalem (Luke 13:34–35) is a prophetic oracle, uttered by Jesus as the final messenger of God to Israel and probably understood to be the fulfillment of the promise in Deuteronomy 18:15–19. The passage directly appealed to, however, is Psalm 118:26, a text widely used in first-century Judaism to refer to the consummation of Israel's hope of the establishment of God's Kingdom,[32] and as such an important feature of the Jewish Feast of Tabernacles. Although Luke understands the lament—or wants his readers to understand it—as a prediction of Jesus' appearance on the occasion of his entry into Jerusalem, Q probably intended it as a mingled lament and warning by Jesus to the nation, represented here by Jerusalem, where the leadership and symbolic center of Judaism were found. If the Jewish leaders did not hear God's message through Jesus, they would have no further opportunity until the Coming One (who for Luke is the risen, vindicated Jesus) appeared in their midst to judge the faithless and to reward the faithful who even now acknowledge him as God's agent of renewal. The city's rejection of Jesus and his message is said to be of a piece with the murders of the prophets that had occurred over the centuries. Although the people of Jerusalem spurn him now, God will vindicate him in the Age to Come.

The sudden coming of the Day of the Lord is stressed in the cluster of words from Q that Luke places immediately after the account of the Pharisee's question to Jesus about the time of the coming of the Kingdom (Luke 17:20–21). The introduction to the Q sayings, "Then he said to the disciples" (17:22), is a form of editorial connection frequently used by the evangelists.[33] From Q come verses 24, 26–27, and 33–37. The appearance of the Son of Man, God's eschatological judge, will be as instantaneous and as public as a flash of lightning; it will not be a hidden event, as some Jewish sectaries expected or claimed with their "Lo, here!" Under the influence of Markan thought, Luke inserts at this point (17:25) a qualification of the unpredictability of the coming of the Son of Man by asserting the apocalyptic necessity of his suffering prior to his revelation as Son of Man. But this viewpoint is not present in Q, which concerns rather the cataclysmic nature of the coming of judgment.

Allied with the theme of the suddenness of the Judge's coming is that of the complacent, preoccupied attitude of the mass of the people. With judgment about to fall, they are concerned only about preserving their possessions. Like the "decent godless people" of T.S. Eliot's "Choruses from *The Rock*," they go about their daily routines oblivious of the catastrophe that is about to destroy the entire present order. So insensitive and self-centered are they that someone must point out to them the vultures swirling about the carcass of a world that passed away without their having noticed.

Eschatological Conflict

Closely linked with the theme of judgment in Q is the portrayal of conflict with the demonic as an essential factor in the fulfillment of God's redemptive purpose through Jesus. As in Mark (1:12–13), the story of Jesus' baptism leads directly into the section dealing with his being tested by the Devil (Luke 4:1–13 = Matt. 4:1–11). The Q version may have had its own narrative introduction, but both Matthew and Luke have incorporated the Markan setting of the incident. The more extensive treatment in Q, however, shows the greater importance attached to this conflict, which sets the tone and the issues for the whole of Jesus' ministry. Whereas in Mark the temptation is only a preparatory experience for Jesus' public activity (analogous to those of Moses, Elijah, and the prophets of the Hebrew Scriptures), in Q it is made the occasion for laying out what is at stake throughout Jesus' ministry: Will Jesus follow God's will in preparing for the coming of the Kingdom, or will he submit to the Devil's schemes for a counterfeit of the Kingdom of God? The temptations are not tests of Jesus' morality but of his dedication to the fulfillment of his mission at whatever cost.

The first temptation calls on him to use his extraordinary powers for his personal comfort by turning stones into bread when he is hungry. In the second testing he is offered immediate access to authority over the kingdoms of this world, if he will only acknowledge the Devil as his sovereign. This temptation not only tests Jesus' dedication to God but also defines his mission: He has been called not to assume power over this world's kingdom but to prepare men for the coming of God's Kingdom. The third temptation is a proposal that Jesus perform a kind of carnival stunt by leaping from a pinnacle of the temple in order to demonstrate God's special care over him, but Jesus would no more put God to the test than he would yield himself to the Devil under pressure of his testings. The Q material portrays Jesus engaged in a cosmic conflict, and the stake is nothing less than God's rule over his creation. The fact that Q places these accounts in what we would call a mythological rather than a historical setting in no way diminishes the importance that the tradition attaches to them. Indeed, the vague mention of locale, "in the wilderness," heightens the sense of mystery and awe that surrounds these vivid vignettes.[34]

The implication of the temptation stories is made explicit in the Q version of the Beelzebub controversy (Luke 11:14–22 = Matt. 12: 22–29). Q adds to the Markan story the detail that the controversy about the source of Jesus' power arose in connection with his having healed a deaf mute. But the more important difference between Mark's and Q's versions of this incident is the fact that in Q the significance of Jesus' exorcisms is made explicit. In Mark, Jesus responds to the accusation that he can perform exorcisms because he is in league with Beelzebub, the prince of demons, by pointing out how foolish it would be for Satan to work through him, since he will bring about Satan's downfall. In the Q account Jesus goes on to say that if everyone who performed exorcisms were in league with Satan, the same would have to be said of the Jewish exorcists, including those associated with Jesus' accusers ("By whom do your sons cast them out?"). Luke 11:20 is one of the most fundamental passages in the entire gospel tradition for understanding the importance of Jesus' ministry of exorcisms:[35]

> But if it is by the finger of God that I cast out demons, then the kingdom of God has come to you.

To the extent that Jesus is defeating the hosts of Satan by liberating men from demonic control, the reign of God over his creation is already becoming an accomplished fact. The phrase "finger of God" comes from the time of God's historic deliverance of Israel from slavery in Egypt in the time of Moses (Ex. 8:19). Now the new liberation "by the finger of God" is cosmic in its import. The exorcisms are signs that the New Age of Israel's eschatological hope is already manifesting its powers in the present through the ministry of Jesus.[36] This is the unequivocal claim embedded in the Q document at this point.

It is not sufficient for anyone merely to be freed from demonic domination, however, for if there were not some superior power to replace the satanic control, one might end up worse off than before— with eight demons instead of one, according to Luke 11:24–26 (= Matt. 12:43–45). Although it is not specifically stated, the implication of the pericope is that the rule of God must assume sway in a human life if the former demoniac is not to slip back under Satan's domination. If the latter disaster were to occur, the possibility of remedy would be even more difficult than before. Thus Jesus' ministry is concerned not merely with removal of Satan's sway but also with replacement of the demonic scheme by the divine will, through the inbreaking of the Kingdom of God.

In the story of the Healing of the Centurion's Servant (Luke 7:1–10 = Matt. 8:5–13) there is, in addition to the matter of Gentile faith, an important element in the account: the authority of Jesus' word. The centurion can appreciate the power of the word of command, since he is himself a man accustomed to authority, presumably both to obeying it and exercising it: "I am a man under authority, with soldiers under me" (Matt. 8:9). But the thrust of the pericope is to depict Jesus as an authoritative figure, who is able to heal disease with a word and thereby to triumph over the powers at work in human life that stand in the way of the fulfillment of God's purpose. Although the terminology is not used, Jesus' healing word is a sign of the inbreaking of the Kingdom of God, as is true in his exorcisms.

Eschatological Promise

In both Luke and Matthew, Jesus' Sermon opens with a series of beatitudes. Although Luke added some material of his own (the woes on the rich, for example—Luke 6:24–26), he seems to have reproduced the Q version of the Sermon more faithfully on the whole than did Matthew, who considerably expanded and modified the tradition.[37] Whereas in Matthew the Beatitudes (5:3–12) are addressed to general categories of persons—"the poor in spirit," "those who mourn," "those who hunger and thirst after righteousness"—in Luke (6:20–23) they are spoken in direct address—"you poor"—and promise future rectification of present injustice. The contrast between present and future has been subdued in Matthew, but it stands out starkly in Luke: "You that hunger now ... shall be satisfied."

Even though in the English translation the announcement of the blessedness of the poor is linked with the statement "yours is the kingdom of God," the point is not that the poor already possess the Kingdom; it is rather that their future possession of the Kingdom is even now assured. The coming of God's Kingdom will reverse all the ordinary human values. Those who are now deprived and despised will be vindicated by God when he establishes his rule in the earth. To say "you shall be satisfied" means "God will satisfy you." The reward in heaven is great, Jesus says; his hearers can count on that, even though they will not enter into the reward until the Day of Judgment when God set things right in his creation. "That day" refers to the day of vindication. The disciples rejoice now at the prospect of the coming events that will set things right.

In the present situation of conflict the followers of Jesus can expect rejection and persecution at the hands of those who consider themselves God's people. To "cast out one's name as evil" is a Semitic expression that means to speak ill of someone. The calumny heaped on Jesus' disciples is not against them individually but is the consequence of their being publicly identified with the Son of Man (Luke 6:22).[38] The use of the term "Son of Man" here heightens the significance of the persecution and suffering that the followers of Jesus are passing through. They are a part of the redemptive suffering that must precede the End of the Age and the coming of God's Kingdom. Luke preserves the original force of the Beatitudes, which are not generalized descriptions of the blessedness of humility but eschatological promises to those who are convinced that Jesus is God's messenger of the coming Kingdom and who are willing to undergo persecution if necessary in standing by their conviction.

The moral appeals to love one's enemies and to respond to injustice with actions of grace (Luke 6:27–36 = Matt. 5:39–42, 44–48) are not based on the shrewd calcuation that in the long run things may work out for one's own welfare if nonretaliatory responses are offered to personal wrongs. Rather, Jesus bases his moral appeal in this Q material solely on the precept that humans are called to act toward others as God has acted toward them. Love is a way of acting, not an emotion or a sentiment. The great paradox lies in the promise that for those who act in love toward their enemies and expect no benefit in return, God has in store a great reward (Luke 6:35). This reward is the goal of the moral life, an eschatological goal: to become a child of the Most High. To move toward this goal, one is called upon to demonstrate concretely the works of mercy that correspond to the mercy that has been received at the hands of God. The final appraisal of human response to God's grace is expected to occur in the Day of Judgment, when works of mercy performed with no eye to recompense will receive the appropriate reward.

As was the case with the Beatitudes, the Lord's Prayer in Luke (11:1–4) is given in its more original form; Matthew expanded it and adapted it for liturgical use (6:9–13). Stripped of the Matthean additions (for example, "Father" instead of "Our Father who art in heaven"), the prayer as it stood in Q manifests a strong eschatological urgency. To call for the hallowing of the name of God is to appeal for a new situation in which men and women will give God the honor that is rightfully his by virtue of his having created the world. The more familiar petition for the coming of God's Kingdom is another way of saying the same thing. Both call for establishment of God's rule in the earth, as Matthew's addition, "on earth as is it is heaven," rightly shows. The requests for bread and forgiveness indicate human beings' fundamental requirements: sufficient food to sustain life and enough of God's grace to make life bearable. They can summon up the grace to forgive others who have wronged them because they have themselves experienced God's forgiveness. In Matthew's version the prayer includes the petition to be delivered from evil, which has been commonly understood as a request that God keep us free of evil influences or from performing evil deeds. If "temptation" in the next line is interpreted as being tempted to commit sin, then the meaning would be plausible and consistent, but noneschatological. Luke's version, however, expresses only the hope that the petitioner will not be led into temptation, a word that probably means an eschatological time of testing rather than a moment in life when one is tempted to commit a sin. "Temptation" is not a random set of circumstances in which one is inclined to do the wrong thing, but a technical term for the ordeal through which God's faithful people will pass in the End Time, just prior to the final judgment. If they hold fast to their trust in God, in spite of persecutions and demonic opposition, they will have demonstrated their right to enter the New Age. Luke's version of the prayer is an understandable expression of hope that it will not be necessary to pass through that time of testing. Matthew's form of the prayer reads like a general request for being kept from lapsing into sin. But if the text of Matthew 6:13 is translated as "from the Evil One" rather than "from evil," the force is the same. The simple human petition is that one might be spared the eschatological woes that will fall upon the earth in the closing days of the present age.

The theme of prayer continues in the same eschatological vein in Luke 11:9–13 (= Matt. 7:7–11). In this Q pericope what is being asked for is admission to the Kingdom of God, not merely some generalized spiritual benefits. The needs of the faithful will be met in the interim. God will give them the "good things" they require.[39] Similar advice is given in Luke 12:22–31 (= Matt. 6:25–33): One should settle for the bare necessities of day-to-day living in the present age in order to gain life in the Age to Come. No goal concerned primarily with sustaining life, or with making life more comfortable or carefree, is to be compared with the highest aim of human existence: seeking God's Kingdom.[40] In Luke 6:33–34 (= Matt. 6:19–21) the disciples are told to rid themselves of earthly possessions, which inevitably become the object of the affections and the force that inclines the will ("where your heart is"). Instead, they are to adopt poverty as a way of life in order that they may devote themselves entirely to carrying out the will of God. Only thus can they claim enduring treasure.

Finally, there is an eschatological promise of vindication contained in a saying attributed to Jesus, found in two quite different forms in Luke 22:29–30 and in Matthew 19:28. Some scholars have expressed doubt that it stood in Q at all. For our purpose, it is enough to focus attention on the main idea of the saying, which is present in both versions: The twelve faithful disciples will participate in the judgment of God's people in the New Age. In Matthew, Jesus addresses his disciples simply as "you who have followed me"; in Luke, however, Jesus calls the disciples "you ... who have continued with me in [eschatological] trials." Matthew promises participation in the renewal of the world; Luke announces a guaranteed place in the Kingdom. But both agree that the twelve disciples will play the role of judge in the day when God sets things right in the creation, as the faithful were promised in Daniel 7:22 and Wisdom 3:8. Discipleship, therefore, involves participation in the work of Jesus, both in this age and in the Age to Come. Jesus is not merely a preacher of the Kingdom's coming; he has a vital role in its establishment.

Eschatological Knowledge

The Q tradition contains not only promises of what God intended to do for his faithful children but also expressions of gratitude to God for having made known these promises. The best known of such passages in Q is in Luke 10:21–24 (= Matt. 11:25–27; 13:16–17).[41] This pericope as found in Luke may consist of what were originally two separate sayings, as Matthew's separation of them suggests. But for Q they belonged together, since they constitute an affirmation that God has given to the inner circle knowledge that prophets and kings have long wanted to possess but have been unable to lay hold of. Knowledge of God resides primarily with Jesus, who alone knows the Father. But he has chosen to reveal this knowledge to his own faithful followers, whose special blessedness is announced here. Although the content of the privileged knowledge is not disclosed, we can infer that it is insight into God's eschatological purpose, which is being achieved through Jesus, his Son. It is important to note that for Jesus to be "Son of God" is here not a matter of his supernatural birth or origin but of his revelatory knowledge of the divine intention for the world, an intention hidden from even the wisest and noblest of earlier generations. The clear implication is that the last days are approaching, in which God's plan is finally to be disclosed.

Eschatological Discipleship

The completeness of identity between Jesus and his followers is the chief mark of discipleship in the Q tradition. To follow Jesus is to give up the security and comfort of one's home (Luke 9:57–58 = Matt. 8:19–20), as well as the obligation to one's family that was from the beginning a central feature of Israel's societal structure (Exod. 20:12). Every other responsibility, however noble and worthy in itself, must take second place to the demands of discipleship. It is significant that in Luke 9:58 and Matthew 8:20, in a context where the radical nature of discipleship is depicted, Jesus is reported to have referred to himself as Son of Man. In Mark and Q (Mark 8:38; Luke 17:22–30) the term is used of the coming Son of Man who will execute judgment on disobedient, preoccupied mankind. Here, however, "Son of Man" is used of Jesus in reference to his earthly rejection by humankind. Although he comes as an authoritative figure, summoning men to leave all and follow him, the widespread rejection he meets means that he cannot offer even a home to his followers:[42] "The Son of man has nowhere to lay his head." Acknowledgment of this hostile reception does not undercut the authority of Jesus; it serves to make his demand more rigorous and to restrict the promise of vindication to the future. There is no ground for encouragement or compensation in the present situation out of which Jesus calls men and women to discipleship.

The claims of discipleship are set forth in Luke 14:25–27 (= Matt. 10:37–38) in absolute terms. First, there is the demand that one who would follow Jesus must "hate" his family. (Matthew tones this down by substituting "does not love more" for "hate," as Luke has it.) In view of the sense of family solidarity that has traditionally characterized Jewish life, it is evident that a demand that would not merely transcend but even violate family ties was about as radical a requirement for discipleship as can be conceived. But Jesus went even beyond that: He called on his followers to be willing to surrender their lives in fulfilling their discipleship. That the writer of Q understood taking up the cross to mean acceptance of martyrdom is obvious from his setting that theme alongside the call to hate life. To take up the cross is to share in the eschatological sufferings that are a necessary prelude to the coming of the Kingdom of God.

Although Matthew (9:37–38; 10:7–15) and Luke (10:1–16) have divergent accounts of Jesus' sending out of the disciples to preach and heal,[43] they agree on the context of the disciples' ministry, the content of their message, and the purpose of their activity. The context is the sense of urgency created by the expectation of "the harvest," that is, the judgment that is about to take place in preparation for the coming of the Kingdom. In light of the imminence of the End of the Age, the disciples are not to concern themselves at all with funds or equipment, with the comfort of their living accommodations, or with the quality of their food. Everything else must move into the background in light of the overwhelming expectation that the end is to come very soon. A single theme is to be the content of their message and to provide the interpretation for the healings and exorcisms they perform: "The kingdom of God has come near to you." Anyone who spurns them or their message invites disaster in the Day of Judgment that is about to come upon the earth. The town that rejects Jesus or his disciples will be worse off than Sodom in the day of its destruction by fire and brimstone (Gen. 18–19).

In a string of sayings (Luke 12:2–12 = Matt. 10:26–33; 12:32) Q brings together warnings and encouragements for the followers of Jesus. For example, it is futile for them to try to hide from God their words or actions: That which they now may suppose can be hidden will be revealed by God in the last days. (Matthew interprets this saying to mean that the disciples are to be free of fear, since even works hidden in darkness will be revealed at the End of the Age.) Their real fear is not those who may put them to death, but those who will cause them to dishonor God and thereby bring about their condemnation. In Luke 12, verses 6 and 7 attest to the loving concern of God for all his creatures, not least of all his own children; therefore they are to be free of fear. But verses 8–10 return to the theme of the judgment. On the one hand, those who publicly confess Jesus as Son of Man will be vindicated by God on the Last Day; on the other hand, those who deny Jesus will stand condemned before God's throne.

In Luke 12:10 (= Matt. 12:32) we have an unusual phenomenon: Q contains a saying of Jesus that appears in an older form in Mark (3:28–30). Mark explains that an insult to one's fellow humans is forgivable but blasphemy against Jesus—specifically the charge that Satan, not the Holy Spirit, is the source of Jesus' power—cannot be forgiven. In Q the Markan phrase "sons of men" has been replaced by "men," only to appear in the next verse transformed into a christological title for Jesus, "Son of Man." Here the penalties for insulting Jesus and for insulting the Holy Spirit are contrasted: The first can be forgiven, the second cannot. The aim of the Q tradition here seems to have been to glorify Jesus by identifying him as Son of Man. But the most meaningful aspect of the saying is the seriousness of the consequences of the individual's present response to Jesus for one's fate in the eschatological judgment. In Luke 12:11–12 (= Matt. 10:19), however, divine aid is promised those who are persecuted in the last days. The Holy Spirit will guide them as they seek to bear their witness during the time of the eschatological woes.

Eschatological Parables

Three closely related parables (Luke 12:39–40, 42–46 = Matt. 24:43–50) make a common point: The coming of the Son of Man cannot be predicted precisely, so it behooves every follower of Jesus to be always ready for his appearance. The owner of the house could have been on guard if he had known the hour that the thief would break in, but he did not know and was robbed. If the servant had known the hour of his master's return, he would not have abused those over whom he had been given authority, but he did not know and was caught. Reward awaits the fully responsible steward, who discharges his duties faithfully in the absence of his master. The lesson is obvious: When the Son of Man comes, he will punish the irresponsible and the disobedient. Sayings that were presumably spoken by Jesus as parables of the eschatological crisis[44] have become allegories of the coming of Christ and the faithfulness of the church's leadership. Although the Q writer has shifted the meaning of these parabolic sayings, he has not lost the eschatological force that they originally possessed; he has only redirected it to the church's situation in his own time.

To the familiar Parable of the Mustard Seed, Q has appended the Parable of the Leaven,[45] since both make the same point: From the most unobtrusive beginnings, wholly unexpected results are certain to come.[46] The parables could also be intended to declare that now that the eschatological process has been launched, its outcome is certain.[47] These two themes are complementary rather than contradictory. Both parables, and both interpretations, look forward to the day when God's purpose is complete, when all the meal will have been leavened.

The Parable of the Great Supper tells the story of the poor and the outcasts who accept an invitation to a feast; those originally invited are too preoccupied with worldly affairs to come. The parable has been preserved in three different forms: Matthew 25:1–10; Luke 14:16–24; and Logion 64 in the Gospel of Thomas.[48] It is possible that the parable is based on an actual incident, as reported in the Palestinian Talmud: When a tax collector's invitation to the town leaders was declined, he invited the poor of the city to be his guests. Luke probably has best preserved the original form of the parable, although he seems to have introduced a two-stage invitation to the outcasts as a way of providing sanction in the teaching of Jesus for the shift of evangelistic focus from outcast Jews during Jesus' ministry to Gentiles in the ministry of the apostles.[49] The narrative setting which Luke gives for the parable (14:15) is suitable and may even be original. Whether original with Jesus or not, it rightly sets the stage for the parable, since it introduces the theme of eschatological fulfillment, depicted under the familiar image of the banquet. The negative reaction to the invitation is consistent with the response of those who hear the gospel and do not respond in faith, as described elsewhere in Q: Those preoccupied with their own daily affairs fail to heed the call to prepare for the coming Kingdom of God.

Similarly, there is an implied justification for extending the gospel invitation to the outsiders—the lost sheep—in the Parable of the Joyous Shepherd (Luke 15:4–7 = Matt. 18:12–14). The basis of this justification, or vindication of the mission to the Gentiles in the face of opposition on the part of strict Jewish Christians, is the nature of God himself, who, like the rejoicing shepherd, is depicted as filled with joy when even a single estranged person repentantly takes his place within the fellowship of God's flock. Apart from the parable's declaration about the attitude of God toward penitents, this pericope implies a criticism of those who pride themselves on being part of the in-group and scorn the religious outsiders with whom Jesus, in Q, is primarily concerned. There is a 99:1 ratio between the insiders and the outcast, but it is over the single penitent that God rejoices. This revolutionary understanding of the nature of God is in keeping with the redefinition of the people of God that this parable, along with other Q material, implies.

Jesus As Eschatological Messenger and Salvation-Bringer

After beginning his presentation of the ministry of Jesus with the coming and preaching of John the Baptist, the Q writer appropriately gives his first direct statement of the significance of Jesus in words describing his relationship to John (Luke 7:19–23 = Matt. 11:3–6). The question as to who Jesus is, is raised by John himself: "Are you he who is to come?" In itself the phrase "he who is to come" does not connote a messianic figure but simply indicates someone whose coming has eschatological significance. Jesus' reported reply recalls portions of the Isaiah apocalypse and of 2 Isaiah (29:18–19; 35:5–6; 61:1), where in each case the prophets are pointing ahead to the last days, when God will establish justice in the land and the oppressed will obtain release from sickness and injustice. The claim of Jesus, according to the Q material, is that the eschatological fulfillment is already taking place in his ministry. The significance of his activity is enhanced by the fact that it is in fulfillment of Scripture; that is, Jesus' ministry is a part of the unfolding of God's redemptive purpose in and for his creation.

Jesus' words about John the Baptist confirm this interpretation of Jesus' activity reported in Q (Luke 7:24–35 = Matt. 11:7–19). Here it is implied that John is the one who prepares the way for Jesus' coming. Matthew makes the explicit claim that John the Baptist is Elijah, whose coming in the last days was predicted in Malachi 4:5 and was widely expected in various forms in the apocalyptic literature.[50] Whereas in Malachi the messenger is to prepare the way for God's, rather than the Messiah's coming, in Q's quotation of Malachi the pronouns have been changed ("ahead of you" instead of "before my face") to imply that the messenger prepares the way for Jesus' coming. Whether we think of Q as representing Jesus to be the kingly Messiah or the prophetic figure of Elijah returned to earth (as Mark seems to have done), he has here a primary role in the coming of the Kingdom of God, whereas John the Baptist has only a secondary and preparatory function.

Accordingly, in the Q tradition John is pictured as worthy of high praise: There is none greater than John among those born of women. Yet John represents the end of the old era, the epoch of the Law and the prophets. He was the one who pointed to the coming Kingdom, but he was not a part of it. The analogy has often been drawn between this view of John and the Old Testament picture of Moses, who was able to see the Promised Land but not to enter it. With the transition from the ministry of John to that of Jesus, there began a new era of conflict. Only through powerful efforts will the Kingdom of God be opened for men and women to enter. The implication is that Jesus' ministry of exorcisms and healings, with the attendant defeat of the demonic powers, is an essential element in the effective manifestation of God's power defeating his adversaries.

Tragically, many of Jesus' contemporaries fail to realize what is taking place in their midst through him. Like petulant children, they are moved neither by the fun of a dance nor by funereal games (Luke

7:32). They are repulsed by both the asceticism of John the Baptist and the conviviality of Jesus, identified here as Son of Man. But as is the case in Luke 9:58 (= Matt. 8:20), the Son of Man is a designation of Jesus not as an apocalyptic figure in disguise but as a sovereign agent of God for the reconstitution of God's people. His cordial association with those rejected by religious standards implies a redefinition of the people of God and a new interpretation of God's Law.[51] The new Law and the new people will alike be vindicated when Jesus is publicly revealed as the Son of Man in the End Time.

The concluding comment (Luke 7:35 = Matt. 11:19), "Yet wisdom is justified by all her children," is an enigmatic statement; not even Matthew ("deeds") and Luke ("children") agree as to what is the central issue here. But more is intended than that both John and Jesus have their places in God's plan and that their roles will be demonstrated by the results of their work. "Wisdom" here means the out-working of God's redemptive scheme for his creation. Knowledge of that plan has been disclosed by Jesus to his followers alone (Luke 10:21–22 = Matt. 11:25–27). The results of the redemptive work launched by Jesus, building on the eschatological message and appeal of John the Baptist, will vindicate Jesus and the wisdom of which he claimed to be the bearer, according to Q. Whoever listens to Jesus, therefore, is giving heed to God's wisdom; whoever rejects Jesus is repudiating God and his redemptive purpose (Luke 10:16 = Matt. 10:40). The results of what Jesus says and does—whether pictured through the image of offspring ("children") or "deeds" (what is accomplished)—will vindicate him.

This inference is confirmed in the Q version (Luke 11:29b–32 = Matt. 12:39–41) of the incident when Jesus' opponents urge him to perform a sign in order to authenticate himself as the agent of God (Mark 8:11–12). Jesus responds by saying he will give none but the sign of Jonah:[52] Jonah came to preach to the Ninevites without credentials or signs to attest to the divine origin of his message of impending judgment. The Ninevites repented because of the power of Jonah's person and message, not because he demonstrated his authority by means of signs.

Jonah is not specifically identified as a prophet in Q, but his role as proclaimer of God's eschatological message and his function as a sign to his generation are both in the prophetic tradition. Nor is Jesus portrayed as another Jonah-like prophetic figure. Rather, he is said to be greater than Jonah, whose preaching was so effective that people repented without his performing any signs to confirm his testimony as originating with God.

Further, Jesus is equated by the Q tradition with the Son of Man, who is depicted here as God's final messenger to what is presumably thought of as the final generation, that is, the last one to have an opportunity to repent now that God's ultimate messenger has come.

Paralleling the role of prophet assigned to Jesus in the Q material is the role of wise man. Jesus is greater than Solomon, whose fabulous wisdom the Queen of Sheba had come from South Arabia to hear at first hand (1 Kings 10:1–13). In late Judaism, Solomon had been venerated even more than in the biblical Hebrew tradition, as is dramatically evident in the widely influential book called the Wisdom of Solomon. This purports to be the writing of David's kingly son but it was written originally in excellent Greek and, using terminology and concepts borrowed from Greek philosophy, it portrays wisdom as a quasi-personal agent by which God created and continues to order the world (Wisdom of Sol. 7:17–8:6). Although in the Q tradition there is no indication of a link between Jesus and this later philosophical wisdom, Jesus is declared to be "greater than Solomon," or at least the enterprise that Jesus represents is greater than that associated with Solomon. The implication is that Jesus is the one through whom the prophetic and wisdom traditions are not merely understood but are in fact moving to their divinely ordained consummation, when the Son of Man is revealed as God's eschatological redeemer. The ancients who in their time heeded God's messengers will give testimony against this generation for having failed to respond in faith to the reality, greater than that of Jonah or Solomon, that Jesus preached and embodied.

In the section of this chapter dealing with eschatological promise we examined the pericope (Luke 22:28–30) in which Jesus speaks of the coming Kingdom, where he and his disciples will be joined in fellowship and in function. Appropriately, Luke placed this saying in the setting of the Last Supper, the occasion on which Jesus is reported to have told the disciples that he would not again share "the fruit of the vine" with them until the Kingdom of God had come (Luke 22:18). Even if Luke had not inserted in the eucharistic passage the promise of participation in the eschatological supper and of the role of judge, the import of the saying would be clear: The Kingdom of God will provide continuity with and consummation of the work that Jesus began during his ministry and that he committed to his faithful followers. Whether one accepts Matthew's "glorious throne" (19:28) of the Son of Man or Luke's "my" appointed Kingdom

(22:30) as the original Q form of the saying, Jesus is in either tradition more than the announcer of the Kingdom's coming: He is the one who has the central role in its establishment. It is by identification with him in his trials that the disciples demonstrate their qualification to share in the exercise of authority when the Kingdom is established.

Whether the pericope of Jesus' lament over Jerusalem (Luke 13:34–35) was originally connected with the Jewish Feast of Tabernacles or not,[53] it includes a passage (Ps. 118:26) that was a central element in the Jewish liturgy for the Feast of Tabernacles, which was celebrated in late Judaism as an anticipation of the rule of God in the future rather than as a mere recollection of the wilderness sojourn.[54] Closely associated in the liturgy was Zechariah 14, where the judgment of God on the nation and its chief city, as well as the appearance of God in the midst of his people, are announced. Although in the mind of the Psalmist, and probably of Jesus (if these are his words), the coming One was God himself,[55] Q and the gospel tradition generally understood this saying as a reference to the vindication of Jesus, either in the Resurrection or on the Last Day. Jesus' appearing in fulfillment of the hope of the coming rule of God was seen as marking the consummation of that hope and the establishment of God's Kingdom in the earth. For Q, therefore, the decisive role in the eschatological fulfillment God has been assigned to Jesus. He is God's final messenger, so the eschatological destiny of his people is determined by their response to him. He is both the bearer of the Good News about the Kingdom's coming and the one who brings to pass that promised Kingdom.

Q has no need of a theological interpretation of the death of Jesus. The Passion of Jesus is for Q a sad fact, since it demonstrates the resistance of Israel to the messengers of God and it breaks off the fellowship of Jesus with his faithful disciples. But the Q tradition looks beyond Jesus' death to the vindication that is to come in the Day of Consummation.

Even more surprising than the absence of a theology of the cross is the lack of any reference to the Resurrection in Q. It is probable that the restoration of the fellowship between Jesus and the disciples that was believed to have taken place in the postresurrection appearances,[56] and that was continued in the church's celebration of the Eucharist, at which Christ was regarded as present, led to the conviction that Jesus was the Son of Man and to the hope that he would return, vindicated by God and in vindication of his followers. This is, however, nowhere explicitly stated in Q. The explanation of the absence of references to the cross and the Resurrection probably lies in the belief represented by Q that the two central factors in God's eschatological purpose were the coming of Jesus as authoritative teacher and agent and God's public confirmation of him in the future as the Son of Man at the End of the Age. The scheme of apocalyptically necessary events, including the suffering, death, and resurrection, essential for Mark, has no place in Q. This is not because Q is concerned only about moral instruction,[57] but because for Q even moral instruction is subordinate to and dependent on the eschatological vindication of Jesus when the present struggle against demonic and unbelieving human forces is at an end. History is perceived in three periods: (1) the old era of the Law and the prophets, which terminated with John the Baptist; (2) the present era, in which Jesus inaugurated the eschatological fellowship and in which man's major responsibility is to recognize in the message and the activity of Jesus God's final word to man; and (3) the Age to Come, in which Jesus will be reunited with his followers as Son of Man and they and he will be vindicated by God.

The Value of Q As an Historical Source

The tradition embodied in Q is more concerned with presenting Jesus as bearer of the eschatological message than as someone whose primary function is to perform deeds that effect salvation, but we have noted the importance attached to his healings and exorcisms. Jesus brings salvation by evoking the response of faith to the word from God that he offers, not by virtue of his saving actions. The result of this emphasis is that while Jesus is pictured in the Q source as historical and as a human individual, rather than as a faceless spokesman for God, there is not sufficient narrative in Q to reconstruct anything like a biographical sequence or overall course of his public career. We have in Q one of our best sources—along with Mark and the special source used by Luke—for recovering the message of Jesus. This is, of course, of primary historical value. But the main thrust of the Jesus tradition in Q is to point forward to the future Kingdom of God rather than to depict the historical life of Jesus.

The Community Behind Q

The segment of primitive Christianity by and for whom Q was produced stood firmly in the tradition of charismatic prophets, with a keen expectation of impending judgment and eschatological vindication. There seems to have been little concern about legal issues; ethical questions were decided more on the basis of divinely revealed wisdom and mutual responsibility within the community than by appeal to legal precepts from Torah. The view of the world that prevailed was sharply dualistic: The powers of Satan were already in process of being overcome by the power at work through Jesus and transmitted by him to his faithful followers. Healings and exorcisms were signs that the era dominated by the devil was coming to an end and that the New Age was dawning.[58] The religious leaders of Judaism were regarded as hypocritical and nitpicking, as exclusive in their attitude toward Gentiles and nonconforming Jews and as hostile toward Jesus and his followers. The Q community, following Jesus' example, was lax in observation of the Law, open and hospitable toward Gentiles, and ready to accept even martyrdom at the hands of the authorities, confident that God would vindicate the faithful in the End Time.

The absence of specific geographical or cultural allusions makes it impossible to locate the community. The fact that the Q material is preserved in Greek and was probably composed in that language—though with traces of Semitic idiom beneath the surface—suggests Syria, but Greek was widely used in Palestine in this period, as many Greek inscriptions and the fragments of Greek manuscripts found at Qumran attest.

We know from the letters of Paul (1 Cor. 15:9; Gal. 1:13; Phil. 3:6) that persecution of the church by Jews began early—perhaps as early as the year 30.[59] Since it presumably did not stop with the conversion of Paul, we can suppose that by the 40s it was a severe problem. This supposition is confirmed by the evidence that conflict within the Jewish community at Rome over the coming of Christian missionaries was so intense as to require imperial intervention and expulsion of the Jews.[60] The concern of the community about persecution and martyrdom was not paranoia but realism. The most honored virtue in the Q tradition is fidelity or perseverance in the face of hostility. For that, the martyred eschatological prophet, Jesus—soon to be vindicated by God—is the paradigm.

Suggestions for Further Reading

A basic necessity for the study of the gospel tradition is *Gospel Parallels: A Synopsis of the First Three Gospels*, 4th ed., ed. B.H. Throckmorton (Nashville: Thomas Nelson, 1979). Various editions of the Greek text arranged in synoptic form are available; the most recent and most complete (including the noncanonical gospel traditions) is *Synopsis Quattor Evangeliorum* available in the United States from the American Bible Society in New York City (4th rev. ed., 1993; Stuttgart: Deutsche Bibelgesellschaft).

Older reconstructions of Q, together with commentary on its contents, have been prepared by F.W. Beare, *Earliest Records of Jesus* (Nashville: Abingdon, 1962), who includes Markan, Matthean, and Lukan material as well as Q, and, by T.W. Manson, "The Sayings of Jesus," in H.D. Major, T.W. Manson, and C.H. Wright, *The Mission and Message of Jesus* (New York: Dutton, 1938). The most influential recent hypothesis about the evolution of the Q source is that of John S. Kloppenburg, *The Formation of Q: Trajectories in Ancient Wisdom Collections* (Philadelphia: Fortress Press, 1987).

Special interest in the Q tradition is shown by H.E. Tödt, *The Son of Man in the Synoptic Tradition* (Philadelphia: Westminster, 1965) and Norman Perrin, *Rediscovering the Teaching of Jesus* (New York: Harper & Row, 1967). The Q parables, as well as all the others, are discussed in detail in Joachim Jeremias, *The Parables of Jesus*, rev. ed. (New York: Scribner's, 1963). A detailed reconstruction of the theology of Q is offered by R.A. Edwards, *A Theology of Q: Eschatology, Prophecy and Wisdom* (Philadelphia: Fortress, 1976). He has also prepared a *Concordance of Q* (Missoula, MT: Society of Biblical Literature, 1975). In *Jesus and the Spiral of Violence: Popular Jewish Resistance in Roman Palestine* (San Francisco: Harper & Row, 1983), Richard A. Horsley describes Q as primarily concerned with a restructured social order in the context of violent conflict that will prepare for the coming kingdom. Important recent analyses of Q are R.A. Piper, *Wisdom in the Q Tradition: The Aphoristic Teaching of Jesus*, SNTSMS 61 (Cambridge: Cambridge University Press, 1989), and Ben Witherington III, *Jesus the Sage: The Pilgrimage of Wisdom* (Minneapolis: Fortress Press, 1994).

NOTES

[1] The current leader in the scholarly effort to deny the existence of Q by demonstrating the priority of Matthew among the synoptic Gospels is William R. Farmer, beginning with his *The Synoptic Problem: A Critical Analysis* (New York: Macmillan, 1964; reprint, Macon, GA: Mercer University Press, 1976).

[2] See the discussion of the origin of this term in C.F.D. Moule, *The Birth of the New Testament* (New York: Harper & Row, 1962), p. 84, n. 1.

[3] *Einleitung in das Neue Testament* [Introduction to the New Testament], 3 vols. (Leipzig: Weidmann'sche Buchhandlung, 1810–1820).

[4]See the excerpts from (and critique of) Eichhorn in W.G. Kümmel, *The New Testament: The History of the Investigation of Its Problems* (trans. S.M. Gilmour and H.C. Kee; Nashville: Abingdon, 1972), pp. 77–79.

[5]An important and thorough discussion of the problem is in W.G. Kümmel, *Introduction to the New Testament* (trans. H.C. Kee; Nashville: Abingdon, 1975), pp. 62–76. W.R. Farmer (in the *The Synoptic Problem*) tries to discredit the theory that Mark is the common element behind the three synoptic Gospels by exposing the fallacy in the argument of such scholars as H.J. Holtzmann (see Chapter 1) that Mark's gospel is historically accurate because it was literarily prior. While his criticism of the assumption made by Holtzmann and others is valid, it is not reasonable to deduce from their efforts to make historical judgments on the basis of the theory of Markan priority that the theory itself is wrong. What Farmer has shown is that any purely literary source theory is inadequate to explain the differences among the first three Gospels. To provide a more nearly adequate explanation, one must use the very methods Farmer avoids: form-critical and redactional studies of the individual gospel writers (see Chapter 1). A useful collection of articles for and against the Q hypothesis and the priority of Mark has been developed by Arthur J. Bellinzoni, Jr., in *The Two-Source Hypothesis: A Critical Appraisal* (Macon, GA: Mercer University Press, 1985). A cautious appraisal of the arguments on both sides is offered by Joseph B. Tyson in that volume (pp. 437–52).

[6]Most departures from Mark's order are in Matthew, and as we shall see in Chapter 5, pp. 160–61, these shifts result from Matthew's arrangement of his material in alternating blocks of action and discourse. See the chart of this material in W.G. Kümmel, *Introduction*, pp. 65–66. J.B. Tyson concludes from an exhaustive study of sequence of material in the Gospels that "the study of sequential parallelism will not dictate any one solution to the synoptic problem" (*New Testament Studies* 22 [1976]: 276–308, 298). But he acknowledges that either Matthew or Luke supports Mark's sequence in nearly every instance, and that even in Q material there is strict agreement or at least relative agreement on order. Mark's failure to use some thirty pericopes common to Matthew and Luke cannot be explained if Mark used Matthew. The most plausible hypothesis remains: Mark and Q are the primary sources for Matthew and Luke.

[7]See pp. 162–66, for Matthew's special sources; for Luke's, see pp. 179–81.

[8]For example, F.C. Grant, *The Gospels: Their Origin and Growth* (New York: Harper Brothers, 1957), pp. 108–09.

[9]J.M. Robinson, "Logoi Sophon: On the Gattung of Q," in *Trajectories Through Early Christianity* (Philadelphia: Fortress, 1971), pp. 71–113. His theories about Q have been adopted and refined by John S. Kloppenborg in *The Formation of Q* (Philadelphia: Fortress Press, 1987), a work which claims to trace the development of Q from its original collection of wisdom sayings to the present mix of references to the age to come and to the miracles of Jesus. Helmut Koester affirms this developmental process for Q in his *Ancient Christian Gospels: Their History and Development* (Philadelphia: Trinity Press International, 1990), pp. 133–34.

[10]The terms "glutton and drunkard" are found in Deuteronomy 21:18–21, where rebellious children are to be killed because their way of life threatens the integrity of the covenant community.

[11]The quotation from "the Wisdom of God" is not found in any known ancient text, but is clearly another example of the personification of Wisdom.

[12]This largely ignored dimension of apocalyptic expectation has been effectively articulated by Richard Horsley in *Jesus and the Spiral of Violence: Popular Jewish Resistance in Roman Palestine* (Minneapolis: Fortress Press, 1993), esp. Chapter 5, "Apocalyptic Orientation and Historical Action," pp. 121–45. He shows that the apocalyptic writers were by no means other-worldly, as they are often portrayed, but that they believed God had given them visions and promises of coming conflict through which the hostile political and social powers will be defeated and God's purpose for his covenant people will triumph.

[13]As noted earlier (p. 35), scholars leading the current Q Seminar perceive Cynic-Stoic philosophy as characteristically aphoristic in its mode of thought and expression, relegating all the apocalyptic features of the Q tradition to later modifications which distort and pervert the original timeless wisdom. My own earlier analysis of the relation between apocalyptic and Stoic thought appeared in the Festschrift for W.G. Kümmel, *Glaube und Eschatologie*, ed. Erich Grasser and Otto Merk (Tübingen: J.C.B. Mohr [Paul Siebeck], 1985), under the title "Pauline Eschatology: Relationships with Apocalyptic and Stoic Thought," pp. 135–58. A subsequent expansion of this proposal is offered in *Who Are the People of God? Early Christian Models of Community* (New Haven and London: Yale University Press, 1995). A similar critique of the proverbial wisdom model for Cynic-Stoic philosophers is offered by Richard Horsley in *Sociology and the Jesus Movement* (New York: Crossroad, 1989).

[14]I have documented this perception of the Cynic-Stoic view in a presentation to the Seminar on the Graeco-Roman Context of Early Christianity, offered at the 1994 annual meeting of Studiorum Novi Testamenti Societas.

[15]David E. Hahm, in *The Origins of Stoic Cosmology* (Columbus: Ohio State University Press, 1977), sketches the cosmic cycles in the Stoic philosophy, which predicted the end of the present cosmic order in a great conflagra-tion and the emergence from it of a Great Year when the order of the cos-mos and the biological species within it would be renewed. One's status in the new order depended on one's moral performance in the present order.

[16]In *De Divinatione* II–III; LIV–LVII vol. 20 (trans. W.A. Falconer) Loeb Classical Library (Cambridge, MA: Harvard University Press, 1929).

[17]So Paul D. Hanson, *The Dawn of Apocalyptic* (Philadelphia: Fortress, 1975).

[18]Martin Hengel, *Judaism and Hellenism*, 2 vols. (Philadelphia: Fortress, 1974), I:180–96.

[19]Ronald A. Piper, *Wisdom in the Q Tradition: The Aphoristic Teaching of Jesus*, SNTSM 61 (Cambridge: Cambridge University Press, 1989); Ben Witherington III, *Jesus the Sage: The Pilgrimage of Wisdom* (Minneapolis: Fortress Press, 1994).

[20]Witherington, pp. 185–87.

[21]Ibid., p. 201.

[22]Ibid., p. 214. Richard A. Horsley, "Questions About Redactional Strata and Social Relations Reflected in Q," SBL Seminar Papers, 1989 (Atlanta: Scholars Press), p. 195.

[23]Josephus, *Jewish Wars*, vol. 2 *Loeb Classical Library* (trans. H. St. J. Thackeray; New York: Putnam's, 1927), pp. 254–63. The importance of this dimen-sion of first century C.E. Jewish life and its relevance for assessing the Jesus

tradition has been highlighted by Richard Horsley and J. Hanson in *Bandits, Prophets and Messiah* (Minneapolis, Chicago, New York: Winston, 1985).

[24]Coined by R.A. Edwards to designate the four Q pericopes (Luke 11:30; 17:24, 26, 28–30) where there is an explicit comparison between a situation in the present and the future time of eschatological fulfillment.

[25]Called by Ernst Käsemann "Sentences of Holy Law" in an essay translated by W.J. Montague and published in Käsemann, *New Testament Questions for Today* (Philadelphia: Fortress, 1969), pp. 66–81.

[26]The capitalized version of this designation for Jesus is used throughout except in quotations from Scripture, which preserve the RSV lowercase style for "man."

[27]This construction is discussed in F.W. Blass and Albert Debrunner, *A Greek Grammar of the New Testament and Other Early Christian Literature*, rev. ed. (trans. R.W. Funk; Chicago: University of Chicago Press, 1961), paras. 130.1, 342.1.

[28]The Zechariah named here is the son of Jehoida the priest, who denounced his contemporaries for having forsaken the commandments of God and was stoned to death by order of King Joash, according to 2 Chronicles 24:17–22. Curiously, Matthew (23:35) identifies this murdered critic as "son of Barachiah," as though he were Zechariah the prophet (Zech. 1:1), who also seems to have been of priestly lineage (Nah. 12:12–21).

[29]The term "scribe," which was used for the professional interpreters of the Law of Moses, is emphasized in Matthew's own reworking of the tradition. See pp. 159, 169.

[30]See pp. 78–80 and pp. 87–107 for discussion of Q's view of Jesus' role as revealer. Scholars have often overlooked or even denied the close links between the roles of prophets and wise men. Both claim to be speaking for God, offering criticisms of the failures of the people to perceive and obey God's will, and conveying what God's purpose is for those who call themselves the covenant community in their special relationship with God.

[31]See the discussion by Joachim Jeremias in *The Parables of Jesus*, rev. ed. (trans. S.H. Hooke; New York: Scribner's, 1963), pp. 42–48.

[32]For the evangelists' adaptation of this saying to the entry of Jesus into Jerusalem and/or the Resurrection, see Barnabas Lindars, *New Testament Apologetic* (Philadelphia: Westminster, 1962), pp. 171–74. A full and illuminating interpretation of the imagery used here is that of Joseph A. Fitzmyer in his commentary on Luke (in The Anchor Bible), *The Gospel According to Luke X–XXIV* (Garden City, NY: Doubleday, 1985), pp. 1033–38.

[33]On this phrase as a characteristic editorial device, see Jeremias, *The Parables of Jesus*, pp. 97–98.

[34]Compare Ulrich Mauser, *Christ in the Wilderness* (Naperville, IL: Allenson, 1963), and a detailed analysis by Joseph A. Fitzmyer, *The Gospel According to Luke I–IX* (Anchor Bible; Garden City, NY: Doubleday, 1981), pp. 506–18.

[35]Although a primary concern for studying Q is not to distinguish authentic sayings of Jesus from those that arose in the early church, it may be noted that even a critical scholar as skeptical about the Jesus tradition as was

Rudolf Bultmann observed concerning Luke 11:20: "The latter [Luke 11:20] can, in my view, claim the highest degree of authenticity which we can make for any saying of Jesus" (*History of the Synoptic Tradition* [New York: Harper & Row, 1963], pp. 162–63).

[36]See the comprehensive survey and analysis of the evidence for exorcisms in Graham H. Twelftree, *Jesus the Exorcist: A Contribution to the Study of the Historical Jesus* [Wissenschaftliche Untersuchungen zum Neuen Testament 2 Reihe] (Tübingen: J.C.B. Mohr [Paul Siebeck], 1993).

[37]Matthew's version of the Sermon runs to three chapters (5, 6, 7) and incorporates extensive material from his own source. See Chapter 5, pp. 166–68.

[38]Luke 6:22 was probably added in Q to the original set of authentic Beatitudes (that is, from Jesus) in 6:20–21 and comes from a time (1) when conflict between church and synagogue was mounting and (2) when Jesus had been identified by the church as the Son of Man. Our present concern, however, is with the viewpoint of Q, rather than with the authenticity of the sayings of Jesus.

[39]"The Holy Spirit" in Luke 11:13 is probably Luke's own addition to the Q saying, which otherwise he preserved quite faithfully.

[40]Matthew adds a special touch in calling for "his kingdom *and his righteousness*" (6:33). For Matthew, righteousness is the mode of life of the covenant people, which he defines in sharp contrast with that called for by rabbinic Judaism, which was shifting into a new authoritative phase in the period following the fall of Jerusalem and the destruction of the temple in 70 C.E. For details, see pp. 168–71. By contrast, Luke's added saying about the Kingdom as God's gift for "the little flock" is wholly in keeping with the intent of the Q saying to which it is appended.

[41]For an older interpretation of this material as proto-Gnostic, see M.J. Suggs, *Wisdom, Christology and Law*, pp. 85–95. The recent attempt to date the Gospel of Thomas, with its Gnostic features, earlier than the Gospel of Mark is part of the larger current scholarly effort to transform Jesus into a purveyor of timeless wisdom. Compare B.L. Mack, *The Lost Gospel* (San Francisco: HarperCollins, 1994).

[42]H.E. Tödt, *The Son of Man in the Synoptic Tradition* (trans. D.M. Barton; Philadelphia: Westminster, 1965), discusses the origin and significance of this Son of Man saying. Precisely because authenticity is not our concern, we can see how useful for Q's viewpoint is such a saying, pointing up as it does the eschatological urgency surrounding the ministry of Jesus.

[43]There are two accounts in Luke (9:1–6 and 10:1–16): The first account mentions twelve disciples; the second mentions seventy. See the discussion in Chapter 6, pp. 179, 186–87.

[44]Jeremias, *The Parables of Jesus*, pp. 48–51.

[45]The Parable of the Leaven follows the Parable of the Mustard Seed in both Matthew 13:33 and Luke 13:20–21.

[46]Ibid., pp. 146–49.

[47]Manson, *The Sayings of Jesus*, p. 123.

[48]In the translation by Beate Blatz included in the revised edition of *New Testament Apocrypha*, ed. R. McL. Wilson (Cambridge: Jas. Clarke, 1991), pp. 125–26, the parable reads as follows:

> Jesus said: A man had guests, and when he had prepared the dinner, he sent his servant to invite the guests. He went to the first,

and said to him: "My master invites you." He said, "I have money with some merchants; they are coming to me this evening. I will go and give them my orders. I ask to be excused from the dinner." He went to another (and) said to him: "My master has invited you." He said to him: "I have bought a house and I am asked for a day. I shall not have time." He went to another and said to him: "My master invites you." He said to him: "My friend is about to be married and I am to arrange the dinner. I ask to be excused from the dinner." He went to another; he said to him: "My master invites you." He said to him: "I have bought a farm; I am going to collect the rent. I shall not be able to come. I ask to be excused." The servant came back (and) said to his master: "Those whom you invited to the dinner have asked to be excused." The master said to the servant: "Go out to the roads, bring those whom you will find, that they may dine. Traders and merchants shall not enter the places of my Father."

[49]The special interest of Luke in the Gentile mission is discussed in Chapter 6.

[50]The coming of the prophet Elijah was to be in preparation for the day of God's judgment, as affirmed when the messenger to prepare the Lord's coming in Malachi. 3:1–2 is identified in 4:5–6 as Elijah. This eschatological role for Elijah is implied in a tiny fragment from one of the caves at Qumran (J. Starcky in *Revue Biblique* 70 [1963]: 498). Later the rabbis claimed that Elijah's return would precede that of the Messiah, but there is no evidence for that belief in the time of Jesus.

[51]See Tödt, *The Son of Man in the Synoptic Tradition*, pp. 114–18.

[52]The interpretation of the sign of Jonah offered by Matthew is awkward and is uniquely his own: The explanation offered there for Jonah's three-day submarine voyage, ending when the fish has an attack of seasickness and vomits up his passenger, is that of a prefiguring of Jesus' burial and resurrection after three days and nights), although this does not fit the Easter tradition of the resurrection "on the third day."

[53]Maurice Goguel used this link between Psalm 118 and the Feast of Tabernacles as the basis for his chronological reconstruction, according to which Jesus came first to Jerusalem at the time of Tabernacles—that is, in September or October—and then returned for the final fatal occasion at Passover—that is, on April 7, A.D. 30 (according to the synoptics) or on April 3, A.D. 33 (according to John). See Goguel's *Life of Jesus* (trans. Olive Wyon; New York: Macmillan, 1946), pp. 226, 250–51.

[54]See the article on the "Feast of Tabernacles" by J.C. Rylaarsdam in G.A. Buttrick, ed., *The Interpreter's Dictionary of the Bible* (Nashville: Abingdon, 1962).

[55]See the discussion in Lindars, *New Testament Apologetic*, pp. 172–73.

[56]H.E. Tödt, *The Son of Man in the Synoptic Tradition* (trans. D.M. Barton; Philadelphia: Westminster, 1965), pp. 251–52, 273.

[57]Decades ago, a thorough but unconvincing description of Q as a collection of sayings brought together for hortatory purposes was given by Martin Dibelius in *From Tradition to Gospel*, 3d ed. (trans. B.L. Woolf; New York: Scribner's, 1965), pp. 233–49, esp. p. 246: "The sayings of Jesus were originally gathered together for a hortatory end, to give the Churches advice, help and commandment by means of the Master's words. This

typical interest was dominant both in the origin of this special source [i.e., Q] and also in the gathering together of the words of Jesus everywhere." As noted earlier (p. 78), this same theory has been revived in recent years, especially by the group calling itself "The International Q Seminar." As noted previously (pp. 34–35), the basic scholarly constructs on which this group builds have been provided by J. Kloppenburg *(The Formation of Q)* and B.L. Mack *(The Lost Gospel: The Book of Q and Christian Origins)*, who begin by eliminating all the Q material which is not aphoristic in mode and then treat the aphorisms as timeless proverbial sayings.

[58]The importance of the miracle tradition in Q and the other gospel traditions is spelled out in my study of *Miracle in the Early Christian World: A Study in Socio-Historical Method* (New Haven: Yale University Press, 1983).

[59]See A.J. Hultgren, "Paul's Pre-Christian Persecutions of the Church: Their Purpose, Locale, and Nature," *Journal of Biblical Literature* 95 (1976): 97–111.

[60]Attested in the decree of Claudius which is reported by the Roman historian, Suetonius (in his *Lives of the Twelve Caesars;* discussed in H.C. Kee, *What Can We Know About Jesus?* [Cambridge: Cambridge University Press, 1990], 9–10).

CHAPTER 4

Jesus As the Culmination of Apocalyptic History
The Gospel of Mark

The term *gospel* as a designation for the early Christian claims about Jesus had been in use for nearly four decades before Mark wrote a work that became known as a gospel and to which he prefixed the words "The beginning of the gospel of Jesus Christ ..." (Mark 1:1). He was apparently the first to write a more or less sequential account of the career of Jesus. Q included only sayings and probably no more than a single narrative, as we have seen. Paul gives no indication of knowing the Gospels, does not quote from them, and disavows interest in Christ "from a human point of view" (2 Cor. 5:16).[1] Why did Mark write such a gospel? What purposes did he intend it to serve? Unlike Paul, whose major interest is the significance of Jesus' crucifixion and resurrection, and unlike Q, where the primary focus is on Jesus' teachings, why is Mark concerned with the life and activity of Jesus prior to his death and resurrection, as well as his message? Why did Mark link what he wrote with the term *gospel* (Mark 1:1)? Our search for answers to these questions requires us to face up to the fact of diversity in the early Christian understandings of Jesus.

The Message of Mark and the Message of Paul

The Gospel of Mark is an account of the public ministry of word and act performed by the pre-cross and pre-resurrection Jesus, whereas the letters of Paul are concerned with the understanding of Jesus that is possible through an apprehension of the significance of the crucified and risen Lord. That there were those in the wider early Christian movement whose primary interest was in what Jesus taught, rather than what he did or what happened to him, is evident from the second-century Gnostic Gospel of Thomas, which relates only Jesus' words without a hint of his deeds or his Passion. Q, as we have seen, does not fit that pattern, since the sayings it includes point to the conflict and suffering that Jesus will experience at the hands of the religious and political authorities. Perhaps the Q document was an alternative to Paul's letters as a way of understanding Jesus, but the fact that it exists only in the form in which it was adapted by the gospel writers indicates that by the later first century the dominant interest was in Jesus as an historical figure. Concurrent with the development of the gospel tradition was exploration of the theological and ethical import of Jesus in the form of letters, of which Paul's were the paradigms. We have seen that in Q there is good evidence that before Mark wrote his gospel there were collections of Jesus material that consisted of sayings alone and possible reports of miracle stories, with reference to conflict and vindication of Jesus, but without explicit reference to a theological understanding of the cross and Resurrection. It seems likely that before Mark wrote his gospel the early church had—in addition to Q—oral or written traditions reporting the sayings of Jesus, including his parables, and his activities—especially his miracles. The question returns: Why was it important for someone to bring these materials together and thereby develop the literary type that we know as the Gospels?

Attempts at Reconciling the Differences Between Mark and Paul

The fact that both the Gospels and Paul's letters are, for Christians, Scripture and have been read in the churches as the Word of God since the first century has obscured the differences between them and tended to lead to simple assumptions about the congruence of these literary types, which are so different in both style and content. Many scholars and theologians have labored to demonstrate their support of this view. Some interpreters of the New Testament have tried to impose unity on the Gospels and the letters or have claimed to find a common ground underlying the differences. For example, in *The Apostolic Preaching and Its Development in the New Testament* C.H. Dodd listed certain propositions about Jesus that he claimed all New

Testament writers affirmed, despite the differences between them.[2] But it is impossible to fit the gospel narratives and teaching materials into such a scheme, since the "common message" reconstructed is often based on a synthesis of Paul and Acts, in both of which the cross and the Resurrection are central and little place is set aside for the public ministry and teaching of Jesus which are primary for the Gospels. Other historians of early Christianity insist that a choice be made between Jesus and Paul. Some treat the message of Paul as a regrettable development that has been superimposed on the simple ethical message of Jesus, which, it is claimed, can be reconstructed from the sayings portions of the first three Gospels. Others think that the message of Jesus in the synoptics—especially Matthew and Mark—is basically an intra-Jewish debate.[3] In the tradition of the Protestant Reformation, it is only in Paul that one finds the essential Christian message. The approach adopted for this book, however, is based on the assumption that the attempt to find *the* central Christian message, however convenient it might be as a theological undertaking, would hinder recognition of the diversity of interpretations of Jesus embodied in the gospel tradition, and in particular of the distinctive contribution of Mark to Christian understanding of the historical role of Jesus. Jacob Neusner makes the point effectively when he points out that there was no single "Judaism" in the first century, nor was there one common "Messiah myth." Rather, "The figure of the Messiah bears within itself the shared views of a society that bonds family to family, village to village, and the whole into 'Israel.' One critical aspect of Israel's self-conception comes to surface in its messianic idea. [In earlier times] he was depicted as whatever people most wanted—king, savior, wonder-worker, perfect priest, invincible general or teacher—but also as the figure of the end and conclusion of history."[4] The inadequacy of approaches that concentrate on the search for *the* central message in the Gospels or in the New Testament as a whole is evident in even a brief survey of the results of investigations of biblical and theological scholars who have taken this as their goal.

The Search for the Central Element in the Christian Message

In the middle of the nineteenth century F.C. Baur proposed a quite specific solution to the problem of the relationship between the message preached by Jesus and known to us through the synoptics and the message preached about him by Paul. In Baur's view, the message of Jesus historically was fundamentally one of "absolute moral command,"[5] according to which "the inner is opposed to the outer, the disposition to the act, the spirit to the letter."[6] Jesus' moral ideal was expressed through Jewish concepts, as we would expect of a historical person living under the intellectual and cultural conditions of first-century Judaism. One group of his followers restricted themselves to "the cramping and narrowing influence of the Jewish national Messianic idea" and therefore were never able "to surmount the particularism of Judaism at all."[7] The wing of the church that launched the Gentile mission, on the other hand, of which Paul was the chief representative, built on the "moral universal in [Jesus], the unconfined humanity, the divine exaltation, which gave his person its absolute significance," and thereby "introduced Christianity to its true destination as a religion for the world, and enunciated, with a full sense of its vast significance, the principle of Christian universalism."[8] Baur found Jesus' moral and spiritual ideal set forth in all the Gospels, and with particular clarity in Matthew's Sermon on the Mount.[9] In Luke, however, he saw an additional development: Luke emphasized the universal element in Jesus' message, modifying the tradition so as to bring out the universal dimension stressed in Paul's message.[10] (Baur assumed that Luke was a companion and disciple of Paul.) Baur saw the culmination of New Testament universalism in the Gospel of John, in which "Christianity is established as a universal principle of salvation; all those antitheses which threatened to detain it within the narrow limits of Jewish particularism are merged in the universalism of Christianity."[11] For Baur there was no essential discontinuity in the conceptual movement from Jesus to Paul and on to the catholic church of the late first and early second centuries. Paul's polemics against the Judaizers were necessary in order to help the church shed its excess baggage of Jewish images and perspectives. Only through such a conflict could the church emerge to the stage of conceptual reconciliation at which the pure, spiritual intention of Jesus was comprehended and expressed in terms freed of the connotations of Jewish particularism.

With his value judgment that Paul's universalism was good and the Jewish particularism of the synoptic Gospels was bad, Baur discouraged serious attention to the interpretations of Jesus embodied in the synoptics. Accordingly, Mark's view of Jesus in history finds no significant place in Baur's critical reconstruction of primitive Christianity, except as it provides evidence of the Jewish particularism that had to be outgrown.

One hundred years after Baur, Rudolf Bultmann was at work on his own formulation of the relationship of the message of Jesus to that of Paul and the later New Testament writers. According to Bultmann, the essential message of the New Testament cannot be found in the message of Jesus in the synoptics; rather, it is to be found in Paul and in the Gospel of John. The preaching of Jesus as we have it in the synoptic tradition is only the presupposition of New Testament theology and is not to be considered *kerygma*, or the proclamation of the Christian message.[12] As an historical person, Jesus should be thought of within the sphere of late Judaism[13] and not as the inaugurator of Christian faith. Christian faith began with Easter; that is, in the rise of the belief that God made the crucified one Lord, the church was asserting that Jesus was present in the kerygma, in the "proclaiming, accosting, demanding and promising word of preaching."[14]

Although the message of Jesus is by no means to be considered kerygma,[15] the synoptics may serve a kerygmatic function: Repetition of Jesus' preaching under the impact of kerygma makes "the past present in such a way that it puts the hearers (or readers) before the decision for (or against) a possibility of self-understanding disclosed in the preaching of the historical Jesus."[16] But it is the Jesus present in the kerygma who is the saving event, not the historical Jesus of the synoptic Gospels. Only to the extent that the post-Jesus kerygma influenced and shaped the present form of the synoptic Gospels can the synoptics be called kerygmatic.

Bultmann made a brilliant contribution to the study of the Gospels through his *History of the Synoptic Tradition*, in which he developed and utilized form criticism to differentiate older from later strata of the tradition incorporated in the synoptic Gospels, but he did not close the gap between the message of Jesus and the message about him. For example, he made no attempt to show the continuity between Jesus' proclamation of the Kingdom of God and Paul's proclamation of Jesus as eschatological event.

That he failed to close this gap is evident too in his brief but highly suggestive analysis of the distinctive features of Mark's editing of the tradition.[17] In discussing Mark's purpose, Bultmann states only that Mark combined the tradition of the story about Jesus with the Hellenistic, or Pauline, kerygma.[18] Thus, according to Bultmann, even in Mark the Pauline message is basic, and the Jesus tradition is little more than an embellishment. He remarks that Mark was "not sufficiently master of his material to venture on a systematic construction himself."[19] As we shall see in this chapter, Bultmann seems not to have recognized that Mark did in fact present a theological construction of his own—one that has some elements in common with the Pauline kerygma, though it does not adopt Paul's cross-resurrection theology as its basis.

In the so-called new quest of the historical Jesus, New Testament scholars have reversed their direction in the search for an answer to the problem of the relationship between Jesus and Paul. Instead of moving from Jesus to Paul, they move from Paul back toward Jesus. Of course, this sequence is required by the fact that in terms of literary chronology alone, the documentation of the cross-resurrection kerygma antedates by thirty-five years the earliest gospel writing. If Paul's claim is accurate that there was no difference between his kerygma and that of the original group of apostle-disciples—Peter and the twelve—is it possible that they too had no more interest than Paul in the kind of material that someone later incorporated in the Gospels? This theory would suggest that the real Christian message was to be found only in the gospel preached by Paul, a message that he shared with the apostles. But then we should be completely at a loss to know why the Gospels were ever written, or why they were included in the same collection—the New Testament—that contained the letters of Paul. Certainly Paul has only a few allusions to sayings of Jesus (for example, 1 Cor. 7:10); Acts attributes to Paul a quotation from the teaching of Jesus that is not otherwise known (Acts 20:35). But Baur long ago recognized the foolishness of those who try to demonstrate Paul's reliance on the Jesus tradition.[20]

Most attempts to trace the links between Paul and the Gospels have proved to be evasions of the problem or blind alleys. Baur's suggestion that Luke was a Paulinized gospel,[21] as well as more recent theories about Mark that depict this gospel as filled with Paulinisms, do not bear up under critical scrutiny.[22] Both the theological concepts and the distinctive vocabulary of Paul are missing from all the Gospels. The extended treatment of the public ministry of Jesus, which is central to the synoptic tradition, has no place in Paul's letters and seems clearly to have no place in his understanding of the central Christian beliefs about Jesus. Even when Paul appeals to a saying of Jesus for purposes of moral instruction, as in 1 Corinthians 7:10 ("I give the charge, not I but the Lord"), he quotes himself with equal authority in the next breath ("I say, not the Lord"—1 Cor. 7:11).

Given the fact that leading historical critics have not differentiated between the Markan message and the message of Paul, it is not surprising that theologians have perpetuated this confusion. For example, Martin Kähler, whose rejection of the attempt to reconstruct a historical picture of Jesus we considered in the first chapter, took a position that has exercised wide influence on the issue of the relationship between the understanding of Jesus recoverable from critical assessment of the Gospels and the understanding of him set forth in the church's kerygma. Having taken as his theological foundation "the kerygma"—which means for Kähler the message of Paul—he declares it invalid even to investigate the differences between Paul and the gospel tradition or to look behind the tradition to its possible historical origins.

> From these fragmentary traditions, these half-understood recollections, these portrayals colored by the writers' individual personalities, these heartfelt confessions, these sermons proclaiming him as Savior, there gazes upon us a vivid and coherent image of a Man, an image we never fail to recognize. Hence, we may conclude that in his unique and powerful personality and by his incomparable deeds and life (including his resurrection appearances) this man has engraved his image on the mind and memory of his followers with such sharp and deeply etched features that it could be neither obliterated nor distorted.[23]

But Kähler's subsequent remarks show that however "deeply etched" the features may be, it is not legitimate for faith to inquire into any of the details with which the gospel portraits have been traced: "It is ... erroneous to make [faith] depend on uncertain statements about an allegedly reliable picture of Jesus that has been torturously extracted by the modern methods of historical research."[24] It is obvious that Kähler is interested in the gospel accounts only as they transmit to the hearts of believers "the mind of Christ."[25] Indeed, the more uncertain the historical reconstruction, the more discernible is the inspiration of the gospel writers. As Kähler puts it, "The more obscure the course of events remains which have preceded the literary activity, all the more certainly can we sense the invisible hand of Providence over the primitive community's carefreeness in the transmission of the tradition."[26]

The systematic theologian Paul Tillich had a more positive attitude than Kähler about historical research, but his conclusions concerning the results of gospel criticism and the differences between the Gospels and Paul are paradoxical, if not downright contradictory. On the one hand, he praised Protestantism for its courage in subjecting its holy writings to critical analysis[27] and for "the immense historical material which has been discovered and often empirically verified by a universally used method of research."[28] He also asserted that it was not enough to reconstruct a *Gestalt* of Jesus after all questionable details have been eliminated: An essential picture "remains dependent on details."[29] But when he spoke of the transforming power of the biblical picture of Jesus as the Christ, through which the New Being is transmitted, he declared: "No special trait of this picture can be verified with certainty. But it can be definitely asserted that through this picture the New Being has power to transform those who are transformed by it."[30] With how little seriousness Tillich took the work of historical criticism—in spite of his commendatory generalities—is evident in this statement: "Harnack was wrong ... about Jesus. There is no substantial difference between the message given by the Synoptic Jesus and the message about Jesus given in Paul's Epistles."[31]

The Different Perspectives of Mark and Paul

By such approaches as these, the problem remains not only unanswered but also unaddressed. The problem is not merely one of historical continuity from Jesus to Paul or from Paul back to Jesus. Theologians have made the easy assumption that there is no fundamental difference between Paul's kerygma and the kerygmatic significance of Jesus in Mark, and this assumption has prevented them from seeing clearly Mark's perspective. To make the distinction between Mark's perspective and Paul's, it may be useful to take up Bultmann's contention that the kerygma announces that a historical event has become an eschatological event. Bultmann used the words "historical" and "eschatological" in a special way that derived from existentialist philosophy. "Historical" concerns not the past, but what he called the historicity of self, which is constituted by an event or a word by which individuals find the meaning of their own existence. Similarly, "eschatological" does not deal with the end of the world at some future date, but describes any moment in the present when the individual is called to make a fundamental decision that requires seeking freedom from reliance on the institutions and powers of the past and to become open to the future. In making the decision, one experiences an event that transforms the outlook on self and the world, upon which one has relied for standards and stability. Making this radical decision, one "dies." But God gives a new life, so that, in the language of the New Testament, one enters "the life of the Age to Come." For Bultmann, it is Jesus' summons to individuals to follow him, in light of his own decision to accept death rather than conform to the political and even religious institutions of his time, that constitutes a historical event which for faith becomes an eschatological event.

Bultmann considered the Gospel of John (in its expurgated form) to embody the purest version of the kerygma: It is the simple declaration *that* God addresses human individuals in a historical man, Jesus of Nazareth.[32] Paul has approached the purity of this insight by leaving out of consideration the ethical and eschatological teaching of Jesus, locating Jesus' obedience in a decision to do God's will made by him as the heavenly Christ before he took the form of the earthly Jesus (Phil. 2:5-8) and limiting his kerygma to the " 'that' of the life of Jesus and the fact of his crucifixion."[33] Through the cross, God announces the end of the old age and the coming of the new; therefore, to accept God's Word through the cross is to enter the life of the Age to Come. Having died to the old world, one is raised by faith to the new life.

Bultmann's representation of Jesus as historical event become eschatological event may be appropriate and illuminating for understanding some of the major aspects of Paul's and John's thought, although it does not provide a satisfactory perspective for dealing with their beliefs about the eschatological future. But for Mark, the axiom is wholly inadequate. It would be useful in interpreting Mark only if both "historical" and "eschatological" were assigned meanings quite different from those that Bultmann intended.

Although Paul does not repudiate the apocalyptic element in the gospel he preaches, he does not give it a central place. Or more accurately, even when he includes the apocalyptic elements of the Christian message, he does so without reference to the past ministry or message of Jesus. The only roles Jesus plays in Paul's eschatological scheme are those of the crucified-exalted Lord and the agent who will bring the cosmos into subjection to the will of God. There is no appeal to precedent or guideline in the activity or message of the earthly Jesus.

For the gospel tradition, as for late Judaism and particularly for Jewish apocalypticism, the coming of the New Age was a far more complicated matter than a shift of self-understanding. Whatever one may think of Albert Schweitzer's reconstruction of the life and message of Jesus, Schweitzer has shown beyond doubt the thoroughly eschatological, and indeed apocalyptic, outlook of Jesus, in terms of which his message of the Kingdom of God was formulated.[34]

In the synoptic tradition the central concerns are precisely what is missing in Paul: Jesus is seen as the eschatological salvation bringer in the context of his *historical* public ministry and without reference to his heavenly existence prior to his appearance as a human or to his *Parousia*, his future coming in glory. No one before Mark had bothered to bring together the tradition in a sequential way; what pre-Markan documents there were seem to have been structured by topical or mnemonic arrangement. Thus, in any study of the Gospels, Mark poses this problem: How in a church that (to judge from most of the New Testament) was dominated by Paul and his kerygma and whose major concern was to proclaim the crucified and risen Lord, did there arise a literary creation like the Gospel of Mark, with the theological understanding of Jesus it embodies?

What Is a Gospel?

The Meaning of Euangelion

The problem of what "gospel" means becomes apparent immediately when we recognize that *euangelion*, or gospel, the word Mark (or the early church for which he was a spokesman) chose as the heading for his little book, was Paul's favorite term for his kerygma. For Paul the word meant the announcement of the eschatological event effected by God through the Crucifixion and Resurrection of Jesus. Therefore, the one who preaches the gospel could be associated with the Deutero-Isaianic messenger of Yahweh, who "proclaims the victory of Yahweh over the whole world."[35] He not only announces it, but his word of good tidings brings about salvation. "By the fact that he declares the restoration of Israel, the new creation of the world, the inauguration of the eschatological age, he brings them to pass."[36]

The noun *euangelion* as used by Mark (1:1) may carry some of the connotation of the verb in 2 Isaiah, but its meaning and use lie closer to the term as it was employed in the imperial Roman cult: It meant an announcement of the benefits the empire enjoyed through the gracious authority of Caesar, the divinely appointed ruler of Rome. Although the fuller documentation for this meaning of *euangelion* comes in part from post–New Testament writers, such as Plutarch (46?–120? C.E.) in *De Fortuna Romanorum*,[37] there is inscriptional evidence going back to the time of Augustus for the use of *euangelion* in connection with the imperial cult: "The birthday of the god was for the world the beginning of tidings of joy *[euangelion]* on his account."[38] Gerhard Friedrich has summarized what the term implied when associated with the saving power and person of the emperor:

> The ruler is divine by nature. His power extends to men, to animals, to the earth and to the sea. Nature belongs to him; the wind and the waves are subject to him. He works miracles and heals men. He is the savior of the world who also redeems individuals from their difficulties.[39]

The emperor's divinity was attested by signs in the heavens at both his birth and his death that showed he belonged among the gods. Although some leading scholars have denied the link between the meaning of *euangelion* as applied to the first four books of the New Testament and the connotation it carries in the imperial cult,[40] the connection has recently and rightly been reaffirmed in an important study of gospel origins by Wilhelm Schneemelcher.[41]

It would be wrong to assume, however, that the primary meaning of *euangelion* was taken over from the Hellenistic conceptual world and that the Old Testament belief in the significance of Yahweh's saving acts as set forth in 2 Isaiah was added later. The likelihood is rather the reverse. For Mark the Hellenistic term was a useful propaganda tool for setting forth his understanding of Jesus' divine kingship, a form of rulership that rested on conceptions of power and divine purpose in the world entirely different from those in non-Christian circles. This radical divergence is explicitly declared in Mark 10:42–45:

> You know that those who are supposed to rule over the Gentiles lord it over them, and their great men exercise authority over them. But it shall not be so among you; but whoever would be great among you must be your servant, and whoever would be first among you must be slave of all. For the Son of man came not to be served but to serve, and to give his life as a ransom for many.

Without assuming that Mark 10:45 is a direct allusion to the Suffering Servant theme of Isaiah 53 (this cannot be demonstrated on philological grounds),[42] we can see that casting Jesus in the role of a servant on the eve of his entry into Jerusalem as a kingly figure (Mark 11:1–10) is clearly intentional. Mark wants to use the terminology of Gentile kingship—including *euangelion*—but to redefine in a radical way what kingship involves. This redefinition, reflecting his understanding of Yahweh's sovereignty, is drawn not from imperial Rome but from the eschatological kingship of 2 Isaiah and the later prophets and apocalyptists.

Although Paul refers to Jesus' turning over "the kingdom" to God after the defeat of the evil powers is complete (1 Cor. 15:24–28), this phrase is not central in Paul's thought. Indeed, he uses it at times in a way that sounds more like its transformation into a state of mind by early twentieth-century Protestant liberals than like Mark: "the kingdom of God does not mean food and drink but righteousness and peace and joy in the Holy Spirit" (Rom. 14:17). Apart from the First Corinthians 15 passage, in which Paul sets forth a kind of eschatological calendar of events, the kingdom plays no significant role in Paul's thought as we know it from his letters. It may be that the eschatological wisdom was kept for the inner core of the theologically mature believers in the Pauline churches,[43] which could account for the brief attention it receives in his public letters. But even if this were the case—and the hypothesis has great plausibility—the central concern for Paul was the message concerning the cross and Resurrection.[44]

What we are confronted with, therefore, is not merely a difference between "gospel" as message in Paul and as a narrative account in Mark, but a different understanding of the meaning of Jesus for faith. The problem is not only the relationship of Jesus' message to that of Paul, but also the understandings of Jesus that underlie the synoptic tradition on the one hand and Paul on the other. It is not enough to say that the gospel form developed by a process of enriching the basic message about the cross and Resurrection. Kähler's oft-quoted dictum that the Gospels are passion stories with extended introductions[45] is likewise inadequate. Although the story of the Passion is an essential element in Mark's scheme, it is not the main event for which the events of Jesus' ministry are no more than inconsequential preliminaries. Nor is Kähler any closer to the truth of Mark's intention when he says that the Gospels are interested not in *what* happened, but in *who* acted and *how*.[46]

Mark's Unique Literary Contribution

What led Mark to arrange the Jesus tradition in the literary form we know as a gospel? Answers to this question were already being offered in the early second century, although there is a certain speciousness about them. Papias of Hierapolis, famed for the low estimate of his intellect advanced by Eusebius[47] and for the tantalizing bits of information about gospel origins attributed to him,[48] reports that Mark is said to have written down the sayings of Jesus as he "remembered *[apemnēmóneuse]*" hearing them from Peter.[49] Justin Martyr (100?–165? C.E.), relying on the testimony of Papias, refers to the Gospel of Mark as the "memoir" of Peter.[50] By the very choice of this designation, Justin elevates the gospel as a literary form into the realm of known types of Hellenistic literature. The implication seems to be that before the apostolic generation passed away, Peter and other apostles (or apostolic associates, such as Luke) authorized or allowed their followers to produce memoirs of their associations with Jesus. These memoirs would guarantee an immediacy of witness to what Jesus had said and done and would serve as the last possible eye-witness accounts. As much as a twentieth-century scholar interested in the origins of Christianity might wish to have access to such documents, it must be acknowledged that the Gospels do not match the description that Justin Martyr offered for them in the middle of the second century C.E. The gospel of Mark is not a "memoir" of Peter, either in the sense that it recounts in a special way the associations of Peter with Jesus or in the sense that Mark reports firsthand recollections about Jesus. The material on which Mark drew passed through a process of retelling, modification, and interpretation, and it reflects less special interest in Peter than does Matthew's gospel. (See, for example, Matt. 16:13–20; verses 17–19, in which Peter is singled out for a special place of authority and which have no parallel in the other gospel accounts of this incident.)

The memoir as a literary type, *apemnēmóneuma*, is best exemplified by the *Memorabilia of Socrates*, written by Xenophon (434?–355? B.C.E.). The analogy between this life of Socrates and the Gospels, first developed by Justin Martyr in his apologetic writings, has been widely discussed for the past century and a half by biblical scholars.[51] Although the theory of apostolic memoirs has been appealed to as a way of ensuring the reliability of the gospel accounts, it does not in fact provide any such guarantee. Indeed, the analogy is not even an appropriate one, since Xenophon's *Memorabilia* represents a conscious literary effort, rather than the popular kind of writing that makes no pretension of being "literature." The distinction is accurately brought out in the contrast between the two German words *Hochliteratur* and *Kleinliteratur* (which might be translated in colloquial terms as "big and little literature"). To make such a distinction is in no way to dismiss the Gospel of Mark as beneath academic notice; it is rather to recognize it for what it is: a propaganda writing produced by and for a community that made no cultural claims for itself and offered its writings as a direct appeal for adherents rather than as a way of attracting the attention of intellectuals or literati of the day.

The attempt has also been made to place the Gospels within a genre of literature reportedly produced in the late Hellenistic–early Roman period (150 B.C.E.–150 C.E.): the aretalogy.[52] This theory has been applied especially to Luke, whose use of contemporary literary conventions shows that the writer wished to be considered an author and a historian[53]—within the genre of the aretalogy. Though the term is not used in Greek, it appears in a Latinized form, *aretalogus*, to designate "one who (professionally) speaks the wondrous deeds of a deity or a divinely gifted human."[54] The aretalogy, then, is the narrative in which a heroic figure is portrayed. Plato's portrayal of Socrates is considered by some scholars, most notably Moses Hadas and Morton Smith, to be "the source for all subsequent aretalogies, pagan and Christian."[55] As artist and teacher, Plato presented Socrates in the *Phaedo* and the *Apology* in such a way as to establish a kind of archetype, in terms of which subsequent ages represented "certain saintly figures, who like Socrates, had selflessly devoted themselves to the spiritual improvement of the community and had accepted the suffering, sometimes the martyrdom [that Socrates had undergone]."[56]

When the detailed evidence is adduced to support this thesis, however, it turns out not to be persuasive. There is no pattern discernible that can be called a common literary element in the "aretalogies" summarized by Morton Smith, nor do three of them—Porphyry's *Life of Pythagoras*, Philo Judaeus' *Life of Moses*, and Philostratus' *Life of Apollonius of Tyana*— depict their respective heroes dying a martyr's death. This is something of a letdown after the moving description of the martyred Socrates as the archetypal subject of the aretalogy. The two elements that seem to be shared by the four biographies are that miracles were attributed to all the heroes and that each had his own kind of divine wisdom to offer his faithful followers. The form and content of these four lives do not demonstrate sufficient similarities as a literary genre to consider the aretalogy—if indeed it is a literary form—as the model for the Gospel of Mark or the other Gospels.[57]

The conclusion reached by K.L. Schmidt in his study of this subject a half-century ago is the only one warranted by the evidence: that the writer of the first gospel, Mark, had no model or precedent to follow. In writing his gospel, he created a new genre of literature for which, as a whole, there was no precedent.[58] He followed the patterns of neither the literary memoirs nor the popular biographies of his time,[59] although analogies to the narrative style can be found in collections of anecdotes in Jewish and pagan folk literature.[60] The chief feature of both the gospel writers (with the exception of Luke) and the authors of anecdotes and miracle stories is the lack of consciousness of being an author or of creating a literature.[61] Stated another way, for the preliterary stages of the origin of the gospel tradition, parallels can be shown in Jewish and pagan sources; for the gospel as a literary whole, there is no real precedent.[62] The analogies with the pagan miracle stories are most evident at the written stage of the development of the synoptic tradition, but Mark has adapted these literary conventions of his contemporary culture in order to serve his own distinctive aims in his portrayal of Jesus. But even where this influence from the wider culture can be observed, as in the heightening of the miraculous element, it is evident only in details of stories and sayings, not in the structure of the gospel or in Mark's goals in writing it.[63]

Chief among Mark's goals was the determination to show that the meaning of Jesus for faith was manifest in the arena of world history. His view of history was derived from that of Jewish apocalypticism,[64] especially from the Book of Daniel. He was not content with the notion that God's purpose for creation was disclosed through the words of Jesus; he wanted to demonstrate that the revelation came through a public person performing public acts in interaction with the civil and religious authorities of his time. For Mark faith did not offer an escape from the world but the divinely granted key to the meaning of the past, the present, and the future of the world. It is in that cosmic context that his report of Jesus is placed. And in the interests of that goal he appropriates the Jesus tradition.

Mark's Use of the Jesus Tradition

The Sources Available to Mark

The theory that Mark is the oldest gospel, as well as the oldest extant gospel, seems to be the most plausible explanation for the literary relationships among the synoptics.[65] As for sources, Mark may have had collections of stories about or sayings of Jesus, but there is no evidence that, before Mark did so, they were woven into a continuous narrative as we now have them. The parables may have constituted one such group of sayings, just as the cluster of shorter miracle stories in Mark 2 and 3, and of longer stories in Mark 4 and 5, may have constituted collections of narratives on which Mark drew. A similar case could be made for sayings or collections offering criticism of the Jewish tradition (Mark 7 and 10), presenting accounts of controversies with Jews (Mark 12), and containing eschatological themes (Mark 13); on the other hand, the present topical groupings could come from Mark. Theories proposed for written sources of Mark are dubious, with the possible exception of collections of miracle stories.[66] Even in the case of the Passion narrative—the only extended narrative sequence in the Gospels—there is no sure evidence (as form critics have assumed)[67] that Mark had access to an existing document for Mark 11–16, or for any part of it. The same characteristics are evident there as are to be found in other parts of Mark. In Mark 11–16 there is pervasive stress on the occurrence of the events as the fulfillment of Scripture, so that the critical reader cannot tell whether the events have been conformed to Scripture or (as seems likely in several cases) the Scripture has been modified to fit the event. Almost everywhere in Mark the connective tissue by which Mark has joined together the sayings and narrative units is secondary; that is, it is the work of Mark himself. Almost certainly he had no sequential or chronological framework available to him, other than the obvious fact that the Baptism of Jesus came at the outset of Jesus' ministry and the Crucifixion came at the end. C.H. Dodd's attempt to prove that there was a traditional sequence of events is not persuasive.[68] There are a few points at which place names may have been preserved in the tradition on the basis of actual historical memory, as in the scene of the confession of Peter, which is located in the theologically and dogmatically insignificant vicinity of Caesarea Philippi (Mark 8:27).[69]

The freedom felt by the gospel writers to rearrange the order of events in the gospel tradition for programmatic or literary purposes is shown by Luke's placing Jesus' rejection at Nazareth at the outset of his public ministry (Luke 4), whereas in Mark it comes in the middle of the story of Jesus' activity (Mark 6:1). The miracle stories of Mark (Mark 1 and 2) are moved by Matthew to a point following the Sermon on the Mount (Matt. 5, 6, and 7) because that best suited Matthew's arrangement of material in alternating panels of activity and discourse.[70] The sense of movement and sequence that the reader receives in Mark's gospel comes from Mark's own arrangement of the tradition, as K.L. Schmidt showed in his pioneering form-critical study *Der Rahmen der Geschichte Jesu* [The framework of the history of Jesus]. Schmidt points out that "in Mark's introductions to the pericopes, there can still be traced vestiges of an itinerary."[71] But only traces of an itinerary remain, and these are confused as a result of Mark's lack of detailed knowledge of Palestinian geography: The report that Jesus went from Tyre and Sidon through the cities of the Decapolis on his way back to the Sea of Galilee sounds as odd to one who knows Palestine as to say that a man stopped off in Boston on his way from New York to Philadelphia. Designations of temporal connections are rare, but where they do occur, as in Mark 9:1—"after six days," that is, one week later—they show us only that Mark may have preserved the few temporal links that he found in the tradition,[72] although these phrases could as well be Markan stylizations intended to impart dramatic movement to the story sequence.

Mark received his material in a period of oral transmission, or perhaps when pregospel documents were available in addition to the oral transmission process, which continued even after the Gospels had been written.[73] But what Mark received probably came to him in isolated pericopes of two main types: sayings tradition and narrative tradition.

Sayings Tradition

1. *Aphorisms.* Example: "He who has ears to hear, let him hear" (Mark 4:9). Mark positioned this type of saying where he thought it fit, a judgment that does not always correspond with the opinion of modern commentators and critics.

2. *Parables.*[74] Example: The Parable of the Productive Seed (= The Parable of the Sower) (Mark 4:3–8). Mark interprets this parable as an allegory of the hearers in the church (Mark 4:14–20).

3. *Sayings clusters.* These are of two types:

   a. *Topical groupings.* Example: The salt words (Matt. 5:13–16).

   b. *Formal groupings.* Example: The Beatitudes and Woes (Luke 6:20–26).

Narrative Tradition

1. *Anecdotes.* Example: The story of the demoniac in the synagogue at Capernaum (Mark 1:23–26). These are brief biographical narratives.

2. *Aphoristic narratives.* Example: The plucking of grain on the Sabbath (Mark 2:23–28). Combining narrative and sayings material, these are narratives that culminate in pithy sayings.

3. *Wonder stories.* Example: Mark 5:1–20. In these stories the main point is the wonder itself, the miraculous as such.

4. *Legends.* These are narratives in which the divine is directly or publicly manifest. They are of two types:

   a. *Biographical legends.* Example: The temptation story, especially in the Q form found in Matthew and Luke. The main interest is in the divine aspect which is disclosed in Jesus' life or activity.

   b. *Cult legends.* Example: The Feeding of the Five Thousand (Mark 6:30–44). The main interest is in authorization of, or grounding for, the church's ritual practice: the Eucharist.

5. *Passion story.* In its present form this is the only extended sequential account preserved in the gospel tradition. The extent to which it preserves pre-Markan reports of the course of events, or to which it has been given this continuity by Mark in the interest of demonstrating Jesus' trial and death as the fulfillment of Scripture, is difficult to determine (see pp. 142–43).

Working with these disconnected elements, it would not have been possible to infer a series of cause-and-effect links that would offer an explanation for the dynamics of Jesus' ministry or the sequence in the events that led to his Crucifixion. Nor is there the slightest possibility of reconstructing the process by which Jesus came to understand his own role in God's plan or in what terms he came to view his own impending death. To the extent that such a developmental pattern can be discerned in the Gospel of Mark, it is almost certainly to be attributed to Mark himself and to the literary method by which he presents and expands his basic themes.

One must distinguish between Mark's themes and the gospel outline he uses to give what is mostly the appearance, but in part also the substance, of a historical sequence of events. Mark placed the traditional material on the following structural framework:

1. Preparation for Ministry (1:1–20)

2. The Kingdom Announced in Word and Act (1:21–8:26)

3. What Messiahship and Discipleship Mean (8:27–10:45)

4. Preparation for the Events of the End (11:1–14:25)

5. The Passion and the Parousia[75] (14:26–16:8)

The sense of urgency and tension in Mark's account is heightened not only in mechanical ways, such as his twelve-times-repeated "immediately," but also in the recurrent juxtaposition of challenge and rejection, of confession and denial, which highlights both the feeling of eschatological imminence and the importance of a faith decision.

Intertwined in the Gospel of Mark (so that more than one theme may be present in a single pericope) are the following major themes:

1. Fulfillment of Scripture

2. Jesus as Son of God and/or Coming Son of Man

3. Coming of the Kingdom and/or Judgment

4. Passion and Parousia

5. Ministry, Ethics, and Cultus in the New Community

Each of these themes, as we shall see, is fundamental to Mark's overall thesis that the eschatological event proclaimed in the kerygma had its beginning in the historical figure of Jesus of Nazareth.[76]

Jesus As the Fulfillment of Scripture

It is tempting to suppose that the gospel writers appealed frequently to Scripture in their portrayals of Jesus as an apologetic tactic, in order to lend authority to the claim of the early church to be the new people of God. This somewhat condescending estimate is made the more appealing by the fact that, gauged by modern interpretive standards, the New Testament writers exercised an embarrassing degree of freedom in applying an Old Testament text to their situation. The fact that the rabbis were performing the same sort of exegetical sleight of hand (or even that similarly fanciful essays in Old Testament hermeneutics have been discovered at Qumran)[77] does not dispel the impression that the methods are artificial. Historically trained Christian interpreters are made more than a little uncomfortable by what they find the New Testament claiming to have happened "according to the Scriptures."[78]

But far more important than the documentation provided by scripture was the power of the belief, shared by the Qumran Essenes and the early church, that the Scriptures were not so much chronicles of the past as blueprints for the future that God had in store for his creation in general and his people in particular. It was the actualization of the eschatological plan laid down in the Scriptures, and now being rightly interpreted in and through contemporary events, that was the ground of the importance of Scripture in the first century C.E. Thus Mark launches into "the beginning of the gospel" (Mark 1:1) with the claim that through Jesus' baptism at the hand of John were fulfilled both the promise of an eschatological messenger (Mal. 3:1) and the announcement of the one who would prepare for the Lord's coming (Isa. 40:3). The fact that the quotation as a whole is wrongly attributed to Isaiah and that 2 Isaiah's expectation was of the coming of Yahweh, not Jesus Christ as Lord, does not obscure the theological assertion that is being made: It is for God's Son, Jesus of Nazareth, that John the Baptist was sent to prepare the way. In a way that could not have been anticipated by the human author of these prophecies, the promise of God is seen as being fulfilled through Jesus.[79] It is impossible to tell how much of the detail given in the tradition concerning John the Baptist is historical recollection about him that is being passed on and how much is Christian interpretation of his role in the light of the Old Testament. If the former, then the Baptist may have modeled his attire after Elijah (2 Kings 1:8), whose coming is announced as an eschatological promise in Malachi 4:5 and was widely expected in late Judaism.[80] If the latter—that is, if Mark shaped his picture of John by recalling the Old Testament allusions to the Lord's forerunner—then we see that in this case also it was the belief that God's redemptive plan was nearing completion that motivated Mark's and the tradition's appeal to Scripture. Early Christian faith deemed it essential that there be discernible correspondence between what the Scriptures announced and what was actually occurring, since the apocalyptic view of history required that the outworking of the divine purpose be seen in current events or in the recent past. Whether the modern reader finds the alleged correspondence convincing is not the point; what was essential at Qumran and for the author of Mark was the demonstration in the realm of observable history of the fulfillment of what God had announced beforehand through the prophets. Only in this way could one be certain that the eschatological schedule was leading on to the redemptive climax.

The form of appeal to the Old Testament in Mark varies widely. In most instances a passage is directly quoted or alluded to quite explicitly. At other times the correspondence between the narrative of the gospel and a prophetic passage must be inferred, as in Mark 11:1–9, where the details of the lowly king's entry match the prophecy of Zechariah 9:9; the link is made explicit in Matthew's expanded version of the incident (Matt. 21:1–9). The apocalyptic discourse in Mark 13 is filled with direct and indirect allusions to Old Testament passages. The Passion story also corresponds closely with the Old Testament; indeed, there are more Old Testament allusions here than elsewhere in Mark. In the details of the Crucifixion alone (Mark 15:24–34) there are at least three recollections of Psalm 22. Thus, the Old Testament may have helped to shape the narrative, although the incidents must have been in some way analogous to Old Testament stories or prophecies from the outset in order for the parallels ever to have been noticed. One gospel passage, however, Mark 9:12, refers to what is "written," as though alluding to Scripture, but no known Jewish writing contains such a prophecy (that is, of the suffering of the Son of Man).

The three major subjects addressed by the Old Testament quotations in Mark are (1) the judgment on Israel, (2) the reinterpretation of the commandments of God, and (3) the fulfillment of messianic hopes. All these are eschatological functions, of course, since the repristination of the Law of God was one of the eschatological functions expected in late Judaism to occur in the End Time. At Qumran it was the Teacher of Righteousness, or the eschatological prophet, who was to fulfill this role. In Mark, Jesus performs this function in denouncing the blindness of the faithless (Mark 4:12 = Isa. 6:9–10); in criticizing the practice of allowing human traditions to supersede the divine command (Mark 7:6 = Isa. 29:13); and in defending belief in the Resurrection (Mark 12:18–27 = Exod. 3:6), even though in this case the weight of the argument is lost on the modern reader. No matter whether the arguments are persuasive or not, the fact remains that Mark presents Jesus as one whose ministry among men was characterized by the work of interpreting anew God's Law, and doing so not in continuity with rabbinic methods of interpretation (1:22) but with his own unprecedented authority. Clearly, Mark wants his reader to see in Jesus of Nazareth the eschatological messenger who restores the true understanding of God's will in the End Time.

Mark spells out this role in relation to specific issues: the precedence of human need over Sabbath observance (Mark 2:26 = 1 Sam. 21:1–6) and the priority of marriage in the created order over divorce, which is a concession to human frailty (Mark 10:2–12 = Gen. 1:27; Deut. 24:1–4). Most important of all, however, is the correspondence that Mark and his tradition see between the Old Testament messianic hopes (as set forth in Psalms 110 and 118 in particular) and the meaning of Jesus. Both these psalms were inter-preted eschatologically in Judaism;[81] by pointing out the fulfillment of them in Jesus' teachings (12:10) and actions (11:9), Mark shows his readers that Jesus, who is worshipped as Lord in the church, was already the eschatological king in the days of his historical ministry, as reported in the synoptic tradition. Something of the difficulties that the early church had in interpreting Jesus in relation to these mes-sianic categories is to be observed in the inconclusive controversy story that Mark pushed back into the ministry of Jesus (12:35–37). Anachronistically, Jesus is thereby depicted struggling with christo-logical questions about himself only a few days before the Crucifixion. But what Mark wants to show is that the christological issue was already implicit in the authoritative earthly ministry of Jesus. The his-torical critic knows, however, that the struggle over titles did not take shape until after Easter.

Jesus As Messiah

The disciples regularly refer to Jesus as "Rabbi" or "Teacher" (*didaskalos*), even in such circumstances as the storm on the lake, when, presumably, their thoughts were not on instructional matters (Mark 4:35–41), but on their survival. Mark's use of these terms may show that he has preserved the actual titles conferred on Jesus by his followers. Paul's favorite title for Jesus, Lord (*kurios*), is rare in Mark (5:19 and 11:3); the occurrences prob-ably betray an unconscious shift to the terminology of the church's post-Easter kerygma: "Jesus is Lord" (Phil. 2:11; 1 Cor. 12:3), which even on Mark's terms is not appropriate until after the Resurrection. Mark's clear preferences as titles for Jesus are Son of God and Son of Man.

Son of God. Because Mark is convinced that the Kingdom of God has begun to break into the old age in the person and ministry of Jesus, it is wholly fitting for him to locate the eschatological titles, Son of God and Son of Man, in Jesus' earthly ministry. In addition to sounding forth the title of Jesus as "Son of God" in his opening words (Mark 1:1), Mark reports that at Jesus' baptism he was acclaimed by a private, divine disclosure to be Son of God (Mark 1:11). The words of the voice of God form a blend of phrases from Psalm 2 and from Isaiah 42: The first was addressed to David (or his successors) as those who ruled in God's stead; the second was uttered to the Servant of Yahweh, who is commended for his humility and persistence and endowed with God's Spirit to enable him to estab-lish justice in the earth among the nations (Isa. 42:1–4). Mark

10:42–45 expresses the view that the one chosen by God to establish the Kingdom of God on the earth accomplishes his mission not by the exercise of brute force but by humble self-sacrificing service. No claim is offered in either Psalm 2 or Isaiah 42 that God's agent of redemption is a divine being, so "Son of God" in Mark 1:1 may not be a metaphysical term. Mark gives no hint of a supernatural birth for Jesus; if there is any belief in the virgin birth abroad, Mary gives no hint of it in Mark's narrative. Indeed, she and her other sons are so unprepared for his authoritative way of commissioning disciples, expelling demons, and accepting acclaim as God's Son (3:11, 14) that they conclude he is crazy (3:21) and try to remove him from the public scene (3:31).[82]

Although the term Son of God is not given (as in Matthew) in connection with the confession of Peter (Mark 8:29), the title used, Christ, refers to the anointed figure or figures who were to reestablish the true kingship and the true cultus in the End Time. The Christian faith in Jesus as a single kingly figure, to whom priestly functions are assigned in a peripheral manner (except in Hebrews, which is itself unique within the canonical New Testament), cannot obscure the fact that in late Judaism there was widespread belief in two anointed figures: the kingly figure from Judah and the priestly figure from Levi.[83] First attested in Zechariah 4 and 6, the theme of two anointed eschatological figures is a dominant one in the Testament of Levi (fragments of which have presumably been found at Qumran).[84] However, since no contrary evidence is present in Mark, we can assume that for him the terms *King*, *Son of God*, and *Christ* are interchangeable: All point to the man divinely appointed to establish God's rule over his people and, through them, over the whole creation. What is new in Mark is his linking this kingly hope with the eschatological servant of 2 Isaiah. The importance for Mark of the servant role of Isaiah 42 is stressed by the fact that Mark sees in Jesus' baptism the fulfillment of the prediction in 42:1, which describes God's pouring out of his Spirit upon the servant to enable him to carry out his redemptive role. At Jesus' baptism he is acclaimed Son of God by a heavenly utterance (Mark 1:10–11).

The other crucial text in which the term *Son of God* is used is Mark 15:39. At the cross, having observed the darkness that covered the earth, the cry of Jesus, the scorn of the crowd, and the ripping of the temple veil, the centurion said: "Truly this man was a son of God!" Although the definite article is not used (not "*the* Son of God"), the pagan soldier's testimony is central for Mark: Through the cross, even Gentiles will recognize in Jesus the redeemer of humanity. The term *Son of God* seems to have carried quite different connotations in Gentile thinking, and Mark's account is not uninfluenced by these. The practice of deifying a great leader or wise man of the past is common throughout the Hellenistic and Roman worlds. It is almost surely too much to claim that there was a fixed type, the *theios anēr*,[85] to which Mark conformed the image of Jesus. This notion, which arose in the heyday of the history of religions school, has been repeated so often that it has come to be accepted as a fact.[86] But in truth, except for a widespread fondness for apotheosis of great men, there is no set type or model of *theios anēr*. That is not to say, however, that the tendency toward apotheosizing Jesus is not at work in Mark, nor in the tradition on which he drew. What is clear is that this does not constitute a major, conscious aim of Mark. The basic function of Jesus as Son of God in Mark is as bringer of the eschatological salvation, in keeping with the expectations of Jewish apocalypticism.

Son of Man. The influence of apocalypticism is even more apparent in Mark's use of the title "Son of Man." Scholarly opinions about the use of this term in the gospel tradition vary widely.[87] Some scholars think that only future Son of Man words are authentic;[88] some are convinced that only the present Son of Man sayings go back to Jesus.[89] Others have been persuaded that all or nearly all the sayings are genuine,[90] and a few think that none of the sayings can be attributed to Jesus.[91] The background of the term, whether used by Jesus of himself, or by the synoptic tradition in its interpretation of him, is Jewish apocalypticism.[92]

The hypothesis with the greatest potential for explaining the development of the various categories of Son of Man words as we now find them in the gospel tradition is the one advanced by H.E. Tödt.[93] According to Tödt, Jesus gathered around himself an eschatological community to whom he announced the coming of the Son of Man, who would judge men on the basis of their response to him and his ministry. His message of the coming Kingdom of God and the signs of its inbreaking, evident in his healings and exorcisms, called men to decision; the Son of Man would confirm that decision in the eschatological judgment (Mark 8:38). When Jesus' fellowship with his own followers was reconstituted in the post-Resurrection appearances, they came to believe that Jesus was himself the Son of Man, whose coming as judge they still awaited. In the light of this conviction, the gospel tradition read back into his earthly ministry this insight into who Jesus was: the Son of Man. The pre-Markan tradition went on from that interpretive point to consider Jesus' suffering as a necessary part of his role as Son of Man (Mark 8:32; 9:31; 10:32–34). But before examining the eschatological framework in which Mark presents the Passion of Jesus, we must look more closely at the description of his public ministry and his message.

Jesus As Salvation-Bringer in His Public Ministry

Mark's understanding of the intention of Jesus' public ministry is expressed succinctly in Mark 1:15: "The time *[kairos]* is fulfilled, and the kingdom of God is at hand; repent, and believe in the gospel [good news]." What is involved in Jesus' gospel is made clear immediately in the story of the demoniac in the synagogue at Capernaum (Mark 1:23–26). A central element in the story is the question of the demon (or the demoniac as his spokesman) "Have you come to destroy us?" The tradition could scarcely make its point more forcefully: To destroy Satan and his hosts is precisely what Jesus has come to do. The interrogative style is replaced by straight declarative in a related passage (Mark 3:22–27) in which a series of sayings points to Jesus' role as the agent through whom Satan's dynasty will be shattered and his posessions plundered. The Q version of this incident makes the point even more explicitly: "If it is by the finger of God that I cast out demons, then the kingdom of God has come upon you" (Luke 11:20). Mark, however, uses a technical term in the exorcism accounts, *epitimáō*, which translates a Semitic word meaning "to utter a commanding word by which an enemy is subjugated."[94] This is the significance attached to Jesus' exorcisms, and perhaps to his healings, in the earliest tradition: By Jesus' powerful acts, Satan's control over the creation was being wrested from him as a necessary step toward the establishment of God's rule. Mark modified this intention of the miracle stories somewhat by shifting the focus at times (especially in Mark 5:1–20) to the thaumaturgic, or wonder-working technique and to the person of the wonder-worker, as in pagan miracle tales. But Mark's changes do not obscure or conflict with his own overall aim of presenting Jesus as the bringer of the message and the signs of the New Age.

Mark shares with Q the belief that Jesus is the eschatological bringer of salvation, but he lays greater stress on Jesus' "mighty works" as manifestations of the inbreaking of the rule of God. Q, as we have observed, holds the same view of the meaning of Jesus' exorcisms, but in fact the Q material does not describe Jesus' miracles but is almost wholly limited to references to Jesus' healing and exorcistic activities. Mark differs from Q also in the sense of apocalyptic urgency that pervades his gospel.

The message of the coming Kingdom is directly set out in the apocalyptic discourse (Mark 13) and metaphorically proclaimed in the parables of the Kingdom (Mark 4). Although Mark reproduced the older—and almost certainly original—form and intent of these parables, with their encouragement to the messengers of the Kingdom to carry out their work without calculating the results (which are, after all, in God's hands), he also added allegorical explanations that turn attention to the inner state of the eschatological community.[95] But the apocalyptic images of the harvest still predominate; by retaining the emphasis on the Judgment, Mark kept the parables within their original eschatological atmosphere. The shorter parabolic sayings, such as those dealing with the bridegroom and the wineskins, are likewise built on apocalyptic imagery and remind the hearer or reader of the day of reckoning that lies ahead (Mark 2:18–22). As a result, the churchly question about whether or not to fast is settled on the basis of an eschatological pronouncement: "The days will come...."

In the context of the announcement by Jesus of his passion (8:27–31), Mark introduces the apocalyptic prediction of the coming in glory of the Son of Man (8:38) and the coming with power of the Kingdom of God (9:1). Precisely because this section of Mark is composite in its present form, we can be sure that Mark placed these materials together with full intent: Jesus' acceptance of the cross and Peter's satanically originated remonstration (8:32–33) are linked with the prophetic words about the coming Son of Man and the coming with power of God's Kingdom. Jesus' message and ministry, as well as his passion and death, are set by Mark within a sequence of apocalyptic events, a schedule of eschatological actions by which God will establish his rule over creation. The direct pronouncement of the apocalyptic role of Jesus is given in Mark 13, which is likewise composite. How much of this apocalyptic discourse goes back to Jesus is variously assessed by scholars,[96] but Mark placed it in a strategic spot—just before the Passion narrative and just after the prediction of the destruction of the Temple—in order to show Jesus' crucial role in the apocalyptic scheme of things: After all these catastrophes have occurred on earth and in the cosmos, "the Son of Man" will be seen "coming in clouds with great power and glory" (Mark 13:26). In keeping with the conventions of apocalyptists, Mark asserts that the end will be soon, within the lifetime of Jesus' hearers (13:30), but that the exact time is known only to God (13:32).

Thus, it is in the interest of documenting his reading of the event of Jesus that Mark, or the tradition on which he drew, assigns to the earthly Jesus throughout his gospel the titles Son of God (king) and Son of Man (eschatological salvation-bringer).

The Apocalyptic Necessity of Jesus' Death

Mark presents Jesus' passion as an essential element in a series of eschatological events rather than as the ground of a developed doctrine of the atonement. From the first prediction of the Passion onward, Mark reports Jesus as describing his impending death in terms of apocalyptic necessity *(deī)*,[97] or simply as certain to occur in the apocalyptic scheme of things ("how is it written of the Son of Man that he should suffer many things...?"—Mark 9:12). Although we know of no such apocalyptic document in which the suffering of the Son of Man is predicted, Mark's appeal to what is "written" suggests that he either had such a document or assumed its existence. In any case, he makes no claim for having originated the idea of the Son of Man who must suffer. From this (hypothetical?) document Mark concluded that the Passion of Jesus was a necessary event in the working out of the divinely determined apocalyptic scheme of "history," both past and future.

The apocalyptic necessity of Jesus' death is underscored in Mark not only in the explicit predictions of the Passion[98] but also in metaphorical allusions to it: the bridegroom taken away (2:20), the cup and the baptism to be endured (10:38). The nearest Mark comes to an interpretation of Jesus' death as an atonement is in 10:45, where the life of the Son of Man is said to be given "as a ransom for many." In spite of learned efforts to link this phrase with Paul or with Isaiah 53,[99] the fact remains that the verse says only that in some unspecified way the death of Jesus will effect release "for many." This notion of the redemptive benefits of the death of a righteous man could be understood in terms of the cult of the martyrs,[100] or simply as a part of the messianic woes or birthpangs that "must" occur before the New Age dawns (Mark 13:7–8). The closest one can come to an interpretation of the death of Jesus in Mark is in the eucharistic word (Mark 14:24–25) and in the Parable of the Vineyard Workers (12:1–11). In the first instance, the life given ("blood ... poured out") is associated with the covenant,[101] a term that is given eschatological significance by Mark's placing beside it the saying about Jesus drinking the fruit of the vine on "that day ... in the kingdom of God." Similar positive meaning is given to the death of Jesus in the Parable of the Vineyard Workers, where his rejection is presented as a necessary step prior to his becoming the "head of the corner," in fulfillment of Psalm 118:22–23. What is at stake, as is shown by (Jesus'? Mark's? the tradition's?) use of the allegorical representation of Israel (Isa. 5:1–7), is the founding of a new people, an eschatological community. In rejecting Jesus as God's final word, the Jewish nation is unwittingly laying the foundation for the new community. This seems to be the fundamental meaning given by Mark, and/or the tradition on which he drew, to the death of Jesus.

Because the cross is not in Mark the basis for a doctrine of the atonement, there is no problem of correlating it with the Parousia or of correlating the Parousia with the Resurrection. Both Resurrection and Parousia are terms Mark uses to represent a single, central apocalyptic event: the vindication of Jesus as triumphant Son of Man and founder of the eschatological community. The explicit predictions of the Passion are also always announcements of the Resurrection (8:31; 9:31; 10:32–33). Jesus' metaphorical warning, couched in apocalyptic language, that the shepherd is about to be struck (14:27)[102] leads directly on to an announcement of his Resurrection and the reassembling of the eschatological community under Peter (14:28), a promise recalled by the supernatural messenger in the post-Resurrection scene (16:6–7) in which the cross is once more presented as a prelude to the reconstitution of the circle of followers: "Do not be amazed; you seek Jesus of Nazareth, who was crucified. He has risen, he is not here.... But go, tell his disciples and Peter that he is going before you to Galilee; there you will see him, as he told you."

Jesus' Relationship to Judaism: A New Understanding of Divine Will

Because Mark regards history as the chain of events by which the divine purpose is worked out through struggle and seeming defeat, it is not surprising that he can discover authorization in the period of Jesus' earthly ministry for the practices that are the concern of the eschatological community as it awaits the final, victorious disclosure of God's redemptive agent, Jesus, the Son of Man. Accordingly, the ethical norms, the missionary practices and pitfalls, and the cultic life of the community are all read out of—or back into—the lifetime of Jesus.

In the course of setting forth his account of Jesus' ministry, Mark addresses himself to the specific problems the early Christian church faced in relation to the conventions and circumstances of the day. Since the church of Mark was so deeply conscious of itself as heir to the promises made to Israel, it could not merely brush aside the distinctive features of Jewish piety. What should the attitude of the church be toward Sabbath observance, fasting, prayer, dietary laws, eating a meal with those who are ceremonially or religiously impure? In addition, problems arose from the historical circumstances of life in first-century Palestine. What should be the relationship of the Christians to Roman authorities? Further, how was a Christian to understand God's seeming judgment on Judaism, as evidenced by the destruction of the Temple? What right had the church to announce the forgiveness of sins? What lay behind the sacraments of Baptism and the Eucharist? Why had not Jesus' claims, which were now so obviously—to the Christians' way of thinking—the fulfillment of Scripture, been recognized by the Jews who knew and searched the Scriptures?

The question of Sabbath observance is dealt with through several stories about Jesus' healings (Mark 1:21–28; 3:1–5): The answer is, meeting human needs takes precedence over Sabbath observance, although the tradition makes the point that Jesus was faithful in worship on the Sabbath. The argument moves beyond the question of human need, however, when Jesus is reported as asserting that, first, the Sabbath was made for the benefit of humans and, second, the Son of Man (= Jesus) is lord of the Sabbath. Even if one assumes that in Mark 2:28 "Son of Man" originally meant simply "man,"[103] the verse still shows that for Mark Jesus has the authority to set aside the venerable Sabbath law and that, indeed, he has done so. Neither the dietary laws nor those forbidding one to eat a meal with impure or unworthy persons are any longer in effect: Jesus has come as the physician for those who are in need and know it, not to confirm the religiously complacent. The dietary laws are unconditionally set aside (7:18–19). This dictum is given in a private session with the disciples, a device that Mark regularly uses for providing his readers with special insight into the intention of Jesus as Mark understands it. The concern of the church, here attributed to Jesus, is for moral qualities (7:20–23), not for ceremonial purity. The clue to the shift away from the laws and traditions, in terms of which Judaism understood the will of God, is given in 2:21–22: A new and powerful reality has come into being in the person and message of Jesus; this reality cannot be pressed into old containers or merely tacked on to what already exists. The eschatological community requires a new understanding of the divine will. Jesus, as Mark represents him, is the bearer of that morality.

The Markan Jesus refuses to become identified with Jewish national or racial exclusiveness. He is willing to perform healings and exorcisms among, and in behalf of, Gentiles (5:1–20; 7:24–30); he refuses to arouse Jewish national hopes by encouraging disobedience to Roman law (12:17). He will not engage in typical rabbinic debate about the interpretation of the Mosaic Law; instead, he confronts his hearers directly with God's radical demand (10:1–12; 10:17–27; 12:28–34). Similarly, the demand of discipleship is total (8:34–37; 9:42–50; 10:28–30), although its reward will be known only in the eschatological judgment. The ministry to which the disciples are called is an extension of Jesus' own eschatological activity: preaching and casting out demons (3:13–14). Both exorcisms (9:14–29) and simple acts of mercy (9:38–41) are to be performed in the name of, and by the authority of, Jesus. Such works will receive their appropriate reward in the eschatological judgment.

The eschatological significance of Christian Baptism is suggested by the words of John the Baptist (1:7–8), through his announcement of the powerful coming one who will bring God's Spirit upon his new people. The eschatological meaning of the Eucharist is made explicit in Jesus' words about drinking wine in the Kingdom of God (14:25), a promise which echoes the words of the Rule of the Future Community at Qumran (125a). The church's eucharistic practice is reflected—and therefore, as Mark intended, authorized in advance—by the twice-told story of the miraculous feeding of the multitudes (6:30–44; 8:1–10). The fact that there is no hint of redemptive or memorial significance in these meals suggests that they are regarded, as is the Last Supper itself, as anticipations of the great eschatological banquet rather than as reenactments of his sacrificial death. The blueprint for the life of the eschatological community, therefore, from cultus to ethics, is provided by Mark, and is placed for purposes of authorization within the ministry of Jesus.

Mark's Apocalyptic View of History

We shall now consider two questions that have been set aside up to this point: What was Mark's historical aim? What historical value does his book have? In juxtaposing these questions, we must recognize that in the first we are asking about Mark's own understanding of history; in the second, about history in terms of modern historiography. Some scholars have attempted to merge these two issues by theorizing that there is identity between a modern conception of historicity as a mode of human self-understanding and Jesus' summons to man to find his true life (or self) by deciding for the will of God and against the world (Mark 8:35). This view implies that by turning away from being obsessed with facts, and toward helping the individual gain self-understanding, the historian is heading toward the same goal as that to which Jesus invited his hearers in his gospel preaching: the achievement of a true understanding of human existence. The existentialist approach, like the attempts to reduce Jesus' role to a mouthpiece for clever aphorisms (as noted earlier in Chapter 1, pp. 33–35), is a distortion of modern historical work, which should seek to understand the life-world of those who produced and used these ancient documents, rather than to transform that world into one with which a modern intellectual feels more comfortable. To coerce the evidence in order to make it conform to what is regarded by the historian as a more satisfactory mode of human understanding, or to concentrate solely on individual self-understanding (as the existentialists have done), is to pervert the historian's task. What is required is to explore, in as comprehensive a manner as the evidence permits, what were the perceptions and assumptions about the role of Jesus in the purpose of God for his people as set forth in the various forms of the gospel tradition.

Accordingly, what must be recognized is that Mark did not have, and could not have had, a post-Enlightenment view of history concerned with cause and effect in a universe governed by natural law, or with a twentieth-century awareness of sociological and psychological factors that shape human decisions and therefore affect human and social movements. The kind of "history" that Mark knew was the apocalyptic variety as it has been preserved for us in such works as the Book of Enoch, the Book of Jubilees, and the Book of Daniel. These apocalypses deal with actual events of the past (or events believed to have occurred, such as the experiences of the patriarchs); they set them in a framework of divine purpose, in the light of which the meaning of the present is grasped and illumined and the hope for the future is specified. Thus Daniel looks back over the fall of world powers —Babylon, Persia, the Hellenistic kingdoms—which had seemed formidable in their time. He encourages his contemporaries not to be intimidated by the present power, the second-century B.C.E. Seleucid king Antiochus IV, for he has confidence that his community is experiencing the final struggle, out of which will come the triumph of God's will and purpose in his cosmos. Both the Apocalypse of Weeks and the Dream Visions included in the Book of Enoch trace the history of Israel from the days of Enoch (who is mentioned in Gen. 5:18–24), through the Exodus and Exile, the restoration and the apostasy, to the founding of what is called the "Plant of Righteousness," (1 En. 10:16). This is the community at Qumran, in whose behalf God is about to intervene. The angelic hosts will aid the earthly army and Belial will go down in defeat; the Kingdom of God will be established in the earth.

It would be easy and natural to dismiss these accounts as fantasy, lacking all claim to be historical documents. Yet the writers believed that they were reporting the past truly; the neat, chronological schematizations were considered not distortions but testimony to the divine order of things. Mark took the synoptic tradition as he found it, largely in scattered units, and worked it into a consecutive account of "history" in which past, present, and future are viewed apocalyptically. He did not have to do violence to his material to set it in this mold, since the basic outlook of Jesus and what seems to have been his understanding of his own exorcisms and healings were also apocalyptically oriented. What was required was for Mark to shift the focus of the record from the implicit meaning of the eschatological signs and words of Jesus to the church's explicit christological claims made in behalf of Jesus and even attributed to him.[104] It is not correct to say, as the Jesus Seminar and other contemporaries do, that the gospel writers created a mythological account of an itinerant philosopher of the Cynic-Stoic variety, whose message was a series of aphorisms encouraging his hearers to liberate themselves from the values and anxieties of their time. Nor is it satisfactory to suppose that Mark tried to transform the Christians' understanding of Jesus by interpreting him on the model of Greco-Roman mystical savior figures such as Isis or Dionysus by attributing to him miracles.[105]

Mark "historicized" the picture of Jesus because his message demanded it. When at Easter the disciples met the risen Christ, they acclaimed him as Son of Man. Through these resurrection experiences the church came to the understanding that the Resurrection was itself a climactic eschatological sign pointing ahead to the consummation of the Kingdom, and it recognized the necessity of tracing the details of the eschatological meaning of the public ministry of

Jesus, including both his acts and his message. As is customary with apocalyptic writing, the symbolic and the factual have a way of merging in Mark, so that the story of the transfiguration, for example, though presented as a historical occurrence, is primarily a symbolic narrative. Much of the activity of Jesus was public; the fact that not all—or even many—of Jesus' contemporaries saw him as the agent of God's New Age is candidly acknowledged by the tradition and by Mark (3:20–27). But Mark provides an explanation for this lack of insight: "To you [Jesus' followers] has been given the secret [mystery][106] of the kingdom of God, but for those outside everything is in riddles"[107] (4:11).

The Markan Community

The community for which Mark is the spokesman or whose traditions he set forth differs from the community of Q in that the Markan group takes with pronounced seriousness the course of history, and while it shares with Q the expectation of an imminent end of the present age, it is much more conscious of obligations for guiding the life of the community in the interim. Therefore, it gives attention to the reinterpretation of the Law, even though its members are not fully familiar with such aspects of Mosaic Law as using ritually clean utensils (Mark 7:3–4). There is more emphasis in Mark than in Q on the esoteric nature of the information revealed to the community, but both groups seek to include the Gentiles in the new community of faith. Most striking, however, is the fact that the Markan community stands on the brink of a major confrontation with Judaism and anticipates as the outcome the destruction of the Temple in Jerusalem and the vindication of the faithful by divine act. The details of the Passion narrative serve to differentiate the Markan group both from the strict adherents to the Law and from the Jewish revolutionaries who seek to establish the Kingdom of God by their own direct action (Mark 10:35–45; 12:13–17). The role of the community is to bear faithful witness, even if it leads to martyrdom, confident of God's sure and soon vindication.

Suggestions for Further Reading

Excellent analytical surveys of the major themes and literary methods of Jewish apocalyptic literature are Paul D. Hanson, *The Dawn of*

Apocalyptic (Philadelphia: Fortress, 1975); Christopher Rowland, *The Open Heaven: A Study of Apocalyptic in Judiasm and Early Christianity* (New York: Crossroad, 1982); John J. Collins, *The Apocalyptic Imagination: An Introduction to the Jewish Matrix of Christianity* (New York: Crossroad, 1987). Useful commentaries on Mark are those by D.E. Nineham, *The Gospel of Mark* (Harmondsworth and New York: Penguin, 1963); E. Schweitzer, *The Good News According to Mark* (London: SPCK, 1971); and Morna Hooker, *The Gospel of Mark* (Black's New Testament Commentary; London: A. & C. Black, 1991).

Adroit use of insights from literary analysis and from sociological perceptions of group identity have been drawn upon by Jerry Camery-Hoggatt in his study, *Irony in Mark's Gospel: Text and Subject* SNTSMS 72 (London: Cambridge University Press, 1992).

My detailed study of the Markan community, *Community of the New Age* (Macon, GA: Mercer University Press, 1983), develops the Markan themes more fully. Surveys of critical questions relating to Mark are available in W.G. Kümmel, *Introduction to the New Testament* (Nashville: Abingdon, 1975), especially pp. 80–101 (and bibliography); and S.P. Kealy, *Mark's Gospel: A History of Its Interpretation* (New York: Paulist Press, 1982).

NOTES

[1] Paul alludes to or quotes from sayings of Jesus, but there is no indication that he knew this material from written Gospels. Rather, it was part of the oral Jesus tradition, which continued to be used and admired down into the second century C.E., as is indicated by Papias' declaration of his preference for the oral tradition ("the things [transmitted] through the living and continuing voice") rather than the written reports in the Gospels (quoted in Eusebius, *Ecclesiastical History* III.39.3 [trans. K. Lake] Loeb Classical Library [Cambridge: Harvard University Press, 1926]).

[2] Earlier attempts to demonstrate that all the New Testament writers affirm the same propositions about Jesus in spite of what are treated as superficial differences are exemplified in C.H. Dodd's *The Apostolic Preaching and Its Development in the New Testament* (New York: Harper Brothers, 1951). But the important differences are overlooked or explained away in such approaches.

[3] This is implied in the title of John P. Meier's, *A Marginal Jew: Rethinking the Historical Jesus*, vol. 1. *The Roots of the Problem and the Person* (Anchor Bible Reference Library; New York: Doubleday, 1991).

[4] Jacob Neusner, *Messiah in Context: Israel's History and Destiny in Formative Judaism* (Philadelphia: Fortress, 1984), pp. xi–xiii.

[5] *The Church History of the First Three Centuries*, 3d ed., vol. 1, (trans. Allan Menzies; London: Williams & Norgate, 1878), p. 29.

[6] Ibid., p. 30.

[7]Ibid., p. 49.

[8]Ibid.

[9]Ibid., p. 29.

[10]Ibid., pp. 78–81.

[11]Ibid., p. 180.

[12]Rudolf Bultmann, *Theology of the New Testament*, vol. 1 (trans. Kendrick Grobel; New York: Scribner's, 1951), p. 3. The term *kerygma* (transliterated from Greek) means "that which is proclaimed." It has become a widely used summary term in biblical and theological circles for the essential Christian message.

[13]Bultmann, *Primitive Christianity in Its Contemporary Setting* (trans. R.H. Fuller; Cleveland: World, 1956); see "The Eschatological Preaching of Jesus," pp. 86–93.

[14]Bultmann, *Theology of the New Testament*, vol. 1, pp. 302–03. See also the subsequent discussion of the presence of Jesus in the kerygma in Bultmann's essay, "The Primitive Christian Kerygma and the Historical Jesus," in C.E. Braaten and R.A. Harrisville, eds., *The Historical Jesus and the Kerygmatic Christ* (Nashville: Abingdon, 1964), pp. 40–42.

[15]Bultmann, *Jesus and the Word* (trans. L.P. Smith and E.H. Lantero; New York: Scribner's, 1934), gives a reconstruction of Jesus' message, but in *Theology of the New Testament*, vol. 1, pp. 33–34, Bultmann asserts categorically that Jesus' message is not kerygma.

[16]Bultmann, "The Primitive Christian Kerygma," pp. 40–41.

[17]Bultmann, *History of the Synoptic Tradition* (trans. John Marsh; New York: Harper & Row, 1963), pp. 338–50.

[18]Ibid., p. 347.

[19]Ibid., p. 350.

[20]Baur, *Church History*, p. 50.

[21]Ibid., p. 81.

[22]A brief discussion and critique of the theory that Mark is a Pauline-oriented document is offered in W.G. Kümmel, *Introduction to the New Testament*, 17th ed. (trans. H.C. Kee; Nashville: Abingdon, 1975), pp. 94–95.

[23]Martin Kähler, *The So-called Historical Jesus and the Historic, Biblical Christ* (trans. and ed. C.E. Braaten; Philadelphia: Fortress, 1964), pp. 89–90.

[24]Ibid., pp. 72–73. The intention of historical criticism in relation to faith is a large question in itself, and one that such subsequent discussions as Gerhard Ebeling's ("the uncertainty created by historical criticism is the reverse side of justification by faith") have scarcely dealt with adequately; see the English edition of Ebeling's collected essays, *Word and Faith* (trans. J.W. Leitch; Philadelphia: Fortress, 1963), pp. 17–61. But historical criticism has the necessary function of bringing into focus the issues that faith alone can decide. One must distinguish between clarity as to what the promise is and certainty that God will fulfill it. The former may be aided by the work of the historian; the latter can rest solely on faith.

[25]Kähler, *The So-called Historical Jesus*, p. 91.

[26]Ibid., p. 90.

[27]*Systematic Theology*, vol. 2 (Chicago: University of Chicago Press, 1957), p. 107.

[28]Ibid., p. 103.

[29]Ibid.

[30]Ibid., p. 114.

[31]Ibid., pp. 117–18.

[32]*Theology of the New Testament*, vol. 2, p. 66.

[33]"The Primitive Christian Kerygma," p. 20. For Bultmann, the essential Christian message resided in *dass* ("that"), the fact that Jesus came, not in *was* ("what"), facts about Jesus.

[34]Schweitzer's position is sketched in *The Quest of the Historical Jesus* (trans. William Montgomery; New York: Macmillan, 1910), Chapter 19. This work is a translation of *Von Reimarus zu Wrede* [From Reimarus to Wrede] (1906). But his basic study of the gospel texts is set out in *The Mystery of the Kingdom of God* (trans. Walter Lowrie; London: A. & C. Black, 1926), which is the second part of *Das Abendmahl im Zusammenhang mit dem Leben Jesu und der Geschichte des Urchristentums* [The Eucharist in relation to the life of Jesus and the history of primitive Christianity] (Tübingen: J.C.B. Mohr, 1901). A posthumously published work of Schweitzer's on the theme of Jesus' eschatology is *Reich Gottes und Christentum* [The Kingdom of God and Christianity] (Tübingen: J.C.B. Mohr, 1967). A critique of Schweitzer's position is given by W.G. Kümmel, available in his collected essays, *Heilsgeschehen und Geschichte* [Salvation-event and history] (Marburg: Elwert, 1965), pp. 328–29.

[35]Gerhard Friedrich, *"euangelizesthai"* ["to proclaim good news"], in *Theological Dictionary of the New Testament*, vol. 2 (trans. G.W. Bromiley; Grand Rapids, MI: Eerdmans, 1965), p. 708.

[36]Ibid., pp. 708–09.

[37]In the Loeb edition of Plutarch the treatise is found in *Moralia*, vol. 2 (trans. F.C. Babbitt; New York: Putnam, 1928), pp. 73–89.

[38]A photograph, transcription, and translation of the 9 B.C.E. text from Priene can be found in Adolf Deissmann, *Light from the Ancient East*, rev. ed. (trans. L.R.M. Strachan; New York: Harper & Row, n.d.), p. 366 and Figure 70. "Whether the ... *[euangelion]* is understood to be the announcement of his birth (so Deissmann) or the fulfillment of the Sibylline prophecies about Augustus" (so Eduard Norden in Deissmann, p. 366, n. 8), the analogy with the use of the term by Mark and the other evangelists is evident. The full Greek text is in Wilhelm Dittenberger, *Orientis Graeci Inscriptiones Selectae* [Selected Greek inscriptions from the Orient], vol. 2, no. 458 (reprinted, Hildesheim: Olms, 1960), lines 40–79 (the point at which the passage under study appears).

[39]Friedrich, op.cit., p. 724.

[40]For example, Bultmann, *Theology of the New Testament*, vol. 1, p. 87.

[41]In *New Testament Apocrypha*, vol. 1, rev. ed. (trans. R. McL. Wilson and others; Cambridge: James Clarke, 1991), pp. 77–87.

[42]See the discussion by C.K. Barrett in his essay in *New Testament Essays*, ed. A.J.B. Higgins (Manchester: Manchester University Press, 1959).

[43]Discussed in an important article by Robin Scroggs, "Paul: *Sophos kai Pneumatikos*" ["wise and spiritual"], in *New Testament Studies* 14, 1 (1967): 33–55. Scroggs suggests that the wisdom issue concerns the merely human wisdom of the Corinthians and "an esoteric Christian apocalyptic-wisdom teaching which [Paul] carefully guarded from immature Christians." Ben Witherington III offers illuminating analyses of the New Testament

hymns, including those in the Pauline tradition, which depict Jesus as the incarnation of divine wisdom. See his *Jesus the Sage: The Pilgrimage of Wisdom* (Minneapolis: Fortress Press, 1994), pp. 249–334.

[44] As Scroggs acknowledges, ibid., p. 54.

[45] *The So-called Historical Jesus*, p. 80, n. 11.

[46] Ibid., p. 81.

[47] *Ecclesiastical History* 3.39.13, vol. 1 (trans. K. Lake) Loeb Classical Library (Cambridge: Harvard University Press, 1949).

[48] Ibid. 3.39.1–17. For a critical evaluation of the significance of the Papias tradition concerning gospel origins, see Kümmel, *Introduction to the New Testament*, pp. 42–44.

[49] Ibid. 3.39.15.

[50] Justin uses the phrase "memoirs of the Apostles" with great frequency in his writings; in Chapters 99–107 of the *Dialogue with Trypho* the term appears twelve times. The "memoirs" are specifically described as documents drawn up by Jesus' apostles and those who followed them (Chapter 103). In *Saint Justin Martyr* (New York: Fathers of the Church, 1949).

[51] A summary of this discussion is given by K.L. Schmidt in his essay "Die Stellung der Evangelien in der allgemeinen Literaturgeschichte" [The place of the Gospels in the general history of literature], in Hans Schmidt, ed., *Eucharisterion* [Essays presented to Hermann Gunkel on his sixtieth birthday] (Göttingen: Vandenhoek & Ruprecht, 1923), pp. 50–134.

[52] Thus Moses Hadas and Morton Smith, *Heroes and Gods* (New York: Harper & Row, 1965).

[53] See Martin Dibelius, "The First Christian Historian" and "The Speeches in Acts and Ancient Historiography," in his *Studies in the Acts of the Apostles* (trans. Mary Ling; London: SCM Press, 1956), pp. 123–85. See also H.J. Cadbury, *The Making of Luke–Acts*, 2d ed. (Naperville, IL: Allenson, 1958).

[54] Moses Hadas and Morton Smith, *Heroes and Gods*, p. 61.

[55] Ibid., p. 63.

[56] Ibid., p. 56. My detailed critique of the aretalogy hypothesis was offered in "Aretalogy and Gospel," *Journal of Biblical Literature* 93 (1973): 408–16.

[57] An effective demonstration of the artificiality of the hypothesis for the aretalogy as the model for the Gospels is offered by W. Schneemelcher in *New Testament Apocrypha*, rev. ed., vol. 1, p. 80, and n. 10, where the great diversity is noted among the literary forms which are glibly called "aretalogy" by some scholars.

[58] Schmidt, "Die Stellung der Evangelien." Also Siegfried Schulz, *Die Stunde der Botschaft* [The hour of the message] (Hamburg: Furche, 1967), p. 36. The nature of this book's contents is described by its subtitle: *Introduction to the Theology of the Four Evangelists.* For a brilliant discussion by an eminent classicist of the uniqueness of the Gospels among Hellenistic literature, see Erich Auerbach, *Mimesis* (Princeton: Princeton University Press, [1953] 1974), pp. 40–49. Analogies have been noted between certain features of the Gospels and Hellenistic literary conventions (see, for example, C.H. Talbert's *Literary Patterns, Theological Themes and the Genre of Luke–Acts* [Missoula, MT: Scholars Press, 1974]), but what is demonstrated is (1) that although the Gospels do share certain stylistic conventions with other writings of the Hellenistic period, (2) the composite product, a gospel, has no real analogy in Hellenistic literature.

[59]Schmidt, "Die Stellung der Evangelien," p. 60.

[60]Ibid., pp. 60–61, 65.

[61]Ibid., pp. 74–75.

[62]Schulz, *Die Stunde der Botschaft*, p. 37; A.N. Wilder, *Early Christian Rhetoric* (New York: Harper & Row, 1964), p. 36.

[63]The phenomenon of miracles in the Greco-Roman world and their function in the biblical tradition are traced in my *Miracle in the Early Christian World* (New Haven: Yale University Press, 1983); and in my *Medicine, Miracle and Magic in New Testament Times* (London: Cambridge University Press, 1986; reprint, 1990).

[64]Fine studies of Jewish apocalyptcism and its import for early Christianity are those of Christopher Rowland, *The Open Heaven: A Study of Apocalyptic in Judaism and Early Christianity* (New York: Crossroad, 1982) and of George W. Nickelsburg, "Social Aspects of Palestinian Jewish Apocalypticism," in *Apocalypticism in the Mediterranean World and the Near East*, ed., D. Hellholm (Tübingen: Mohr [Siebeck], 1983), pp. 641–54.

[65]See the discussion of the priority of the Gospels, pp. 127–30.

[66]Among the attempts to reconstruct sources behind Mark are W.L. Knox, *The Sources of the Synoptic Gospels*, vol. 1: *St. Mark*, ed. Henry Chadwick (London: Cambridge University Press, 1953); P.J. Achtemeier, "Pre-Markan Miracle Catenae," *Journal of Biblical Literature* 89 (1970): 265–91, who makes a good case for Mark's having used collections of miracle stories.

[67]Bultmann, *History of the Synoptic Tradition*, pp. 275, 279; Martin Debelius, *From Tradition to Gospel*, 3d ed. (trans. B.L. Woolf; New York: Scribner's, 1965), pp. 22–23, 178–217. For evidence that Mark has created this sequential narrative, see my essay, "The Function of Scriptural Quotations and Allusions in Mk 11–16," E.E. Ellis and E. Grasser, eds., *Jesus und Paulus* (Göttingen: Vandenhoeck B. Ruprecht, 1975).

[68]"The Framework of the Gospel Narrative," in his *New Testament Studies* (Manchester: Manchester University Press, 1953), pp. 1–11.

[69]In contrast, for example, to references to Galilee, which R.H. Lightfoot and Ernst Lohmeyer suppose to have reflected a special interest of a hypothetical Galilean wing of the primitive church that was clearly differentiated, theologically and otherwise, from the Jerusalem church. For details, see R.H. Lightfoot, *Locality and Doctrine in the Gospels* (New York: Harper Brothers, 1938).

[70]A summary of Matthew's rearrangement of Markan material is given in H.C. Kee, *Understanding the New Testament*, 5th ed. (Englewood Cliffs, NJ: Prentice-Hall, 1993), pp. 137–39. Details can be found in W.G. Kümmel, *Introduction to the New Testament*, pp. 59–61, 106–09.

[71]*Der Rahmen der Geschichte Jesu* (Berlin: Trowitsch & Sohn, 1919; reprint, 1964), p. 317.

[72]Ibid., pp. 222–24.

[73]See for example H. Köster, *Synoptische Überlieferungen bei den apostolischen Vätern* [Synoptic traditions in the apostolic fathers] (Berlin: Akademie Verlag, 1957).

[74]A fine survey and analysis of the parables of Jesus is by John R. Donahue, *The Gospel in Parables* (Minneapolis: Fortress Press, 1988).

[75]*Parousia* is a Greek word which means "presence" and was used for the formal public appearance of an authority figure, such as a governor or a king. Paul uses it to refer to the arrival of visitors from churches in other cities

(1 Cor. 16:17), or his own future visit to a church (Phil. 1:16), but especially of the appearing of Christ in triumph at the end of the present age (1 Cor. 15:23; 1 Thess. 2:19; 4:15; 5:23). Among the Gospels, the term is found only in Matt. 24:3, 27, 37, 39.

[76]Hans Conzelmann, "Gegenwart und Zukunft in der synoptischen Tradition" [Present and future in the synoptic tradition], in *Zeitschrift für Theologie und Kirche* 54 (1957): 288–96 (see esp. p. 294), adopts a view of Mark that is formally similar to the one proposed here; the substantial difference lies in the understanding of the aim of the wonder stories. Their intent is not to present Jesus as a *theios anēr* ("divine man") but to show him as the bearer of the eschatological power to defeat Satan. On the imprecision of the term *theios anēr*, see D.L. Tiede, *The Charismatic Figure As Miracle Worker* (Missoula, MT: Scholars Press, 1972).

[77]See Krister Stendahl, *The School of St. Matthew* (Philadelphia: Fortress, 1966), where the use of Scripture in the first-discovered Qumran documents is discussed.

[78]A candid and illuminating discussion of this problem has been written by Barnabas Lindars in his *New Testament Apologetic* (Philadelphia: Westminster, 1961).

[79]This lack of exact correspondence between the prophetic promise and the Christian claim of fulfillment has been stressed by Wolfhart Pannenberg in his contributions to Pannenberg, ed., *Revelation As History*, 3d ed. (trans. David Granskou; New York: Macmillan, 1968).

[80]See article on Elijah by Jerome T. Walsh in the *Anchor Bible Dictionary*, ed. David N. Freedman, vol. 2 (New York: Doubleday, 1992).

[81]See Sigmund Mowinckel, *He That Cometh* (trans. G.W. Anderson; Nashville: Abingdon, 1956), esp. pp. 155–86.

[82]The phrase *hoi par' aoutou* in Mark 3:21 is wrongly translated in some editions of the RSV as "his friends." It means "his family," as 3:31–35 shows and as NRSV accurately renders the phrase.

[83]A fundamental essay on this subject is by K.G. Kuhn, "The Two Messiahs of Aaron and Israel," in Krister Stendahl, ed., *The Scrolls and the New Testament* (New York: Harper Brothers, 1957), pp. 54–64. Subsequent criticism of Kuhn's interpretation has not set aside his basic position. See Matthew Black, *The Scrolls and Christian Origins* (New York: Scribner's, 1961).

[84]On the theory that the Testaments of the Twelve Patriarchs originated at Qumran, see F.M. Cross, *The Ancient Library of Qumran*, rev. ed. (Garden City, NY: Doubleday, 1961), pp. 198–206. My own analysis of this document points to a Greek origin for the document as we know it in its complete form; my translation and introduction are in *The Old Testament Pseudepigrapha*, vol. 1, ed. J.H. Charlesworth (New York: Doubleday, 1983).

[85]It is treated along with christological titles by Ferdinand Hahn in *Christologische Hoheitstitel* [Christological titles] (Göttingen: Vandenhoeck & Ruprecht, 1963).

[86]See my discussion of *aretalogy* and *theios anēr* in "Aretalogy and Gospel," *Journal of Biblical Literature* 93 (1973): 408–16, and in "Aretalogies,

Hellenistic 'Lives' and the Sources of Mark," *12th Colloquy of the Center for Hermeneutical Studies in Hellenistic and Modern Culture* (Berkeley, CA: Center for Hermeneutical Studies in Hellenistic and Modern Culture, 1975).

[87] Excellent surveys of the evidence about the Son of Man, and of the variety of scholarly interpretations of the term, may be found in H.E. Tödt, *Son of Man in the Synoptic Tradition* (London and Philadelphia, 1956); in F.W. Borsch, *Son of Man in Myth and History* (London and Philadelphia, 1967); and in R.G. Hamerton-Kelly, *Pre-existence Wisdom and the Son of Man* (London: Cambridge University Press, 1973).

[88] See for example Bultmann, in his *Theology of the New Testament*, vol. 1, pp. 30–32.

[89] Eduard Schweizer, "Son of Man," *Journal of Biblical Literature* 79 (1960): 119–29. Also Norman Perrin, *The New Testament: An Introduction* (New York: Harcourt Brace Jovanovich, 1974), pp. 76–77, 156–57; now replaced by 3d ed., revised by Dennis Duling (Harcourt Brace, 1994).

[90] For example, Vincent Taylor, *The Names of Jesus* (New York: St. Martin's, 1953). With many Anglo-Saxon scholars, Taylor believed that Jesus' messianic consciousness was formulated through his combining the traditional kingly messianic idea of Israel with the apocalyptic Son of Man notion and the Suffering Servant concept of II Isaiah.

[91] Philip Vielhauer, "Gottesreich und Menschensohn in der Verkündigung Jesu" [Kingdom of God and Son of Man in the preaching of Jesus], in his *Aufsätze zum Neuen Testament* [Essays on the New Testament] (Munich: Kaiser, 1965) pp. 55–91. Also H.B. Sharman, *Son of Man and Kingdom of God* (New York: Harper Brothers, 1943).

[92] The most thorough and convincing survey of the history-of-religions background of "Son of Man" is still Carsten Colpe's article on the term in *Theological Dictionary of the New Testament*, vol. 8, pp. 400–77.

[93] *The Son of Man in the Synoptic Tradition*, esp. pp. 222–83.

[94] See my article on this term in *New Testament Studies* 14, 2 (1968): 232–46.

[95] A fundamental work on the parables remains that of Joachim Jeremias, *Parables of Jesus*, rev. ed. (trans. S.H. Hooke; New York: Scribner's, 1963). Useful analyses of Mark in terms of conflict concerning power in the first century C.E. are J.D. Kingsbury, *Conflict in Mark: Jews, Authorities, Disputes* (Minneapolis: Fortress Press, 1989) and Herman E. Waetjen, *A Reordering of Power: A Socio-political Reading of Mark's Gospel* (Minneapolis: Fortress, 1989).

[96] A comprehensive, readable commentary on Mark, including an analysis of the apocalyptic section, is by Morna Hooker in Black's New Testament Commentary series (London: A. & C. Black, 1991). For a survey of views concerning the origin of Mark's apocalyptic discourse, see my *Community of the New Age*, pp. 43–45.

[97] The relevant texts are 8:31 ("must suffer"), 9:11 ("Elijah *must* come first"), and 13:10 ("the gospel *must* first be preached to all nations," i.e., before the End).

[98] Mark 8:31; 9:12; 9:31; 10:33–34.

[99] See note 97, above.

[100] Edward Lohse, *Märtyrer und Gottesknecht* [Martyr and servant of God] (Göttingen: Vandenhoeck & Ruprecht, 1955).

[101]Although the King James Version and a great many of the Greek and other ancient manuscripts read "new testament" (= covenant) at Mark 14:24, the New Revised Standard Version follows the oldest and best Greek manuscripts in omitting the word "new." Nevertheless, the implication of this saying of Jesus is that the new basis of man's relationship to God that Jesus is establishing will replace the Jewish covenant. Whether the claim of newness arose with Jesus or with the early church, it is clearly dependent on Jeremiah 31:31–34:

> Behold, the days are coming says the Lord, when I will make a new convenant with the house of Israel and the house of Judah, not like the covenant which I made with their fathers when I took them by the hand to bring them out of the land of Egypt, my covenant which they broke, though I was their husband, says the Lord. But this is the covenant which I will make with the house of Israel after those days, says the Lord: I will put my law within them, and I will write it upon their hearts; and I will be their God, and they shall be my people. And no longer shall each man teach his neighbor and each his brother, saying, "Know the Lord," for they shall all know me, from the least of them to the greatest, says the Lord; for I will forgive their iniquity, and I will remember their sin no more.

Read against the background of these words of Jeremiah, the implication of this saying of Jesus (Mark 14:24) is that his death in some way seals or ratifies the (new) covenant and effects the forgiveness of sin.

[102]This passage is built on the imagery of the proto-apocalyptic book of Ezekiel (esp. Ezek. 34) and the apocalyptic oracle of Zechariah 13:7.

[103]See for example C. Colpe, in his analysis of *huios tou anthropou* [son of man] in Kittel, *Theological Dictionary of the New Testament*, vol. 8.

[104]A long-enduring theory proposed at the beginning of the present century by William Wrede, in *Das Messiasgeheminis in den Evangelien* (Göttingen: Vandenhoeck & Ruprecht, 1901 [trans. by J.C.G. Grieg, *The Messianic Secret*, Greenwood, SC: Attic Press, 1971]), was that Mark invented the notion that Jesus told his followers to be silent about his messiahship in order to explain the fact that Jesus never publicly claimed to be the messiah.

[105]See the discussion of the differences between the meaning attached to the miracles of Jesus and those attributed to the Greco-Roman mystical savior figures in my *Miracle in the Early Christian World* (New Haven: Yale University Press, 1983), pp. 78–173.

[106]An important technical term in apocalyptic literature. Compare 1 En. 16:3; 51:3; 103:2; 104:12; 106:19; Lev. 2:10; 1QS 4; 6; 1QH 1:21; 2:13; 1QpHab 7.5; 8.14.

[107]See Jeremias, *Parables of Jesus*, pp. 14–17. Although used by Mark in relation to the parables, this explanation is fittingly applied to the whole of his representation of Jesus.

CHAPTER 5

Jesus in the History of the Church
The Gospel of Matthew

As we have noted earlier (Chapter 4), in the last two decades of the first century C.E., at least three writers in addition to Mark undertook to produce Gospels of their own, utilizing Mark's literary form, but modifying it each in his own way. Two of these evangelists, Matthew and Luke, not only adopted the literary genre but took over nearly the whole of Mark's content as well, expanding it with Q and other traditions to which they had access and shaping the Markan material to suit their own special ends. John, however, borrowed the genre but utilized the substance of Mark's traditions hardly at all. Throughout the present century scholars have often discussed the question of the literary dependence of the gospel writers. But only in recent decades has attention been paid to the unmistakable fact that Matthew, Luke, and John modified for their own purposes Mark's understanding of history.

None of the other gospel writers utilized unchanged Mark's apocalyptic view of history. Matthew carried over, and at some points intensified, the apocalyptic language and the sense of urgent expectancy, but he also significantly altered the historical outlook as we shall see. Luke introduced sayings into the gospel tradition that lay even more stress on the coming Son of Man than does Mark, but his schematic view of history is far removed from Mark's apocalypticism. The *language* of apocalypticism is scattered throughout John's gospel, but with almost none of its substance. Each of the evangelists has recast the tradition in such a way as to present his own understanding of the place of Jesus in history.

One of the important elements that contributed to the reshaping in each case was the fact that the church was now an organized community. In Mark and Q we find a strong social sense of community, expressed in recognition of the followers of Jesus as the eschatological people to whom God has granted special wisdom and promised redemption; but there is little evidence of the process of development within the community of a structure of leadership or for assignment of responsibilities for leaders and members. There are in these two older sources mostly challenges as to how the individual is to relate to the group and guidelines for the tasks that discipleship involves, but few hints about emerging community organization or structure. The tradition has been oriented more toward bringing about the eschatological fulfillment than toward giving guidance to an ongoing institution. In each of the other three Gospels, however, the situation of the church with respect to inner organization and external relations has changed, or at least the writer's understanding of the church's situation has altered.

In Matthew the problems of authority within the community and of the moral responsibility of its members are explicitly raised, and the question about the nature of the continuity between the Christian church and Jewish tradition is directly addressed. Closely related to this is Matthew's concern for the place of Jesus and his community in God's historical plan for creation—an interest he shares with Luke, although the two Gospels differ in important detail, as we shall see. Matthew emphasizes the church as the ongoing instrument through which God is calling the nations of the world to repentance and faith (Matt. 25:32; 28:19), even though there is full acknowledgment that not everyone who hears the message will respond in faith (25:32, 41–46). Full opportunity to hear the gospel is to be extended initially to Israel, as the traditional people of God and the possessors of the Law and the prophets (10:5–6). With the official rejection of Jesus by the civil and religious authorities, as depicted symbolically in the Parable of the Wedding Banquet (22:1–14), the missionary call is to go out to those who might be considered unworthy by standards of the Law of Moses (22:9), and disciples are to be invited into the new community from all the nations of the world (28:19). As a result, the membership of the new community according to Matthew is mixed, ethnically, ethically, and ritually (22:10). Luke has less to say about the community structure and rules than does Matthew, but much more to say concerning the present age as the epoch of the new covenant people in the divine plan of the ages. Luke goes beyond Matthew in his stress on Gentile participation in the church as a major factor in the outworking of God's plan of redemption for his new people.

The Gospel of John evidences no interest in the organizational aspects of the church's life, preferring to portray the church under a series of metaphors or images—children, flock, vine—in which dependence on God and on others is the chief characteristic of the people of God. The Johannine author's view of history concerns the person and one's relationship to the new community: One must come to understand oneself as a moment-by-moment participant in the story of Jesus and the emergent community, rather than as merely a spectator of past events. As will become evident in the more detailed analyses of the three Gospels offered in this chapter and the next two, the distinctions sketched here are in many instances differences of emphasis, and some common elements are shared by all three writers.

The Continuing Importance of Jewish Tradition

Matthew's two major convictions, both of which are made explicit in his gospel, are (1) that the Law of God, as given to ancient Israel, is eternally valid and (2) that Jesus is the final agent of power through whom God's purpose as announced in the Scriptures is being consummated (Matt. 5:17–18).[1] Putting the two beliefs together, one can say that, for Matthew, Jesus is the inaugurator of the true Israel, the people through and among whom God's ultimate purpose for the human race is to be achieved. The requirements for God's people set forth in the Scriptures are to be carried out fully by the new community. The demands on the members go beyond those made by the two major groups engaged in showing the relevance and articulating the demands of the law: the scribes and the Pharisees.

The Law of Jesus and the Law of Moses

Interpreters have frequently drawn attention to the parallels between Moses in the Old Testament and Jewish tradition and Jesus in the Gospel of Matthew. Both of them appear on the mountain to interpret God's Law to his people. In the Sermon on the Mount, Jesus sets his authority over against that of Moses: "You have heard that it was said [that is, by Moses].... But I say to you...." The important common elements are not only the figures of Moses and Jesus as the agents through whom God discloses his purpose for his people, but also the Law itself as the expression of what God expects of them.

The "book" of Matthew—as it calls itself (1:1)—has been variously outlined by scholars. If one takes as the principal clue to the structure of Matthew the twice-repeated phrase "From that time Jesus began ..." (4:17 and 16:21), then Matthew has arranged his gospel in a chronological way, beginning in Galilee and culminating in Jerusalem.[2] If, on the other hand, the five-times repeated phrase "when Jesus had finished ..." is taken as the clue to Matthew's intention, then the book may be divided up thematically, with five major discourse sections, each of which is paired with a narrative section.[3] There are other recurrent phrases throughout the gospel, however, such as the so-called fulfillment quotations from Scripture, in terms of which divine justification or determination is offered for important details in Matthew's account of Jesus' career (1:23; 2:15, 18, 23; 4:15–16; 8:17; 12:18–21; 13:35; 21:5; 27:9–10). Each is prefixed by a variant of the phrase "This was done in order that it might be fulfilled as was spoken by the prophet." Some have tried to argue from this recurrent phrase that the structure of Matthew's gospel manifests his developing portrait of Jesus as the Christ.[4]

If the fivefold phrase "When Jesus had finished ..." is adopted as the key to the structure of the gospel, then perhaps it is best explained as the result of a conscious imitation of the structure of the Torah, the first five books of the Old Testament, which are attributed by Jewish tradition to Moses. On this theory, Matthew's gospel could be divided as follows:

1. The Coming of Jesus As God's Messiah (1–2)

2. The Ministry of the Messiah and His Followers (3–25)

    a. *Narrative:* The Beginning of the Ministry in Galilee (3:1–4:25)
       Discourse: The Sermon on the Mount (5:1–7:29)

    b. *Narrative:* The Authority of Jesus' Ministry (8:1–12:50)
       Discourse: The Messianic Mission (9:36–10:42)

    c. *Narrative:* The Kingdom and Its Coming (11:1–12:50)
       Discourse: The Parables of the Kingdom (13:1–52)

    d. *Narrative:* The Life of the New Community (13:53–17:27)
       Discourse: Greatness and Responsibility (18:1–35)

    e. *Narrative:* Conflict and Consummation (19:1–24:3)
       Discourse: Revelation of the End (24:4–25:46)

3. The Humiliation and Exaltation of the Messiah (26–28)[5]

Supporting this approach is the fact that transitions from narrative to discourse are marked off at 4:23 and 9:35 by summarizing statements about the healing ministry, although this element is missing elsewhere. Problematical for this structural hypothesis, however, is the fact that the contrast in 2d between narrative and discourse is not at all clear, while 2e contains a potent discourse denouncing the Pharisees (23:1–36), one which is separated by theme and locale from the apocalyptic discourse that follows. The pattern is not altogether clear probably because Matthew's purposes are multiple, including apologetics in behalf of his community's understanding of Jesus and the Law, controversy with Pharisees over its interpretation, and the need for provision of norms and guidelines for the church as an ongoing institution, especially in view of its mounting conflict with Jewish authorities. The disagreement with Judaism was not over the enduring validity of the Law (which is, in fact, affirmed—5:17–18) but rather over the interpretation of the Law and the purity of heart with which it is obeyed. New studies of Matthew's gospel offer reconstructions of his community and the nature of its continuities and tensions with emergent rabbinic Judaism.[6]

The Jewish Law, as analyzed by modern scholarship, falls into two categories: (1) apodictic laws, which are based solely on God's decree ("Thou shalt ... thou shalt not ...") and (2) casuistic laws, which state the consequences of obeying or disobeying ("Honor thy father ... that thy days may be long ..."). The apodictic form of ethics that Matthew attributes to Jesus, particularly in the Sermon on the Mount, seems to be a conscious paralleling of the giving of the Law through Moses on Mount Sinai, even though the actual contents of the moral declarations may have arisen through the words of Christian prophets in apostolic times.[7] If the ethics in Matthew did, in fact, develop in this way, then this process would parallel the development of Jewish ethics within the embryonic rabbinic movement, whereby the process of interpreting the Law of Moses was an ongoing task of the community under the guidance of its authoritative teachers. It was believed, at least in principle, that the link could be traced, from what became authoritative rabbinic interpretations, back through earlier generations of interpreters to Moses himself. In practice, no sharp distinction was made between the Law of Moses and the subsequent interpretation of it: Both were equally binding. Similarly, the words of Jesus and the later interpretations carried an equally authoritative obligation for Matthew's church. As Jacob Neusner's brilliant analyses have shown, however, it was only in the post-Maccabean period, when the nationalistic hopes failed and the priesthood was dominated by the Roman rulers, that the interpretation and appropriation of the Law through voluntary gatherings launched what was subsequently to become postbiblical Judaism.[8] As we noted previously (pp.157–58), the initially informal gatherings for study and worship, and the leadership of the movement, became increasingly structured and formal following the destruction of the Temple and the failure of the Second Revolt under Bar Kochba.

The Outworking of the Divine Purpose

In order to heighten the aura of the supernatural that surrounds Jesus, Matthew portrays his birth as climaxing a development that began with Abraham, the progenitor of the Hebrew people, included such eminent figures in Israel's history as David, the ideal king, and Solomon, the ideal man of wisdom, and culminated in Jesus' birth from a virgin in fulfillment of the prophecy of Isaiah 7:14.[9] Even the movement of the stars in the heavens is altered by the appearance of a star that guides the astrologers (Magi) from the East (presumably Mesopotamia, where astrology is supposed to have flourished) to Jesus' birthplace (Matt. 2:1–2), Bethlehem, a city that was predetermined by the divine plan laid down in the Scriptures (cf. Matt. 2:5–6 with Mic. 5:2). It is possible that mention of the star results from Matthew's literal understanding of the prophecy of Numbers 24:17, in which the future ruler of Israel is called a Star from Jacob, a title that figured in the expectations of the Qumran community,[10] as it did in the brief but fervent Jewish nationalism of the Second Revolt against the Romans in 130–135 C.E. The leader of that revolt, Bar Kosibah, took the Bar Kochbah, meaning "Son of the Star," apparently to associate himself in the popular mind with the promise of Numbers 24. But Matthew's primary interest in the star at the birth of Jesus is to imply his place, not in Jewish political aspirations, but in the cosmic scheme.

The notion of supernatural preparation for the coming of Jesus is further heightened by the dreams that Matthew describes: Joseph is advised about the pregnancy of his betrothed, who is still a virgin; the Magi are warned against reporting back to Herod as he had requested them to do (Matt. 2:12); Joseph is counseled to flee with the child to Egypt in order to escape the wrath of Herod, as later, after Herod's death, he is instructed to move with his family to Nazareth in Galilee, where he would be out of the jurisdiction of Archelaus, the son of Herod.[11] Unlike Luke, who pictures Joseph as residing in Nazareth but required to go to Bethlehem for enrollment in the Roman census, Matthew mentions Joseph's "house" in Bethlehem, as though he had lived there permanently until forced to flee by Herod's decrees aimed against Jesus (Matt. 2:11).

Each of these "historical" moves was ultimately dictated not by the dreams themselves but by the divine plan laid down in Scripture. The return from Egypt is said to be the fulfillment of Hosea 11:1. The grief of the mothers whose children were slain by Herod is seen as predicted in Jeremiah 31:15. The move to Nazareth is said to accord with "what was spoken by the prophets": "He shall be called a Nazarene" (Matt. 2:23). There is no text corresponding to this declaration, but it is likely a reference to Isaiah 11:1, as noted below. Matthew has no interest in the actual historical situation out of which the prophets spoke these words, nor does he make any attempt to show a direct correlation between the historic events in biblical times and the situation in the time of Jesus. Hosea was describing the Exodus from Egypt, when God delivered his people ("my son") and led them into the land of Palestine. Jeremiah's words probably refer to the fall of the northern kingdom of Israel in 722 B.C.E., some 100 years before his own time. Jeremiah's prophecies come from the last quarter of the seventh century B.C.E., shortly before Judah, the southern kingdom, likewise fell. The word *Nazarene* does not occur in the Hebrew Bible, but is probably to be traced to Isaiah 11:1, where the shoot *(netser)* from the stump of Jesse is mentioned as God's agent in establishing his just rule on earth. The metaphor in Isaiah is that of a tree cut down, which signifies the end of the Davidic dynasty. The prophet foresees the appearance, from the seemingly lifeless stump, of a shoot that will both signal and effect the reestablishment of the Kingdom. Conceivably, Matthew could have found in this prophetic word a prediction pointing to the kingly role that was assigned by Christians to Jesus. Instead, Matthew used the Isaiah 11 passage to prove that it was ordained in Scripture that Jesus' residence should be in Nazareth. (The Hebrew letters would be *n-ts-r;* the language was written in consonants, and the reader supplied the vowels; hence, Na-TSa-Rene.) The writer of Matthew did not ask what Isaiah intended by his words; he was interested in finding what they might mean to him and his readers. Since the Bible was held to be divinely inspired, its sacred letters were subject to multiple interpretations, limited only by the talent and ingenuity of the interpreter. The discovery of obscure meanings in Scripture was regarded as a tribute to its divine origin, not a falsification of the intention of the biblical writer. The question of the Old Testament writers' intentions was for Matthew as well as for Jewish interpreters of his age an irrelevant one, because they believed that the God who had spoken through the prophets in the past was still in control of human affairs and was shaping them in accord with his own purpose, which the skillful interpreter of Scripture could discern in the present and correlate with the writings from the ancient past. What was significant was continuity of divine purpose, not precision of historical knowledge.

Because this redemptive purpose of God was seen as being worked out through Jesus, not only in his mission but even in the circumstances of his birth, Matthew gave him in a particularly explicit way superhuman titles and prerogatives. He affirmed Jesus' sinlessness and his superiority to John the Baptist in his brief addition to the baptismal story (3:14–15), in which John acknowledges his inferiority to Jesus and suggests the inappropriateness of Jesus' receiving a baptism for repentance. In the apocryphal Gospel of the Hebrews (quoted by Jerome in his fourth-century treatise *Against Pelagius* 3.2), the problem of Jesus' baptism for repentance is handled more explicity than in the canonical Gospels: Jesus directly disclaims any consciousness of having committed sin. In Matthew the heavenly voice that speaks at the moment of the descent of the Spirit makes a public declaration rather than a private disclosure to Jesus (as is the case in Mark 1:11): "This is my beloved Son, with whom I am well pleased" (3:17). These words are repeated in Matthew 17:54 on the occasion of the transfiguration of Jesus. Again they are uttered by the heavenly voice, and again they are in an expanded form, as compared with the parallel account in Mark 9:7 (Matthew's source!). A similar development occurs in Matthew's account of Peter's confession (16:17), and he is promised both a foundational role in the establishment of Christ's church (a word used only by Matthew among the evangelists) and an authoritative function in its administration. Whatever the origins of this passage added by Matthew may have been,[12] he used the pericope to assert unequivocally the messiahship of Jesus and his central place in God's plan as one assigned to establish the new people of God. The Greek word for church, *ekklesía*, has long been recognized as a translation of the Semitic word used in the Old Testament for the covenant community of Israel, *qahal*.[13]

The healing ministry of Jesus is presented by Matthew as prime evidence of Jesus' divine authority, in that the miracles are explicitly linked in Matthew with the fulfillment of Scripture in order to underscore the connection between Jesus' activity and the plan of God. In reproducing Mark's summary of Jesus' healing in Galilee (Mark 1:32–34 = Matt.

8:16–17), Matthew connects it directly with Isaiah 53:4: "This was to fulfill what was spoken by the prophet Isaiah, 'He took our infirmities and bore our diseases.'" Similarly, in Matthew 12:15–21 there is a parallel with Mark 3:7–12. In Mark a full summary is given of the response to Jesus' ministry in Galilee and the surrounding regions; Matthew added an extended quotation from Isaiah 42:1–4, and the whole passage has the effect of identifying Jesus with the Servant of Yahweh in 2 Isaiah and of explaining, by appeal to the Scriptures, the shift from Jewish to Gentile audiences for the hearing of the gospel and the acceptance of its power: "And in his name will the Gentiles hope."

The Divine Authority of Jesus

In his handling of the miracle-story aspect of the gospel tradition,[14] Matthew asserts that Jesus is endowed with divine authority and that he exercises his power in relation to the community of faith. Many details are intended to heighten the miraculous element. For example, Matthew reports that Jairus' daughter, whom Jesus makes well, is not just at the point of death (Mark 5:23) but already dead (Matt. 9:18); he doubles a miracle by reporting that, in Jericho, Jesus healed not one blind man (Mark 10:46) but two (Matt. 20:29). The details of the discovery of the empty tomb in Mark 16:1–8 are expanded to include an earthquake, a descending angel, and a band of soldiers on guard who fall unconscious (Matt. 28:1–4). Matthew also modifies the miracle-story tradition in such a way that the stories deal with problems of faith in the church in his own time. Accordingly, the stories of Jesus stilling the storm (8:23–27) and walking on the water (14:22–33) include a rebuke to the disciples (= the church of Matthew's time) for being men of little faith, an element not found in the Markan and Lukan parallels.

The heightening of the sense of Jesus' authority is further seen in Matthew's allegorical modification and elaboration of the parables. For example, Matthew appended to the Parable of the Weeds (13:24–30) an allegorical explanation in which Jesus is identified as the Son of Man, whose present task of proclamation of the gospel will be brought to completion by the work of judgment that he will carry out at the End of the Age (13:36–43). Indeed, Jesus' teaching in parables is seen by Matthew (13:35) as the fulfillment of a predetermined role announced by the prophets (actually the Psalmist, in Ps. 78:2). Matthew reworked parables that he received from the tradition in such a way as to make more nearly explicit the christological meaning he found in them; for example, the Parable of the Supper (Matt. 21:1–14; cf. Luke 14:16–24) he made into a marriage feast (= the eschatological banquet in the End Time) given by a king (= God) for his son (= Jesus). But Matthew also added from his own source(s) parabolic material that is even more explicit in depicting Jesus as the criterion by which God will judge the human race and as the one designated Judge and Son of Man in the Day of Consummation (Matt. 25:31–46).

Jesus As Preeminent Interpreter of God's Will

The church of Matthew is faced with problems of identity, discipline, and proper interpretation of Scripture in the interim between its Lord's vindication in the Resurrection and the time when he will return to vindicate the faithful, while judging their opponents. Meanwhile, the members are to live in obedience to his words and in confidence of both his presence and his return (Matt. 28:20).[15] Thus, Matthew recognizes the crucial role of Jesus in the coming Day of Judgment, but this is not his main point. More important is the fact that Jesus, the Christ, is now authoritatively active in the ongoing life of the true Israel, the church. He is the "one teacher" of the church, its sole "instructor"[16] (23:7–10). As in emergent rabbinic Judaism, it is essential that there be distinct guidelines for the instruction that is to be carried on within the community. It is wholly fitting that the mission call of 28:19 be for the apostles to "make disciples"— those under instruction, learning the significance of Jesus and his role as communicator of the true Law for the true people of God. A major feature of the task assigned by him to the apostles is to engage in the correct interpretation of the Law of God, which Matthew presents as the ultimate expression of the divine will for his people.

Matthew sounds this theme near the beginning of his version of the Sermon on the Mount (5:17–20). Jesus' mission under God was not to destroy the Law and the prophets, but to bring to completion the will and purpose of God contained in them. From what follows in the Sermon, it is clear that "fulfill" refers not only to the outworking of a purpose in history—though that is surely an important factor— but also to the obedience of the true Israel to the moral demands of the Law and the prophets. The Pharisees are attacked in Matthew, not because they are too demanding and legalistic, but because there is a hypocritical gap between their demands on others and their own

moral performance (5:20; 23:2–4). The rigor of the moral requirement of the Law is not to be relaxed in the slightest degree.

Unique to Matthew is the series of antitheses mentioned earlier,
in which Jesus contrasts the words of the Mosaic Law with his own
interpretation of God's will: "You have heard that it was said ... But
I say to you ..." (Matt. 5:21–48). Without exploring the details of
Matthew's ethics, we can see two important elements emerge: (1)
Jesus is cast in the role of the teacher whose authority transcends
and supplants that of Moses, the ultimate interpreter of the divine will
in Judaism, and (2) the moral requirements laid down by Jesus exceed
the severity of the demands contained in the Torah, the Law of
Moses. Not only murder but even anger toward others is outlawed.
God requires more than abstention from the act of killing; he requires
the positive act of reconciliation (5:21–26). Similarly, it is not enough
for Matthew's Jesus that a man refrain from committing adultery.
He is to exercise such self-control that he avoids even lustful looks
(5:27–30). Divorce and oath-taking are likewise ruled out (5:31–37),
since all these practices give the appearance of honoring the Law
and the purpose of God while they actually are violations of God's
will that his people should remain in marital union and speak only the
truth (19:4–9). But according to Matthew, Jesus went beyond even
this rigid view to enjoin celibacy as a higher way of life (19:10–12).
Matthew's call for a righteousness exceeding that of the Pharisees is
carried to great lengths. For example, only Matthew reports Jesus as
saying, "You must be perfect ..." (5:48). On the more humane side,
Matthew also reports Jesus as calling for acts of kindness in response
to maltreatment or exploitation (5:38–42) and for works of love even
toward one's enemies. But the standard for one's behavior is nothing
less than the perfect character of God himself (5:48).

The true Israel is to be characterized by the same forms of
religion that are practiced in Judaism, but the church is to avoid
the kinds of display of piety that can make a mockery of true religion. Almsgiving and prayer are purely private matters, not occa-
sions for religious ostentation (6:1–8). Likewise, fasting is to be
practiced in secret, as a discipline directed toward God alone, not
as a means of drawing attention to one's religious devotion
(6:16–18). The primary aim of the life of the member of the true
Israel is to seek God's Kingdom and the righteousness he demands
(6:32).

The problem of conflict within the Christian community is
obviously one of the most serious for Matthew. In 18:15–35 he has

brought together a series of tradition units, some from Q but mostly from his own source(s), through which he describes the conciliatory attitude Christians are to adopt toward one another. On the other hand, he sets forth the structured procedure the church is to follow when dealing with recalcitrant members. Those who refuse to listen to the church face excommunication. What is perhaps surprising here is that Matthew views both the procedure of reconciliation and the exercise of authority as manifestations of the continuing presence of Christ in the midst of his people (18:20). For Matthew the place of Jesus in history is quite specific: His invisible presence is the ground of the fellowship and the exercise of authority that are to characterize the corporate life of the true Israel.

Matthew gives Jesus' assignment of authority to the disciples new force by bringing together not only the parallel passages from Mark (6:6–11; 3:13–19), where the disciples are commissioned by Jesus, but also other pericopes selected from Q and from the apocalyptic discourse of Mark 13. The disciples are specifically called apostles (Matt. 10:2), as they are in Mark 6:30, but the transposition of the material from the apocalyptic discourse (in Mark 13) back into the section portraying the public teaching of Jesus has the effect of establishing an identity between the ministry of Jesus and that of the church in the apostolic age. From the standpoint of the modern historian, one could say that Matthew has falsified the account by depicting Jesus as warning his disciples that they will be required to appear at hearings before kings and governors (10:18), since these circumstances did not arise until apostolic times and even later. But Matthew is making precisely the opposite point: The living Christ is present and active in his church in apostolic times. It is not a matter of Matthew's placing the history of the church back into the ministry of Jesus, but of placing the history of Jesus within the ongoing life of the church.

The Church As the True Israel

As we noted, there is a distinction between the limitation of the disciples' mission in Matthew 10:6 to the "lost sheep of the house of Israel"[17] and the command of the resurrected Christ to the disciples to undertake worldwide evangelism in 28:19. Presumably, Matthew's depiction of the activity of Jesus was influenced by the geographical and ethnic limitations of Jesus' actual ministry to Galilee, Judea, the vicinity of Tyre and Sidon, and the cities of the Decapolis. The gospel and Acts are at one in describing the initial activity of the apostles as taking place in Jewish territory, which is then contrasted in Acts with the Gentile mission launched in the subsequent period. One could argue that since Paul, within a few years of the Crucifixion of Jesus, was so disturbed by the presence and apparent success of a group in Damascus claiming to be the heirs of the covenant tradition that he went there intending to destroy the movement (Gal. 1:11–17). Even so, Jesus historically seems to have concentrated his activity chiefly on Jewish territory and to have had Jewish people as his primary audience, although his outreach into the region of the Decapolis and Gentile cities is also reported in Mark. Only in the time after his death was the wider mission launched into the Gentile world, first Syria and Asia Minor, and then Greece and Rome. For Matthew, however, the attempted evangelism of the Jewish people seems to have been a necessary initial phase; its relative lack of success was interpreted as being in keeping with a divine plan to have the new community reach beyond ethnic and regional Judaism. Twice in the report of the teaching of Jesus in the final days before the Passion, Matthew introduces the saying "The first will be last, and the last first" (19:30; 20:16); that is, the Gentiles will one day outnumber the birthright Jews as those who share in the life of God's new covenant people. The second occurrence of the saying leads directly into the third and final prediction of the Passion (20:17–19) and thus seems to point to the impending rejection of Jesus by Jewish officialdom in Jerusalem. The conviction that God will open the gospel invitation to the Gentiles when the Jewish officials have spurned it is again expressed in the Parable of the Supper (Matt. 22:1–14). It is made even more explicit in the long and bitter discourse in which Jesus reportedly denounces the scribes and Pharisees (23:1–36). This culminates in the announcement that judgment for the persistent rejection and murder of God's messengers will fall "on this generation." The acceptance of this responsibility is attributed by Matthew to the Jewish leaders in the dreadful words of Matthew 27:25: "His blood be on us and on our children!"

Matthew took advantage of details in such unlikely places as the miracle stories to strengthen his case for the lack of responsiveness of many in historic Israel and the openness to faith of those who comprise the true Israel. In the story of the Healing of the Centurion's Servant (8:1–13), for example, he took out of another context in Q (= Luke 13:28–30) a pericope that contrasts the participation of

Gentiles in the benefits and privileges of the New Age with the outcast state of the unrepentant in Israel (Matt. 8:9–11). That Matthew placed this tradition at this point is confirmed by his addition of one of his favorite phrases describing the unrepentant—those who "weep and gnash their teeth." What is little more than a hint of the Gentile mission in Q became, in Matthew's hand, a part of his polemic against the Jewish leadership. This does not lead to complete abandonment of Jews, and certainly not of the Jewish heritage in the Law and the prophets. What has happened is an ethnically inclusive emphasis and the recasting of the traditions of Israel concerning the accomplishment of God's purpose for his people.[18]

The shift of primary attention from those born in the Jewish tradition to the inclusion of Gentiles is directly declared in Matthew's addition to the Parable of the Vineyard Workers (21:43): "Therefore I tell you, the kingdom of God will be taken away from you [Jews] and given to a nation producing the fruits of it." The new "nation" is, of course, the church, composed of Gentiles and believing Jews. To the extent that Matthew is at all interested in what modern scholars might call the course of history, he seeks to show that the focus of God's concern has shifted from major occupation with those who were Jews by birth to a new undertaking in which there is a universal potential for participation in the people of God, or the true Israel.

In the final verses of his gospel (28:16–20), Matthew draws together several strands that run through his work: (1) the worldwide mission for which the disciples are commissioned, (2) the continuing presence of the risen Christ, who is the sole source of the church's authority and the chief agent of its teaching ministry among "all nations," and (3) the reminder that the present age will come to a close when the Kingdom of God is finally established. The present age is designated by Matthew as the Kingdom of the Son of Man, during which time the church is composed of good and bad (13:41); it will end in the judgment (13:49; 25:31–46). The Age to Come will be the Kingdom of God or, as Matthew prefers, the Kingdom of the Father (13:43; 25:34).

Eschatological expectation figures in Matthew's understanding of the course of history, so that heavy stress is laid on the need for the community to be ready when the Last Day comes. For example, Matthew appended to the apocalyptic discourse that he took over from Mark 13 an extended series of sayings (24:37–41); he also included parabolic words (24:42–51) and parables (25:1–46), two of which are found only in Matthew: the Ten Maidens (25:1–13) and the Last Judgment (25:31–46). There are two main themes that run through all this material as Matthew reproduced and edited it: (1) the need to be ready ("Watch therefore, for you know neither the day nor the hour," 25:13), and (2) the severity of punishment of the unworthy:

> For to all those who have, more will be given, and they will have an abundance; but from those who have nothing, even what they have will be taken away. As for this worthless slave, throw him into outer darkness; there will be weeping and gnashing of teeth. (Matt. 25:29–30)

The inference to be drawn from this representation of the conclusion of Jesus' ministry in these solemn words of warning is that for Matthew the most important consideration is the purity of life and faithfulness of the church, which has now become the true, ethnically inclusive Israel. The concept of the judgment is retained from the older tradition, and readiness is repeatedly enjoined, but the aim throughout Matthew's gospel is by every means to encourage righteous living on the part of Christians *in the present*. Mark's eschatological outlook, and even his apocalyptic words and imagery, have been retained. But the primary focus has shifted from the future consummation to present churchly responsibilities, so that even the announcements of the coming judgment are an appeal to present moral obligation. For Matthew, Jesus' purpose and authority are to be manifest in the history of the church. He is its master; he will be its judge. But its obedience to him and his understanding of the Law of God now will determine the destiny of humanity in the future judgment, which will also take place at his hands.

The Community Behind Matthew

In what segment of early Christianity could the Gospel of Matthew have originated? Clearly, in a place where the issues and decisions of the burgeoning rabbinic movement were taken seriously, both by the Jewish community and by those who were opposed to the point of view in the process of formulation by the rabbinic leaders in Palestine. It is inconceivable that Matthew was written in Hebrew or Aramaic in an earlier version, since it used the Greek Mark as one of its basic sources. Furthermore, its frequent quotations from Scripture are in the Greek version, and in some instances the argument turns on the details of the text as found in the Septuagint (LXX). The quotation from Psalm 8:2 in Matthew 21:16, for example, makes sense in the Greek wording of the LXX but would not in the Hebrew original. Matthew could have been written in any Greek-speaking Jewish center, although it likely came from a city with close ties to Palestine, since the issues reportedly based in Jewish sources on rabbinic decisions at Jamnia seem to be important in this gospel. Recent archaeological and literary evidence of the widespread use of Greek among Jews in Palestine in the first and second centuries mean that this gospel's having been written in that land cannot be ruled out. The earliest witness we have to Matthew's gospel is from Ignatius of Antioch, who died as a martyr in the early second century. A reasonable conjecture for the provenance of Matthew is a city in the eastern Mediterranean, whether in Palestine, Phoenicia, or in another city of western Syria. Wherever it was, the community was locked in fierce debate with Greek-speaking Jews on the issues of scriptural authority and qualifications for covenantal participation which the subsequent rabbinic tradition traces back to a council at Jamnia at the end of the first century C.E.

Suggestions for Further Reading

An earlier comprehensive and erudite study of the background of Matthew's thought is W.D. Davies, *The Setting of the Sermon on the Mount* (Cambridge: Cambridge University Press, 1964). Important recent studies of Matthew and the community in and for which it was written are those by J. Andrew Overman, *Matthew's Gospel and Formative Judaism: The Social World of the Matthean Community* (Minneapolis: Fortress, 1993); and Anthony J. Saldarini, *Matthew's Christian-Jewish Community* (Chicago: University of Chicago Press, 1994). Excellent commentaries on this gospel are those of R.H. Gundry, *Matthew: A Commentary on his Literary and Theological Art* (Grand Rapids, MI: Eerdmans, 1982); and E. Schweizer, *The Good News According to Matthew* (London: SPCK, 1976). Fundamental essays on the theology of Matthew are in Günther Bornkamm, Gerhard Barth, and H.J. Held, *Tradition and Interpretation in Matthew* (Philadelphia: Westminster, 1963). Other useful studies of Matthew include R.E. Brown, *The Birth of the Messiah: A Commentary on the Infancy Narratives in Matthew and Luke* (Garden City, NY: Doubleday, 1977); and R.A. Guelich, *The Sermon on the Mount: A Foundation for Understanding* (Waco, TX: Word, 1982). Important comparisons between the Qumran community and that of Matthew are in Krister Stendahl, *The School of St. Matthew* (Philadelphia: Fortress, 1968), and A.R.C. Leaney, *The Rule of Qumran and Its Meaning* (Philadelphia: Westminster, 1966).

A comprehensive survey of critical questions on Matthew, with full bibliography is available in W.G. Kümmel, *Introduction to the New Testament*, 17th ed. (trans. H.C. Kee; Nashville: Abingdon, 1975), pp. 101–21; see also Norman Perrin (rev. by Dennis C. Duling), *The New Testament: An Introduction** (Fort Worth, TX: Harcourt Brace, 1994).

*Available in a paperback edition.

NOTES _____

[1]Found only in Matthew, although a variant of Matthew 5:18 appears in Luke 16:17. Luke's version of the saying is probably the earlier form, making the same point: that the promises of God reported in Scripture ("the Law") are going to come to pass.

[2]Proposed by J.D. Kingsbury, in *Matthew: Structure, Christology, Kingdom* (Philadelphia: Fortress, 1975).

[3]The phrase occurs at the conclusion of each of the main sections, which begin with narrative about Jesus' activities and end with an extended discourse by him, as indicated in the outline on p. 160. The fivefold structure of Matthew was identified by B.W. Bacon (*Studies in Matthew* [New York: Holt, Rinehart & Winston, 1930]).

[4]See for example J.D. Kingsbury, *Matthew*, passim, but esp. p. 36.

[5]Based on my analysis of Matthew in *Understanding the New Testament*, 5th ed. (Englewood Cliffs, NJ: Prentice-Hall, 1993) M.J. Suggs proposed that Matthew's aim was to set the true Torah of Israel, regarded as embodied in Jesus as incarnate Wisdom, in contrast to the Pharisaic Torah; see his *Wisdom, Christology and Law in Matthew* (Cambridge, MA: Harvard University Press, 1970), pp. 106–08.

[6]Important analyses of Matthew's critique of other Jewish interpretations of the application of the Law in the contemporary situation are by J. Andrew Overman, *Matthew's Gospel and Formative Judaism: The Social World of the Matthean Community* (Minneapolis: Fortress, 1990); and Anthony J. Saldarini, *Matthew's Jewish-Christian Community* (Chicago: University of Chicago Press, 1994).

[7]Persuasively argued by Ernst Käsemann, "Sentences of Holy Law in the New Testament," in his *New Testament Questions of Today* (trans. W.J. Montague; Philadelphia: Fortress, 1970), pp. 66–81. The contrasts between the concurrent attitudes toward the law in emergent formative Judaism and in the wing of early Christianity represented by Matthew's gospel are set forth by J. Andrew Overman in *Matthew's Gospel and Formative Judaism*.

[8]A useful summary of Neusner's conclusions on this subject is offered in his essay, "The Formation of Rabbinic Judaism," in ANRW 2.19.2:3–42. The

basic insights were set out in his ground-breaking work, *The Rabbinic Traditions About the Pharisees Before 70* (Leiden: Brill, 1971).

[9]In Isaiah 7:14 the Greek word for virgin, *parthenós*, is essential for Matthew's representation of Jesus as supernaturally born, but the Hebrew text here contains the word *almah*, which means simply "young woman." It is evident that Matthew is writing in and for a Greek-speaking community, since without *parthenós* his citation of the Old Testament quotation would be pointless.

[10]In the document known as 4Q 174, or the Florilegium, Numbers 24:17 is quoted in connection with the messianic expectations at Qumran. A translation with brief notes is offered by Geza Vermes, in *The Dead Sea Scrolls in English*, 3d ed. (Harmondsworth and New York: Penguin, 1987), pp. 293–94.

[11]Herod the Great was ruler of the whole of Palestine at the time of Jesus' birth. It was only after his death that the puppet kingdom was divided among his sons; Archelaus for a time ruled Judea, and Herod Antipas governed Galilee (along with Perea, the area east of the Jordan).

[12]For a full interpretation of this passage see Oscar Cullmann, *Peter: Disciple, Apostle, Martyr*, 2d rev. ed. (Philadelphia: Westminster, 1962). Cullmann thinks this is an authentic saying of Jesus spoken at the Resurrection appearance of Jesus to Peter, but it is more likely added by Matthew to confirm the emergent structure of authority in his community.

[13]On the use of *ekklesía* in this passage, and in the New Testament in general, see K.L. Schmidt, *"kaléo,"* in Gerhard Kittel and Gerhard Friedrich, eds., *Theological Dictionary of the New Testament*, vol. 3 (Grand Rapids, MI: Eerdmans, 1965), pp. 487–536.

[14]See my analysis of the miracles in Matthew, in *Miracle in the Early Christian World* (New Haven: Yale University Press, 1983), pp. 183–90.

[15]See on this Günther Bornkamm, "End-Expectation and Church in Matthew," in Bornkamm, Barth, and Held, *Tradition and Interpretation in Matthew*, pp. 15–51.

[16]The word translated "instructor" here *(kathēgētēs)* is of special interest since it is primarily a scholastic term. It means "school teacher" in the Greek of New Testament times (see J.H. Moulton and George Milligan, *The Vocabulary of the Greek Testament* [Grand Rapids, MI: Eerdmans, 1949]), as it did in the patristic period (see G.W. Lampe, ed., *A Patristic Greek Lexicon* [New York: Oxford University Press, 1961–1968]), and as it does in modern Greek (= professor). When linked with *didaskalos*, as in Matthew 23:8, it is clear that Matthew's aim is to ascribe to Jesus the central role of instructor. The verb from which *kathēgētēs* is derived means "to explain, show the way." This is precisely what the church of Matthew understands Jesus to be doing in the life of the Christian community, which is another way of saying that it sees its own task as instructional. The school atmosphere of Matthew has been discussed by Krister Stendahl in his *The School of St. Matthew* (Philadelphia: Fortress, 1966). W.D. Davies, in his study *The Setting of the Sermon on the Mount* (London: Cambridge University Press, 1964), pp. 297–98, suggested that the scholastic controversy implicit in Matthew 23:8–10 reflects an historical tension between emergent rabbinic Judaism and an emergent structured Christianity. Later Jewish tradition reports the existence of a Council at Jamnia, near the Palestinian coast, which reacted to the destruction of the

Jerusalem Temple by striving to consolidate Jewish faith and to safeguard the integrity of the Hebrew Scriptures against all actual and potential threats. The scholarly theory is that, in reaction against the Jamnian exclusivist truth claims, Jesus was declared by the Matthean tradition to be the sole teacher of truth. The historicity of this council has been called into question. See the challenging analysis by N.T. Wright in *The New Testament and the People of God*, vol. 1 (London: SPCK, 1993), pp. 161–66.

[17]This limitation is of fundamental importance for Albert Schweitzer's reconstruction of the career of Jesus, especially when Matthew 10:6 is linked with 10:22 and the inference drawn that Jesus, expecting the End of the Age to occur in a matter of weeks, tried to force God's hand when Israel did not repent. See Schweitzer's *The Quest of the Historical Jesus* (trans. William Montgomery; New York: Macmillan, 1910), p. 357. A fuller development of this historically dubious conclusion is found in Schweitzer's *The Mystery of the Kingdom of God* (trans. Walter Lowrie; New York: Macmillan, 1956), pp. 219–42. But in the posthumously published work *Reich Gottes und Christentum* [The Kingdom of God and Christianity] (Tübingen: J.C.B. Mohr, 1967), pp. 127–31, Schweitzer puts more stress than in his earlier works on Jesus' voluntary participation in the messianic woes that must precede the coming of the Kingdom, giving less attention to the notion of forcing God's hand to act within a brief period of time.

[18]This point is made effectively in the two recent works on Matthew by J. Andrew Overman and Anthony J. Saldarini mentioned on p. 173, note 6.

CHAPTER 6

Jesus and the Church in the History of the World
The Gospel of Luke

Luke has been called "the first Christian historian."[1] In at least two fundamental ways, that is an accurate designation. First, he is the only New Testament writer who set about presenting the story of Jesus in the forms and categories in use among secular historians of the first century. In the Gospel of Luke and in the Book of Acts, which from the similarity of style and vocabulary as well as from the specific claims of the opening paragraphs (Luke 1:1-4; Act 1:1) we recognize to be two parts of a single work, Luke[2] gives an account of events from just before the birth of Jesus to the climax of Paul's missionary activity in Rome, on the eve of his trial (Acts 28). In presenting his historical narrative, Luke uses the methods and conventions of the Hellenistic historians of his time. Writing in an age that lacked a universally accepted absolute chronology, Luke dates certain crucial events in his work by referring to the monarchs and governors in power at the time:

> In the fifteenth year of the reign of Tiberius Caesar, when Pontius Pilate was governor of Judea, and Herod[3] was ruler of Galilee, and his brother Philip ruler of the region of Ituraea and Trachonitis, and Lysanias ruler of Abilene, during the high-priesthood of Annas and Caiaphas, the word of God came to John the son of Zechariah in the wilderness. (Luke 3:1–2)

The reference to Lysanias is of no help in establishing the date of the beginning of Jesus' ministry, since we do not know which Lysanias Luke meant.[4] But what the paragraph does show is that Luke wanted to represent the career of Jesus as a real event that occurred in a historical time and place, along with other known and observable events. In Acts he takes pains to describe the conversations of Paul and the other apostolic leaders with various pagan rulers in Cyprus, Corinth, Caesarea (13:7; 18:12; 23:24), and elsewhere. The famous interrogation of Paul by the council of the Areopagus in Athens pictures Paul encountering the leaders of pagan culture as well (Acts 17:16–34). In this synchronization of the history of Jesus with that of the pagan world, Luke is following the literary patterns of his time, and is thereby—at least implicitly—making a claim for Christianity to be considered seriously by pagan observers.

The second aspect of Luke's historical work is more subtle. The very fact that his story line does not end with the death and resurrection of Jesus means that not only literarily but in terms of his view of history he is in a different category from the writers of the other two synoptic Gospels. It is true that in the other Gospels each author has reworked the tradition so that the significance of the Jesus tradition for the Christian community of the evangelist's own time is evident. However, in Mark and Matthew the focus remains on the End of the Age, at which time the mission will be completed and there will ensue a judgment wherein the faithful will be vindicated, the wicked punished, and the rule of God established. Luke's distinctive interests, however, are in the church's ongoing work in the present age, its expansion to the ends of the earth (Acts 1:6), and its image as a literate, appealing enterprise. For Luke, God's redemptive purpose in history is evident not only through present appropriation of the effects of events in the past (Jesus' teaching, miracles, death, and resurrection), but also through the progress of the gospel in the widening circles of the Roman world. This is portrayed in a mixture of the literal and the symbolic in Luke's two-volume narrative that begins with the divine preparations for the birth of Jesus in Bethlehem and ends with the divine exploitation of Roman judicial process that brings Paul to launch his Christian mission in the capital of the empire itself (Acts 28).

Some scholars have suggested that Luke placed the story of Jesus in this larger historical framework as a way of overcoming the embarrassment felt in the early church when the Parousia of Jesus did not occur in the first generation of Christians as expected.[5] The Gospels of Mark and Matthew, however, had already come to terms with the needs of their respective communities as ongoing enterprises, with Matthew offering norms and regulation for members and pointing up the correspondences between Jesus' work and their own. The new feature in Luke is the adoption of an epochal view of history, according to which the story of the human race is depicted as moving through successive stages.

Luke's Epochal View of History

The writing of periodized historical accounts became common in the Hellenistic period, probably through influences from Iran. Already in Hesiod (eighth century B.C.E.) there appeared a scheme of successive ages of the world. In Daniel 7–12, four visions of Daniel depict in symbolic form the powers which dominated the Middle East: The lion is Babylon; the bear is Media; the leopard is Persia; and the strange horned beast represents Alexander and his successors, culminating in the "little horn," who is Antiochus IV Epiphanes, the Seleucid king who desecrated the Temple in Jerusalem and sought to coerce the people of Israel to offer him honors as divine. In contrast to these beasts, the human leader ("one like a son of man," or human being, Dan. 7:13–14) is the one who will establish the eternal Rule of God, which will be administered for and through "the people of the holy ones of the Most High" (Dan. 7:27). Luke represents Jesus as offering a schematic view of history that is unfolding in three stages. The first of these focuses on the events that immediately precede the establishment of God's Rule:

> The law and the prophets were in effect until John came; since then the good news of the Kingdom of God is proclaimed, and every one tries to enter it by force. (Luke 16:16)

The first epoch is presented as preliminary and anticipatory of later events, covering the time of the Law and the Prophets. The second is the present age, when the coming of the Kingdom of God is being proclaimed in words and acts, first by Jesus (phase one) and then by his emissaries (phase two). This period is characterized by conflict: between Jesus and the powers of evil in preparation for the coming of God's Rule, as evident in his exorcisms (Luke 11:20). It will culminate in the third stage: the coming of the Son of Man and the judgment of the world, resulting in the establishment of the Kingdom of God throughout the earth (Luke 17:22–30).[6]

The consummation of God's purpose is variously described as "your redemption" (Luke 21:28), or simply "the Kingdom of God" (21:31), in which Jesus' followers share with him in exercising authority over the twelve tribes of Israel (22:28–30). The transition from the present age into the eschatological age will be marked by the coming or "day" of the Son of Man (17:22–26; 21:27). Another way of referring to the end of the current age is as the fulfillment of "the times of the Gentiles" (21:24). Surprisingly, the destruction of Jerusalem is not seen by Luke as marking the end of this age, as is the case in Mark 13:14–27. Rather, the Roman army's attack on Jerusalem is a warning of the impending "desolation" (Luke 21:20) and of its continuing occupation by pagan rulers until God's Rule is fully established in the world (21:24).

Luke sketches these eschatological events, but his primary interest is in the present age, during which Jesus' followers carry forward the work of preaching and healing for which he commissioned them. That missionary charge was in two stages: The first concerns Jews exclusively; the second includes Gentiles, as is shown by the narrative accounts in Luke (9:1–6, where twelve are sent, presumably to Israel; 10:1–16, where seventy are sent on the Gentile mission) and also in Luke's variant of the Parable of the Supper (14:15–24), where those first invited refuse and the outsiders are welcomed. These include, presumably, both those regarded by strict Jewish ritual standards as outcasts (14:21) and Gentiles (14:23). The central epoch of redemption is inaugurated by the coming of Jesus (Luke 1:2). The redemptive scheme begins with his birth (Luke 2) and will be consummated by his coming in glory (21:27). As we shall see, Luke's two-volume work is occupied with showing how the work of the gospel was launched so that the objective might be ultmately achieved: "All flesh shall see the salvation of our God" (3:6; cf. Mark 1:3; only Luke continues the quotation from Isaiah 40 that far). In his two opening chapters Luke shows how the epoch of redemption, the present age, began.

The Inauguration of the Epoch of Redemption: The Baptist and Infancy Stories

Luke opens his gospel with a report about the childlessness of an aged Jewish couple, Zechariah, a priest, and Elizabeth (Luke 1:5–25). The account is reminiscent of the Old Testament story of Elkanah and Hannah (1 Sam. 1). In each case a son is born to a pious priest after it seemed that his wife was barren; in each case the son is especially dedicated to God, although his greatest task is to prepare the way for someone else—Samuel to anoint Israel's first king, Saul, and John to prepare the way for Jesus. The rhetoric of the prophets (echoing the words of Malachi 4:5, which predict the coming of Elijah before the Last Day) is recalled in the hymn of the angel before Zechariah, the father of John the Baptist:

> With the spirit and power of Elijah, he [John] will go before him
> [Jesus] to turn the hearts of the parents to their children, and the

disobedient to the wisdom of the righteous, to make ready a people prepared for the Lord. (Luke 1:17)

Similarly, the other hymns of Luke's infancy narratives are based on the diction and prophecies of the Old Testament. Mary's Magnificat (1:29–32) closely parallels Hannah's hymn of praise in 1 Samuel 2:1–10.[7] Zechariah's prophesying (Luke 1:67) is patterned after the Psalms of the Old Testament and draws for its content on the prophecies of Isaiah 9 and Malachi 4. Simeon's blessing of God on the occasion of the presentation of the infant Jesus in the Temple incorporates themes from 2 Isaiah:

Master, now you are dismissing your servant in peace,
according to your word;
for my eyes have seen your salvation,
which you have prepared in the presence of all peoples,
a light for revelation to the Gentiles,
and for glory to your people Israel.[8] (Luke 2:29–32)

The point of Simeon's prayer is not merely that prophecy is being fulfilled, but that God's redemptive plan for all humanity—Gentile and Jew—is about to be fulfilled. In short, the long age of preparation that stretched from creation through the days of the prophets is now drawing to a close, not in disappointed hopes, but in eager expectation of fulfillment. Simeon's hymn is not only his own adieu but also a farewell to the age that lived by hope alone. Similarly, John the Baptist[9] has the final role in preparing Israel (Luke 1:80) to receive the one whose coming is to be a source of joy "to all the people" (2:10). The last of these prophetic figures to be described by Luke is Anna, who is God's representative who addresses "all who were looking for the redemption of Jerusalem" (2:38).

But Luke goes beyond the theme of prophetic fulfillment in depicting Jesus' place in God's plan of history. Prophecy drawn from the Hebrew Scriptures was, after all, limited to the Jews. Luke sees God's hand at work in the routine operations of the Roman government, as in the decree attributed to Caesar Augustus requiring all persons to return to their ancestral homes in order to be enrolled in a census. Although such decrees were issued by Augustus in various parts of the empire during his long reign (30 B.C.E.–14 C.E.), the only sure evidence that he did so in Syria-Palestine dates from after the probable time of Jesus' birth.[10] The significance of the event for Luke is that the official action of a pagan ruler became the occasion for Jesus to be born in Bethlehem, the city of David, in fulfillment of the Hebrew prophecy in Micah 5. God's sovereignty over history is thus fully demonstrated. In spite of attempts to explain away Luke's error,[11] it must be concluded that Luke's interest in setting the events of Jesus' life in the context of world history led him to make what is probably an innocent mistake in assigning to the year of Jesus' birth a census that actually occurred a decade later.[12]

The Central Redemptive Events, Phase One: Jesus' Public Career

The launching of the first phase of Luke's second and central epoch, the career of Jesus, is effected in the sermon of Jesus in the synagogue in Nazareth (Luke 4:16–30). It is important to note the Janus-like nature of the sermon and its immediate sequel: The passage looks back to the Old Testament, whose prophecies are seen as being fulfilled in Jesus, and it looks forward to the events of Jesus' ministry, in which the fulfillment itself takes place. With a few quick strokes, Luke paints a picture of Jesus at the synagogue, observing the traditions of worship as they had developed in postexilic Judaism: his habit of regular attendance, his being asked to read and interpret the Scripture as a layman who was presumed by the synagogue community in Nazareth to have something to say worth hearing, the attendant's selection of the scroll of Scripture from its place, the unrolling of the unwieldy scroll to the appropriate point at which to begin reading, and Jesus' sitting down to begin his extemporaneous exposition of the Scripture.[13] More significant than these details, however, is the position of the scene in the gospel: By placing this sermon at the beginning of Jesus' public activity (instead of later on, as in Luke's major source, Mark 6), Luke provides the context and the grand aim for all that Jesus does. The passage chosen to be read, Isaiah 61:1–2, is one of the great eschatological poems of the Old Testament. Its appropriateness here is heightened by the fact that Jesus reads it shortly after he has been anointed with the Spirit at baptism (Luke 3:21–22); thus the words of 2 Isaiah epitomize the gospel that Jesus preached and enacted:

> *The Spirit of the Lord is upon me,*
> *because he has anointed[14] me to bring good news to the poor.*
> *He has sent me to proclaim release to the captives*
> *and recovery of sight to the blind,*
> *to let the oppressed go free,*
> *to proclaim the year of the Lord's favor. (Luke 4:18–19)*

The quotation that Luke takes from Isaiah serves as a kind of program for the ministry of Jesus as Luke represents it. The final element, proclaiming the acceptable year of the Lord, is important for Luke's schematization of history, which is depicted here as unfolding in accord with the divine plan. The link between the prophecy of Isaiah and the activity of Jesus is made explicit in the words attributed to Jesus (Luke 4:21): "Today this scripture has been fulfilled in your hearing." The details of the miracles, especially specific features of thaumaturgic or exorcistic technique, tend to be played down in Luke, with the result that the emphasis in his miracle stories is more often on the power of faith than on the act of healing (cf. Luke 7:1–10 with Matt. 8:5–13), or on the miracles as the fulfillment of Scripture (as in the location of the string of miracle stories following the report of Jesus' sermon in Nazareth).

Stress on fulfillment of Scriptures makes all the more appropriate Luke's appeal to two of the most familiar miracle workers of the Old Testament as paradigms for Jesus' activity: Elijah and Elisha. In the face of the opposition that Jesus' claim immediately arouses, Luke (4:25–27) appeals to two incidents in their lives. Each prophet, rejected in his own land and among his own people, turned to non-Jews (or non-Israelites) as the beneficiaries of the prophetic healing power. It was in the land of Sidon (Phoenicia) that Elijah and the hospitable widow were miraculously sustained during a long drought (1 Kings 17:8–16). It was a leprous Syrian officer who benefited from the restorative powers of Elisha (2 Kings 5:1–14). The illustrations chosen by Jesus, with their implicit criticism of Israel's lack of faith, evoke hostility from the worshipers in the synagogue who try to destroy Jesus. Thus, at the very outset of Jesus' career, his rejection by some of the Jews and his acceptance by some Gentiles are portrayed as an outworking of the ancient pattern laid down in Scripture and now fully revealed in the "acceptable year of the Lord."[15]

Just as Elijah and Elisha carried out their work by the power of God's Spirit (1 Kings 18:12; 2 Kings 2:9–16), so the Spirit empowers Jesus and his followers. In the second volume of his work Luke gives a summary of the career of Jesus (Acts 10:36–43) that moves from the launching of Jesus' activity of preaching and healing, through his confrontation with the authorities in Jerusalem, his death and resurrection, and his commissioning of his followers as "witnesses" whose work will continue until he is manifested as the "one ordained by God to be the judge of the living and the dead." This account presented as a sermon by Peter, which is an essential step by which Luke depicts the transition from the ministry of Jesus to that of his apostles: They are sent forth in Jesus' name and in the power of the same Spirit (Acts 1:8) that came upon him at the outset of his career (Luke 3:22; 4:18).

The description of Jesus' ministry begins at 4:31, at the point where Luke resumes the sequence of the Markan narrative (cf. Mark 1:21). The general strategy of the ministry has already been indicated in the transitional verses, Luke 4:14–15, where Luke turns from the preparatory phases (birth, baptism, temptation) to the appropriate scene of Jesus' activity: Galilee.

> Then Jesus, filled with the power of the Spirit, returned [that is, from the Jordan Valley] to Galilee, and a report about him spread through all the surrounding country. He began to teach in their synagogues, and was praised by everyone. (Luke 4:18–19)

The Ministry in Galilee

For Luke, Galilee is the place of public manifestation and favorable response, just as Jerusalem is the place of rejection and passion. The geographical movement of Jesus, therefore, is not simply historical recollection, nor is it even strictly accurate. Rather, it functions in a symbolic way and as evidence of a divinely determined scheme as Luke understands it.[16] We shall see how important for Luke is the shift of scene from Galilee to Jerusalem.

The straightforward Markan account of Jesus' calling of the disciples (Mark 1:16–20), which is reproduced with little change in Matthew (4:18–20), becomes in Luke (5:1–11) an extended miracle story, rich in symbolic detail pointing to the world mission of the church. The nearest parallel in the gospel tradition is the story in John 21:1–11, where the risen Lord commissions the church to carry out its "fishing" task in obedience to this word, not merely in reliance on its own resources.[17] Far from preserving, as a fiction writer would, the illusion that the ministry of Jesus unfolded in a series of events that could not have been anticipated by the participants, Luke (5:4) tips off his reader well in advance, in Jesus' words to Simon, as to the divinely intended scope of the church's mission: "Put out into the deep...." The rest of Luke–Acts tells how this enlargement of scope came about, first through Jesus and then through the apostles, and especially Paul.

Luke follows with only slight variation Mark's order from 5:12 (= Mark 1:40) to 6:16 (= Mark 3:19). But just before introducing his

Sermon on the Plain (6:20–49), Luke modifies slightly the list of names of the disciples and identifies them also as apostles (cf. Mark 3:13–19 with Luke 6:12–16). Although Luke's version of the Q material in the Sermon is not nearly so full as Matthew's Sermon on the Mount (Matt. 5–7), Luke presents it in the same sequence as Matthew, which suggests that they used a common document as the basis for their reconstructed sermons. The Q material continues in Luke from 7:1 to 7:35, with the insertion at 7:11–17 of a uniquely Lukan pericope (the Widow's Son at Nain), which is the first of a long series of stories about women that are found only in Luke. This story of Jesus healing a widow's son is reminiscent, as were Jesus' words at the end of his sermon in the Nazareth synagogue, of the miracles of Elijah and Elisha in 1 Kings 17 and 2 Kings 4. It is not surprising, therefore, that Luke reports that Jesus was acclaimed as a "great prophet." Luke's version of Jesus' answer to the question of John the Baptist about his possible role in the purpose of God ("Are you the one who is to come?" 7:18–13) makes explicit the link between Jesus' healing of the ailing and his preaching "good news to the poor" and the saving role promised in the prophets (Isa. 29:18–19; 35:5–6; 61:1).

Two more stories about women follow immediately. One (Luke 7:36–50) reads like an expanded variant of Mark's story (Mark 14:3–9 = Matt. 26:6–13) in which a woman anoints Jesus on the eve of his crucifixion, "beforehand for burying" (Mark 14:8). But in keeping with Luke's emphasis on Jesus' message of God's gracious forgiveness, the story demonstrates Jesus' accepting stance toward a sinner. Elsewhere in the gospel tradition, "Your faith has saved you" means "Your faith has made possible your being healed," but in Luke 7:50, it means "You have been granted divine forgiveness." The theme of forgiveness as the chief feature of salvation was sounded in the prophetic oracle of Zechariah in the infancy narrative, where salvation is linked with the forgiveness of sins, light in darkness, and access to the way of peace (Luke 1:77–79). It is emphatically repeated in the apostles' preaching in Acts (10:43; 13:38; 26:18), and the theme of penitent Gentiles turning to God brings Acts to a close (28:27–29). In this way Luke underscores the continuity between the message of Jesus and that of his apostolic messengers in the author's own time.

Luke resumes Mark's sequence at the point where the parables of the Kingdom are introduced (Mark 4:1 = Luke 8:4). Whenever Luke departs from the Markan order here, he includes that material (Mark 3:19–35) at later points (Luke 11:1–23) where it better serves his purpose of demonstrating the mounting conflict in the period after Jesus turns toward Jerusalem (Luke 9:51). The miracle stories follow in the Markan order, from the Stilling of the Storm (Mark 4:35–41 = Luke 8:22–25) to the Raising of Jairus' Daughter (Mark 5:43 = Luke 8:56). And with a few omissions,[18] the sequence continues through the story of the Feeding of the Five Thousand (Luke 9:10–17 = Mark 6:30–44). From that point, Luke leaps over the Markan material to the account of the confession of Peter and the first prediction of the Passion.[19]

Luke usually condenses the narrative taken over from Mark, although he underscores the divinity of Jesus, as in 9:20, where Jesus is expressly called "the Christ of God," and in 9:43, the story of Jesus' healing the epileptic child, which is described as a manifestation of "the majesty of God." At one crucial point, however, an extended Lukan addition to Mark (cf. Luke 9:30–31 with Mark 9:4) discloses the subject of the conversation of Jesus, Moses, and Elijah at the transfiguration: Jesus' departure *(exodos)* from this life, which was soon to take place in Jerusalem, and which will be an event analogous to the historic Exodus of Israel from Egypt by which the covenant people was initially formed. Luke is offering his reader clear indications not only of the fact of Jesus' passion but also of the place where it will occur, and assuring them that all this was in accord with the divinely determined plan for the creation of the new covenant people. That Moses and Elijah are able to converse on the subject shows that it is predicted in Scripture, which for Luke is tantamount to saying it is predetermined by God.

As we have observed, it is in keeping with Luke's conviction that the Jews had the first opportunity to hear the gospel.[20] The twelve disciples are reported as being sent out to preach, to heal, and to perform exorcisms, presumably among Jews, though Luke does not say so explicitly. The number twelve (Luke 9:10–17) is probably intended to symbolize the twelve tribes of Israel, as it does in Acts 6:1–2, where the "twelve" are chosen from among the Hebrews. In contrast, after Jesus has begun his final, fateful journey toward Jerusalem, another mission is launched; but this time its intended audience is the Gentiles, as reflected in the selection of seventy disciples, symbolizing the number of Gentile nations according to Jewish tradition of the period (Luke 10:1–20).[21]

The Journey to Jerusalem

The first prediction of the Passion (Luke 9:18–22) provides the beginning of the transition to Luke's section on the journey to Jerusalem, but the locale of the Passion is not specified until the transfiguration story, as we have seen. It is in Luke 9:51, however, that the journey actually gets under way. Twice in the pericope (9:51–56) Luke declares that Jesus "set his face to go to Jerusalem." Clearly, Jesus is dedicating himself to the outworking of the divine plan, as Luke sees it, which requires that the death of God's messenger occur in Jerusalem. But it is not until 13:31–33 that the link between Jerusalem and the Passion is made explicit: "It cannot be that a prophet should perish away from Jerusalem."

The material between these two statements about Jesus' going to Jerusalem is drawn almost entirely from Q and from Luke's own special source.[22] There is very little actual narrative, apart from the story of the sending of the seventy messengers and their return. The pericope about Mary and Martha, the devoted sister and the diligent sister, respectively, is more like a parable than a narrative (Luke 10:38–42). The single miracle story (13:10–17) is seemingly less concerned with the health of the woman (that problem is handled in three verses) than with Jesus' setting aside the Sabbath law, since his act of healing was regarded as a form of work. The story clearly reveals the influence of controversy between church and synagogue in the writer's time, in addition to preserving part of the record of Jesus' healing activity.

The rest of this section contains eight parables, some of them quite brief: the Good Samaritan (10:29–37), the Friend at Midnight (11:5–8), the Rich Fool (12:13–21), the Faithful Servants (12:35–38), the Servant's Wages (12:47–48), Settlement Out of Court (12:57–59), the Unproductive Fig Tree (13:6–9), and the Late Guest (13:25–27). In addition, Luke includes many short parabolic words or phrases. There are two major themes in this material. The first is the call to be compassionate toward those who are in need. The second is the urgency of repentance, a point that is made explicitly in the sayings about the sign of Jonah (11:31–32) and in Jesus' reply to the question about whose sin it was that resulted in certain catastrophes (13:1–5): "Unless you repent you will all likewise perish."

Another theme that runs throughout this section is that of the disciples' blessedness, revealed in the special insight into God's purpose that he has granted to them. As we might expect, this motif is drawn largely from such Q passages as Luke 10:21–24 and 11:9–13, where the privileges of the true children of God are described. Luke adds to the gifts of grace the promise of the bestowal of the Holy Spirit (11:13). The term *Spirit* probably did not appear in the Q version, but it does figure prominently and pervasively in Luke's second volume, the Book of Acts, from the promise of the Spirit and the vivid account of the outpouring of the Spirit at Pentecost through the rest of the book. From Acts 2:16–21 we learn that the outpouring of the Spirit is to be regarded as an eschatological sign in fulfillment of the prophecy of Joel 2:28–32. In both Acts and Luke's gospel, the Spirit is accessible for all of humanity ("all flesh"), a point that fits nicely with the prominent position Luke gives to the promise of the Spirit in the gospel narrative, just after the mission of the seventy to the Gentiles. Luke follows the pericope with his own modification of the tradition so that it now announces God's offer of the gift of the Spirit:

> How much more will the heavenly Father give the Holy Spirit to those who ask him? (Luke 11:13)

Similar declarations of the blessedness are present in sayings unique to Luke. In Luke 11:27–28 Jesus pronounces more blessed than the mother that bore and nurtured him the follower who obeys God's word. In 12:32, the Kingdom is spoken of as a gift of God to his own flock. Mention of God's "good pleasure" recalls the message of the angel (2:14) "On earth peace among those whom he favors!"[23]

The promise of the Kingdom leads into a series of sayings, widely scattered in the Matthean parallels, which Luke has brought together and in which the recurrent theme is that of preparedness for the coming of the Judgment (12:33–13:9). The urgency of the decision of faith is stressed in parables and sayings, culminating in a final pericope—reportedly spoken by Jesus on the way to Jerusalem (13:22)—in which the finality of the Judgment is depicted under the image of the closed door (13:25). Only the truly faithful will be admitted to the eschatological feast, at which will be gathered the ancient worthies, Abraham and the other patriarchs, and the faithful Gentiles ("from east and west"). But those who heard Jesus—and those who heard his messengers—and failed to repent will not be invited to "sit at table in the kingdom of God." Luke is letting his reader know what the end of the final epoch will be like, since one's response to Jesus now will be the decisive factor in how one fares on the Day of Judgment.

The transition to the third phase of Jesus' ministry, the Passion in Jerusalem, is extensive. Although there is no indication in the narrative of actual progress from Galilee to Jerusalem once the journey through the Samaritan villages has been described (9:51–56), Luke reminds his readers repeatedly that Jerusalem is now Jesus' goal. The vivid account of the Pharisees' rumor that Herod Antipas intends to kill Jesus and Jesus' response to the rumor suggest that Jesus left Galilee not to escape Herod but to conform to the divine plan:

> At that very hour some Pharisees came and said to him, "Get away from here, for Herod wants to kill you." He said to them, "Go and tell that fox for me, 'Listen, I am casting out demons and performing cures today and tomorrow, and on the third day I finish my work. Yet today, tomorrow, and the next day I must be on my way, because it is impossible for a prophet to be killed outside of Jerusalem.'" (Luke 13:31–33)

By enumerating the days, Luke is pointing to the divinely ordained sequence of events, not presenting a literal timetable. Jesus' ministry must continue until the Passion takes place, and the Passion can occur only in Jerusalem. Luke follows the announcement of the Jerusalem journey with the Q pericope, the lament over Jerusalem (13:34–35), which Matthew included in his expanded version of the prediction of the destruction of the Temple (Matt. 23:37–39). Luke is telling his reader that Jesus' death is part of the outworking of God's plan of history and that Jesus foresees it in this way throughout the second half of his ministry. The general implications of the predictions of the Passion that Luke takes over from Mark are made more specific so that in Luke they detail the inexorable movement from Galilee to the place of the Passion, Jerusalem.

As was true in the section between 9:51 and 13:33, Luke has strung together parables and sayings (many of which are parabolic), nearly all of which point to eschatological judgment or blessing. Exceptions are the Healing of the Man with Dropsy (14:1–6) and the sayings about divorce (16:18), temptations to sin (17:1–2), forgiveness (17:3–4), faith (17:5–6), and fidelity (17:7–10). Otherwise, even sayings that seem to concern ethical questions, such as the parable about humility (14:7–14), the saying about children (18:15–17 = Mark 10:13–16), and the reply to the ruler's question (18:18–30 = Mark 10:17–32), are set in a context where the issue is one's fate in the eschatological judgment. The parables are either explicitly eschatological, as in the Great Supper (14:15–24), the Prudent Builder and the Prudent Warrior (14:28–33), the Unjust Steward (16:1–13), the Rich Man and Lazarus (16:19–31), or else they depict the joy of God over a sinner's repentance, as in the Joyous Shepherd, the Joyous Housewife, the Joyous Father (15:1–32). The Parable of the Unjust Judge (18:1–8) is given eschatological connotations by the addition of the concluding question, "When the Son of Man comes, will he find faith on earth?" Similarly, the generalizing conclusion to the pericope about the Pharisee and the Publican (18:9–14) reminds the reader that God is the one who will do the final humbling of the impenitent and the exalting of the faithful on the Last Day.

The Passion

The final section of Luke's account of Jesus' ministry begins with the third prediction of the Passion (18:31–33), as taken from Mark (10:32–34) and adapted by Luke:

> Then he took the twelve aside and said to them, "See, we are going up to Jerusalem, and everything that is written about the Son of man by the prophets will be accomplished." (Luke 18:31)

The rest of the prediction Luke reproduced from Mark without important change, except that he added the statement that the disciples did not and could not understand this prediction because its meaning was "hidden from them" (18:34). This implies that God concealed its meaning from them, even though the fate of Jesus (= the Son of Man) was in fulfillment of the words of the prophets. There is nothing in the Old Testament prophets about the suffering of the Son of Man, and in the late (probably first century C.E. or later) apocalyptic writings where the Son of Man appears, he is a triumphant figure and nothing is indicated of his suffering.[24] Luke uses the title Son of Man for Jesus in terms of his earthly authority, suffering, and return in triumph, just as Mark does (pp. 126, 139–40). Whether this meaning originated with Jesus or is read back into the account of Jesus' earthly ministry is impossible to determine. In either case, Luke's use of the saying makes it serve his purpose well, since the fact that it was written by the prophets shows it to be a part of the divine plan for history, and the fact that it is being fulfilled shows that God is achieving his purpose through the death of Jesus and his resurrection "on the third day" (18:33).

On the whole, the narrative of Jesus' journey through Jericho follows that of Mark, but with some highly significant departures. The story of the tax collector, Zacchaeus, who received Jesus (Luke 19:1–10) is an instance of the receptivity to the gospel on the part of the outcasts ("the poor" are the outsiders, not merely the economically deprived) who hear it and respond in faith. The collaboration of the tax collectors with the Romans, the physical contacts they inevitably had with ritually unclean material being shipped through the land of the Jews, and the wealth they were able to gain from taking on this role made them despicable in the eyes of pious and nationalistic Jews. The point of this story contrasts sharply with that of the parable, originally from Q, that Luke inserted at this point (19:11–27) and drastically reshaped to suit his purpose, adding details about the man who journeyed far to have himself confirmed as king. Matthew's version is probably more original,[25] but Luke tells his reader that the parable is relevant for those who expect the End of the Age immediately (19:11). This can only mean that Luke understands the parable as an allegory in which Jesus has gone to heaven to await his installation on earth as king. The citizens who hate him are unbelieving religious leaders, who collaborate with the Romans to maintain their status, and who claim to possess for themselves the Kingdom of God. When the king (Christ as judge) returns at the End of the Age, he will reward the faithful and slay the wicked, "who did not want me to reign over them" (19:27).

For dramatic effect, Luke inserted in the Markan narrative of Jesus' entry into Jerusalem an oracle spoken just as Jesus reached the crest of the Mount of Olives, where he could see the city of Jerusalem spread out below. The prophecy (19:39–44) is very specific about the siege of the city and the ramparts thrown up to prevent the escape of the besieged people of Jerusalem ("Your enemies will cast up a bank about you and surround you"), which is a description that coincides with the fate of the city as Josephus depicts it in his *Jewish Wars*.[26] The slaughter of the inhabitants of the city and the destruction of its marvelous buildings are likewise fully attested by Josephus. What Luke did was to amplify the theme in Mark 13:1–2 concerning the destruction of the Temple (which is reproduced in Luke 21:5–6) in such a way as to make Jesus envision the ruin of the city as a whole. It is clear that this event had already occurred at the time Luke was writing. Far from sensing anything unethical in representing this description as a prediction, Luke seized the opportunity to demonstrate how the course of such visible, worldly events as the sacking of a provincial city by the Roman legions was the outworking of God's plan.

Luke picked up this theme again in his version of the apocalyptic discourse (Luke 21:20 = Mark 13:14), where he replaced Mark's vague reference to "the desolating sacrilege" with the concrete "Jerusalem surrounded by armies." The succeeding verses continue the theme of the destruction of the city, rather than portending the

End of the Age. Indeed, Luke reports Jesus as predicting that there will be an extended period of indefinite extent, "the times of the Gentiles," during which "Jerusalem will be trodden down by the Gentiles" (21:24). Only when this time is "fulfilled" will the end come. The Markan notion of the imminent end has been played down; instead, Luke calls for patient and pious waiting—and in Acts, for intensive and extensive mission activity throughout the world (Acts 1:8)—until the Son of Man appears (21:34–36).

It is important for Luke's purpose to report that during the days of Jesus' witness in Jerusalem, "early in the morning all the people came to him in the temple to hear him" (21:38). His testimony was available to the entire populace, Luke suggests, so that Jerusalem can never offer the excuse that it had no opportunity to hear Jesus' message. This is, of course, an important ingredient in Luke's understanding of the divine scheme of the spread of the gospel, beginning "in Jerusalem ... and [extending] to the end of the earth" (Act 1:8).

The detailed differences between Luke's and Mark's passion narratives are such that some interpreters think Luke used a source other than Mark in this part of his gospel.[27] It is more likely that he amplified Mark's account by drawing on his own written or oral sources, and that he modified the whole to suit his theological aims. We can find three "historical" motifs in the service of Luke's theological aims at work in Luke 23:4–16. First, to the Markan account of Jesus' hearing before Pilate (Mark 15:2–5) Luke adds Pilate's remark that he can find no crime in Jesus,[28] thereby strengthening his case that no Gentile ruler was ever able to show that Jesus or his followers were lawbreakers, so that Christianity is not to be regarded as a subversive force in history. This same claim is made of the apostles, and especially of Paul, as they are brought before the civil authorities and in each case exonerated from charges of fomenting civil disorder. The second point is seen in Luke's historical tracing of the geographical movement in the two main phases of Jesus' ministry, which he summarizes for his readers as follows: "... teaching throughout all Judea, from Galilee even to this place" (23:5). All parts of Palestine were covered by Jesus during his ministry, culminating in the confrontation with the religious authorities in Jerusalem. The third motif is the care with which Luke seeks to show how Jesus and the beginnings of Christianity were involved with the secular rulers of the time; hence, it is important to report the hearing held by Herod Antipas (Luke 23:6–16), who felt authorized to examine Jesus on the ground that he was tetrarch of the territory where Jesus' public activity had begun. No charges were made, and the accused Jesus was returned to Pilate with no evidence of his guilt.

Luke's version of the Crucifixion of Jesus differs considerably from those in the other Gospels. Jesus addresses the women of the city, warning of the destruction that is going to fall on the city of Jerusalem because the religious leaders refuse to accept him as God's agent of renewal (23:27–31), and from the cross he asks God to forgive those who are putting him to death (23:34–35). Instead of the declaration by the leaders that Jesus cannot save himself, though he claims to be the Christ (Matt. 27:42; Mark 15:31), Luke reports that they challenge him to save himself (23:35). Joining in the scoffing is one of the criminals (23:39), but his remark is countered by the other criminal's declaration of Jesus' innocence and a petition to him for remembrance when he enters his kingdom (23:40–42). There is an ironic convergence in Luke's story between the scoffing denial of Jesus' messiahship and the inscription placed above the cross, identifying him as "King of the Jews."

Instead of the lament that precedes his death in Mark 15:34 and Matthew 27:46, in Luke's account Jesus simply entrusts his spirit to God (23:46; quoting Psalm 31:5). His response to the penitent criminal makes an important point for Luke's understanding of the program for God's purpose in the world: Jesus at death will go directly to be with God, where there will also be present those who died in faith (23:43). The Galilean identity of the women at the cross, as indicated in Mark 15:40–41 is repeated in Luke (23:49, 55), in keeping with Luke's testimony that his report is based on eyewitnesses "from the beginning" (1:4). Although the redemptive work of Jesus began in Galilee, it is in Jerusalem that it reaches the next, crucial stage in its unfolding: the appearance of Jesus risen from the dead.

Phase Two: Rejection in Jerusalem Brings Opportunity for the World

According to Luke, it was near Jerusalem, not in Galilee, that the disclosure of the risen Lord occurred (Luke 24:13–53). The obtuseness of the disciples in their initial conversation with Jesus after the Resurrection is apparent: They had thought of him as a mighty prophet, who might redeem Israel on its own terms. It is in the exposition of the Scriptures that the meaning of Jesus and of God's purpose through him is communicated to the disciples. But, significantly, it is in the Eucharist that he is "made known" to them (24:35). Except for apologetic lines, which seek to combat a purely spiritual concept of the Resurrection of Jesus and which therefore offer proof of the corporeality of the risen Jesus, the main force of the concluding section of Luke is to affirm the real presence of Christ among his people: in the interpretation of the Scriptures and in the Eucharist. That the threefold Hebrew canon—Law, prophets, and Psalms—has its fulfillment in Jesus attests that he is the one through whom the redemptive purpose of God is being consummated.

But there is one further evidence of the invisible presence of Christ among his people, as Luke perceives it. This is the Holy Spirit, which is promised to the faithful (24:49) and which will provide the power for them to carry out their world mission, "beginning in Jerusalem." The Book of Acts is the account of how that mission was launched, following the outpouring of the Spirit (Acts 2).

To the modern reader, it might seem incongruous to alternate accounts of Jesus' postresurrection appearances (Luke 24:13–49; Acts 1:3) with presentations of his Ascension (Luke 24:50–53; Acts 1:6–9). It is important for Luke's purposes, however, that all these elements stand in his report. Of first importance is the Ascension, which is an essential element in Luke's scheme, since he must show that Christ is now bodily removed from the earthly scene and bodily present at God's right hand, and that he will bodily return:

> This Jesus, who has been taken up from you into heaven, will come in the same way as you saw him go into heaven. (Acts 1:11)

It is in such a framework of space and time that Luke placed the earthly and the risen Jesus, the central figure in the unfolding of God's plan of history.

In the distinctive narratives of the appearances of the risen Christ are several other motifs that were clearly of special importance for the Lukan community. There is a stress on the bodily nature of the resurrected Jesus, who invites his followers to inspect his hands and his feet as well as to handle him, so that they can be assured that "it is I myself" and not a "ghost." In addition to serving to combat the view that flourished in the early second century that Jesus' resurrection was not bodily but purely spiritual, this story makes all the more emphatic his absence from earth and his ongoing presence in heaven. That is the point of Acts 1:11: Just as he went up to heaven, so he shall return. Furthermore, by the heavenly vision of a dying martyr, Stephen, he can be seen to be in heaven in the present age of the church (Acts 7:55). This provides a dimension of concreteness to the church's expectation of his appearance in glory at the Consummation of the Age.

Furthermore, these postresurrection stories show how the community saw itself as sustained in the period of waiting: through sharing in the Eucharist (Luke 24:30, 35) and in the Christian exposition of the Scriptures (24:25–27, 32). The issue of fidelity was a paramount concern for Luke's community, as may be inferred from the special emphasis placed on faithfulness and perseverance (18:8; 12:46; 21:36; 9:57–62). The sufferings of the faithful are pointed to specifically, as in 22:28, and are exemplified by the faithful messengers of Jesus in Acts, from Stephen through Paul, both of whom are martyred (Acts 7:59; 20:18–38).

Finally, Jesus is portrayed as "a prophet mighty in word and deed" (Luke 24:19), who commissions his followers to carry forward his work (24:47–49) by the power of the Spirit. The Kingdom of God, whose consummation is eagerly awaited, was already manifested through the words and acts of Jesus during his earthly ministry (8:1; 11:20; 16:16; 17:20–21). The program sketched in Jesus' sermon in Nazareth ("good news to the poor … sight to the blind … release to the captives" [Luke 4:18]) is assigned to the members of the community. The story of the miraculous catch of fish became for Luke an allegory of their mission (5:1–11). His expanded version of the story of Jesus' call to his disciples (Mark 1:16–20) gives richly symbolic meaning to the work he is calling them to do. The astonishing results of their evangelistic activity will force them to acknowledge their own limitations and the necessity for them to rely on the power God provides. Yet, Luke also reckons with the fact that the protraction of the period before the Consummation will result in the lapse of many from their commitment to Jesus (12:42–46) and even in the fall of some into profligate life-styles ("weighed down with dissipation and drunkenness and cares of this life," 21:34). The faithful, however, rest confident in God's vindication of them (18:8).

In spite of his call for unswerving devotion to the Kingdom of God and to its consummation on the earth, Luke carefully points out that neither Jesus nor the followers whose story is told in Acts were ever accurately charged with political subversion. The details of the trials of Jesus before Jewish and Roman authorities have been carefully modified by Luke to remove "any semblance of legitimacy" in his interrogation by the religious leaders and to show that Roman involvement was minimal. The rare lapse in Roman justice that resulted in the death of Jesus was an unusual succumbing "to the chaos of unlawful men," but it occurred "in order to set in motion the plan of God" for human redemption. Whenever Jesus or the apostles were brought up before the civil authorities, political charges could not be made to stick (Acts 16:39; 18:14–16; 19:37; 23:29; 25:8; 25:25; 26:32). This does not suggest that Luke–Acts was written as a political apology for Christianity, but rather that Christians were being counseled to maintain a nonpolitical stance, in keeping with the tradition that went back to Jesus and Paul.[29]

Luke As Historian

Luke had historical interests and skills that went beyond the scheme of theological history outlined in this chapter. He was able to write with verisimilitude, especially in the infancy stories, using an intentionally archaic language echoing the Septuagintal version of the Jewish Scriptures in order to give the flavor of an era and a culture—early first-century Palestine—that were not his own.[30] He possessed the historian's imagination. But he also possessed the historian's concern for careful use of his sources. We are under obligation to him for reproducing faithfully most of the Q document, as well as the parables and sayings that he alone has recorded, which give us some of our most important clues concerning the message of Jesus.

Although in a broad way Luke manifests greater kinship with formal literature of his time than do the other evangelists, the material itself was not easily transposed into formal history, since it was dependent on the traditions and social needs of the community for whom Luke was writing.[31] The stylistic feature by which parallels are drawn implicitly between central characters in the narratives—between Jesus and John the Baptist, between Jesus and Paul, between the activities of Jesus and those of the apostles—suggests that Luke is consciously following the pattern used by Hellenistic writers for presenting the lives of philosophers. But the absence of the typical summaries of the "philosophical doctrines" of Jesus and Paul shows that literary analogy is at best approximate.[32] The narrative portions of Acts have as their model the so-called Hellenistic romances, which were written as propaganda for the worship of various deities in the Greco-Roman world, especially Isis and Dionysus.[33]

In spite of some inaccuracies, Luke furnished what slim evidence we have for correlating the rise of Christianity chronologically with the history of the period. By modifying the tradition to make it more comprehensible for non-Jewish readers, he made more effective the

communication of the gospel to Gentiles. But perhaps most important of all, by replacing the Markan apocalyptic scheme of an imminent End of the Age with an epochal pattern of an ongoing church
with its own place in the economy of God, Luke must have helped
to prevent many early Christians from despairing when their apocalyptic hopes were not realized. And his perspectives on the church in
the divine plan gave it an understanding of itself and its mission that
has enabled it to function in spite of the passing of nearly two millennia since the prediction was reportedly uttered, "This generation
will not pass away before all these things take place" (Mark 13:30).
Whereas Matthew placed Jesus in the history of the church, Luke
placed the church and Jesus in the history of the world.

By using the popular narrative and other literary styles of its
time, by linking the events of Jesus with those of the empire and the
wider world, by underscoring the public nature of the life and work of
Jesus (and of the apostles in Acts), the Lukan community was making the point expressed indirectly in Acts 26:26: "This did not take
place hidden away in a corner!"

Suggestions for Further Reading

Pioneer work on the special aims of Luke was done by H.J. Cadbury,
The Making of Luke–Acts, 2d ed. (Naperville, IL: Allenson, 1958),
and Martin Dibelius, *Studies in the Acts of the Apostles** (London: SCM
Press, 1956). On the theological interests of Luke, see especially
Hans Conzelmann, *The Theology of St. Luke* (New York: Harper
Brothers, 1961), and Helmut Flender, *Saint Luke: Theologian of
Redemptive History* (Philadelphia: Fortress, 1967). Jacob Jervell, *Luke
and the People of God* (Minneapolis: Augsburg, 1972) stresses that (1)
Paul's evaluation of the faith of the local congregations as essential
to the spread of the gospel was in line with Luke–Acts' portrayal of a
developing apostolic tradition; and that (2) Luke regarded Israel
alone as God's people, so that the conversion of Jews provided the
essential transition to the inclusion of Gentiles within "Israel." Since
the parables are especially revealing of Luke's aims, see the relevant
portions of Joachim Jeremias, *The Parables of Jesus,* 6th ed. (New
York: Scribner's, 1971); for Luke's special version of the Passion
narrative, see also Joachim Jeremias, *The Eucharistic Words of Jesus,*
2d ed. (Naperville, IL: Allenson, 1966). An excellent survey of the

thought of Luke is by Joseph A. Fitzmyer, *Luke the Theologian: Aspects of His Teaching* * (Mahwah, NJ: Paulist Press, 1989).

Important studies of the community in and for which Luke–Acts was produced, with attention to social and political features are P.F. Esler, *Community and Gospel in Luke–Acts: The Social and Political Motivations of Lucan Theology* (Cambridge: Cambridge University Press, 1987); and Paul S. Walaskay, *"And So We Came to Rome" The Political Perspective of St. Luke* (Cambridge and New York: Cambridge University Press, 1983).

Two useful older commentaries on Luke are E.E. Ellis, *The Gospel of Luke* (London: Thomas Nelson, 1967), and G.B. Caird, *The Gospel of St. Luke* * (Baltimore: Penguin, 1964), but the most comprehensive and insightful are the two-volume work of Joseph A. Fitzmyer, *The Gospel According to Luke (I–IX)* (Garden City, NY: Doubleday, 1981) and *The Gospel According to Luke (XII–XIV)*, 1985; and Luke Timothy Johnson, *The Gospel of Luke* in Sacra Pagina Series, ed. D.J. Harrington (Collegeville, MN: Liturgical Press, 1991). Useful are the *Studies in Luke–Acts*, ed. J.L. Martyn and L.E. Keck (Nashville: Abingdon, 1966), which includes essays on Luke and on the relationship between Luke's viewpoint and the viewpoints of other New Testament writers; and C.H. Talbert, ed., *Perspectives on Luke–Acts* (Danville, VA: Association of Baptist Professors of Religion, 1978).

*Available in a paperback edition.

NOTES

[1] See for example Martin Dibelius, *Studies in the Acts of the Apostles* (trans. Mary Ling; London: SCM Press, 1956), p. 136. For a survey of Lukan studies and theories about the origins of the Gospel of Luke, Joseph A. Fitzmyer, in the Anchor Bible, *The Gospel According to Luke (I–IX)* (Garden City, NY: Doubleday, 1981). An important series of studies bearing on Luke and Acts is being edited at Tyndale House, Cambridge, under the general title *The Book of Acts in Its First Century Setting*. Of the projected six volumes, three have appeared: Vol. 1, *The Book of Acts in Its Ancient Literary Setting*, ed. Bruce W. Winter and Andrew D. Clarke; Vol. 2, *The Book of Acts in Its Graeco-Roman Setting*, ed. David W.F. Gill and Conrad Gempf (Carlisle, Cumbria: Paternoster Press; and Grand Rapids, MI: Eerdmans, 1993, 1994); Vol. 3, *The Book of Acts and Paul in Roman Custody*, by Brian Rapske; soon to appear is Vol. 4, *The Book of Acts in Its Palestinian Setting* by Richard Bauckham; to be published later are Vol. 5, *The Book of Acts in Its Diaspora Setting* and Vol. 6, *The Book of Acts in Its Theological Setting*.

[2] "Luke" is used here to designate the writer of the single two-volume work, *Luke–Acts*, but the authorship of the work is in fact unknown. Attribution

to Luke is perhaps nothing more than an ancient conjecture. The assumption that *Luke–Acts* was written by a companion of Paul (note the "we" passages in Acts 16:10 and 20:5) is an inference from Colossians 4:14 and 2 Timothy 4:11. For a discussion of the work's authorship, see W.G. Kümmel, *Introduction to the New Testament*, 17th ed. (trans. H.C. Kee; Nashville: Abingdon, 1975), pp. 122–51. The finest and most detailed recent study of Luke is that of Joseph A. Fitzmyer, in *The Gospel According to Luke I–IX* and *The Gospel According to Luke X–XXIV* (The Anchor Bible 28 and 28A; New York: Doubleday, 1981 and 1985).

[3]Not Herod the Great, who died in 4 B.C.E., but Herod Antipas (reigned 4 B.C.E.–39 C.E.).

[4]Lysanias was the name of a governor of Abilene executed by Mark Antony in 36 B.C.E., but Josephus mentions that a territory called "Abila of Lysanias" was assigned to Herod Agrippa I in 42 C.E., thus implying that Lysanias was a recent ruler. If the reference were to the earlier Lysanias, Luke's reference would be an anachronism. See Josephus, *Antiquities of the Jews* XIX.5.1, vol. 9 (trans. L.H. Feldman) Loeb Classical Library (Cambridge, MA: Harvard University Press, 1957). Joseph Fitzmyer has noted that several Greek inscriptions from Syria mention a Lysanias, but Abilene was a tiny district and there is no clear indication why Luke mentions it, unless he was from that place. For details see Joseph Fitzmyer, *The Gospel of Luke I–IX*, pp. 457–58.

[5]Ernst Käsemann noted in one of his essays published under the general title *New Testament Questions of Today* (Philadelphia: Fortress, 1969) that Luke is "the first representative of nascent early catholicism." Käsemann thus places Luke in the period of "transition from earliest Christianity to the so-called ancient church, which is completed with the disappearance of the imminent expectation [of Jesus' coming at the End of the Age]." In his view, primitive Christian eschatology, which was the dynamic force of New Testament preaching, is in eclipse in Luke and in other later New Testament writings, where it survives solely as a formal, doctrinal statement about the Last Things. But in Luke the focus has shifted from the imminent End of the Age to the task that the new community and its leaders are to perform in spreading the Good News "to the ends of the earth" (Acts 1:8). This theme is traced by Jacob Jervell in *Luke and the People of God: A New Look at Luke–Acts* (Minneapolis: Augsburg, 1972) and by myself in *Good News to the Ends of the Earth: The Theology of Acts* (Philadelphia: Trinity Press International, 1990).

[6]Hans Conzelmann (in *The Theology of St. Luke* [New York: Harper Brothers, 1961], pp. 202–06) developed the idea that Luke saw history as the unfolding of God's plan in three successive and sharply distinguished periods of time: (1) the epoch of Israel; (2) the career of Jesus as the center of history; (3) the epoch of the church. In this way the author was supposed to have removed the problem of the delay of the Parousia, since the third epoch was not yet complete. But the scheme presented in Luke–Acts, rather than sharply differentiating epochs, emphasizes the importance of the continuity between what Jesus launched (in the Gospel of Luke) and what the apostles are enabled to do by the power of the Holy Spirit (in the Book of Acts) and the

worldwide mission to which the church is called, and for which Jesus' inclusive attitude and activity set the precedent. The open-ended way in which Luke leaves the reader at the conclusion of the Book of Acts is intended to show that the preparation for the coming of God's Rule is not yet completed.

[7] Raymond E. Brown, in *The Birth of the Messiah* (Anchor Bible Reference Library; New York: Doubleday, 1979), pp. 350–55, proposes that the Magnificat (Luke 1:46–55) was composed by a group of Jewish Christians who called themselves "the poor ones," regarding themselves as the faithful remnant of God's people (as in Isa. 11:4; 14:30; 29:19; 61:1). The last of these texts is quoted by Jesus in his inaugural address to the synagogue (4:18–19).

[8] Compare Isaiah 40:5; 52:10; 49:6.

[9] It has been suggested by C.H. Kraeling, *John the Baptist* (New York: Scribner's, 1951), pp. 16-23, that all the hymns incorporated by Luke into the first two chapters were originally used in the Baptist movement, which saw John as the redemptive figure, but were modified by the Christians so as to place John in the subordinate position and Jesus in the central role. See also C.H. Scobie, *John the Baptist* (Philadelphia: Fortress, 1964), pp. 54–55.

[10] Josephus (*Antiquities* 18.1.1) reports that Quirinius conducted the census about 6 C.E. Joseph Fitzmyer has examined in great detail the historical and inscriptional evidence about Quirinius' term as governor of Syria, and finds support for this date of the census (*The Gospel of Luke I–IX*, pp. 399–406).

[11] Such as that by Jack Finegan, *Handbook of Biblical Chronology* (Princeton, NJ: Princeton University Press, 1964), pp. 235–38, where Quirinius' participation in the earlier census is described as "not unlikely."

[12] See the summary of evidence and bibliography in the notes to Josephus, *Antiquities* 18, vol. 9 (trans. L.H. Feldman) Loeb Classical Library (Cambridge, MA: Harvard University Press, 1965), pp. 2–3.

[13] The nature of the synagogue as community gathering, rather than special sacred building with formal procedures is sketched in my essays "The Transformation of the Synagogue after 70 C.E." (*New Testament Studies* 36 1, 1990) and "Early Christianity in Galilee: Reassessing the Evidence from the Gospel," in *The Galilee in Late Antiquity*, ed. A.J. Levine (New York and Jerusalem: Jewish Theological Seminary, Harvard University Press, 1991).

[14] The Greek verb here, *chriō*, is the base of the adjectival title *christos* ("Christ"); the underlying Semitic root is commonly transliterated as "Messiah."

[15] The theme of outreach to Gentiles by Jesus and the apostles in Acts is traced by Stephen G. Wilson in *The Gentiles and the Gentile Mission in Luke–Acts* (SNTS Monograph Series; Cambridge: Cambridge University Press, 1973).

[16] Luke's knowledge of Palestinian geography is not precise, as is evident from his reference to Jesus' passing between Galilee and Samaria (Luke 17:11), since the latter lies just to the south of the former. For older discussions of the symbolic significance of Galilee and Jersualem, see R.H. Lightfoot, *Locality and Doctrine in the Gospels* (New York: Harper Brothers, 1938) and Hans Conzelmann, *The Theology of St. Luke*, Part I, esp. pp. 60–65. The symbolic centrality of Jerusalem in Luke–Acts for the launching of the worldwide mission of the church is evident in both volumes.

[17]An informative study of the disciples as fishers of men is Wilhelm Wuellner, *The Meaning of "Fishers of Men"* (Philadelphia: Westminster, 1967).

[18]Luke's seeming omission of Mark 6:1–6 is only an apparent one, since he has reworked and expanded the incident into a programmatic event at the outset of Jesus' ministry (Luke 4:16–30). Luke's failure to include the pericope on the death of John the Baptist is more difficult to account for, since it would seem to be precisely the kind of "historical" incident that would serve Luke's aims well.

[19]The longer omission—from Mark 6:45 to 8:10—is probably best explained by assuming that Luke had a defective or incomplete copy of Mark, since elsewhere he either follows Mark's narrative carefully or adapts it to his own purposes.

[20]In addition to the implication of the two-stage invitation in the Parable of the Supper (Luke 14:15–24), the shift of focus for the preaching of the apostles from primarily Jews to including Gentiles among their hearers is anticipated in Acts 2:21 when Peter quotes Joel's promise that "*everyone* who calls on the name of the Lord shall be saved"; it becomes apostolic policy following the success of Peter's mission at the house of Cornelius (Acts 10:1–48). This means that Israel's destiny is redefined to include Gentiles, so that evangelism of non-Jews and engagement of Jews in discussion and invitation to share in the new community continue (Acts 28:23–31). See Jacob Jervell, *Luke and the People of God* (Minneapolis: Augsburg, 1972), esp. pp. 41–69. The insistence that Gentiles now may share in the new community, which is "the restored and true Israel" and that they must observe the Law if they are now to participate in salvation "are the distinguishing marks of the Israel that Moses and the prophets predicted as the people of the promises of salvation" (p. 147). In Acts 15, however, the specifics of Christian conformity to the law of Moses are radically redefined.

[21]Some of the ancient manuscripts read "seventy-two" instead of "seventy," but this does not affect the symbolism, since a variant of the Jewish tradition claimed that there were seventy-two nations rather than seventy. The fact that in the Letter of Aristeas the Greek translation of the Old Testament was reportedly accomplished by seventy-two scholars and was intended for Gentile readers is further evidence of the symbolic force of the number. Apparently this number became reduced in popular understanding to seventy, which was then used as the popular designation for this second century B.C.E. Greek translation of the Jewish Bible: the Septuagint.

[22]The only Markan materials in this section are (1) the lawyer's question, (2) the Beelzebub controversy, and (3) the Parable of the Mustard Seed.

[23]The meaning of the word in 2:14, *eudokía*, sometimes translated as "goodwill" (that is, toward men), has been clarified through a parallel expression in the Thanksgiving Hymns of the Essene community of Qumran, where the comparable term in Hebrew refers to God's good will and pleasure toward those on whom he showers benefits, as shown by Joseph Fitzmyer, *The Gospel According to Luke I–IX*, pp. 411–12.

[24]The Son of Man is mentioned in 1 Enoch and in 4 Ezra ("the Man"), but in each case the term occurs in parts that scholars have proposed are Christian in

origin. The fragments found at Qumran include all parts of Enoch (known from later translations into Ethiopic and Greek preserved by Christians) except the section called the Similitudes of Enoch. From this absence, J.T. Milik (*Ten Years of Discovery in the Wilderness of Judea* [trans. John Strugnell; Naperville, IL: Allenson, 1959], p. 33) has concluded that the Similitudes are later than the time of Qumran and that they are Christian in origin. That view is challenged by André Dupont-Sommer, *The Essene Writings from Qumran* (trans. Geza Vermes; Cleveland: Meridian, 1962), and by others who assign the Similitudes to the first century B.C.E. or to the turn of our era. It has also been found in other Dead Sea texts (1QapGen 21:13; 11QtgJob 9:9; 26:3). See Barnabas Lindars, "Re-enter the Apocalyptic Son of Man," New Testament Studies 22 (1975): 54-60 and Martin Hengel, *Judaism and Hellenism*, vol. 1 (Philadelphia: Fortress, 1974), p. 200. There is nothing distinctively Christian about the role of the Son of Man in the Qumran texts, and it appears to be a development from the use of the term in Daniel 7, whereby the collective term for humans ("mortal man") has become a designation of an agent of God through whom his purpose for his people will be achieved. Joseph Fitzmyer offers a full and illuminating analysis of the term and its possible origins in *The Gospel According to Luke I–IX*, pp. 208–11.

[25]The parable was probably originally intended as a criticism of the scribes, to whom the Word of God had been entrusted, but who had failed to allow it to work in a fruitful way; thus Joachim Jeremias, *The Parables of Jesus*, 6th ed. (trans. S.H. Hooke; New York: Scribner's, 1963), p. 62. Matthew has placed the emphasis on the Day of Reckoning (Judgment), which suits well his setting of it in 25:14–30, which is his version of the synoptic apocalypse. The Lukan addition, about the nobleman traveling (to Rome?) to have his kingship confirmed, may reflect an actual occurrence in 4 B.C.E., when Herod's son, Archelaus, who had gone to Rome to try to gain his official designation as king of Judea from Caesar Augustus, was followed by a Jewish delegation requesting the denial of his appointment (Josephus, *Antiquities* 17.8–11). Augustus compromised by giving Archelaus half his father's realm, but he was so incompetent that he had to be replaced by a Roman governor in 6 C.E.

[26]5.262, vol. 3 (trans. H. St. John Thackeray) Loeb Classical Library (Cambridge, MA: Harvard University Press, 1957).

[27]An older theory on this issue is that of Vincent Taylor, in *Behind the Third Gospel* (Oxford: Oxford University Press, 1926), where he developed B.H. Streeter's hypothesis that a writer first combined Q and L (Luke's special source, which included a non-Markan passion story) to produce a document that Streeter designated as Proto-Luke. Only later, his thesis ran, was Proto-Luke combined with L to form Luke as we now know it. For the arguments against this hypothesis, see Kümmel, *Introduction to the New Testament*, pp. 131–37.

[28]A similar verdict is attributed—in Luke only— to the centurion at the foot of the cross (Luke 23:47).

[29]Paul W. Walaskay, "The Trial and Death of Jesus in Luke," *Journal of Biblical Literature* 94 (1975): 93. Detailed analysis of the special features of the trial of Jesus are offered by Joseph Fitzmyer, in *The Gospel According to Luke X–XXIV*, pp. 1447–92. Walaskay has developed the thesis that Luke's depiction of the civil authorities as exonerating Jesus and the

apostles is aimed to show the commendable justice of the imperial author-ities, rather than to convince the latter that Christians are not violators of the law, in *"And So We Came to Rome": The Political Perspective of St. Luke* (SNTS Monograph Series; Cambridge: Cambridge University Press, 1983).

[30]His literary style in Acts, especially when Paul is encountering Greek intellectu-als and Roman authorities, is much more sophisticated in style and vocabu-lary, especially in Paul's address at the Areopagus (Acts 17) and in his defense speeches in Acts 21–26, where first-century rhetorical style is reflected. See Bruce W. Winter, "Official Proceedings and the Forensic Speeches in Acts 24–26," in *The Book of Acts in Ancient Literary Setting*, ed. Bruce W. Winter and Andrew D. Clarke (Grand Rapids, MI: Eerdmans, 1993), pp. 305–36.

[31]The classic studies of Lukan style and aims are both by H.J. Cadbury: *The Style and Literary Method of Luke* (Cambridge, MA: Harvard University Press, 1919–1920); and *The Making of Luke–Acts*, 2d ed. (Naperville, IL: Allenson, 1958).

[32]Analyses of these parallel accounts in Luke–Acts, as well as in Hellenistic and Roman literary conventions of the time, are offered by C.H. Talbert, in *Literary Patterns, Theological Themes, and the Genre of Luke–Acts* (Missoula, MT: Scholars Press, 1974). The details Talbert presents are impressive; the case he seeks to make for Luke–Acts as a Hellenistic-style biography is not.

[33]Prime examples of the romance as religious propaganda are *Chaereas and Callirhoe* by Chariton of Aphrodisias and *Ephesiaca* by Xenophon of Ephesus. The latter describes the journeys of devotees of Isis. Apuleius' *The Golden Ass* (or *Metamorphoses*) recounts the religious experience of a man who becomes dedicated to the Egyptian goddess Isis. The relevance of this kind of literature for New Testament study is indicated by Douglas Edwards, *In Roman Greek East* (New York and Oxford: Oxford University Press, forthcoming).

CHAPTER 7

The Story of Jesus As
Mystical Participation
The Gospel of John

From the moment the reader first comes on the stately cadences of John's hymn to the Word of God (John 1:1–18), it is apparent that this gospel stands apart from the other three, despite the superficial similarity of content. To be sure, all four Gospels move through a sequence of events, from the launching of Jesus' public career to the report of instructions to his followers after his passion, and carry accounts of his teachings. But the radical differences between John and the other three Gospels have long been recognized.

The Greek Christian theologian Clement of Alexandria wrote in the second half of the second century that "John, last of all, conscious that the outward facts had been set forth in the other Gospels, was urged on by his disciples, and, divinely moved by the Spirit, composed a spiritual gospel."[1] Irenaeus, who left his native Asia Minor for Rome and by 180 C.E. was Bishop of Lyons in Gaul, likewise connects the Gospel of John with the Spirit. John predicts the coming of the Spirit and describes his work (John 14–16). According to Irenaeus, the Spirit's activity in the Gospel of John is like that of an eagle hovering over the church, protecting it with his wings.[2] The same perception of this gospel as a spiritual mode of communication is evident in the Commentary on John by the learned Christian scholar, Origen of Alexandria (185–354 C.E.), who used elaborate allegorical methods to show the compatibility of John with Platonic philosophy, especially its distinction between the impermanent physical world and the eternal concepts and models on the basis of which it was created. But Irenaeus declares that John also aimed to combat the teaching of the Gnostic Cerinthus,[3] by asserting the oneness of the God of creation and redemption. (These functions were assigned to two gods

203

by the Gnostics, as we shall note in Chapter 8.) Ironically, however, as Irenaeus was obliged to acknowledge, it was the Gospel of John that was seized upon by Valentinus and the later second-century Gnostics to document their own view of Jesus as the heavenly possessor of secret knowledge (also noted in Chapter 8, pp. 257–59).[4] John's claim that the purpose of the Holy Spirit's coming was to offer private knowledge to the inner circle of Jesus' followers (14:17; 16:13) was an invitation to the Gnostics to exploit John's gospel for their own ends.

Why did John especially lend itself to exploitation by the heretics, with their claims of superior revelations? Throughout the gospel there are allusions to the heavenly origin of Jesus and to the links he had with a transcendent realm that is inaccessible to most human beings. The heavenly connection is expressed, for example, in the following:

> Very truly, I tell you, you will see heaven opened, and the angels of God ascending and descending upon the Son of Man. (John 1:51)

Jesus affirms here that his ultimate destiny will receive heavenly confirmation. But his heavenly origin is likewise attested, when he declares that he "came down from heaven" (6:38, 41, 62). Indeed, he asserts that his existence is eternal (8:23, 58) and that he is not subject to death (10:17–18; 11:25). Under what circumstances and by what sort of person was such a representation of Jesus produced?

The Authorship of the Gospel of John

Of the historical origins of the Gospel of John, unfortunately, nothing is known with certainty. The early traditions of the second century attribute it to the apostle John, son of Zebedee, who is reported to have lived to an advanced age in Ephesus.[5] Modern proponents of this authorship theory have claimed that John's Greek reveals that he worked from or translated an Aramaic source.[6] In fact, however, a careful analysis of the Greek text of John shows that the language and vocabulary are paralleled in pagan usage of the first century C.E.[7] and that the scriptural quotations are regularly based on the Greek translation of the Old Testament, the Septuagint,[8] which suggests that the author's primary language was not Hebrew or Aramaic. The Greek is smooth, though not at a sophisticated literary level, and it does contain many expressions that sound Semitic. Its poetic style, especially in the prologue, may also show Semitic influence. It is most likely, therefore, that John's gospel was written in a bilingual area, where both Greek and a Semitic language were spoken. Syria is a possibility, since the intensive Hellenization process there under the Seleucids dated back to the fourth century B.C.E. and Greek language and culture had become fully integrated with the native Syrian culture by the second century C.E.[9]

Far more plausible than the theory that John was written in its entirety by a single creative individual is the hypothesis that this gospel is the cumulative product of a distinctive Christian tradition that developed within an ongoing community. Studies of philosophers and the schools they founded in the Hellenistic period indicate that these movements were characterized by a strong sense of fellowship among the disciples, concern for the preservation and interpretation of a tradition, devotion to learning, and/or a deep commitment to the teacher or founder of the movement. The organization of a group might have been loose or formal, but the activities consisted of instruction, study, and writing.[10] The itinerant teacher-preachers of the Cynic-Stoic philosophical school which flourished in Syria in this period are in some ways analogous to the wandering preachers sent out by Jesus, and their emphasis on coming judgment and cosmic renewal, as we have noted (pp. 33–35), is likewise akin to Jewish and Christian apocalyptic. At the same time, John's use of symbolic and allegorical methods of interpreting Scripture have their closest analogy in the works of Philo of Alexandria, where the Jewish community was powerfully influenced by Hellenistic philosophy and literature. There is no clear indication whether John was written in Syria or in Egypt, since in both contexts Judaism had accommodated to Hellenistic culture.[11] Unlike the loosely organized Cynic-Stoic movement, however, the community that lies behind John appears to have had a long and closely knit common life. Out of this esoteric study, worship, and contemplation came a variant form of the Jesus tradition that borrowed terminology from the wider Hellenistic world and employed it to reinterpret the language and concepts of the Jewish and earlier Christian communities along mystical lines. The result was a unique understanding of Jesus.

The Background of John's Portrayal of Jesus

Although John shares with the synoptic Gospels the accounts of Jesus' miracles as well as of his trial and crucifixion, these features and others are presented in a way that is noticeably different from those of the other Gospels. The narrative accounts, for example, do not come to a conclusion in the expected sense. Jesus approaches John the Baptist (John 1:29), but there is no report of Jesus' having been baptized by John. Instead we have general statements about who Jesus is and why his disciples followed him (1:36–51). In the synoptics, Jesus' action in cleansing the temple is the last straw that determines the Jerusalem leaders to seek his death (Mark 11:18), but in John the incident takes place at the outset of his public activity (2:13–22). The gospel account then shifts abruptly to a conversation with Nicodemus (John 3), which ends, again unexpectedly, with a discourse on God's love and eternal life. The text thus moves from narration to considerations of cosmic and mystical significance.

This kind of literary movement is fairly typical of John's gospel as a whole. John uses the history of Jesus not so much to convey information as to point beyond the outward events of Jesus' career to the eternal, spiritual meaning that faith can discern in them. This does not mean that John is primarily interested in presenting an allegory, where each person or event represents some abstract idea. Rather, his purpose is to create a kind of metahistory, in which the nature of God and the outworking of his purpose are disclosed through historical events. The presentation of Jesus' miracles in John's gospel highlights this tendency to move from public event to private significance for faith.

Jesus As Miracle Worker

Jesus' action in turning the water into wine at Cana is designated by John as "the first of his signs" (2:11); only after two extended narrative sections (Jesus' conversations first with Nicodemus and then with the Samaritan woman, in John 3 and 4) does John refer to the second sign: the healing of the official's son (4:54). In 20:30–31 John mentions the "many other signs" that Jesus did "in the presence of the disciples." On the basis of these references to signs, many commentators have assumed that John had access to a Signs Source, which he incorporated into his gospel.[12] There is no consensus, however, about what was included in the original Signs Source. Some think that it was merely a collection of miracles, while others contend that it contained narratives that reported what are not strictly miracles, such as Jesus' call of the disciples in 1:35–49.[13] Still others consider the Signs Source to have been a miniature gospel, which included a passion narrative.[14] No matter what the extent of the document may have been, proponents of the Signs Source hypothesis assume that it presented Jesus as a Hellenistic-style "divine man" of a type supposed to have been common in the Hellenistic world of the first century C.E. In fact, the charismatic miracle workers of the period—the so-called divine men—were variously represented, so that no single model can be presented for them, nor can any single set of inferences be drawn concerning their significance.[15] A more serious problem for the Signs Source, however, is that it is impossible to differentiate between the alleged source and the evangelist's adaptation of it.[16] Since some of the miracles in John resemble those in the synoptic tradition, both may have drawn on the same tradition, or John may have used one or more of the synoptics for his miracle stories.[17] But there is no unambiguous evidence in John that he or the source on which he drew was trying to put Jesus in competition with other miracle workers of that epoch, or conversely, that John was trying to combat such a notion by linking the stories of Jesus' miracles with that of his passion. The present state of the text of John moves for the most part so smoothly from narrative to discourse, and in both cases manifests so many common stylistic features, that there are no solid criteria for reconstructing either a Signs Source or a pre-Johannine picture of Jesus as miracle worker.[18] Since the isolation of John's sources is a highly subjective and inconclusive undertaking, we shall group together in our analysis much of the narrative in John, because it serves John's "sign" purpose, even when it is not presenting miracle accounts.

The fullest clue to the meaning of the signs is given, somewhat surprisingly, at the end of the narrative:

> Now Jesus did many other signs in the presence of the disciples, which are not written in this book; but these are written so that you may come to believe that Jesus is the Messiah, the Son of God, and that through believing you may have life in his name. (20:30–31)

It is difficult to determine whether John intends for his recounting of the signs to evoke faith among unbelievers or to enrich insight among those who already believe. The latter seems more probable, since throughout his gospel he shows that Jesus' miracles aroused hostility rather than faith among those who were not disposed to see in him the messenger and agent of God. The gospel, then, would be a book for the church, rather than an evangelistic appeal to the world. This impression is supported by the book as a whole, especially in the farewell chapters:

> I am asking on their behalf; I am not asking on behalf of the world,
> but on behalf of those that you have given me. (John 17:9)

John's narrative about the disciples (1:35–51) points up for us several of John's favorite themes. One is the emphasis on the earthly origins of Jesus, as son of Joseph, whose home is in Nazareth (1:45). Another is the perception of Jesus as the fulfillment of the Scripture. But most striking is the prophecy of Jesus:

> Very truly, I tell you, you will see heaven opened, and the angels of God ascending and descending upon the Son of Man. (1:51)

The scene recalls the experience of Jacob described in Genesis 28:12, where in a dream Jacob saw a ladder reaching to heaven and heard the voice of God promising him the land and posterity under the blessing of Yahweh, the God of Abraham and Isaac. The title "Son of Man" recalls the promise given to Daniel in a dream that to "the saints of the Most High" God would give his Kingdom (Dan. 7:13–14, 27). Since Nathanael has just acclaimed Jesus "the Son of God, the King of Israel" (John 1:49), one cannot miss John's point here: Jesus is the one through whom God's Kingdom is to be established and the new people of God assembled to share in its rule. Only the *terminology* of apocalyptic expectation remains, however; nothing of the substance is to be found here— neither the urgency of the moment nor the shortness of time until the promise is fulfilled. Even the conflict with the demonic, which is so characteristic of the apocalyptic outlook, has all but vanished in John, except for a trace in the report that the devil put it into Judas' heart to betray Jesus (13:2). The real power that consigns men to the realm of darkness is their misguided will, not the power of Satan or demons:

> People loved darkness rather than light, because their deeds were evil. For all who do evil hate the light, and do not come to the light, so that their deeds may not be exposed. (John 3:19–20)

The power that will achieve the divine purpose in history is God disclosing himself to men and women of faith. It is through word, sign, and symbol that this revelation takes place for John. The outward course of history, including tensions with the principalities and powers of this world order (as in Acts 4 or Rom. 13), is of no concern to him.

In the first miracle story, the Changing of Water into Wine at the Wedding in Cana (2:1–11), the symbolic intent of the narrative is evident. The best wine coming at the end of the feast reminds the reader familiar with Jewish tradition of the eschatological meal when the new wine of the New Age will be available (Amos 9:13; Jer. 31:10–12; and in the apocalyptic literature, 1 En. 10:19 and 2 Bar. 29:5). In what purports to be a quotation from Jesus, the early second-century bishop Papias tells of the marvelous fruitfulness of the vines in the Kingdom of God:

> The days will come in which vines will grow, each having ten thousand branches, and on each branch ten thousand twigs, and on each twig ten thousand shoots, and on each one of the shoots ten thousand clusters, and on every one of the clusters ten thousand grapes, and every grape when pressed will give ten thousand measures of wine. And when any one of the saints shall lay hold of a cluster, another shall cry out, "I am a better cluster, take me; bless the Lord through me." (Quoted by Irenaeus, *Against Heresies* 5.33.3)

In contrast to Papias' expectation that the best comes last, John reports Jesus as reversing the expected order: He brings the best wine (= eschatological joy) now. One need not wait until the End of the Age; the goal of history is already present in Jesus.

The second sign (by our count, not John's) is the Cleansing of the Temple (2:13–22). Its link with the signs is given in the story itself, in which Jesus' opponents ask him what *sign* he can give as authorization for his audacious assumption of the right to cleanse the Temple courts (2:18). But the overturning of tables and the expulsion of the money changers—who, after all, were necessary for the continuance of proper offerings in the Temple—are not for John the important facts. The interest shifts in 2:18 from the cleansing to the destruction and rebuilding of the Temple, and then to the raising up of the body of Jesus. But even this is not an unequivocal reference to the Resurrection of Jesus, since "his body" could as well be the church. And it is the establishment of a new people of God through whom the true worship of God will be carried out ("in spirit and truth," 4:23) that is a major theme in John. For John's community, as for the one that the Dead Sea Scrolls claim was being formed at Qumran, the eschatological people of God was already taking shape in the postresurrection situation. The end of history was present in the life of faith as the new temple, the church, was being erected.

Another narrative that may be included among the signs (the third in our numbering system) is the recounting of the conversation between Jesus and Nicodemus (3:1–15), who appears in the latter part of the gospel as a secret follower of Jesus (19:39). Nicodemus recognizes the power of Jesus and attributes his authority to God, even though he thinks of Jesus as a teacher ("Rabbi," 3:2) rather than as Messiah or prophet. The conversation moves along on the basis of three words with double meanings: again (= from above), wind (= spirit), and lifted up (= crucified and/or exalted). Nicodemus assumes that to be born again means to begin life over again on the same basis (3:4); Jesus' meaning is that to be born from above is to enter into a new kind of life, which can be called (using the traditional eschatological terminology) the Kingdom of God (3:5). Nicodemus can make nothing of new life through "wind"; Jesus means, of course, the life given through the Spirit (3:8). The life is given through the lifting up of the Son of Man,[19] in an act analogous to the lifting up of the serpent of brass in the wilderness on the day of God's Judgment on faithless Israel (Num. 21:9). In the days of ancient Israel, a look in faith toward the snake on the pole brought recovery from the otherwise fatal bite of the serpents in the camp of Israel. Jesus is now saying that a look in faith toward the Son of Man lifted up (that is, on the cross) brings eternal life (3:14).

As we have remarked, the conversation shifts here abruptly to a discourse (by Jesus? by John?) on the gift of eternal life to those who recognize Jesus to be the Son of God (3:16–17). The Judgment is not something that has already fallen, as in the plague of serpents (Num. 21:6), nor is it something that will come in the last days, in accord with apocalyptic teaching (Mal. 4:5–6); it is rather something that occurs in the moment when an individual makes the decision of faith in Jesus as the Son of God (3:18). The traditional view of the Day of Judgment at the End of the Age has been transformed into the present moment of decision.

Jesus' encounter with the woman at the well in Samaria (4:1–42)—a fascinating story in itself—is likewise filled with double and symbolic meanings. There is the implied contrast between the head of ancient Israel, Jacob, who provided the well at which succeeding generations could quench their thirst, and Jesus, whose gift of the Spirit is a source of eternal life, not merely the means of sustaining life on its old terms. Another contrast is presented concerning the true worship of God. The woman raises the ancient controversial issue between Jews and Samaritans as to the proper place for the worship of God: Jerusalem, where the Jewish temple was located, or Samaria, where the Samaritan temple stood on Mt. Gerizim (4:20–22)? Finally (4:25), the woman tries to demonstrate her piety by declaring her faith that the Messiah is coming, but Jesus' reply is that he for whom she is looking has already come (4:26). This series of exchanges is intended to confirm Jesus' claim that he is the one through whom true life may be gained and sustained, that he is the one who has established the true worship of God apart from a pridefully localized setting (Jerusalem or Gerizim), and that this Jew, whose thirst seemingly overcomes his Jewish reluctance to have dealings with Samaritans (4:9), is in fact the Messiah (4:26), the Savior of the world (4:42).

The fifth sign (the second by John's enumeration) is the Healing of the Official's Son (4:46–53). In one of the few Johannine passages with clear synoptic parallels (= Matt. 8:5–10 and Luke 7:2–10), the point of the story is not that Jesus' miracle of healing evoked faith, but that the official trusted Jesus' word before the miracle was performed. The details of the healing—that it occurred at the precise hour that Jesus had spoken (4:52–53)—confirmed the man's faith, but they were not the cause of his faith. John wants his reader to see beyond the son's recovery of physical health to the belief that, at the word of Jesus, true life becomes a reality (4:53).

Jesus' Healing of the Lame Man at the Pool of Beth-zatha (5:1–18) is for John far more than a work of mercy that happens to violate the Jewish Sabbath restriction. It is, in the first place, a vivid way of showing the inadequacy of the ordinary way of doing things. The man has waited in vain throughout a lifetime (5:5) to be healed, counting on the bubbling of the pool (caused perhaps by an intermittent spring) to restore his health. Even when Jesus asks him if he wants to be healed, his reply is that he wants someone to help him into the pool (5:7). But at the word of Jesus, responded to in faith, the man receives the gift of health. The second point is also the more important one: Jesus' opponents understandably assume that to violate the Sabbath law is to break God's rule. But Jesus turns the argument around. He justifies his violation of the Sabbath regulation by identifying his work with God's work (5:18). He dismisses Sabbath desecration by what his opponents can regard only as a blasphemous claim: He identifies his work with God's. It is important to note that, for John, Jesus' oneness with the Father is not a matter of metaphysical substance, as it came to be formulated in the creeds of the church, but of identity of work, word, and will.

In the sequence of the seventh and eighth signs, Feeding of the Five Thousand (6:1–14) and Walking on the Water (6:16–21), John comes closest to following the synoptic order (Mark 6:32–44 and 6:45–51; also Matt. 14:13–33 and Luke 9:10–17, although Luke omitted all the Markan material, including the story of Jesus'

Walking on the Water, from Mark 6:45 to 8:27). The details of the events vary from the synoptic accounts slightly, as though John were drawing on a variant of the tradition or perhaps recalling it from memory, with some embellishment of his own, such as the detail that a lad provided the fish and that the loaves were of barley. Most striking, however, is the response of the people, who first acclaim Jesus to be "the prophet" (= the eschatological prophet of Deut. 18:15–19) and then determine to make him king. Apparently the prospect of a king who can provide food without anyone working to produce it has irresistible appeal for the populace. Jesus rejects the offer of kingship on these terms, in a manner analogous to his struggle against Satan in the temptation stories of the synoptics.

John's only addition to the synoptic version of Jesus' Walking on the Water (Mark 6:45–52; Matt. 14:22–33) is the concluding detail: As soon as Jesus was aboard, the boat immediately reached its destination (6:21). This detail heightens the element of the miraculous in the story, but it is clearly intended here as a manifestation of Jesus' divine power in his lordship over nature.[20] His words addressed to the disciples, "it is I" (in Greek, *ego eimi*), are the same as those by which he identifies himself to them in the synoptic accounts. But there is no mistaking the intentional link between the "I am" phrase here and elsewhere in John and the distinctive name of God in the Greek Bible in Exodus 3:14: "*Ego eimi*" (= I am). John uses this phrase throughout his gospel to disclose one facet after another of the revelation of God in Jesus.

In contrast to the story of Jesus' Walking on the Water, which simply reports an epiphany (a manifestation of the divine), the story of the Feeding of the Five Thousand sets forth an understanding of Jesus as the food that God supplies to feed his own people (6:25–58). The imagery builds on the Jewish tradition of the bread from heaven (manna) that sustained the life of Israel during its desert wanderings from Egypt to Palestine.[21] Philo of Alexandria, and later the rabbis, elaborated on this story and gave it an interpretation related to God's care of his people in the End Time, when they would be restored in his Kingdom.[22] But for John, the bread from heaven has already come in the person of Jesus (6:41). John uses this image to refer not only to the spiritual strength and growth that come from living by faith in Jesus but also to the Eucharist. This is clear from the rather shocking words:

> Very truly, I tell you, unless you eat the flesh of the Son of Man and drink his blood, you have no life in you. Those who eat my flesh and

drink my blood have eternal life, and I will raise them up on the last day. (6:53–54)

The shocking quality of these words is heightened by John's use of a word for eating that is normally found only in connection with animals feeding. John's aim may have been to combat the notion that to partake of Christ was a purely spiritual experience. But more important is his eagerness to stress the necessity for participation in the Eucharist.[23] "Eating the flesh" is participation in the sacrament, though it may also be a metaphor for meditation and devotion. But the intended meaning is clear: To feed on Christ by sharing his sacramental "flesh and blood" is to partake of eternal life, not merely to have life sustained as it was in the wilderness by the bread from heaven. John is telling his reader that Jesus is one whose meaning and power transcend the greatest redemptive events in Israel's history.

Jesus' Healing of the Man Born Blind (9:1–41) resembles the story of the Healing at the Pool in at least two ways: It occurs on a Sabbath day, and it raises the question of the link between Jesus' work and God's work (9:4, 14). Of all the sign narratives in John, this one has the highest degree of verisimilitude. The reader can sense the incredulity of the neighbors when the man receives his sight (9:8–10), the sinister motives of the Pharisees in questioning him (9:13–17), and the timidity of the parents in refusing to acknowledge anything more than that he is their son and that he once was blind (9:20–23). They want to shift the responsibility to their son when they say, "Ask him; he is of age, he will speak for himself" (9:21). The Pharisees' interrogation of the man becomes an indictment of the interrogators, when they insist that a violator of the Sabbath law cannot be an agent of God, no matter how marvelous his healing powers (9:24). The climax of the story comes in the words of Jesus:

> I came into this world for judgment, so that those who do not see may see, and that those who do see may become blind. (9:39)

The very fact that Jesus has come precipitates the Judgment: the time of decision. There is no question of waiting until a day in the future when human deeds will be appraised, rewards and punishments meted out. The decisive moment is now, when men and women are confronted by Jesus' words and works. Those who know their own shortcomings, who acknowledge their need of God's revelation, are enabled to "see." On the other hand, those who pride themselves on their grasp of what they take to be the truth, are confirmed in their "blindness." The passage is a variation on the theme of Isaiah 6:10, in which God blinds those who refuse to repent at the word of God's messenger:

> Make the mind of this people dull, and stop their ears, and shut their eyes; so that they may not look with their eyes, and listen with their ears, and comprehend with their minds, and turn and be healed.

The story of Lazarus' Being Raised from the Dead (John 11) is generally regarded as the last of the sign narratives. It is not a *resurrection* account, since Lazarus is merely restored to the life of this age rather than permitted to enter the life of the Age to Come. Jesus' power to restore life to a friend is, however, a sign of the resurrection; the act points to Jesus' ability to give eternal life, which is qualitatively different from the conditions of ordinary human life, to which Lazarus is brought back.

In the narrative Martha speaks for the orthodox Pharisaic point of view that there will be a resurrection of the dead in the End Time (11:24). She and her sister, Mary, also have faith in the ability of Jesus to heal those who are sick, and she regrets that Jesus' delay in arriving prevented him from restoring Lazarus to health (9:21, 32). Jesus' intention is not to enable life to continue on its old basis, however, but to give a new kind of life that enables the faithful to share in eternity now in the midst of time (11:25–26). The grant of true life is not merely a future prospect but a present possibility.

The macabre details of the burial, the four-day period during which decay has set in, and the burial wrappings help to make John's point: Lazarus was really dead; Jesus revived him. John does not deny the reality of the resurrection at the Last Day; indeed, he refers to it repeatedly: 5:28–29; 6:35, 44, 54.[24] He continues to affirm the traditional beliefs in eschatological fulfillment in the End Time, including judgment and resurrection, but he sets over against this view the conviction that the important factor for the individual of faith is the decision for or against Jesus made in the present moment. In that moment the individual is judged and may be raised to new life. The Greek root *krisis* can mean either to judge or to make a decision. John capitalizes on both meanings at the same time. He reports Jesus as saying in 5:24:

> Very truly, I tell you, anyone who hears my word and believes him who sent me has eternal life, and does not come under judgment, but has passed from death to life.

A person's decision *(krisis)* delivers him from the judgment *(krisis)*.

Jesus As Gnostic Redeemer

The signs material in John does not help us to determine the precise religious background against which John is offering his interpretation of Jesus. Especially perplexing is the motif of Jesus as one who comes "from above" (3:7, 13; 6:62). Bultmann, among others, claimed that this feature of John was to be accounted for as John's adaptation of a pre-Christian myth of a heavenly redeemer, according to which an agent of God came down to liberate humans from their entanglement in the material world.[25] Through this redeemer, one who attains true knowledge is supposed to be able to return to his or her true and proper place, heaven. It was Bultmann's contention that the Logos hymn in John (1:1–18) is a Christianized version of this myth. Although some components of what became this redeemer myth are found in late first-century C.E. literature, such as 4 Ezra, in which the redeemer is hidden in heaven and preexistent, the surviving Gnostic texts in which the fully developed Gnostic redeemer that Bultmann constructed come from the second century C.E. and later, and hence are too late to have been used by the author of the Gospel of John. Of Gnosticizing Jewish sources, the parallels with John most often pointed to are the second-century C.E. Odes of Solomon[26] and Mandaean writings, which were preserved by a Gnostic sect, originally Jewish, that apparently still survives in southern Iraq and in Iran.[27] When the Odes of Solomon were first discovered early in the present century, it was assumed that they were Jewish in origin and Gnostic in content. Careful subsequent analysis has shown that they were probably written by Syrian Christians in the late first or early second century, in reaction to the destruction of the Jerusalem temple. They are akin in conceptual outlook to the Gospel of John, with comparable emphasis on the Word of God as the agent of redemption. Wholly unlike Gnosticism, however, the Odes affirm the creation of the world (Ode 16) and picture such physical aspects of Jesus as the incarnation (7:3–6), his crucifixion (27:1–3), and his resurrection (42:6). As in the prologue of John, the Word descends from God and comes into the fully human sphere (12:12; 22:1).

Detailed examination of the relevant texts, however, shows that none of the links between John and these allegedly pre-Christian Gnostic sources can be maintained. Careful analysis of the Mandaean material has discredited the notion that John the Baptist fulfilled an incarnational-redemptive role for that sect,[28] and the Mandaean texts from Iran do not document the myth of the redeemer who is himself redeemed and offers redemption to the faithful, as Bultmann had conjectured from his "reconstructed" version of John.[29] The Odes of Solomon have been shown to share with John the light-dark imagery and the modified ethical dualism that is found in the Qumran documents.[30] The source of that dualism is not Gnosticism, however, but Jewish apocalypticism and certain other features of Jewish wisdom, as we shall observe shortly. There is some evidence that the self-presentation style of Jesus in the Johannine discourses ("I am") is similar to his revelatory claims made in some of the Coptic Gnostic materials discovered and studied since 1945,[31] but once more the earliest of those documents is later than John's gospel. The Coptic material, in fact, may have drawn on John's discourses. Whether this is true or not, neither appears to have kinship with the redeemer myth invented by twentieth-century scholars, and both probably represent sectarian Jewish developments of the Wisdom tradition. It is to the specifics of the content of the Johannine discourses and their background that we now turn our attention.

Jesus As Revealer of God

The series of revelatory discourses, most of which are readily identifiable by the phrase "I am," constitutes the second major cycle of material in John. In each case, the words "I am" are followed by two other terms: (1) a noun or noun phrase, in which some aspect of the redemptive function or the revelation that Christ brings is asserted; (2) a parallel phrase or sentence, in which either the function of Jesus as revealer is further defined or the response to the revelation is described. These elements can be seen clearly in the first of the revelatory sayings:

> I am the bread of life; whoever comes to me will never be hungry, and whoever believes in me will never be thirsty. (6:35)

These words are presented in the setting of a controversy between Jesus and the crowd that followed him because they thought he would provide them with free meals. The issue turns very quickly to the question of the source of his authority (6:30). The contrast is explored between the manna given by God to the children of Israel in the Sinai desert (Exod. 16) and the bread that Jesus gave on the occasion of the miraculous feeding (6:1–12). In the Jewish tradition, the bread from heaven in the manna story was understood as a symbol for the Torah, the will of God embodied in the Law. By feeding on it, a person might learn how to live properly. As it is expressed in Deuteronomy:

> You must follow exactly the path that the Lord your God has commanded you, so that you may live, and that it may go well with you, and that you may live long in the land which you are to possess. (5:33)

Obeying the Law guaranteed life, prosperity, and longevity. But the bread that Jesus offered promised a new kind of life—true obedience and life "forever" (John 6:58).

There are two significant factors in the first of these revelatory speeches. The first is the form of the speech itself, which has its closest parallels in the speeches of the Mandaean writings and the Odes of Solomon, where the revealer addresses the community in the first person. The second is the direct description of Jesus as a revealer who has "come down from heaven" (6:38, 50, 58) and who is yet to ascend back to the Father (6:62). Although in the prologue John speaks only of the preexistence of the Logos, not directly of Jesus' preexistence, he asserts here that Jesus came from God and is going back to God. His departure "out of this world to the Father" is announced in 13:1 on the eve of the Passion. In the postresurrection appearance of Jesus to Mary Magdalene (20:1–18), he tells her, "Do not try to hold me, for I have not yet ascended to the Father . . . I am ascending to my Father and your Father. . . ." Thus John follows through consistently on the picture of Jesus as the one who came from God and returns to God when his work is completed. This picture of Jesus has no parallel in the synoptic tradition. What image has provided the model for this understanding of Jesus? As an initial step in determining the probable background of this ascending-descending figure, we must examine other discourses in which the transcendent significance of Jesus is displayed.

In John 7:37 Jesus is represented as following up on the promise made in 6:35, "Whoever believes in me shall never be thirsty," which is in turn a development of the statement made to the Samaritan woman at Jacob's well:

> Every one who drinks of this water will be thirsty again, but those who drink of the water that I shall give them will never be thirsty; the water that I will give will become in them a spring of water gushing up to eternal life. (4:13–14)

John brought together in 7:37–39 a whole series of allusions to Old Testament and later Jewish traditions. The feast day referred to is the Feast of Tabernacles, an autumn feast. When rain fell at that time of year, it gave promise of good winter rains and therefore of good crops in the following spring. But a symbolic meaning arose, according to which the concern was not for literal crops but for the pouring out of eschatological blessing in the End Time. John linked with this hope the experience reported in Exodus 13 and 14, which tell of God sustaining his people in the desert by causing water to flow from the rock at the command of Moses. This, too, was associated with the messianic age, as we can see from the Jewish interpretations of the passage and from Paul's comment in 1 Corinthians 10:1–3. The eschatological outpouring of the Spirit, which figures so prominently in the prophetic tradition (e.g., Isa. 61 and Joel 2:28–29), is seen here as already occurring through Jesus. Or, more accurately, it is described as about to occur when the Spirit comes, following Jesus' departure to be with the Father (John 16:5–11). To believe in Jesus is not only to share in the water of life that he provides but also to be a channel through which it is conveyed to others.

Jesus' declaration of his superiority to Abraham reaches a climax in the words "before Abraham was, I am" (8:58) in a passage that does not follow the pattern of the revelatory speeches. The ostensible question voiced by Jesus' opponents is one of physical lineage. The distinction in the Greek verbs is crucial here. A literal translation would be "Before Abraham became" or "came to exist, I am." The latter phrase implies "I share in timeless being." In addition to this linguistic and philosophical distinction between becoming and being, the phrase "I Am" echoes God's answer to Moses about the name of the deity who was sending him to lead Israel out of Egypt: "I Am who I AM" (Exod. 3:13–14). Jesus builds on their challenge to his identity and the enduring power of his words by questioning whether they really are children of Abraham (8:39) and whether they indeed know the God of Abraham, the progenitor of the people of God. Their response to him indicates that they are children of the devil, whose sons do the father's work (8:39–44). Jesus here dissociates himself from traditional, ethnically exclusive Israel, as may be inferred from his mentioning Abraham as "your father" rather than *our* father (8:56). The offspring of Abraham are supposed to enjoy "length of days" if they keep the words of Moses; Jesus promises not an extended period of earthly existence but eternal life to those who keep *his* word (8:51). Jesus' opponents react by stoning him (8:59). Their violent, hostile action is readily understandable, given their perception that Jesus is truly subversive of the foundations of Judaism: obedience to the Law of Moses and preservation of physical descent from Abraham. Add to this his seemingly blasphemous claim of eternal existence (8:58), and one can see why the religious leadership would seek to destroy Jesus.

Jesus places himself, as John here describes him, in the context of eternity rather than of chronological history. It is idle to speak of historical causes or antecedents when dealing with one who is portrayed as enjoying existence from before the founding of the ages. The history of Jesus is linked with the history of Abraham as fulfillment is linked with promise, since Abraham looked forward in faith to the day of Jesus' coming. But just as the Logos "was in the beginning," so Jesus "was" before Abraham. John has moved beyond the limits and categories of historical knowledge into assertions concerning eternal reality.

The metaphors of food and drink are replaced in John 10 by those linked with shepherd and flock. The first of these figures is somewhat strained:

I am the gate; whoever enters by me, he will be saved, and will come in and go out and find pasture. (10:9)

Apparently what John intended to say here is that the only means of access into the flock of God is through Jesus, though the detail of moving in and out shows that the sheepfold is a place of group identity, not of refuge or withdrawal. We shall see later in this chapter that the church is understood as an agent of mission, not as an exclusivist conventicle concerned only with its own spiritual welfare. The shepherd metaphor is all but self-explanatory: Those who follow Jesus constitute the true flock of God. John adds two surprising elements to the Old Testament image of God's flock, however. One is the fact that the shepherd must die in order to benefit the sheep. The other is the merging of two flocks into one. Any doubt about the meaning of the latter detail disappears when the reader realizes that John is speaking of bringing together Jew and Gentile ("other sheep") into the one fold. In short, the theme of the reconstitution of the people of God is present in John 10 under an image which expands upon, and hence is different from, the simple notion of Israel as the flock and God as the shepherd.

Jesus anticipates his death and resurrection in the words of John 10:17–18 about laying down his life and taking it again. There is no provision offered in the saying attributed to Jesus for historical development in the customary sense of the term that would indicate the specific circumstances and events that led to his death. Everything is predetermined in accord with the divine will: "This command I have received from my Father" (10:18). John has only secondary historical interest in the actual sequence of events leading up to the Crucifixion; he is primarily concerned with posing the issue of the theological understanding of Jesus in order to show how, given traditional Jewish presuppositions, Jesus could be regarded as a subversive, whereas, given Christian presuppositions, he could be seen as the agent of God.

Again, John's transcending of historical concern is evident in the revelatory speech (11:25–26) in which Jesus declares, "I am the resurrection and the life." The characteristic response, faith, is called for: To trust in Jesus is to receive life. The life received is not historical existence under conditions of space and time, but participation in a mode of spiritual existence in the midst of, but beyond the limitations of, ordinary life. Even death cannot bring it to an end: "Even though they die, yet shall they live" (11:25). John sees this life not merely as something that Jesus gives but as what he *is*. Faith is therefore not belief in an idea or acceptance of certain spiritual values; it is a relationship of communion with and trust in a person. The way of knowing for John is accordingly not primarily by historical information about a life in the past, but by some kind of mystical participation with one who is thought to live in the present. This is dramatically stated in the promise attributed to Jesus in 14:2–3 that he is now preparing a place in his "Father's house" where he will take his own people to be with him. Mystical union of Jesus, the Father, and believers is also asserted in 17:11, 21, 23, 25–26, where Jesus prays that God will preserve them in unity in the world. This has as its model the complete unity of Jesus and God, which serves as witness to the world and which enables the members to experience the encompassing divine love.

Jewish precedent for the mystical aspiration to ascend to heaven and see God is evident in the *Merkebah*, or throne mysticism of Judaism.[32] Building on the accounts of transforming visions of God in Isaiah 6 and Ezekiel 1, and especially Ezekiel's commissioning based on his having seen visions of God seated on his throne, a mystical movement developed in Judaism in Hellenistic times. It promised the faithful that they would have visions of the throne in the present, sustenance of their existence now, and transport to the divine presence when life ended. That theme pervades John, from the opening hymn, with its remarks about beholding God's glory (1:14) and seeing God (1:18), through the promises that Jesus will take his own to be with God (14:1–2; 17:24), to the postresurrection announcement of Jesus' ascent to God (20:17). This outlook was later taken over and adapted by the Gnostics in conformity with their radical dualism of spirit and matter, but the influence on Johannine thought seems to have come directly from the Jewish mystical sect. It is not surprising, therefore, that the final discourses in John are taken up with the theme of the union between Jesus and his community.

In contrast to the common mystical ways of knowing—that is, through direct communion with God—John declares in 14:6 that Jesus is "the way, and the truth, and the life." He is the only means of access to knowledge of God. "No one comes to the Father, but by me." Jesus' claim to be the sole revealer of God is also found elsewhere in John, for example, in 10:8, where Jesus brands as thieves and robbers all who before him claimed to be revealers. Knowledge of God comes not through direct historical information concerning the events of Jesus' life, but through God's indwelling Spirit, whom the Father will send after Jesus has left (14:16–17) and who will guide God's people into "all truth" (16:13).

The most obvious mystical image used by John in the revelatory discourses is that of the vine (15:1–17). The life of the vine (= Jesus) flowing into the branches is what produces the fruit of obedience, which manifests itself in mutual love. There is little hint here of the Christian's responsibility toward the world. In fact, Jesus tells his followers in 15:19 that they should expect to be hated by the world. In the prayers of John 17, petitions in behalf of the world are explicitly excluded (17:9), although the unity of the people of God is a demonstration to the world that God sent Jesus into the world. The reader of John receives the impression that there is to be a sharp cleavage between the church and the world, and that the church's chief testimony in the world is to be communicated through the mutual love within the group and the sense of unity that is to characterize the church's corporate life. Through the testimony of the members of the community, others will come to believe (17:20). But John envisions no comprehensive scheme of world history, no cataclysmic change by which the rule of God will be established in the world. The Kingdom of God is for John that new sphere of life into which a person enters now by faith upon being baptized (3:5). God loves all the world (3:16) but does not intend to redeem it together with all its inhabitants. Rather, only the faithful are delivered, as by a new birth, from the present world with its limitations and its empty standards and values, and brought into a new order, which is eternal life. There will be suffering in the new life (15:18–21; 16:1–4; 17:13–18), but the faithful will be patient and obedient in the midst of difficulties, standing firm in the faith in spite of outward circumstances.

Jesus As the Fulfillment of God's Plan

In spite of his emphasis on mystical union, John is not wholly devoid of a sense of events moving toward the completion of God's purpose. Referring to Jesus as the fulfillment of Scripture and redefining traditional messianic and redemptive categories, John shows that what happened to and through Jesus was the result of the outworking of God's plan in the world of time and space.

The Fulfillment of Scripture

John explicitly claims that Jesus actualizes what was promised in Scripture. There are at least twenty-five quotations from the Old Testament in John; six are quoted in such a way as to make clear that a claim of fulfillment is being made, and fourteen begin with a formula such as "scripture is fulfilled," "scripture says," "the word was fulfilled," "it is written," "Isaiah says." Five times the phrase "in order that it might be fulfilled" is used.

The Scriptures appear in John as the divine blueprint for the work of Jesus, especially in his passion (12:15; 12:40; 13:18; 15:25; 19:28; 19:36, 37) and in his special redemptive-revelatory role (1:51; 6:31; 6:45; 10:16). It is worth noting that much of the detail of the passion story is provided by, or at least conforms to the words of, the Psalms. In some cases there is exact correspondence between what is said in the Scriptures and what is reported as happening in the career of Jesus, as in 19:37 (= Zech. 12:10, "they look on him whom they have pierced"). In other cases the interpretation of fulfillment claim seems forced, as in John 10:34, in which Jesus, defending his use of the term *Son of God*, refers to Psalm 82:6. In Psalm 82 the whole point is that, though created in the image of God, humans are mortal. Thus, it is scarcely a convincing passage in confirmation of Jesus' alleged claim to divinity. Strangely, the Old Testament quotations in John are not appealed to in confirmation of Jesus' messianic claims, with the possible exception of 12:13–15 (= Zech. 9:9). In at least one instance (7:42), John argues against the interpretation of Jesus' messiahship according to the traditional messianic notion of the restored Davidic kingly line (= Mic. 5:2). John's conviction is that perceptive reading of Scripture will show that the basic pattern of God's purpose as laid down in Scripture is now moving toward completion. However, the freedom to achieve this purpose rests solely with God, so traditional forms of expectation must often be revised or even rejected in view of the fulfillment that is already occurring through Jesus.

Redefinition of Traditional Messianic and Redemptive Categories

John's use of the messianic and redemptive categories drawn from the Old Testament and Jewish traditions is both continuous and discontinuous with Jewish ideas and hopes. Messiah was by no means a fixed or even a well-defined concept in first-century Judaism, but John introduces four different conceptions or images of messianic figures in his gospel—Prophet, Son of Man, Son of God, and Savior of the World—all of them in polemical contexts. Thus in 1:19–23, three questions are addressed to John the Baptist in an effort to determine what his role is. He is asked if he is the Christ (= Messiah), or Elijah, or the Prophet. Later in the same chapter, Jesus is described as Lamb of God and as Son of Man. In addition, Nathanael acclaims him Son of God and King of Israel, both of which are synonyms for Messiah. Similarly, the question initially raised by the woman at the well (4:29) is whether or not Jesus is the Messiah. But at the end of the narrative he is acclaimed by the Samaritans, not as Messiah, but as "Savior of the world" (4:42). The redefining of the traditional messianic categories is implied by the tension between Martha's declaration that Jesus is the Christ and her reluctance to have the tomb of Lazarus opened, which shows that she does not understand the full implications of her own confession of faith.

The significance of John's use of these traditional messianic categories is that though in some sense Jesus is seen as their fulfillment in another sense he does not fit any of them. The title Messiah (= Anointed One) is a kingly designation, associated with David and his successors. Israel's basic presupposition was that God was king (Ps. 5:2; 10:16; 93; 96; 97; 99; 103:19). Perhaps the clearest statement of this is in the familiar words of Psalm 24:7–10:

> *Lift up your heads, O gates!*
> *and be lifted up, O ancient doors!*
> *that the King of glory may come in.*
>
> *Who is the King of glory?*
> *The Lord, strong and mighty,*
> *the Lord, mighty in battle!*
>
> *Lift up your heads, O gates!*
> *and be lifted up, O ancient doors!*
> *that the King of glory may come in!*
>
> *Who is this King of glory?*
> *The Lord of hosts,*
> *he is the King of glory!*

Although God was king, he was understood to have granted royal authority to his viceregent, David, as Psalm 110:1 affirms:

> *The Lord says to my lord:*
> *"Sit at my right hand,*
> *until I make your enemies your footstool."*

In Psalm 72 the king is to be enabled to carry out the justice of God by vindicating the oppressed, and by defending those who have been mistreated. In behalf of the king, the Psalmist requested length of days and wide dominions.

As the Davidic dynasty came to an end, however, with the captivity of the tribes of Judah in the sixth century B.C.E., the prophets began to project the hope of the messianic reign into the future, as can be seen in Isaiah 9:6–7 and especially in 11:1–10, in which the prophet depicts the Davidic royal house as a tree cut down and reduced to a stump. But from that stump he foresees a shoot or a branch coming forth. Unexpectedly, the hope of renewal of the kingship is revived through the descendant of David who appears like one from the dead; accordingly, the divine spirit will come upon him and grant him the understanding and wisdom to discharge his kingly duties with justice and with effective authority over his enemies. The consequence of this eschatological kingship will be to bring about the renewal of the whole creation, as symbolized by the cessation of hostility among the beasts of the field:

> The wolf shall live with the lamb, and the leopard shall lie down with the kid.
>
> . . .
>
> They will not hurt or destroy in all my holy mountain for the earth will be full of the knowledge of the Lord as the waters cover the sea.
>
> (Isa. 11:6, 9)

One of the specific details of this kind of expectation of the king was that he would be born in Bethlehem, the hometown of David, Israel's ideal king (Mic. 5:2). John, however, explicitly dissociates Jesus from that prophecy, asserting that Jesus' place of origin is Nazareth. It is possible that John knew nothing of the Christian tradition of Jesus' birth in Bethlehem (as it is seen in Luke and Matthew) or that if he knew it, he rejected it. While he unequivocally declares Jesus to be the Messiah (1:41), he emphasizes his purely human birth ("son of Joseph," 1:45) and the insignificance of his place of birth ("Can anything good come out of Nazareth?" 1:46). But John goes even further to show that Jesus is not to be identified with popular kingly hopes. In 6:15 Jesus escapes from a crowd eager to acclaim him king. Before Pilate, Jesus' replies concerning his role as king are ambiguous, but he directly repudiates kingship by any ordinary definition (18:36).

In Zechariah 4, especially 4:14, the prophet describes two messiahs: an anointed king and an anointed priest. Further documentation for the messianic dyarchy is presented in the postbiblical Jewish writings,[33] such as the Testaments of the Twelve Patriarchs[34] and the Manual of Discipline.[35] The latter is a document found at Qumran in which the structure and expectations of the community are outlined. The kingly and priestly functions are combined in Jesus, as John depicts him, since he is both the King of Israel (1:49) and the Lamb of God who takes away the sin of the world (1:29). But unlike the Jewish priest who offers the sacrifice, the Lamb is himself the sacrificial victim. The mingling of priestly and kingly imagery is surely characteristic of John's picture of Jesus, but he has modified the expectation in the light of the reality of Jesus, as faith understands him.

A second redemptive figure mentioned in John's gospel is Elijah. The Jewish understanding of Elijah was primarily built not on the account in 1 Kings 17–19, but on the prophecies of his return at the End of the Age in Malachi 3:1 and 4:5. In the (Wisdom of) Sirach

48:1–11, Elijah is extolled as one who was God's agent, who raised the dead, who "brought kings down to destruction" and anointed others "to exact retribution," and whose coming is expected to turn the hearts of the nation to its God. Significantly, Elijah's role is described by Malachi 3:3–4 as reforming the priesthood—that is, "purifying the sons of Levi" and making their worship acceptable to Yahweh. To associate the Messiah with Elijah, or to see Elijah as taking the place of the Messiah, is to lay stress on the purificatory, judgmental function of God's agent in the End Time. The synoptic tradition emphasizes the preparatory role of Elijah, who makes ready the Lord's way (Isa. 40 and Mal. 3), and therefore equates Elijah with John the Baptist. In John's gospel, however, John the Baptist rejects the title of Elijah (1:21). Although Jesus is not *identified* as Elijah in the Gospel of John, it is perhaps implied that he *is* Elijah, by his being referred to as "the prophet," the term used of Elijah at times in the rabbinic sources.

According to John 1:21, John the Baptist also rejects the title of the eschatological "prophet" of Deuteronomy 18. But it is linked to Jesus by the populace after the Feeding of the Five Thousand (6:14) and by those who heard Jesus' announcement about the Spirit being poured out (7:37–40). And the fact that the title "prophet" is followed by the question concerning Jesus' being Messiah (7:41) shows that both titles carry significance in John's gospel as redemptive roles. That impression is confirmed by the note that Jesus' detractors exclude the possibility that he could be a prophet since he comes from Galilee (7:52). Once more, then, John is showing that Jesus both fulfills the categories of Jewish redemptive expectation and transforms them. John summarizes his own point of view well in the words of Philip:

> We have found him about whom Moses in the law and also the prophets wrote, Jesus son of Joseph from Nazareth. (1:45).

Other titles are used for Jesus, such as "the Holy One of God" in 6:69, which is presented as the confession of faith in Jesus by the disciples. But the climax of all the confessions is attributed to the one disciple whose doubt has become proverbial: Thomas. After seeing for himself the reality of the Resurrection of Jesus and the corporeality of Jesus' body, Thomas exclaims, "My Lord and my God!" (20:28). In both the Greek-speaking and the Aramaic-speaking branches of the early church (Phil. 2:10–11 and 1 Cor. 16:22, respectively), Jesus was from the beginning acclaimed as Lord. It is widely recognized that the earliest Christian confession was "Jesus is Lord."[36] The fact that the Septuagint translated the holy name of God, YHWH (or Yahweh), as *kurios* (= lord), combined with the fact that the church designated Jesus as Lord, encouraged the interpretation of the Old Testament through Christian eyes, and many of the attributes and functions of God were assigned by Christian faith to Jesus. These include the creation of the world (John 1:3) and the renewal of God's people.

Probably the most important christological title in John's gospel is Son of Man. In Daniel 7 the Son of Man is a corporate figure—representing the faithful remnant of the Jews in the Maccabean period—who appears on the clouds of heaven at the End of the Age to establish God's Kingdom. The Son of Man moves, therefore, from heaven to earth, where God's rule is established. In John, however, the Son of Man has already come to earth (1:51) and will complete his work when he returns to heaven (6:58, 62). In 2 Esdras 13:3, 26, the man who comes with the clouds of heaven (as does the Son of Man in Dan. 7:13) is explicitly said to be the agent of redemption "whom the Most High has been keeping for many ages." That is to say, he is a preexistent being, just as Jesus is represented in John. Unlike the figure in Daniel and 2 Esdras, however, Jesus' final action is declared by John to be his return to the Father (6:61; 20:17). Indeed, for John the Kingdom of God has to do with "heavenly things" (3:12). It was disclosed by one who came from heaven and will be entered only by those who are "born from above" (3:3). What moved John to use this apocalyptic title, Son of Man, in a manner that has so little to do with traditional Jewish apocalyptic expectations? The answer lies in the wisdom tradition of Hellenistic Judaism.

Jesus As Wisdom Incarnate

In the late biblical tradition, as well as in Jewish writings of the Hellenistic period, there is another figure in addition to the Son of Man who is depicted as preexistent: Wisdom (Prov. 8:22–23; Sir. 24:9; Wisd. of Sol. 6:22). Wisdom not only preexists but has a role in the creation of the world (Prov. 8:23–31), since she serves as God's companion in the bringing of the world into existence (Wisd. of Sol. 8:4–6; Sir. 1). As R.E. Brown has shown, Wisdom is portrayed in this literature as the effulgence of divine glory (Wisd. of Sol. 7:25, 26), as the illuminator of mankind (Wisd. of Sol. 7:10, 29), as descended from heaven (Prov. 8:31; Sir. 24:8; Wisd. of Sol. 9:10), as returning to God (1 En. 42:2), as having the chief role in instructing mankind concerning heavenly things (Job 11:6–7; Wisd. of Sol. 9:16–18), as taking the initiative to engage hearers of her message (Prov. 1:20–21; 8:1–4; Wisd. of Sol. 6:16), and as experiencing rejection (Prov. 1:24–45; Bar. 3:12; 1 En. 42:2).[37] All these features and functions are also discernible in John's picture of Jesus. However, instead of identifying Jesus with the feminine figure Wisdom (= *Sophia*, in Greek), John links Jesus with the masculine figure Logos (= Word).[38]

For John, the Logos is the divine purpose for the Creation and the Redemption of the world. It is not an expedient that God came up with when matters went out of control. The Logos is eternally with God (1:1) and partakes of the divine nature, but is not simply to be equated with God. The Logos is essential to God's purpose but is not merely another name for God. Rather, the Logos is the means by which the purpose of God for the Creation and for his people is formulated, articulated and put into operation. Unlike the Neoplatonic philosophers and the Gnostics of the second century, there is for John no scorning of the physical world, as though it consisted of inherently inferior matter. Rather, it is the very nature and purpose of God to create the world and then to redeem it (1:3). This divine intention, shining like a light among humans, has always been disclosing itself, although opposition has sought to extinguish it (1:4–5, 9). The Logos has been present and active in the world, but it was not recognized for what it was (1:10), either by the created order or by its own people (1:11). Possibly John shifts at this point from describing the Logos as impersonal to depicting the Logos as manifest in human form in Jesus of Nazareth, in which case the translation would be "He came to what was his own, but his own people received him not." In 1:14, John states explicitly that the Logos is manifest in human form. The revelation of God that the Logos brings is accessible to all who are willing to receive it, not just to those who by ethnic descent or by pious mode of life consider themselves to have some special claim on God (1:12–13).

This possibility of universal recognition of God's purpose for all humanity and its sociocultural world has been given a new basis in the advent into the world of the Logos in a human form, the Word become flesh (1:14), through whom the glorious purpose and nature of God are disclosed for the faithful. Jews traditionally assumed that the full revelation of God was available through the Law of Moses, but John declares that the full knowledge of God's gracious purpose and the final disclosure of his truth have been granted by God through Jesus Christ (1:17). The incarnation, therefore, is the crucial moment in the whole of history. God's purpose has always been present and operative, though in a partly hidden way, but now it is fully revealed, at least for the faithful, who "have seen his glory, glory as of a father's only Son" (1:14).

Martin Hengel has drawn attention to a development in Jewish understanding of the Law during the Hellenistic period that resembles John's representation of the Logos. Although the influence was probably not conscious, the equating of Law with Wisdom (Bar. 4:1; Sir. 24 [esp. vs. 23]) led to the view that Law is cosmic in its meaning and absolute in its demands. Like the Stoics, devotees of the Law of Moses sought to live their lives in conformity to it. It came to be regarded as coexistent with God and an object of devotion, even of love, as is evident in Psalms 119:47–48, 97, 113, 159, 163, and 176. Its existence as an eternal paradigm is reminiscent of the Platonic concept of the ideal world. This view of revelation as timeless contrasts with the traditional view of God's self-disclosure as historical, as set forth in the biblical narratives and as summarized in passages such as Deuteronomy 26:5–9, Joshua 24, Psalms 78, and Sirach 44–50. Although the Law originates with God, it was said to have a distinct ontological status of its own, whereby it serves as "the mediator of creation and revelation between God and the world."[39] What distinguishes this view of Law from John's view of Logos, however, is that only the Logos "became flesh," appearing in human form. The Law, though personified at times, is never identified as an historical person, as the Logos is with Jesus.

In John, the concept of incarnate Wisdom has been further enriched by its association with three great figures of Israel's past: Jacob, Abraham, and Moses. The stage is set for this transformation of the Jewish tradition in John 1:51, where the imagery of angels ascending and descending on the progenitor and eponymous hero, Israel, in Jacob's dream (Gen. 28:12) is linked with Jesus, who is identified as the Son of Man. In Genesis 28:13, Abraham is mentioned as the one with whom God first entered into the covenant relationship; in John 9:51–58, Jesus claims that Abraham as a prophet foresaw and rejoiced in his coming, and that he existed before Abraham. But the most extensive set of comparisons and contrasts with a figure out of ancient Israel is with Moses.

In 1:17, John contrasts the revelation that came through Moses (the Law) with that given through Jesus (grace and truth). According to John, the coming of Jesus was foretold in Moses and the prophets (1:45). Moses' act of deliverance of his people from the deadly serpents has its analogue in Jesus' crucifixion and exaltation (3:14). Rejection of Jesus is tantamount to rejection of Moses, whose writings—correctly understood—tell about Jesus. Jesus' provision of bread in the desert (John 6) surpasses the provision of manna through Moses (6:32). Jesus' acts of healing are contrasted with the surgical act of circumcision as required in the Law of Moses (7:22–23). In addition to these explicit links, Jesus is presented in John as the fulfillment of the roles of prophet (6:14) and King of Israel (1:49), assigned in Jewish tradition to Moses.

John's understanding of Jesus as king and prophet converge in John 6, which is an adaptation of the synoptic account of Jesus' Feeding the Five Thousand (cf. Mark 6:32–44), developed on the basis of the Old Testament miracle of the manna in the desert (Exod. 16:11–35; Num. 11:7–9; Ps. 78:23–35). John's account represents an interpretive expansion of the biblical text of a type known from Qumran sources of the period and subsequently developed in Jewish expository texts (Midrash).[40] In Deuteronomy 33:5, and in rabbinic and other Jewish exegetical texts building on this passage, Moses is depicted as king of Israel.[41] His role as prophet is linked with his performance of "signs and wonders" in Deuteronomy 34:10–11:

> Never since has there arisen a prophet in Israel like Moses, whom the Lord knew face to face. He was unequaled for all the signs and the wonders that the Lord sent him to perform in the land of Egypt.

The attribution of signs and wonders to Moses is found in the Wisdom of Solomon 10:16 as well. The Johannine portrayal of Jesus builds upon this picture of Moses. In John 6:14–15, Jesus is acclaimed as prophet and king as a consequence of a miracle, which parallels but transcends the biblical account of God's deliverance of his people: Moses' miracle sustained human life, but Jesus' bestows eternal life (6:5). Jesus, referred to in 6:14 as the "prophet who is to come," is thus seen as fulfilling the promise made through Moses (Deut. 18:18) of an eschatological prophet.[42] John's comprehensive title for this eschatological redeemer is Son of Man (6:27, 53, 62).

John's Understanding of History

John's gospel is theological interpretation of Jesus with belief in the incarnation at its core. This does not imply, however, that John had no interest in historical information. In fact, it is because the idea of incarnation is so central to his thought that John uses the gospel form and recounts the facts of Jesus' earthly, human life. Not only does he adapt the synoptic tradition to serve his own ends, but he also supplies additional valuable historical information of his own. Throughout his gospel, John's purpose is to instruct his community about its resources and responsibilities and to articulate its role in the wider world.

John and the Synoptics

The relationship of John to the synoptic tradition is complex. On a number of points John actually supplements or even corrects the synoptic accounts. For example, John records the importance of John the Baptist, both for the launching of Jesus' ministry and for the tensions that arose after Jesus' death between his followers and John's.[43] John 1:35–42 shows that Jesus took over the nucleus of his followers from the disciples of John the Baptist. The parallel between Jesus' activity and John's, including baptisms performed by both, is only thinly disguised behind the rather ambiguous or even contradictory language of 3:22–26 and 4:1–3. John 3:22 mentions the baptizing activity of Jesus in Judea while John and his followers were baptizing in the Jordan Valley or one of its tributaries.[44] It is plausible to assume that historically there was a period of direct competition between Jesus and John, and that Jesus accordingly withdrew from public activity (4:3) until John's imprisonment (3:24) made it clear that there would be no further rivalry between the two men. Their respective disciples seem to have perpetuated the conflict, however, as is apparent from the anti-Baptist polemic inserted into the Logos hymn. If we omit verses 6, 7, 8, and 15 from John 1, the prologue moves along smoothly and is symmetrically structured:

> God's Logos: verses 1, 2, 3
>
> Logos and Light: verses 4, 5, 9
>
> Logos and World: verses 10, 11, 12
>
> Logos and God: verses 14b, 16, 17
>
> Logos As Revelation: verses 14a, 18

It seems clear that John was writing his gospel at a time when a claim was being made that the Baptist came before Jesus and therefore should be considered superior to him. The interpolated verses are intended to show not only that John is subordinate in his role, but also that Jesus originated before him: "He who comes after me ranks before me, for he was before me" (John 1:15). The argument is based on John's claim that the Logos is preexistent. Thus, John combined a historical fact about Jesus—his situation of dependence on and then tension with John the Baptist—with a fact about the history of the church: the competition between the followers of the Baptist and those of Jesus. We see concretely how John understands history: as a dialectic between what happened in the past and the meaning of those events in the life of the church in his own time.

Another historical point already noted is John's stress on the humble birth of Jesus in Nazareth. He gives no hint of belief in the virgin birth. Instead, as noted above, he states directly that Joseph is the father of Jesus (1:45; 6:42). John took for granted Jesus' Galilean origins (7:40–42), as did the Jewish opponents of the early church who attempted to discredit Jesus because he was not born in Bethlehem according to the traditional Jewish messianic expectation. For John, however, birth in Nazareth was quite in keeping with Jesus' nature: The true and full humanity of Jesus as it was evident in the ordinariness of his birth and the insignificance of his birthplace were essential elements in his role as the Word made flesh (= human).

A third area in which John may be more accurate than the synoptics is the chronology of the passion story, which combines historical tradition and symbolic meaning. In the synoptic accounts, the Last Supper is a Passover meal, and Jesus dies in the closing hours of the Passover, on the eve of the Sabbath, which would have begun at sundown on Friday. In John, however, Passover and the Sabbath coincide, so that Jesus takes his last meal with his followers the night before the Passover, and he dies on Friday at the very hour the faithful Jews were slaughtering the lambs in preparation for the Passover, which was to begin with the Sabbath at sundown. John is most explicit in declaring that Jesus' final meal was before the Passover, not on the feast itself (13:1; 18:29; 18:39; 19:31). In addition to preserving a more accurate historical recollection (in Luke, there is an apparent conflict between 22:8, which describes the Last Supper as a Passover meal, and 22:15, which implies that Jesus will not live to eat the Passover), John heightens the symbolic meaning of Jesus as the Passover lamb by setting his death outside the city at the moment the lambs are being killed in the Temple enclosure.

Elsewhere, John alters the probable historical facts, or at least the sequence of events, in order to bring out more forcefully the theological meaning he sees in them. The contrast between John as the one who baptizes with water and Jesus as the one who baptizes with the Spirit is intensified by omitting the report that Jesus was baptized at all. We should expect it to take place in 1:31, but only the coming of the Spirit upon Jesus is described.

In the synoptic accounts, one of the factors that brings the resentment of the Jewish leaders against Jesus to a head is his unauthorized action in cleansing the Temple courts (Mark 11:15–17 = Matt. 21:12–13 and Luke 19:45–46). Although some scholars think that this incident may have actually occurred earlier than Jesus' final week in Jerusalem,[45] it was a turning point in the minds of the Jewish authorities; afterward, his execution was inevitable. But in John's narrative (2:13–22), as noted earlier, both the cleansing of the Temple and the discussion of its destruction occur at the beginning of Jesus' ministry. The function that they serve for John is not to provide a climax to the hostility of official Judaism toward Jesus, but to point out from the outset (1) that Jesus intends nothing less than the complete transformation of the worship of God, and (2) that his death and resurrection will be the actions of God by which the new community of faith will be brought into being as the true locus for the worship of God, where God will meet his people (= temple). Once more John moves from reporting the event (Jesus' announcement of the new temple) to describing the situation of the early church (to which the meaning of that event was disclosed) "when . . . he was raised from the dead" (3:22).

According to the synoptic accounts, Jesus spent nearly the whole of his ministry in Galilee and other adjacent northern regions, but according to John, he was active primarily in Jerusalem and vicinity, although the geography and sequence of his movements to and from Jerusalem are not always easy to follow. John's preference for Jerusalem as the setting for Jesus' ministry may be an actual historical recollection, but it is more likely intended to serve a polemical purpose, since Jesus' conflict with the Jewish leaders and challenge to the Jewish institutions seems to serve a clearer symbolic function when it is located in Jerusalem, the central focus of Judaism.

Because John is depicting a human life as the vehicle of divine revelation, he is concerned for action as well as word, for sequence as well as significance. Accordingly, his gospel is a real narrative, not merely a collection of sayings, as is the apocryphal Gospel of Thomas (see pp. 260–64). The course of the story moves from the beginnings in the baptism by the Spirit, through the public career of teaching and healing and controversy, to the cross and Resurrection. As such, it is in a general way similar to the other gospel narratives. But the differences from the synoptics are more evident. From the very outset of Jesus' ministry, according to John, the hour of his death is predetermined. Nothing can happen to him apart from this divinely ordained plan. That theme is merely announced without explanation in 2:4: "My hour has not yet come." But it is made clear in 7:6, and especially 7:30 and 8:20, that no one can seize Jesus until the designated hour. The climax of this series of sayings comes in 12:23, on the eve of the Passion, when Jesus announces that the hour has arrived for him to be "glorified," which in 12:32 is interpreted to mean the hour of his being lifted up (crucified) in death. There is at this point in John's account a vestige of the struggle in Gethsemane, when Jesus is facing the prospect of death and prays for the "cup" of suffering to pass from him (cf. Mark 14:32–42 and parallels). But in John the question is no more than a rhetorical one: "And what shall I say, 'Father, save me from this hour'? No, for this purpose I have come to this hour" (12:27). John is asserting that the force at work in Jesus' fate is not that God has established a series of inevitable future apocalyptic struggles and suffering, as is the case in Mark's view, but that there has already begun a calm unfolding of the predetermined course of events in accordance with the divinely established schedule.

Jesus' Significance for the Johannine Community

At the same time that John wants to place Jesus at the point of intersection of the historically concrete and the timeless, he seeks also to interpret Jesus in such a way as to demonstrate his meaning for John's own community and its situation in life. The very emphasis that John gives to the corporeality of Jesus—"the Word made flesh" (1:14), Jesus as weary and thirsty (4:5–7), "put your hand . . . in my side" (20:27)— is aimed in part at the need of his community to combat the heretical notion that Jesus was a purely spiritual being. Or it may have had as its target an incipient Gnosticism that denied the goodness of the created world. But in either case, its historical context is the Johannine community, not the original historical setting in the time of Jesus.

We can infer from John that there were serious problems confronting his community as a result of outside opposition, especially from the emergent rabbinic leadership around the end of the first century C.E., which resented the Christians' claiming as their own both Scripture and the covenant relationship with God. Further, the new community opened its membership to non-Jews and dismissed the temple as the central locus of God's presence on earth, as is indicated by the tradition's recalling the words of Jesus to the Samaritan woman about the impossibility of locating the true place of worship in Jerusalem or elsewhere (4:21–23), and by the admission of "other sheep" (10:16) into the flock of God. In all probability the hostility between the synagogue and the Johannine church had mounted to the point at which the Christians demanded public confession of Jesus and the Jews excluded from the synagogue those who made such a witness. This tension is reflected in such passages as 9:22, 12:42, and 16:2. The conclusion of the story of the Healing of the Man Born Blind (9:8–41) illustrates vividly the mutual antipathy that must have been a feature of the situation of John's community.[46]

Both the hostility from without and the mystical bent within seem to have led John's community to turn in upon itself in sectarian fashion. Wayne Meeks has noted that the inconclusiveness of the dialogues, the use of double-meaning words, and the statements in riddles, as well as the evident misunderstandings of Jesus and his words on the part of the disciples and others, are evidences of a theory of knowledge that supported this sectarianism.[47] Truth is not transmitted by direct communication based on public information but is arrived at by meditation, reflection, dialogue, and above all by spiritual revelation within the community itself. Meeks has characterized the Gospel of John as "a book for insiders . . . to provide reinforcement for the community's social identity. . . . It provided a symbolic universe which gave religious legitimacy, a theodicy, to the group's actual isolation from the larger society."[48]

The Johannine school engaged in adapting and reappropriating the Jesus tradition in the way that it thought would best serve its own needs. This is evident in the editing process that was apparently not yet completed when the Gospel of John assumed its present form.[49] Many scholars have noted the rough transitions in John and even some apparent contradictions. For example, did Jesus perform baptisms (John 3:22) or did he not (4:2)? Attempts have been made to account for these irregularities on the ground that John was using sources that he did not fully assimilate. More plausible is the proposal that this gospel is the product of an interpretive school, like the Qumran community, which was in process of reinterpreting the Scriptures in light of its group experience and its hopes for divine vindication in the future. In some cases the tensions in the text reflect issues still under discussion within the community and points of controversy with opponents. In other cases the abrupt shifts seem to be awkward literary transitions.

Evidence of such awkward editorial connections can be seen, for example, in 4:54 and 5:1. At the end of Chapter 4 Jesus is in Galilee, having recently come back from Jerusalem (4:43). But in 5:1 he is back in Jerusalem, even though in 6:1 he is suddenly in Galilee once more and crossing the sea. The transition from 4:54 to 6:1 would be smooth, but from 4:54 to 5:1 it is inexplicably abrupt; thus Chapter 5 seems to be out of place. Equally rough transitions can be seen between 7:52 and 8:12[50] and between 8:59 and 9:1. Additionally, although 14:25–31 reads like a farewell to the disciples and ends in the injunction "Rise, let us go hence," there are three long discourse chapters to be uttered by Jesus before he actually sets out for the garden (of Gethsemane, although the name is not mentioned in John 18:1; see Mark 14:32). Some commentators try to get around this difficulty by designating these discourses as having been "spoken on the way to the garden," which hardly seems convincing.

A clear case of inconsistency as a product of controversy can be seen in 3:25 and 4:1. In both passages, it looks as if there were disputes between Jesus (together with his followers) and the disciples of John the Baptist. The implied question in 3:26 ("What are you [John] going to do about it"?) concerns Jesus' success in finding candidates for baptism, not a dispute with an unspecified Jew. The apparently contradictory statements mentioned earlier about Jesus' baptizing are also part of this controversy. What seems to have happened is this: (1) The conflict with the Baptist's followers has been toned down, and (2) the presumably undignified act of performing a baptism has been attributed to Jesus' disciples, rather than to him personally.

A special, unmistakable case of editing that was not completed can be seen in John 21, which by style and vocabulary has long been recognized as an appendix. John 20:30–31 forms an appropriate conclusion to the rest of the gospel, whereas John 21 is rather lame as an end to the book. All the manuscripts of John include this chapter, however, so it must be as old as the gospel in its present literary form, even though it is not integrated into the gospel in form, content, or style, and probably represents a later development than the material John assembled and synthesized more completely for the main part of his gospel.

The passage of time and the heightening of hostility did not bring discouragement to the Johannine community. The members' perception of God and themselves freed them from anxiety about conflicts in the present life: God had guaranteed to preserve them from both the world and the Evil One (17:6–19). They were to be apprehensive about neither death (12:24) nor the delay in the Parousia, which they continued to believe would occur "in a little while" (12:35–36). The Last Day, with resurrection and judgment, would come in its own time (5:28–29). Meanwhile, they were conscious of the preparations even now in progress that would usher them into the presence of God (14:3).

John's Concern for the Church in the World

John replaced the concern for the End of the Age, which is dominant in the synoptic tradition, with a concern for the church's fulfillment of its mission in the world. Jesus is reported to have prayed not for deliverance of Christians from the world but for their preservation in the midst of the world.[51] Christians are to see to it that the flock is fed and cared for, as the epilogue of John (Chapter 21) phrases it ("Feed my sheep," 21:17). With the disappearance of the sense of an imminent Parousia, it is anticipated that the witness of the church will continue from generation to generation: "Blessed are those who have not seen and yet believe" (20:29). The bounds of the church are to be extended beyond Judaism ("I have other sheep, that are not of this fold; I must bring them also," 10:16).

The work of the church in the world is primarily that of standing faithful to Jesus' command to obey his commandment of love:

> By this everyone will know that you are my disciples, if you have love for one another. (13:35)

His followers are to be set apart in the truth (17:17), although they are not to withdraw from the world. Rather, they will experience joy in the midst of the world's hostility toward them (17:13). The unity of their community will be the chief witness to the oneness of Jesus with God (17:11). There is no suggestion of a mission to convert the world totally, and no call to become the instrument through which God will defeat the evil powers. The history of the world will not be altered by their work; it is their own personal history and the history of those who come to have faith that will be transformed through Jesus.

The Relationship of Theology and History in John's Gospel

For John it is essential that Jesus be portrayed as a historical person, truly human, with human birth, parentage, needs, and even limitations. At the same time, Jesus is more than human, according to John, and at many points can also transcend human limitations, as he does in performing the many signs John attributes to him. In some ways, as we have seen, John seeks to supplement or even to correct the historical tradition preserved in the synoptic Gospels. But the narrative framework of John is not an end in itself, through which John seeks to present a primarily historical account of Jesus. John's gospel is rather a theological essay in the form of a gospel. The historical dimensions of his account are of use to him, but his main concern is his theological understanding of Jesus as the Word of God becoming human (1:14).

John does believe that the intention of God to reveal himself to man took place in the historical reality of Jesus, but he has no interest in the unfolding course of history as such. He has no scheme of the ages, such as we have found in Mark and Luke and, to a lesser extent, in Q. It is the history of the self as a member of God's new people that is John's primary focus. The awesome prospect of death, resurrection, and judgment does not lie in the unpredictable future for John; these events occur again and again in every moment when the claim of Jesus calls the individual to a decision for or against the will of God.[52] John does not deny that there will be a resurrection or a judgment in the future, but the anxiety is removed from these future events by the belief that the decisive factor is the decision of faith that is made in every present moment. Using the form of historical narrative and locating the goal of history in the moment of decision, John succeeds in presenting his story of Jesus in terms of mystical participation in the new life that God has provided for his people.

Suggestions for Further Reading

Still useful are two older studies of the background of John's thoughts by C.H. Dodd: *The Interpretation of the Fourth Gospel** (Cambridge: Cambridge University Press, 1953); and *Historical Tradition in the*

Fourth Gospel* (Cambridge: Cambridge University Press, 1963). The most original theological interpretation of John was offered by Rudolf Bultmann, *Theology of the New Testament*,* vol. 2 (New York: Scribner's, 1955), even though his basic understanding of John has been called into question. Three fine commentaries on John are C.K. Barrett, *The Gospel According to St. John* (New York: Seabury, 1956); R.H. Lightfoot, *St. John's Gospel: A Commentary** (Oxford: Oxford University Press, 1956); and more recently the learned, detailed but readable two-volume work by Raymond E. Brown in the Anchor Bible, *The Gospel According to St. John* (Garden City, NY: Doubleday, 1966 [vol. 1], 1970 [vol. 2]). Brown's subsequent study, *The Community of the Beloved Disciple* (New York: Paulist Press, 1979) constitutes a superb analysis of the evidence for this community and a brilliant reconstruction of its origins and evolution.

Special studies of particular aspects of Johannine thought are Peder Borgen, *Bread from Heaven* (Leiden: Brill, 1966), in which the influence of Jewish Passover interpretations on John's story of the Feeding of the Five Thousand are traced; J.L. Martyn, *History and Theology in the Fourth Gospel* (New York: Harper & Row, 1968); D.M. Smith, Jr., *Johannine Christianity* (Columbia, SC: University of South Carolina Press, 1984); *John and Qumran*, ed. J.H. Charlesworth (London: Geoffrey Chapman, 1972); R.A. Culpepper, *Anatomy of the Fourth Gospel* (Philadelphia: Fortress Press, 1983); Robert Kysar, *John's Story of Jesus* (Philadelphia: Fortress Press, 1984); and A.E. Harvey, *Jesus on Trial: A Study in the Fourth Gospel* (London: SPCK, 1976).

*Available in a paperback edition.

NOTES

[1] Quoted by Eusebius, *Ecclesiastical History* 6.14.4–9, vol. 1 (trans. Kirsopp Lake) Loeb Classical Library (Cambridge, MA: Harvard University Press, 1957), from Clement's *Outlines* (of Holy Scripture), preserved only in fragments by other writers.

[2] Irenaeus, *Against Heresies* 3.11.8–9, in *The Ante-Nicene Fathers*, vol. 1 (trans. Alexander Roberts and James Donaldson; New York: 1899; reprint, Grand Rapids, MI: Eerdmans, 1953).

[3] Ibid., 3.11.1.

[4] Ibid., 3.11.7.

[5] The identification of the apostle John, the son of Zebedee, with the disciple who, according to the fourth gospel, was especially close to Jesus and the assumption that he is the disciple who wrote the fourth gospel are implied

by Irenaeus in *Against Heresies* 3.1.1; moreover, in 5.33.4 he describes Papias, bishop of Hieropolis in Asia Minor in the second century, as one who was a "hearer of John"—apparently meaning John the son of Zebedee. But Papias himself distinguishes this John from another, John the Presbyter (or Elder), who is classed among "other of the Lord's disciples" (quoted in Eusebius, *Ecclesiastical History* 3.39.4). Probably Irenaeus confused these two men; John the Presbyter (see 2 John 1 and 3 John 1) is, then, the man who is identified with the Johannine literature from the second century on, but there is no sure tradition linking him or the gospel with Ephesus or Asia Minor.

[6]Long ago C.F. Burney, in *The Aramaic Origin of the Fourth Gospel* (Oxford: Clarendon, 1922), attempted to show that Jesus taught in poetic form and that Aramaic poetry lies behind the Greek text of the Gospel of John. His intent was thereby to demonstrate the authenticity of the gospel as the actual words of Jesus.

[7]E.C. Colwell, *The Greek of the Fourth Gospel* (Chicago: University of Chicago Press, 1931).

[8]See for example G.D. Kilpatrick, "The Religious Background of the Fourth Gospel," in F.L. Cross, ed., *Studies in the Fourth Gospel* (London: A.R. Mowbray, 1957), p. 36. Also Barnabas Lindars, *New Testament Apologetic* (Philadelphia: Westminster, 1962), p. 269.

[9]See the further discussion in W.G. Kümmel, *Introduction to the New Testament*, 17th ed. (trans. H.C. Kee; Nashville: Abingdon, 1975), pp. 188–247. Raymond E. Brown, in his commentary in The Anchor Bible, *The Gospel According to John (I–XII)* (Garden City, NY: Doubleday, 1966), pp. cxxix–cxxx, concludes that there may have been Aramaic traditions drawn on by the author, but that the gospel as we have it was composed in Greek.

[10]On the schools in the Hellenistic-Roman world see R.A. Culpepper, *The Johannine School: An Evaluation of the Johannine School Hypothesis Based on an Investigation of the Nature of Ancient Schools* (Missoula, MT: Scholars Press, 1976) pp. 61–225; also Martin Hengel, *Judaism and Hellenism*, vol. 1 (Philadelphia: Fortress, 1974), pp. 65–83, where the impact of Greek education on Jewish culture is discussed.

[11]The features of charismatic itinerant preachers in the Cynic-Stoic tradition are described by Martin Hengel in his *Nachfolge und Charisma* [Discipleship and charisma] (Berlin: Töpelmann, 1968). See my discussion in *Community of the New Age: Studies in Mark's Gospel* (Macon, GA: Mercer University Press, 1983), pp. 89–90.

[12]See, for example, Rudolf Bultmann, *Gospel of John: A Commentary* (Philadelphia: Westminster, 1971), pp. 113, 180, 203, 205, 211, 238, 289, 329, 393, 395, 410, 698, 705. The source has been reconstructed by D.M. Smith, *The Composition and Order of the Fourth Gospel* (New Haven, CT: Yale University Press, 1965), pp. 38–44. For a summary and critique of source theories, including Robert Fortna's (see note 14 below), see W.G. Kümmel, *Introduction to the New Testament*, pp. 200–17.

[13]Bultmann includes this passage with his Signs Source.

[14]Robert T. Fortna, *The Gospel of Signs: A Reconstruction of the Narrative Source Underlying the Fourth Gospel* (Cambridge, MA: Cambridge University

Press, 1970), pp. 235–45, includes in his Signs Source a prologue and epilogue; the witness of John the Baptist; the call of the first disciples; seven signs; the Cleansing of the Temple (which Fortna thinks was placed in this source just before the Passion, as in the synoptics); the anointing; the entry into Jerusalem; the Last Supper; Jesus' arrest and hearings; and his crucifixion, burial, and resurrection. Only the teachings are omitted, which implies the existence of a kind of gospel that did not recount Jesus' teaching activity—in sharp contrast to Q, which consisted almost wholly of teachings material.

[15]The term *divine man* no longer enjoys the vogue it once had in biblical studies, since its imprecision as a term has been shown by scholars such as David L. Tiede, *The Charismatic Figure As Miracle Worker* (Missoula, MT: Scholars Press, 1972). For a summary of the evidence see my *Medicine, Miracle and Magic in New Testament Times* (SNTS Monograph Series; Cambridge: Cambridge University Press, 1986; reprint, 1990), pp. 84–85.

[16]Smith, *The Composition and Order of the Fourth Gospel*, convincingly argues that the stylistic unity of the gospel as it stands is such as to show that whatever sources the evangelist had access to have been so thoroughly reworked as to render indecisive any appeal to them as a clue to interpretation (p. 114). He questions both the logic of converting an inconsistent and frequently awkward text into a unified and consistent version and the usefulness of an interpretation that is based on what the interpreter thinks the author/editor ought to have said (p. 241).

[17]See for example R.E. Brown, *The Gospel According to John I–XII* (Garden City, NY: Doubleday, 1966), pp. xliv–xlvii.

[18]Barnabas Lindars, *Behind the Fourth Gospel* (London: SPCK, 1971), pp. 27–42.

[19]For John's interpretation of this term, see p. 227.

[20]The older form-critical designation for this type of pericope is that of Martin Dibelius: an "epiphany story," since it functions to disclose the divine nature of Jesus. In *From Tradition to Gospel*, 3d ed. (trans. B.L. Woolf; New York: Scribner's, 1965), pp. 94–96.

[21]God's provision of food for Israel in the wilderness is described in Exodus 16:1–16 and Numbers 11:4–9.

[22]Fully discussed in Peder Borgen, *Bread from Heaven* (Leiden: Brill, 1965).

[23]In earlier discussion of this feature of John's gospel, Bultmann asserted that John wanted to eliminate all references to the sacraments and to treat them as purely spiritual. See his *Theology of the New Testament*, vol. 2 (trans. Kendrick Grobel; New York: Scribner's, 1955), pp. 54, 58–59. At the opposite extreme, Oscar Cullmann found the sacraments pervasively present in John. See his *Early Christian Worship* (trans. A.S. Todd and J.B. Torrance; Naperville, IL: Allenson, 1953). In his masterful commentary on John, Raymond E. Brown has shown that some allusions to the sacraments in John are the work of later redactors, but he insists that "among the four Gospels, it is to John most of all that we owe the deep Christian understanding of the purpose of Baptism and the Eucharist," which is "an indispensable means of transmitting God's life to men through Jesus." No longer is the gaining of eternal life "the result of believing in Jesus: it comes from feeding on his flesh and drinking his blood" (6:54), in *The*

Gospel According to John I–XII (Garden City, NY: Doubleday, 1966), pp. cxii–cxiv and 284.

[24]Bultmann considered these references to the future resurrection to be incompatible with the basic outlook of John and therefore explained them as interpolations by a redactor who sought to make John's eschatology more orthodox. Compare his *Theology of the New Testament*, vol. 2, p. 39, and *History and Eschatology* (Edinburgh: University of Edinburgh Press, 1957), p. 47, n. 1. There is no manuscript evidence that these passages are later additions, however. And, more importantly, they demonstrate that John was concerned with correcting an eschatology that concentrated solely on the future, not with replacing it entirely by translating it without remainder into terms of an existentialist theology of present decision.

[25]Bultmann summarizes this myth in *Primitive Christianity in Its Contemporary Setting* (trans. R.H. Fuller; Cleveland: Meridian, 1957), pp. 163–69, and in *Theology of the New Testament*, vol. 1, pp. 166–68, and vol. 2, pp. 12–13.

[26]*The Odes of Solomon*, J.H. Charlesworth, with translation and notes (Oxford: Clarendon, 1973). See also his "Qumran, John and the Odes of Solomon," in *John and Qumran*, ed. J.H. Charlesworth (London: Geoffrey Chapman, 1972), pp. 107–36.

[27]There is a vast literature concerning this tiny sect of the Mandaeans, which presumably still exists at the lower end of the Tigris-Euphrates valley. A Semitic-speaking group, the sect traces its origin to a migration from Palestine. John the Baptist is an important figure for the Mandaeans. They claim to possess special revelation, which is preserved within the sect in the form of sacred writings. Some of their documents have long been known, but through the indefatigable efforts of a learned British woman, Lady D.S. Drower, many of their documents have been translated and published. An account of the sect, including a compendium of its teachings, is given in Lady Drower's *The Mandaeans of Iraq and Iran: Their Cults, Customs, Magic, Legends, and Folklore* (Oxford: Oxford University Press, 1937).

[28]Kurt Rudolph, *Die Mandäer*, [The Mandaeans] vol. 1 (Göttingen: Vandenhoeck & Ruprecht, 1960), p. 69.

[29]See the devastating critique of Bultmann in Carsten Colpe, *Die religionsgeschichtliche Schule: Darstellung und Kritik ihres Bildes vom gnostischen Erlösermythus* [The history-of-religions school: Sketch and critique of its image of the Gnostic redeemer myth] (Göttingen: Vandenhoeck & Ruprecht, 1961), pp. 186–89.

[30]J.H. Charlesworth, "A Critical Comparison of the Dualism in 1 QS 3:13–4:26 and the Dualism Contained in the Gospel of John," in *John and Qumran*, pp. 76–106.

[31]George MacRae, "The Ego-Proclamation in Gnostic Sources," in *The Trial of Jesus*, ed. Ernest Bammel (London: SCM, 1970), pp. 123–39.

[32]The basic studies of this movement are by Gershom G. Scholem: *Major Trends in Jewish Mysticism* (New York: Schocken, 1954); and *Jewish Gnosticism, Merkebah Mysticism and Talmudic Tradition* (New York: Jewish Theological Seminary of America, 1960). The apocryphal work *The Testament of Job* consists of retelling of the Job story from the standpoint of *Merkebah* mysticism, as I have shown in a study of this document, "Satan, Magic and Salvation in the Testament of Job," in *Society of Biblical*

Literature 1974 Seminar Papers, ed. George MacRae (Cambridge, MA: Society of Biblical Literature, 1974), pp. 53–76.

[33]By "postbiblical Jewish writings" is meant the Jewish works purported to have been written by biblical characters but actually written later than the second century B.C.E. They were not recognized by the whole of the Jewish community as authoritative. The writings have been called by Christians "Apocrypha" (including the so-called Deuterocanonicals) and the "Pseudepigrapha." Scholarly translations of the former writings with introductions and notes are available in the *Cambridge Annotated Study Apocrypha,* ed. H.C. Kee (Cambridge: Cambridge University Press, 1994); and of the latter in *The Old Testament Pseudepigrapha,* ed. J.H. Charlesworth, vol. 1, 1983, and vol. 2, 1985 (Garden City, NY: Doubleday).

[34]My translation and notes for the Testaments of the Twelve Patriarchs are in the *Old Testament Pseudepigrapha,* vol. 1, pp. 775–828. Some of the most directly relevant texts are Testament of Judah 21:2; 25:1–2; Testament of Issachar 5:7; Testament of Levi 8:14; Testament of Dan 5:4, 7; Testament of Naphtali 8:2.

[35]A fine translation of the Manual of Discipline, or Community Rule, or Scroll of the Rule (1QS) is in *The Dead Sea Scrolls in English,* trans. G. Vermes, 3d ed. (London and New York: Pelican Books, 1987). There are two messianic figures in the Manual of Discipline (1QS 9:10–11), and a king and an anointed priest in the Annex to the Manual (1QSa 2:11–22). See the essay on this theme by K.G. Kuhn, "The Two Messiahs of Aaron and Israel," in Krister Stendahl, ed., *The Scrolls and the New Testament* (New York: Harper Brothers, 1957), pp. 54–64.

[36]Joseph Fitzmyer, in his analysis of the synoptic passage in which Jesus links the role of Messiah with God's exaltation of David's son to his right hand (Luke 20:41–44; Mark 12:35–37a; Matt. 22:41–46), proposes that this interpretation may have originated with Jesus, since there are no clear precedents for it in Jewish sources. "Luke implies that the full understanding of Jesus' relation to David and of the nature of his lordship comes only with resurrection-faith." *Gospel According to Luke X–XXIV,* pp. 1309–1314.

[37]Brown, *The Gospel According to John I–XII,* pp. cxxii–cxxv.

[38]As noted earlier (p. 1), recent feminist interpreters of the New Testament have begun to promote the claim that the historical Jesus was actually a female named Sophia, and that male chauvinists soon took over the movement and portrayed Jesus as a male, as he appears uniformly throughout the gospel and other early Christian traditions. The theory is that Paul inadvertently revealed the feminine identity of Jesus when he spoke of "her" as "Christ the power of God and the wisdom *(Sophia)* of God" (1 Cor. 1:24). By this line of reasoning, one could also infer that Jesus' original name was *Dynamis,* which happens also to be feminine. Ignored is the fact that in Greek, as in many other languages, the gender of words and sexual distinctions are not directly correlated, so that use of an abstract term of feminine gender implies nothing about the sexual identity of the one with whom that term is associated. The theory is sheer conjecture, contrived in violation of the linguistic structures of Greek, and runs counter to all the evidence about Jesus from the early Jewish, Christian,

and Roman sources. The motivation for this recent proposal that Jesus is really Sophia is ideological, not logical or linguistic.

[39] Hengel, *Judaism and Hellenism*, vol. 1, pp. 169–75. R.G. Hamerton-Kelly, *Pre-Existence, Widsom, and Son of Man* (Cambridge: Cambridge University Press, 1973), also emphasizes the Jewish Wisdom myth as the primary historical precedent for the development of the Johannine Logos–Son of Man figure (pp. 206–09). See also James M. Reese, *Hellenistic Influence on the Book of Wisdom and Its Consequences* (Rome: Pontifical Biblical Institute, 1970), who graphically demonstrates the verbal similarities between the portrayal of divine Wisdom in the Jewish tradition and the Hellenistic veneration of Isis as the stabilizer of the cosmos and the guardian of the human race, who also speaks in "I am" language, resembling Johannine discourses (pp. 45–49).

[40] This insight has been developed fully by Peder Borgen in *Bread from Heaven* (Leiden: Brill, 1965).

[41] The biblical, rabbinic, Philonic, and Hellenistic Jewish literature on the theme of Moses' dual role as prophet and king has been illuminatingly treated by Wayne Meeks in the *The Prophet-King: Moses Traditions and the Johannine Christology* (Leiden: Brill, 1967), esp. pp. 186–95.

[42] In the Qumran Community Rule (1QS 9:11) and in 4Q Testamonia, the collection of messianic texts, there is a clear reference to the eschatological prophet.

[43] On the probable historical connections between Jesus and John the Baptist, see C.H. Kraeling, *John the Baptist* (New York: Scribner's, 1951); and Maurice Goguel, *Life of Jesus* (trans. Olive Wyon; New York: Macmillan, 1946), pp. 264–79.

[44] East of the site of ancient Shechem in the district that was known as Samaria are some springs near a village called Salim, in a valley that leads down to the Jordan. "Aenon" probably derives from the Semitic word for springs. This location would suggest that John the Baptist was inviting even the hated Samaritans to share in the new community that he was forming (John 3:23).

[45] Some scholars have conjectured that Jesus withdrew to Perea, east of the Jordan, after predicting the temple's destruction (see M. Goguel, *Life of Jesus*, p. 418). But a more plausible interpretation is to see it as receiving enhanced symbolic significance in John's gospel, as sketched below.

[46] J.L. Martyn, *History and Theology in the Fourth Gospel* (New York: Harper & Row, 1968), pp. 18–27.

[47] W.A. Meeks, "The Man from Heaven in Johannine Sectarianism," *Journal of Biblical Literature* 91 (1972): 52–65.

[48] Ibid., 49.

[49] See Smith, *The Composition and Order of the Fourth Gospel*, p. 239, and Kümmel, *Introduction to the New Testament*, p. 216.

[50] It is almost universally accepted that 7:53–8:11, the story of the adulterous woman, does not belong in the text of John. It does not appear in any of the oldest manuscripts of John, and in some manuscripts it is found in Luke, after 21:38.

[51] The evolution of the Johannine community from before the Gospel of John was written to the period of the Letters of John and subsequently has been

brilliantly traced by Raymond E. Brown in *The Community of the Beloved Disciple* (New York: Paulist Press, 1979).

[52]See Bultmann, *Theology of the New Testament*, vol. 2, pp. 38–40, and *History and Eschatology*, pp. 47–55, where this theme is elaborated.

CHAPTER 8

The Gospels in the History of the Early Church

It is not possible that the Gospels can be either more or fewer than they are. For, since there are four zones of the world in which we live, and four principal winds, while the church is scattered throughout the world, and the "pillar and ground"[1] of the church is the Gospel and the Spirit of Life; it is fitting that she should have four pillars, breathing out immortality on every side, and vivifying men afresh.[2]

Thus wrote Irenaeus in the second century in an effort to justify the church's use of four different Gospels.

The Attitude of the Early Church Toward the Gospels

That Irenaeus had to strain so hard shows that the existence of these diverse documents was an embarrassment to the church. The problem was not so much that the divergences among the four Gospels raised questions for the church or its critics, but that elements in the church tended to seize upon one or the other of the Gospels to the exclusion of the rest. Irenaeus noted that each of four different heretical groups of his day had selected one of the Gospels to justify its position. Those who considered Christianity a special form of Judaism, and accordingly laid heavy stress on the Law, chose Matthew.[3] The second-century church leader Marcion, who denied that the God and Father of Jesus was the creator and who sought to rid Christianity of all its Jewish elements, settled on the Gospel of Luke, although he had to expurgate it in order to render it totally non-Jewish. Another heretical group, called by their opponents the "Docetists"—the "Seemists," who denied the true humanity of Jesus

Christ by claiming he only "seemed" to have a body—used the Gospel of Mark as the basis for their distinction between the heavenly Christ and the earthly Jesus, who was no more than a phantasm.[4] As is noted below, there is a current trend among scholars dealing with the historical Jesus to demonstrate precisely the opposite position from the Docetists: that the real Jesus made no divine claims and displayed no divine capacities.[5] The Gospel of John was the favorite of Valentinus, one of the early Gnostics, whose elaboration on and speculative additions to the Christian faith are documented in the Gospel of Truth.[6] As we have noted,[7] the kinship between the mystical approach to truth represented by the Gospel of John and Gnosticism of the second century C.E. is so close that scholars have conjectured that John and the Gnostics employed, in different ways, certain Jewish concepts (e.g., preexistent Wisdom) and Gentile religious forms (e.g., the self-revealing speeches of Isis). In both these types of literature the reader is addressed as an individual in the first person singular and invited to share in the life of the divine—approaches which may have influenced both the prologue and the "I am" speeches of John's gospel. The Gospel of John differs radically from the Gospel of Truth, however, in its insistence on the bodily, physical existence of Jesus, even following his resurrection (John 20:27).

The point that Irenaeus was making in the quotation with which this chapter began is not that there is anything wrong with the four Gospels separately, but that the only guarantee that they will be interpreted in accordance with true catholic faith is to hold them together so that the faith may be grasped in its fullness. His defense of the four-part combination of the gospel literature excludes by implication other documents that claimed to be of equal authority, such as the noncanonical Gospels, but does not address itself to the problem of the differences among the four gospel accounts. The inclination to choose one of the Gospels or a particular strand of the gospel tradition and to establish it as the norm, against which Irenaeus was protesting, has its modern counterpart in groups like the Jesus Seminar who are selecting out of the Gospels—including those outside the canon—what they find comfortable and intellectually compatible.

It might seem appropriate to account for this diversity on the ground that each of the four Gospels represented a local tradition that originated in a different center of the primitive church. Such a theory was developed in the early church and has had its proponents down into the present century: Mark is assigned to Rome, John to

Ephesus, Matthew to Antioch, and Luke to Rome, their respective places of writing. Scholars earlier in the present century undertook similar designations of origins for the Gospels.[8] But Matthew and Luke used Mark, and probably John did too.[9] Thus the notion that any one gospel is a product of purely local origin and therefore reflects local theological or historical preferences cannot be sustained.

Indeed, there is some evidence that all four Gospels may have originated in Syria, which might account for the fact that it was there in the late second century that the first known attempt was made to resolve the problem of the multiplicity of the Gospels by weaving them together into a single consecutive narrative, called the Diatessaron, that is, "through the four" (see pp. 266–73). Mark and Luke have traditionally been assigned to Rome, but on the dubious grounds that they were supposed to have been written by men who were, respectively, the companions of Peter and Paul, both of whom met martyrdom in Rome. Actually, Syria is a more likely place of origin for Mark[10] and has been proposed as well for John.[11] An eastern Mediterranean origin is also possible for Luke, but there is no clear evidence.[12] That Matthew was written in Antioch or at least in Syria has long been maintained,[13] but J. Andrew Overman has proposed that it was written in Galilee—probably Sepphoris—concurrent with "nascent rabbinic Judaism."[14] The plausible theory that all four Gospels were written in Syria might suggest that the gospel tradition was first preserved and then propagated in the churches of Syria because of a special understanding of the meaning of Jesus that flourished there.

It may well be that the type of theological outlook represented by Mark and Q, for example, flourished in the Syrian church, where, in spite of the Semitic-language culture that stretched back into antiquity, Greek was widely spoken and understood, as it was in Palestine.[15] This could account, on the one hand, for the preservation there of an oral tradition in Aramaic (a Semitic dialect closely related to Syriac) and, on the other hand, for its early translation and recording in Greek, which from the time of Alexander the Great had been the language of culture and international relations. Yet the mounting evidence of the pervasive influence of Greek and of Hellenistic culture in Galilee in the first century C.E. indicates that a Palestinian provenance for Matthew and Mark cannot be ruled out.[16] The authority of these Gospels was established, however, by associating each of them with one of the apostles: Each was purportedly authored by either an apostle (Matthew and John) or someone perceived as an apostle's companion (Mark of Peter, and Luke of Paul). The fact that critical analysis of the Gospels now discredits these claims for apostolic authorship makes no difference in the matter of their authority for the early church as testimonies of faith: It was as books bearing the weight of apostolic origin that they found their way out from their actual place of origin into the wider church.

By the end of the second century, the four—and only these four—were widely recognized as canonical,[17] or authoritative, and this recognition is attested in the main areas of the empire: by Irenaeus in Gaul, by Tertullian in North Africa, by Clement of Alexandria in Egypt, and by an ancient document preserved in what is known as the Muratorian Canon, which originated in Rome.[18] Discoveries of other Gospels dating back to the second century, including the Gospel of Thomas discovered in a Coptic version in Egypt in 1945, have led some scholars to assert that these noncanonical Gospels offer older and more reliable traditions about Jesus than the four canonical Gospels do.[19] But their conclusions are reached only because they have decided antecedently that the historical Jesus was a teacher of timeless wisdom, rather than one who performed healings and exorcisms and announced the coming of the New Age of God's rule. Although there may be a few authentic sayings of Jesus preserved in noncanonical Gospels and sayings collections,[20] none of the other Gospels or collections has been able to establish a wide claim for canonicity. Even these supposedly authentic sayings are judged so only by reference to the material contained in the four familiar, canonical Gospels. The chief concern of the church seems to have been to preserve the authority of the four Gospels by demonstrating their apostolic origin rather than to raise questions about divergences between the accounts. Specifically, the church was more embarrassed by having to show why four authoritative Gospels were necessary than by having to explain how the discrepancies among them were to be accounted for.

Before the question of the canonicity of the Gospels was more or less settled—that is, before the first half of the second century—the sayings of Jesus and stories about him that had already been incorporated into the Gospels were still being circulated orally. As a result, different variations of these gospel traditions were preserved in the memories of Christians and thus found their way into the church leaders' writings—including both New Testament writings and others that were omitted from the canon but prized by the early church.[21] The persistence of a free process of transmitting the gospel tradition helps to account for the wide range of variations found in the most ancient manuscripts of the Gospels, the earliest of which are fragmentary and date from the second century, and the most important of which are from the fourth century.[22] The variants now found among the ancient manuscripts, as well as those variants that seem to have developed while the gospel tradition was transmitted orally and then were written down during the second century, are of a relatively minor nature and for the most part do not introduce additional information or modify substantially the historical evidence available from the canonical Gospels.[23]

The early church clearly regarded our four canonical Gospels as the basic source for knowledge about Jesus. And, in spite of large numbers of variants in the manuscripts of the Gospels, a remarkably reliable text of these Gospels can be reconstructed. But, can we obtain additional information from the noncanonical sources? The surge of interest in the noncanonical gospel tradition began with the discovery of the Gospel of Thomas but continues at an astonishing pace.[24]

Filling the Gaps in Knowledge of Jesus

The Infancy Gospels

Curiosity about the circumstances of Jesus' birth and childhood beyond the limited information available in the canonical Gospels aroused pious imaginations to fill in the gaps. Legendary stories arose. By the second half of the second century, they had been brought together in a form roughly resembling the canonical Gospels. These works were concerned, however, only with the background, birth, and childhood of Jesus. Of these infancy Gospels, two have survived: the Protevangelium of James and the Infancy Gospel of Thomas (not to be confused with a document bearing the same name but consisting entirely of hidden sayings of Jesus[25]).

The Protevangelium of James.   In this infancy gospel, the miraculous stories depicting the circumstances of Jesus' birth in the canonical Gospels of Matthew and Luke were expanded and some miraculous details were projected backward into the life of Mary and her family. At times the very words of the canonical gospel accounts are used, but they are applied to Jesus' supposed ancestors. For example, the report of the annunciation to Anna that she is to have a child (= Mary) uses the exact words of Luke 2 and builds on the tradition of the birth of Samuel, just as the author of the infancy story in Luke did:[26]

> And *behold an angel of the Lord came to her* and said: "Anna, Anna, *the Lord has heard your prayer. You shall conceive and bear,* and your offspring shall be spoken of in the whole world." And Anna said: *"As the Lord my God lives,* if I bear a child, whether male or female, I will *bring it as a gift to the Lord my God,* and it shall *serve him all the days of its life."* (Prot. of Jas. 4:1)[27]

It is obvious that this passage is based on the canonical Greek Gospels and the Old Testament and therefore is not earlier than the canonical infancy stories; nor was it written in Hebrew or Aramaic, as has sometimes been supposed by scholars wanting to claim that very old tradition lies behind the Protevangelium. It is instead composed of phrases taken from 1 Samuel 1 and 2 and from Luke 1 and 2, in sections dealing with the miraculous circumstances surrounding Hanna, Elizabeth, and Mary at the births of Samuel, John the Baptist, and Jesus, respectively. Not only phrases but also the basic ideas of the birth and childhood accounts were taken over from the older Greek Gospels. In addition, the author included some fantastic tales. For example, there is the story that Mary, sent by her parents to serve in the Temple and fed there by the angels (Prot. of J. 8:1), was assigned the task of weaving the veil of the Temple, which was later torn at the moment of Jesus' death (10:1–2). Another passage reports that as Joseph was out looking for a midwife in Bethlehem, the stars stood still and all earthly activity, human and animal, came momentarily to a halt. Not surprisingly, the account weaves together elements from both the Lukan and Matthean versions, a procedure that, as we shall see later in this chapter, was to be widely adopted, with far-reaching consequences for the church's understanding of Jesus.

The Infancy Story of Thomas. In this second infancy gospel, which seems to have been written only slightly later than the Protevangelium of James, the miraculous element was further expanded and the incredibility of the stories for the modern reader increased. Jesus is portrayed as a powerful wonder-worker, whom people are well-advised not to trifle with. Rebuked for fashioning clay sparrows on the Sabbath, he clapped his hands and made them fly away (Inf. Thos. 2:1–5). When taunted, he caused his opponents to wither or die, although on occasion he did a kind deed for a playmate:

> Now after some days Jesus was playing on a roof in the upper story, and one of the children who were playing with him fell down from the roof and died. And when the other children saw it they fled, and Jesus remained alone. And the parents of him that was dead came and accused him of having thrown him down. And Jesus replied, "I did not throw him down." But they continued to revile him. Then Jesus leaped down from the roof and stood by the body of the child, and cried with a loud voice: "Zenon"—for that was his name—"Arise and tell me, did I throw you down?" And he arose at once and said: "No, Lord, you did not throw me down but raised me up." And when they saw it they were amazed. And the parents of the child glorified God for the miracle that had happened and worshipped Jesus.[28] (Inf. Thos. 9:1–3)

Jesus performed the miracle, however, not as an act of compassion of the sort familiar from the synoptic accounts, but as a peevish way of vindicating himself in the face of the false accusation that he was responsible for the child's death.

Somewhat more worthy motives appear in other miracle stories, such as the one in which Jesus heals a man's foot that has been split by an ax (10:1–3). Among the more charming stories are those of Jesus bringing water home to his mother in the fold of his garment after the pitcher had broken (11:1–2) and of his helping his father finish a furniture-making assignment by stretching a board that had mistakenly been cut too short (13:1–2). Elsewhere (19:1–3), an entire pericope is taken over, with only slight changes, from the Lukan account (2:41–52) of Jesus among the teachers in the Jerusalem Temple.

The conclusion to be reached from an examination of the infancy Gospels is clear: They contain no independent historical information. This inference is confirmed when we consider the differences between the portrayal of Jesus in the canonical Gospels and in the noncanonical narratives. The latter make no attempt to show how the miracles of Jesus were performed in the interests of his serving others, and, significantly, the miracles are not interpreted as signs of the inbreaking of the Kingdom of God. In the infancy Gospels the miracles are portrayed precisely as forms of Jesus' public authorization—something the Jesus of the synoptic tradition refuses (Mark 8:11–12). The overwhelming impression the reader receives from the canonical

Gospels—namely, that all of Jesus' teachings and actions are made to serve the interests of the coming reign of God—is totally missing from these second-century documents. Instead, Jesus is portrayed as a precocious prig, revolting and ruthless in the exploitation of his supernatural powers. Such a picture simply cannot be brought into congruity with the image of Jesus that comes through the canonical accounts. The fact that the writers of these infancy narratives heaped miracle on miracle, with no awareness that they might strain the credulity of their readers, indicates that the modern questions of historical accuracy and credibility simply did not figure in literature of this type. The major aim was to heighten the aura of supernatural mystery around the figure of Jesus[29] and thus to make of him an even more noteworthy figure than he would be on the basis of the gospel accounts alone, replete with miracles though they are too. By the very effort to make the story of Jesus more spectacular, the writers removed him even further from the sphere of ordinary humanity than did, for example, the author of Mark, who sought to place Jesus the man in a scheme of apocalyptic history.

Stories of Jesus' Trial and Death

The Acts of Pilate.   Another narrative that was produced by pious imagination to fill the gaps in historical knowledge about Jesus is the Acts of Pilate, purportedly translated by a certain Ananias, who identifies himself merely as an official of the guard and a faithful Christian. "Ananias" claims that he took his translation from Hebrew documents that originated with Nicodemus, the secret disciple of Jesus, who, with Joseph of Arimathea, claimed Jesus' body and buried it. He dates his translation during the reign of Emperor Theodosius II, or about 425 C.E., but of course the document translated goes back, according to "Ananias," to the time of Jesus. The work is, however, demonstrably dependent on the canonical Greek Gospels, especially on John and to a lesser extent on Matthew, and cannot therefore be regarded as an independent source. According to one theory, it originated as a Christian reaction to pagan documents purporting to be Pilate's records concerning Jesus, in which Jesus is portrayed in a bitterly hostile light.[30] These spurious official "annals" were used at the beginning of the fourth century C.E. to obtain popular support for the persecution of Christians ordered by Emperor Galerius, and primary-school teachers required their pupils to commit them to memory.[31] But in spite of ferocious efforts to coerce

Christians into participating in the sacrifices connected with the cult of the emperor—including forcing them to taste the sacrificial offerings—popular feeling turned against Galerius' nephew and protégé, Daia, during his reign as emperor Maximinus Galerius Valerius (308–314 C.E.) for his excessively harsh attempts to suppress Christianity.[32]

More likely than the theory that Christians developed their own Acts of Pilate in response to those promulgated by Maximinus, however, is the supposition that Justin Martyr's references to reports of Jesus' hearing before Pilate, as well as Pilate's confirmation of Jesus' miracles of healing the sick and raising the dead, were a part of a document called the Acts of Pontius Pilate[33] that was already in existence in Justin Martyr's day (100?–165? C.E.). Although the Gospel of Nicodemus, which contains our oldest version of the Acts of Pilate, was written in the early fifth century, it probably incorporates much older material, going back to the first half of the second century.[34] Working primarily from Matthew, as we can infer from details in the Passion story (Pilate washing his hands) and the Resurrection appearances (in Galilee), the author has introduced miraculous details (the soldiers' standards bow of themselves when Jesus enters the judgment hall) and has gone even further than Matthew to exonerate Pilate of blame for Jesus' death. The work reads like a Hellenistic romance, therefore, and only in those passages where the author is most heavily dependent on Matthew can we consider seriously the possibility of a basis in the early Jesus tradition. The heightening of both the miraculous features and the anti-Jewish elements renders the document of value only for understanding the history of the church in the third and fourth centuries. As a primary historical source, the Acts of Pilate are valueless.

The Gospel of Peter.   On the basis of the common use of the phrase "friend of Pilate" in a fifth-century C.E. copy of the Gospel of Peter and in a fragmentary late second-century manuscript (Oxyrynchus Papyrus 2949), J.D. Crossan declares that the "latest date for the Gospel of Peter is the late second or early third century."[35] But he goes on to claim that this gospel includes three elements in its account of Jesus' crucifixion and resurrection which antedate those features in the four canonical Gospels: (1) the Crucifixion and deposition of Jesus' body; (2) the description of the tomb and the guards; and (3) the Resurrection and confession. This gospel also includes three items which are derived from the canonical Gospels, Crossan asserts (1) Joseph and the burial of Jesus, (2) the women and youth at the tomb, and (3) the disciples and Jesus' appearance to them. The earlier version of the Gospel of Peter, which contained only the first three elements is, he declares, the source drawn upon by the canonical Gospels. The argument is completely circular, building as it does on the wholly undocumented assumption that there was a Passion narrative that antedates what is found in the New Testament Gospels. The far more plausible thesis is that Mark's account of the Crucifixion and his anticipation of the Resurrection were the basic source which was later developed independently by the other gospel writers, canonical and extracanonical. The absence of quotes from the Gospel of Peter in the early second-century Christian writers and from Tatian's Diatessaron indicate that it was not in existence until late in that century, and hence could not have served as a source for the canonical Gospels.

The Gnostic Gospels

Another attempt to fill in the gaps in knowledge of Jesus was undertaken by those who were persuaded—or at least sought to persuade their readers—that the reason Jesus was not more fully known by his contemporaries in general was that he had disclosed fuller knowledge of himself to his inner circle of followers only after his resurrection. This idea was not new in the second century; rather, it developed from at least two factors that were present in the synoptic tradition in the first century. The first of these is the claim, so basic to Mark, that only Jesus' most intimate followers understood the hidden meaning of his words and actions. Mark believed that they had been given special insight so that they could discern in Jesus' teaching and activity the inbreaking of the End of the Age, which was soon to take place. What they possessed was not special information but revealed insight, which enabled them to recognize the true meaning of Jesus. While others found him threatening, offensive to, or even subversive of the established religious and political values and institutions, his disciples saw in him the inbreaking Kingdom of God.

Second, in the canonical Gospels Jesus does make private disclosures to his inner group of followers both during his public ministry—in the transfiguration scene, for example—and after the Resurrection. One postresurrection appearance is promised in Mark 14:28, and another in 16:7, in which the young man who appears at the empty tomb says to the distraught women, "Go, tell his disciples and Peter that he is going before you to Galilee; there you will see him, as he told you." Some of the ancient manuscripts—although none of the most ancient and reliable ones—include a description of this appearance, given in the King James Version and other versions as Mark 16:9–19.

Matthew inserted at this point in his gospel (28:8–20) a report of Jesus' appearance to the disciples in Galilee after the Resurrection, when he greeted them and then commissioned them to carry out their mission to the world, promising to be present with them until the Consummation of the Age. The fact that Mark hints at, and Matthew recounts, a postresurrection appearance in Galilee, whereas the postresurrection appearances in Luke 24 and John 20 take place in Jerusalem or its vicinity, may reflect a tradition preserved by the primitive church in Galilee. The question of the significance of the different locations for the appearances of Jesus has received scholarly attention,[36] but what is important for historical inquiry is the implication of these gospel records that the full meaning of Jesus was not grasped by the disciples until after they had seen him risen from the dead. In Luke especially, the disciples are depicted as "foolish men, and slow of heart to believe" (Luke 24:25). On confronting the risen Lord, their minds were "opened . . . to understand" not only the Scriptures as such but also the intention of God through Jesus (Luke 24:45).

The knowledge imparted in each of these briefing sessions is not secret. What Jesus discloses is as much a part of the church's public tradition as what he taught in the Capernaum synagogue (Luke 4) or on the Mount (Matt. 5). Information for the inner circle is a characteristic feature of apocalyptic understanding. The visions of Daniel, for example, receive private interpretation for him so that he can prepare the faithful community ("the holy ones"; Dan. 7:22) for the disaster which is going to fall on the nations of the world and on the disobedient majority of those who claim to be God's people, and for the vindication by God that the faithful will receive (Dan. 9; 12:1–4). Jesus is reported to have made private disclosures to his followers (Mark 4:10–11; 13:3 ff.). In this way the precedent was established for esoteric knowledge of Jesus and for private sessions in which the risen Lord disclosed hidden truth to his own, which became widely understood only after he was raised from the dead. It is this pattern of postresurrection disclosures, which were seen to have made possible a fuller grasp of the significance of Jesus, that were developed further in the second century in so-called Gospels that had no interest in the earthly activity of Jesus but concentrated solely on his secret revelations, granted to the faithful after his crucifixion and resurrection. Indeed, neither the cross nor the Resurrection figures in most of these accounts. The esoteric revelation is the paramount concern.

Although we cannot trace the stages in the development of Gnosticism, the interest in hidden knowledge evident in the second-century expansion and modification of the gospel tradition is related to the emergence of that movement. In our study of the Gospel of John we considered the antecedents of Gnosticism as seen in the Jewish concepts of personified Wisdom and the ascent of the soul to union with God. But by the time the apocryphal Gospels now under consideration began to appear, some of the features of mystical philosophy—which helped to create Gnostic thought with its claim of access to direct knowledge of the divine—are evident in mainstream Christian thinking, as in the mystical theology of Origen of Alexandria. But in its more radical form, there was a movement within the church to transform Jesus into a heavenly redeemer who brought secret knowledge (*gnosis*) to earth so that men could be freed from their enslavement in the world of matter and thus be able to ascend to the world of spirit. The major conceptual factor in the second century C.E. which contributed to this attempted alteration of Christianity—and which clearly transformed secular philosophy as well—was Neoplatonism. The revival of Pythagoreanism in the later first century C.E. had been part of a process which reached its climax in Poseidonius' early second-century radical dualism of matter and reason and the corresponding heightening of the function of the human will. Combining these philosophical developments were features of Iranian dualism, which had come to be understood as ontological dualism of spirit and matter rather than as ethical dualism of good and evil. Also influential was Chaldean theosophy, with its positing of successively ascending spheres of being. Although these conceptual developments achieved more precise definition only in the third century C.E. under Plotinus, the antecedents were powerfully operative earlier. A major feature in this conceptual evolution was the belief in the ascent of the soul from the multiplicity of the material world to the vision of the ultimate One. The adaptation of some Christian thinkers to this intellectual trend, building on earlier dualistic modes in Jewish and Christian thinking, most likely gave rise to what came to be called Gnosticism.

One important step in the Gnostic direction was taken by certain Christians who became persuaded that the bodily urges, especially the sexual drive, were evil. A man of true faith would be able to overcome the sexual urge, they maintained, by abstaining from marriage or sexual intercourse. Those who shared this view became known as *Encratites* (from the Greek, meaning "those who exercise self-control"). The asceticism of the Encratites also forbade drinking wine or eating meat. Their negative estimate of the body, and of the material creation, was an important factor in the developing Gnosticism of the period, although one cannot be sure if the Encratites took over this view from an existing movement or if this was their contribution to incipient Gnosticism. Several of the apocryphal Gospels show the influence of Encratitism, and accordingly they were adopted by the Gnostics as their own. So numerous are the Gospels that show the influence of Encratitism and Gnosticism that only representatives of the various types can be given here.

The Infancy Gospel of Thomas.   The development of the occult knowledge tradition is seen in the Infancy Gospel of Thomas, which we have examined in relation to stories of Jesus' childhood. In this gospel Jesus sets his teacher straight on the hidden meaning of the letters of the alphabet:

> When Joseph saw the understanding of the child and his age, that he was growing to maturity, he resolved again that he should not remain ignorant of letters; and he took him and handed him over to another teacher. And the teacher said to Joseph: "First I will teach him Greek, and then Hebrew." For the teacher knew the child's knowledge and was afraid of him. Nevertheless he wrote the alphabet and practiced it with him for a long time; but he gave no answer. Then Jesus said to him: "If you are indeed a teacher, and if you know the letters well, tell me the meaning of the Alpha, and I will tell you that of Beta." And the teacher was annoyed and struck him on the head. And the child was hurt and cursed him, and he immediately fainted and fell to the ground on his face. And the child returned to Joseph's house. But Joseph was grieved and commanded his mother: "Do not let him go outside the door, for all those who provoke him die."[37]

Apart from the despicable behavior attributed to the boy Jesus in this story, interest centers on the implication that he possesses certain occult knowledge of the letters of the alphabet. This claim that Jesus possessed esoteric information represents the reshaping of the gospel tradition in the direction more fully developed in the Gnostic Gospels.

The Apocryphon of James.   Dating from the middle of the second century[38] is a work recounting an extended conversation between the apostles and the risen Jesus. Known as the Apocryphon of James, its style and contents represent an important stage in the development of Gnostic understanding of the role of Jesus and the consequent recasting of the gospel tradition. A major factor is the interpretation of obedience in terms of radical asceticism and self-denial phrased as seeking death:

> [The risen Christ said] "Remember my cross and my death, and you shall live!" But I answered and said to him, "O Lord, do not preach to us the cross and death, for they are remote from you." The Lord answered and said, "Truly, I tell you that none will be saved unless they believe in my cross. For those who have believed in my cross, theirs is the kingdom of God. Therefore, seek death, like the dead who seek life! For that which they seek will be revealed to them. And what is there to trouble them? If you turn your attention to death, it will teach you about election. Truly, I tell you . . . none will be saved who fear death. For the kingdom of God belongs to those who are killed. Become better than I! Make yourselves like the son of the Holy Spirit!"[39]

At the end of this dialogue with the risen Jesus, those are pronounced blessed who "through faith and *gnosis* have received life." James and Peter thereupon gave thanks and sent their "hearts upward to heaven":

> And when we had passed beyond that place, we sent our mind further upwards. And we saw with our eyes and heard with our ears hymns and eulogies of angels and rejoicing of angels, and heavenly majesties singing praises, and we too rejoiced. After this we wished once more to send up our spirit to the majesty. And having ascended we were not allowed to see or hear anything.

> For the other disciples called us. They asked us, "What did you hear from the Master?," and "What did he say to you?", and "Where did he go to?" But we answered them, "He has ascended" and "He has given us a pledge and promised life to all and has revealed to us children who will come after us, after commanding us to love them since we would be saved for their sakes." And when they heard this, they believed indeed in the revelation.[40]

This Apocryphon of James is an elaboration of the postresurrection scenes in the canonical Gospels, building on the traditional saying of Jesus about taking up the cross or losing one's life in order to find it (Mark 8:34–35) in a radical way that calls for total self-denial and is aimed at finding death (= liberation from bodily existence), not life. The document embodies a radical kind of dualism between existence in the material body and new life in the Spirit.

The Gospel of Thomas.   Another gospel which originated about the middle of the second century appears to stand closer in content to the synoptic Gospels: the Gospel of Thomas. Until thirty years ago this gospel was known only by name, through references to it by the fathers of the early church in their lists of heretical books, but about 1945 a virtually complete text was found among the codices from Nag Hammadi in Upper Egypt in a translation in Coptic, a late form of Egyptian used chiefly by Christians in Egypt. The editors of the text have divided it into 114 sayings, or *logia*, which, apart from a brief introductory word and the repetition of the title at the end, comprise the entire text of the gospel. The introduction runs as follows:

> These are the secret words which the Living Jesus spoke and Didymos Judas Thomas wrote down.[41]

The designation of Jesus as "the Living Jesus" implies that he is regarded as risen from the dead, an implication that is almost certainly confirmed by the first logion, which follows immediately:

> And He said: He who shall find the interpretation of these words shall not taste death.

The representation of Thomas as the special custodian of the hidden teaching of Jesus is paralleled in the description of him that is given in the Acts of Thomas, a work of the early third century,[42] in which he is depicted as a fellow initiate in the hidden word of Christ[43] and the receiver of his hidden mysteries.[44] It is not likely, therefore, that one would look to the Gospel of Thomas as a source of historical knowledge about Jesus, since by definition, the sayings included are those of the risen Christ, not the earthly Jesus.

The situation is more complex, however, because the Gospel of Thomas contains logia that stand very close to those attributed to Jesus in the canonical tradition. Some scholars insist that the Gospel of Thomas contains older forms of Jesus' sayings than those known from the synoptics.[45] Since the early years of this century, scholars have known of the existence of collections of Jesus' sayings that resemble those preserved in the synoptic Gospels, although in many instances, the significance of crucial terms has been radically altered, as in Logia 22 and 46, discussed later (p. 263). The first such group of sayings, known as Oxyrhynchus Papyri from the place of their discovery in Egypt, was published by G.P. Grenfell and A.S. Hunt in 1903.[46] They were subsequently studied by H.G. Evelyn-White[47] and later by Joachim Jeremias.[48] The fact that Thomas is mentioned in the preface to the first logion of the Oxyrhynchus sayings (known to scholars as Papyrus Oxy. 654) had raised the possibility that this fragmentary collection was part of the Gospel of Thomas, but it is now clear that indeed three of these papyri—Oxy. 1, 654, and 655— are parts of what was originally one work, which is preserved in the Coptic version of the Gospel of Thomas. J.A. Fitzmyer has reconstructed the Greek text behind the Coptic version and has published a detailed comparison of it with sayings from the Oxyrhynchus Papyri.[49] What he has rendered highly probable is that the Coptic Gospel of Thomas is a version of a Greek original. What cannot be demonstrated persuasively is that the Greek Gospel of Thomas contains material that is independent of or older than that preserved in the synoptics.[50] Clear evidence of Thomas' dependence on, and alteration of, the older synoptic tradition is offered below (p. 261–64).

Some of the logia do little more than reproduce what is found in the synoptics, and without significant change, as the following logia (31–35), with synoptic parallels in the margin, reveal:

Matt. 13:57	⎫	Jesus said: No prophet is acceptable in his
Mark 6:4	⎬	village; no physician heals those who
Luke 4:24	⎭	know him.

Matt. 5:14;
7:24–25 }
	Jesus said: A city being built on a high
	        mountain cannot fall nor
	        can it be hidden.

Matt. 10–27	Jesus said: What thou shalt hear in
Luke 12:3 Mark 4:21 }	thine ear and in the other ear, that preach on the housetops; for no one

Luke 8:16
Matt. 5:15
Luke 11:33 }
	lights a lamp and puts it under a bushel,
	        nor does he put it in a hidden place, but
	        he sets it on a lampstand so that all who
	        come in and go out may see its light.[51]

Matt. 15:14 Luke 6:39 }	Jesus said: If a blind man leads a blind man, both of them fall into a pit.

Mark 3:27
Matt. 12:29 }
	Jesus said: It is not possible for me to
	        enter the house of the strong man and
	        take him by force unless he binds his
	        hands; then he will ransack his house.

Other logia, such as logion 44, alter the synoptic tradition in doctrinally significant ways:

> Jesus said: Whoever blasphemes against the Father will be forgiven, and whoever blasphemes against the Son will be forgiven; but whoever blasphemes against the Holy Ghost, will not be forgiven, either on earth or in heaven.

Logion 44 is obviously a development from Mark 3:28–29, which reads:

> Truly, I tell you, all sins be forgiven the sons of men, and whatever blasphemies they utter; but whoever blasphemes against the Holy Spirit can never have forgiveness, but is guilty of an eternal sin.

What has happened is that the reference to grossly insulting remarks about other men (= "sons of men") has been transformed into a reference to Jesus as Son (of Man), while a third term, "the Father," has been prefixed to the saying. The result is a statement strongly influenced by the doctrine of the Trinity, a teaching that is found only in the latest stratum of the synoptic tradition (for example, in Matthew's epilogue, 28:19, where the Trinitarian baptismal formula is given).

Similarly, the idea of becoming like a child in order to enter the Kingdom is retained in the Gospel of Thomas (logia 22 and 46) on the basis of Mark 10:15, but the force has been fundamentally altered.[52]

> Jesus said: From Adam to John the Baptist there is among the children of women none higher than John the Baptist, for his eyes were not destroyed. But I have said to you that whoever among you becomes small will know the Kingdom, and will be higher than John. (Logion 46)

Except for the curious expression about the eyes not being destroyed, the logion sounds like a combination of Jesus' word concerning John (Matt. 11:11 = Luke 7:28) with the saying from Mark 10:15 about becoming like a child in order to enter the Kingdom. But logion 22 shows that far more is involved.

> Jesus saw infants who were being suckled. He said to his disciples: These infants being suckled are like those who enter the Kingdom. They said to him: If we then become children, shall we enter the Kingdom? Jesus said to them: When you make the two one, and when you make the inside as the outside and the outside as the inside, and the upper as the lower, and when you make the male and the female into a single one, so that the male is not male and the female is not female, when you make eyes in the place of an eye, and a hand in the place of a hand, and a foot in the place of a foot, and an image in the place of an image, then shall you enter [the Kingdom].

The meaning of this string of curious contrasts was investigated by A.F.J. Klijn, who showed that to become a "single one" means to return to the androgynous state of Adam before he was divided into male and female, when Eve was fashioned from his side.[53] But the other image in the Gospel of Thomas for regaining the theoretically primal human condition of asexuality is to "become as a child."[54] What was in the earlier Jesus tradition a metaphor of acceptant simplicity or childlike trust has become in the Gospel of Thomas a Gnosticizing appeal to divest oneself of sexuality in order to return to the primordial state of innocence. Far from representing an older form of the synoptic tradition, the Gospel of Thomas represents the gospel material at a later stage of its development, when it has been adapted to serve the interests of Encratites (who abstained from sex, wine, and meat) or even Gnostic groups.

There are, however, simpler and therefore possibly older versions of the parables in the Gospel of Thomas. For example, logion 57 reads like an earlier form of the Parable of the Weeds found in Matthew 13:24–30:

> Jesus said: The Kingdom of the Father is like a man who had [good] seed. His enemy came by night, he sowed a weed among the good seed. The man did not permit them [the workers] to pull up the weed. He said to them: Lest perhaps you go to pull up the weed and pull up the wheat with it. For on the day of harvest the weeds will appear, they [will] pull them and burn them.

There are fewer details in Thomas than in Matthew, and there is no hint of the allegorical interpretation that Matthew introduces in 13:36–43.[55] This may well be one of the instances where the Gospel of Thomas preserves a more primitive form of the gospel tradition, although even here we can see the influence of the gospel writer's theology when he uses the phrase "Kingdom of the Father" rather than the simple Matthean "kingdom of heaven" (= God).

The Parable of the Supper, which occurs in Q (Matt. 22:2–10 = Luke 14:16–24), may also appear in an older form in Thomas, logion 64. But the conclusion, with its warning that "Tradesmen and merchants [shall] not [enter] the places *[topos]* of my Father," shows beyond question that the parable serves a Gnostic viewpoint,[56] since *topos* is for Gnostics a technical term for the place of redemption.[57]

Even if we were to assume that in some places Thomas preserves older forms of the sayings of Jesus, these instances do not materially change our understanding of the message of Jesus in the canonical gospel tradition, nor do they tell us anything about the context of meaning and action in which Jesus first proclaimed his message, or in which the first-century church came to understand that message. Rather, the sayings are used in a way that serves the interests of a Gnostic viewpoint, which has no concern for the historical but is intended instead to help deliver humans from their involvement in the material world. As such, the Gospel of Thomas has no important contribution to make to our understanding of Jesus in history. Its concern is rather to show how through Jesus one may escape from history. The potent, though unacknowledged ground of preference by some contemporary scholars for the Gospel of Thomas and their theory of its more primitive form of the Jesus tradition is that it does not contain features of the canonical gospel tradition which they as post-Enlightenment scholars find embarrassing, such as miracles, exorcisms, bodily resurrection, and predictions about an Age to Come.

Attempts to Impose Unity on the Gospel Tradition

Although various parts of the church in specific areas of the Roman Empire seem to have preferred one of the canonical Gospels above the others, there was an inclination on the part of some Christians in the second century to choose one gospel and eliminate the others. In the first half of the second century, Marcion, a native of Pontus on the Black Sea, was apparently active in the church at Edessa, an important center of Syriac-speaking Christianity. In 138 C.E. he left the church to form his own group, for whom he prepared his own canon, which included a single gospel, generally thought to have been a drastically edited version of the Gospel of Luke.[58] Whether he began with Luke as his basis or worked from the mass of gospel tradition including Luke,[59] he removed any elements from the story of Jesus that he regarded as Jewish perversions of the true gospel.[60] Although Marcion's brilliance and effectiveness as a leader gave him a large following in his own day, his chief enduring contribution seems to be that he moved the church to form its own official canon, including the four Gospels,[61] as a way of combatting his anti-Judaic canon. The impact that he had on the church at Edessa, even though he was regarded as a heretic, is evidenced by the fact that Marcion is mentioned in the official history of the church at Edessa: the Edessene Chronicle.[62]

It was another prominent man connected with the second-century church in Edessa and, like Marcion, considered a heretic, whose handling of the problem of the plurality of the Gospels had the most enduring influence on the church's understanding of the story of Jesus. That man was Tatian. He called himself an Assyrian, and he probably was a native of Adiabene, a district that lay east of the Tigris and had long been a buffer zone between the eastern edge of the Roman Empire and the territory of the Parthians, although it was included as a Roman province of Assyria after Trajan's defeat of the Parthians in 116 C.E. By at least the middle of the second century, the Greek Gospels had been translated for the use of the church in northern Syria and Mesopotamia into Syriac, which in spoken form closely resembled the Aramaic of Syria and Palestine, though it was radically different in script. It was these Syriac Gospels that Tatian later wove together into his harmony of the Gospels, the Diatessaron (meaning, "through four").

The Diatessaron

The discovery of a fragment of the Diatessaron in Greek at Dura-Europos[63] revived the supposition that Tatian originally composed his harmony in that language. It is widely agreed, however, that he did the work in his native Syriac. Until rather recently, no copies of the work in that language were known to have survived. And the Commentary of Ephraem on the Diatessaron, written in Syriac in the fourth century, had also disappeared, except for a few fragments.[64] In the past few decades, however, the original text of Ephraem's Commentary, and through it, of the Diatessaron itself, has become available in the Syriac original. The Armenian version, which had long served as one of the important sources for reconstructing the text of the Diatessaron, is now known to diverge from the Syriac. The major English translations currently available, however, are still based on yet another version (Arabic) of Tatian's influential harmony of the Gospels.[65] The original, almost certainly written in Syriac, was composed in all likelihood after Tatian returned to Mesopotamia at the end of his extended stay in Rome.

Very little is known of Tatian's life. Irenaeus reports that he was a pupil of Justin Martyr in Rome, but that he erred in denying, as did the Gnostics, both the salvation of Adam and the sanctity of marriage.[66] He was also the teacher of Clement of Alexandria, presumably after the martyrdom of Justin, who was largely responsible for Tatian's conversion to Christianity. Tatian's mastery of Greek and knowledge of Greek philosophy are well attested in his *Oration to the Greeks*, which is the only one of his writings that has been preserved. His espousal of the Encratite position led to his being discredited and probably to the destruction of his writings. Indeed, Theodoret, Bishop of Cyrrhus on the Euphrates, in 423 C.E. set about systematically destroying all the copies of Tatian's Diatessaron that he could find.[67] He boasted:

> He [Tatian] composed the so-called Diatessaron by cutting out the genealogies and whatever goes to prove the Lord to have been born of the seed of David according to the flesh. And this work was in use not only among his own party but even amongst those who follow

the tradition of the Apostles, who used it somewhat innocently as a compendium of the Gospels, without recognizing the craftiness of its composition. I myself found more than 200 copies in reverential use in churches of my diocese, all of which I removed, replacing them by the Gospels of the Four Evangelists.[68]

It is impossible at a distance of 1800 years to determine the motive Tatian had in weaving together the four gospel records. Even from such learned opponents of Christianity as Celsus, a Platonist of the late second century who denounced the incarnation as absurd and whose detailed attacks on the credibility of the Gospels were the most serious intellectual challenge the church had encountered until then, there is no evidence that the differences among the accounts raised for Tatian any serious questions about the trustworthiness of the records. We must constantly remind ourselves that devotion to what are regarded as objective facts is a relatively modern dimension of human thought and that precise analysis of historical sources is largely a development of the post-Enlightenment period in the West. Celsus did scoff at certain aspects of the gospel narrative because he found the miraculous claims incredible. He preferred the Jewish account of Jesus' birth—as the illegitimate child of an adulterous village woman[69]—to the gospel report of the virgin birth. The story of the descent of the Holy Spirit in bodily form struck Celsus as especially preposterous. But, significantly, Origen, the learned leader of the Christian School in Alexandria (c. 185–254 C.E.), who devoted a full-scale book *(Contra Celsum)* to answering Celsus, did not respond with a rational explanation of the miracles, nor was he willing to set them aside as not integral to the gospel record. Rather, he showed that the reader of every myth-filled history must exercise his own judgment "as to what statements he will give assent to [that is, as historically accurate], and what he will accept figuratively, seeking to discover the meaning of the authors of such inventions."[70] Origen's quite sophisticated method of handling the miracle accounts—as mythical or figurative[71]—anticipated the method of analyzing the Gospels that developed 1600 years later in the work of David Friedrich Strauss. But neither Origen nor Celsus seems to have been troubled by divergent accounts in the various Gospels.

Tatian's aim was to include the whole of the four Gospels, with three notable exceptions: (1) The genealogies from Matthew and Luke are missing, as are the story of the woman taken in adultery and the preamble to Luke (Luke 1:1–4); (2) pericopes found only in

Mark, such as the Parable of the Seed Growing of Itself (Mark 4:26–29), are included, but connective phrases are omitted; and (3) where Mark has a fuller account of a miracle performed by Jesus, as in the Healing of the Woman with the Hemorrhage (Mark 5:21–43, esp. 29–34), Tatian has included all the Markan detail.

The Diatessaron shows a preference for John, whose Passovers provide the chronological structure for the entire narrative. Otherwise, the order of events comes closer to following Matthew's sequence than that of any other gospel. But Tatian felt free to shift positions radically when it served his aims. For example, the Johannine account of the cleansing of the Temple, which comes at the beginning of the gospel (John 2), is blended with the synoptic account and is placed at the time of Jesus' last journey to Jerusalem. Similarly, the story of Jesus' dialogue with Nicodemus, which comes early in John (John 3), is assigned in the Diatessaron to the section dealing with the controversies between Jesus and the Pharisees, that is, with material found in Matthew 21. Because the lengthy Johannine discourses must be positioned prior to the Passion narrative, the incident of cleansing the Temple is found in the Diatessaron slightly past the halfway point, although it comes toward the end of each of the synoptic accounts (Mark 11; Matt. 21; Luke 19). The story of Jesus' washing the disciples' feet (John 13) is merged with Jesus' promise of a Kingdom to his disciples (Luke 22:27–30). Tatian skillfully linked it with both the preceding and subsequent narratives by placing it just after the Markan saying about preparing for the Passover (Mark 14:12), which then leads directly into the meal which is eaten "before the Passover" (John 13:1). Similarly, in 44:10–33, John 13:20 ("He that receives me receives him that sent me") blends smoothly with Luke 22:27 ("Which is greater, he that reclines [at the table] or he that serves? I am in the midst of you as he that serves").

Tatian's work does not add to our store of information about Jesus, since his procedure limited him largely to the four canonical Gospels as sources, although there is some evidence that he had access to other Gospels or to oral tradition as well.[72] But what makes his work of such great importance for the study of the Gospels is that he set the pattern for the vast majority of subsequent readers of the Gospels by his program of harmonization. Only when we look at the interwoven text of the Diatessaron with marginal references to the individual gospel sources do we realize how much thinking about Jesus has been shaped by the unconscious blending of the different, or even disparate, accounts.

The following extended excerpt from the Diatessaron (from an English translation of the Arabic version)[73] shows with what care Tatian went about his task. The references to the gospel material, which are given in the margin, reveal Tatian's great skill at blending his four sources into a single flowing account.

Matt. 3:13	Then cometh Jesus from Galilee to the Jordan unto John, to be baptized of him.
Luke 3:23	And Jesus was about thirty years of age, and was supposed to be the son of Joseph.
John 1:29	Now John saw Jesus coming unto him, and saith, This is the Lamb of God, which
John 1:30	taketh away the sin of the world. This is he of whom I said, After me shall come a man, which is preferred before me,
John 1:31	for he is before me. And I knew him not; but that he may be made manifest to Israel, for this
Matt. 3:14	cause am I come baptizing in water. Now John was forbidding him, saying, I have need to be baptized of thee, and comest
Matt. 3:15	thou to me? Jesus answered him, and said, Consent to it now: thus it becometh us to fulfill all righteousness. Then he consented.
Luke 3:21	And when all the people were baptized,
Matt. 3:16	Jesus also was baptized; and he went up straightway from the water: and the heaven
Luke 3:22	was opened unto him. And the Holy Spirit descended upon him in the form of a dove's
Matt. 3:17	body: and lo, a voice from heaven, saying, This is my beloved Son, in whom I am well
John 1:32	pleased. And John bore witness, saying, Furthermore I saw the Spirit descending as a dove out of heaven; and it abode upon
John 1:33	him. And I knew him not; but he that sent me to baptize in water, he said unto me, Upon whomsoever thou shalt see the Spirit descending and abiding, this is he
John 1:34	that baptizeth in the Holy Spirit. And I have seen, and have borne witness, that this is the Son of God.

Matt. 21:12	And when Jesus had entered Jerusalem,
John 2:14	he went up into the temple of God; and he
Matt. 21:12	found there oxen, sheep, and doves. And
John 2:14	when he saw them that sold and bought,
John 2:15	and the money changers sitting, he made
	for himself a scourge of cords, and cast all
	of them out of the temple, the sheep also,
	and the oxen, and the money changers,
	whose money he poured out, and overthrew
Matt. 21:12	the tables, and the seats of them that sold
Matt. 21:13	the doves; and he was teaching and saying
	unto them, Is it not written, My house is a
	house of prayer for all nations: but ye have
John 2:16	made it a den of robbers? And to them that
	sold the doves, he said, Take these things
	hence; and make not my Father's
Mark 11:16	house a house of merchandise. And he
	suffered not that any man should carry
John 2:17	vessels through the temple. And his disci-
	ples remembered the scripture, The zeal
John 2:18	of thine house hath eaten me up. The
	Jews answered and said unto him, What
	sign shewest thou unto us, that thou
John 2:19	shouldest do this? Jesus answered, and
	said unto them, Destroy this temple, and in
John 2:20	three days I will raise it up. The Jews said
	unto him, In forty and six years was this
	temple built, and wilt thou raise it up
John 2:21	in three days? But he spake unto them of
	the temple of his body: that when they
	destroyed it, he would raise it up in three
John 2:22	days. And when he rose again from the
	dead, his disciples remembered that he had
	said this; and they believed the scriptures,
Mark 12:41	and the saying that Jesus spake. And Jesus
	sat down over against the treasury: and
	observed how the multitudes cast their
	offerings into the treasury: and many that
Mark 12:42	were rich cast in much. And there came a
	poor widow, and she cast in two mites.

Luke 21:3	And Jesus called his disciples, and said unto
	them, Verily I say unto you, This poor
	widow cast in more than they all into the
Mark 12:44	treasury: for all these did cast in of the
	superfluity of their substance into the ark
	of the offering of God; but she of her
	want did cast all that she possessed.
Luke 19:28	And when he had said these things, Jesus
	went forth slowly to proceed to Jerusalem.
Luke 19:29	And when he was arrived at Bethphage and
	Bethany, near the mount that is called the
Matt. 21:1	mount of Olives, Jesus sent two of his
Matt. 21:2	disciples, saying unto them, Go into the
Mark 11:2	village that is over against you, and when
Matt. 21:2	ye are entered into it, ye shall find an ass
Luke 19:30	tied, and a colt with her, whereon no man
Matt. 21:2	ever yet sat: loose it, and bring *them* unto
Luke 19:31	me. And if anyone say unto you, Why do
Matt. 21:3	ye loose them? say thus unto him, We seek
	them for the Lord; and straightway send
Matt. 21:4	them both hither. All this is come to pass,
	that it might be fulfilled which was spoken
	through the prophet, saying
Matt. 21:5	Tell ye the daughter of Sion,
	Behold, thy King cometh unto thee
	Meek, and sitting upon an ass, and upon a
	colt the foal of an ass.
John 12:16	This understood not his disciples at that time:
	but after Jesus was glorified, his disciples
	remembered that these things had been
	written of him, and that they did these
	things unto him.
Matt. 21:6; Luke 19:32 }	And the disciples went, and found even
Matt. 21:6	as he had said unto them, and they did as
Luke 19:33	Jesus had commanded them. And when
	they had loosed them, the owners thereof
Luke 19:34	said unto them, Why loose ye them? They
	said unto them, We seek them for our Lord;
Mark 11:6	and they let them go.

Matt. 21:7	And they brought the ass and the colt, and put their garments upon the colt, and
Matt. 21:8	Jesus rode thereon. And the most part of the multitude spread their garments before him on the ground; and others cut branches from the trees, and spread them in the way.
Luke 19:37	And when he drew near his descent of the mount of Olives, all the disciples began to rejoice and praise God with a loud voice for all the mighty works which they had seen;
Matt. 21:9	saying, Glory in the highest: glory to the son of David: blessed is he that cometh in the
Mark 11:10	name of the Lord: and blessed is the kingdom
Luke 19:38	which cometh, even our father David's: peace in heaven, and glory in the highest.
John 12:12	And a great multitude that had come to the feast, when they had heard that Jesus
John 12:13	was coming to Jerusalem, took the branches of the palm trees, and went forth to meet him, and cried out, saying, Praise: blessed is he that cometh in the name of the Lord,
Luke 19:30	even the King of Israel. And some of the Pharisees from the multitudes said unto him,
Luke 19:40	Master, rebuke thy disciples. He saith unto them, Verily I say unto you, If these held their peace, the stones would cry out.

It is evident that Tatian went about his task with enormous literary dexterity and with profound respect for the gospel tradition itself. Even though Theodoret saw a sinister motive in Tatian's failure to include the genealogies—as if for docetic reasons he were denying the true humanity of Jesus—there are only occasional evidences that Tatian altered his canonical sources out of theological prejudice, as in the modification of Matthew 11:19 to avoid depicting Jesus as a drinker of wine.[74] Irenaeus may well be correct in labeling Tatian an Encratite and attributing to him Gnostic notions, but there is no trace of Gnosticism in the Diatessaron. One must infer either that he arranged his harmony before he became heretical in his views or that his devotion to the text of Scripture led him to incorporate it unchanged in content even though its message was not compatible with his own theological outlook. However, if he was an Encratite at the time he prepared the Diatessaron, it is striking that the tradition was not adapted to serve Gnostic aims as it was in the contemporaneous Gnostic Gospel of Thomas, which seems also to have originated in a Syrian church.

The influence of Tatian's work was of two kinds: direct and indirect. The direct influence is seen in the gospel harmonies preserved in the church in many languages and over a wide geographical range, which blended together the features of the four Gospels and eliminated differences. The popularity of the Diatessaron is further attested by the fact that commentaries on it were translated into other languages, among them the Armenian version of Ephraem's Commentary. There are two Arabic versions of the Diatessaron, one of which included the genealogies Tatian omitted.[75] The presence or absence of the genealogies does not seem to have affected the use made of the harmony in the church. It functioned as the vehicle of a unified representation of Jesus, which simply eliminated any questions about differences among the interests of the evangelists. The sequence of events in the Diatessaron came to be regarded as not merely useful but canonical. The implications of any discrepancies that might appear from the study of the individual Gospels were forgotten in favor of the harmonious whole.

The basic Tatianic pattern was influential for centuries; it was adopted by Victor, Bishop of Capua (d. 554), whose harmony either provided the norm for, or employed the same norm as, the subsequent harmonies developed in Western Europe. The structure of Dutch, Italian, French, German, and English harmonies can thus be traced back to Tatian.[76] In the East, a Coptic harmony preserved by a heretical group known as the Manicheans can be shown to rest on the structure and even the Syriac text of the Diatessaron.[77] Although the general pattern of the Diatessaron may lie behind the Heliand, an Old Saxon epic poem apparently written to give the Christian faith competitive appeal with the pagan Teutonic heroes, the case is weak for the notion that one can reconstruct the text of Tatian from this medieval poetic work.[78]

As for its indirect effect, Tatian's work set the pattern from the second century on for regarding the harmonized gospel accounts as historically trustworthy in both sequence and content. Popular passion plays and nativity pageants—both ancient and modern—wove together quite disparate elements from the divergent records, and both writers and audiences ignored the implications of the fact that there were differences. From Augustine to Calvin, however, profound thinkers in the church were aware of the difficulties raised by differences among the gospel accounts but they regarded these divergences either as capable of reconciliation or as indications of special interests on the part of the individual evangelists.[79] In the case of Calvin, the priority on questions of order of events was usually decided in favor of Matthew's sequence. But since all parts of Scripture were thought to have equal authority, the order of events did not really matter. Though one writer might find more meaning in one sequence than another, every pericope was a part of Holy Scripture, and all were equally to be believed. Readers might have personal preferences among the Gospels—mystics for John and moralists for Matthew—but if they had doubts about seeming discrepancies, their doubts reflected on their faith, not on the gospel record.

Prior to the rise of modern critical methods in the nineteenth century, there were available no analytical tools by which the student of Scripture could differentiate the aim of one writer from another.[80] The question of the historical credibility of any given narrative could be decided only by the predilection of individual readers, since there were no norms of critical historiography by which to evaluate historical texts. Even those ancient historical and religious texts that were known to early Christians and might have been studied on a comparative basis for critical analysis of the New Testament were not so utilized, since the Gospels were understood by Christians to be sacred books and therefore beyond comparison with pagan writings. All but rare minds such as Origen accepted the Gospels as factual in all their miraculous and supernatural detail. Any historical questions raised were quickly decided by appeal to authoritative accounts of Jesus written down by, or on the authority of, the apostles. This view of the authority of the Gospels as equal and unassailable continued unchallenged until, beginning in the eighteenth century, the supernatural factor in general was examined critically in relation to the central philosophical and natural scientific concept of natural order and until the notion of the Gospels as narratives of divine origin was set aside under the impact of emerging critical study of mythology and history.

It was not until more than a century later, however, that the critical tools were developed that made possible a detailed historical analysis of the history of the gospel tradition. These included careful study of Jewish and Greco-Roman writings contemporary with the New Testament—especially those dealing with the development of religious concepts, practices, and societies—as well as theoretical methods for conceptual and literary analysis of the New Testament in light of its historical background. The implications of the social sciences, and especially of sociology of knowledge, for gaining perceptions about the nature and diversity of the early Christian communities that produced the Gospels, have been developing fruitfully in recent years.[81] But does the emergence of new critical methods and newly found sources enable us to settle with finality our questions about the place of Jesus in history?

Suggestions for Further Reading

Older theory on the origins of Gnosticism were offered by Rudolf Bultmann, in *Primitive Christianity in Its Contemporary Setting** (Cleveland: World, 1956); and by R.M. Grant, *Gnosticism and Early Christianity,** rev. ed. (New York: Harper Brothers, 1961). The Gnostic documents discovered in Egypt have been published in *The Nag Hammadi Library in English*, ed. James M. Robinson, 3d ed. (Leiden: Brill, 1988). The apocryphal Jewish and early Christian writings are available in *The Old Testament Pseudepigrapha*, ed. J.H. Charlesworth (Garden City, NY: Doubleday; vol. 1, 1983; vol. 2, 1985); and the writings known as *New Testament Apocrypha* are available in a new and more complete edition with superb introductory essays and full bibliography in W. Schneemelcher, *New Testament Apocrypha*, vols. 1 and 2 (trans. R. McL. Wilson; Cambridge: James Clarke, 1991; and Louisville, KY: John Knox/Westminster, 1992).

Essays on the Diatessaron and its influence are included in B.M. Metzger, *Chapters in the History of New Testament Textual Criticism* (Grand Rapids, MI: Eerdmans, 1963); and in Paul Kahle, *The Cairo Genizah* (Oxford: Oxford University Press, 1947).

---

*Available in a paperback edition.

NOTES ───

[1] From 1 Timothy 3:15.

[2] Irenaeus, *Against Heresies* 3.11.8, in the *The Ante-Nicene Fathers*, vol. 1. (trans. Alexander Roberts and James Donaldson; New York: 1899; reprint, Grand Rapids, MI: Eerdmans, 1953).

[3] These were the Ebionites, though Irenaeus' statement is not accurate since they actually had their own gospel or Gospels. Of the Gospel of the Ebionites mentioned by Epiphanius in his *Panarion* (sec. 29), Philip Vielhauer and Georg Strecker, in *New Testament Apocrypha*, ed. W. Schneemelcher, vol. 1 (trans. R. McL. Wilson (Cambridge: James Clarke, 1991), p. 140, show that it could not have been the Gospel of Matthew, but was at most a "falsified and abridged" version of it. It was a later book composed in Hebrew, which Epiphanius called the "Hebrew Gospel." Introduction and excerpts are given on pp. 166–71.

[4] Denial of the reality of Jesus' humanity developed early in the church, as the warning against this notion in 1 John 4:2 suggests. The term *Docetist* is derived from the Greek word *dokeo*, "to seem."

[5] See the discussion of the Jesus and Q Seminars, pp. 1–2.

[6] An English translation of the *The Gospel of Truth* is available in *The Nag Hammadi Library in English*, ed. James M. Robinson (Leiden: Brill; 3d ed. 1988), pp. 40–51.

[7] Chapter 7 on the Gospel of John.

[8] Thus B.H. Streeter in *The Four Gospels* (New York: Macmillan, 1925). On the provenance of Mark and Matthew, see pp. 485–527; of Luke, pp. 531–40; of John, pp. 431–61. Streeter assigns M, the Matthean source, to Jerusalem and L, the Lukan source, to Caesarea in Palestine.

[9] The much-debated question of John's dependence on Mark was decided negatively by C.H. Dodd in *Historical Tradition in the Fourth Gospel* (Cambridge: Cambridge University Press, 1963), esp. pp. 423–32, but positively by C.K. Barrett, *Commentary on John* (London: SPCK, 1956), pp. 34–45. A more recent cautious affirmation of John's use of pre-Markan, and especially Lukan tradition, is offered by R.E. Brown, *Commentary on John, I–XII*, pp. xliv–xlvii.

[10] See W.G. Kümmel, *Introduction to the New Testament*, 17th ed. (trans. H.C. Kee (Nashville: Abingdon, 1975), p. 98; and H.C. Kee, *Community of the New Age: Studies in Mark's Gospel*, pp. 100–104.

[11] R.E. Brown summarizes the theories about the origin of John's Gospel in Antioch, but opts instead for Ephesus *(Gospel of John, I–XII)*, pp. cii–civ.

[12] Joseph Fitzmyer, after surveying the proposals for the place of origin of Luke-Acts concludes that "It is anyone's guess," although he notes that the author's seeming lack of knowledge of Palestine indicates that it was not written there (*Commentary on Luke I–IX*, pp. 53–57).

[13] The earlier scholarly consensus, as stated by B.W. Bacon in his *Studies in Matthew* (New York: Henry Holt, 1930), pp. 24–36, and supported by W.G. Kümmel in *Introduction to the New Testament*, pp. 119–20, is affirmed by Anthony Saldarini in *Matthew's Christian-Jewish Community* (Chicago: University of Chicago Press, 1994), p. 26.

[14]In *Matthew's Gospel and Formative Judaism: The Social World of the Matthean Community* (Minneapolis: Fortress Press, 1990), p. 159 and n. 20.

[15]The widespread use of Greek in first-century Palestine is indicated by John E. Stambaugh and David L. Balch in *The New Testament in Its Social Environment* (Philadelphia: Westminster Press, 1986), pp. 87–88. A letter found at the headquarters of the Jewish revolt in the second century, written in Greek by its leader, Bar Kochba, includes the explanation which should probably be translated "No one was found to write in Hebrew." What is remarkable is that the leader of the Jewish nationalist movement would write to his colleagues in Greek.

[16]The excavations at Sepphoris in recent years have shown how thoroughly Hellenized that city, the capital of Galilee, was in the time of Jesus and throughout the first century C.E., during the period when Galilee was becoming the center for formative rabbinic Judaism.

[17]On the development of the concept of canon, see Kümmel, *Introduction to the New Testament*, pp. 475–501. For the specifics of the process of decision as to which Gospels were to be regarded as canonical, see Schneemelcher, *New Testament Apocrypha*, vol. 1, pp. 15–50, where translations are given of the ancient sources and lists from which the development of the canon can be traced. See also Hans von Campenhausen, *The Formation of the Christian Bible* (Philadelphia: Fortress, 1971).

[18]A brief description and a translation of the Muratorian Canon are given in Schneemelcher, *New Testament Apocrypha*, vol. 1, pp. 34–36. Unfortunately, the first part of the canon, in which Matthew and Mark were certainly described, is now lost.

[19]A leader among those making such assertions is Helmut Koester, who after noting close correspondence between Thomas and what he regards as the earlier stage of Q (devoid of eschatological and christological features), asserts that "the Gospel of Thomas and Q must belong to a very early stage of the transmission of Jesus' sayings" (*Ancient Christian Gospels: Their History and Development* [Philadelphia: Trinity Press International, 1990], p. 163).

John Dominic Crossan is more cautious, concluding simply that Thomas embodies a tradition independent of the canonical Gospels. His test case, the Gospel of Thomas 54, however, rather than showing an independent tradition, clearly demonstrates that the author made use of both Matthew ("the poor" and "Kingdom of Heaven") and Luke ("yours") in his adaptation of the Beatitude from Matthew 5:3 and Luke 6:20. Other indications that these Gospels are adaptations of the canonical tradition are offered, pp. 255–64.

[20]The earlier conclusion of Joachim Jeremias that there was a "very small residue of [isolated] sayings in the case of which content, form and attestation justify the opinion that they stand on a level with the sayings of our Lord (themselves historically of very differing value) contained in our four Gospels" (Joachim Jeremias, "Isolated Sayings of the Lord," in the earlier edition of *New Testament Apocrypha* [Schneemelcher] vol. 1, p. 87) has been reduced in the revised edition of that work to four sayings which are "not derivative in terms of tradition history" (*New Testament Apocrypha*,

rev. ed. by W. Schneemelcher [trans. R. McL. Wilson; Cambridge and
Louisville, KY: James Clarke, and Westminster/John Knox, 1991],
pp. 88–90).

[21]A survey of this process of development of the gospel tradition is offered by
Helmut Koester in *Ancient Christian Gospels* (Philadelphia: Trinity Press
International, 1990). A comprehensive analysis of the development of the
noncanonical gospel tradition is set out in *New Testament Apocrypha*, 2
vols., ed. W. Schneemelcher (trans. R. McL. Wilson; Cambridge: James
Clarke, 1991).

[22]A concise discussion of the causes of error in the transmission of the text of the
New Testament is provided by B.M. Metzger, *The Text of the New
Testament* (Oxford: Oxford University Press, 1964), pp. 186–206. Although
Metzger takes into account unconscious (p. 193) and conscious (p. 197)
harmonization of the various gospel accounts, he does not seem to allow
for another important factor that contributed to the rise of textual variants:
the continuing influence of oral tradition after the Gospels were available
in written form. Presumably, copyists introduced into the text variants that
they recalled and preferred to the version in their master copy, based on
the authority of living memory rather than on the written record, even
though producing written records was the source of their own livelihood.

[23]The question of alterations of the text of the Gospels was treated in an illuminating way by C.S.C. Williams, *Alterations of the Words of Jesus As Quoted
in the Literature of the Second Century* (Cambridge, MA: Harvard
University Press, 1952).

[24]The recently heightened attention to the other Gospels is evident not only in
the multiple publications of the texts (as in the new edition of the *New
Testament Apocrypha* [Cambridge: James Clarke, 1991]), but also in the
analyses of these sources, ranging from the popular appeal approach of
Robert Funk in *The Five Gospels* (New York: Macmillan, 1993) to the more
scholarly strategy of Helmut Koester in *Ancient Christian Gospels*
(Philadelphia: Trinity Press International, 1990).

[25]See pp. 260–64.

[26]The Lukan and Matthean infancy stories were themselves influenced by the
legends that arose from pious speculation about Jesus' birth. Such speculation produced accounts of miracles attending his birth and of his miraculous
powers, even as a child, that are similar to stories which developed over the
centuries about Buddha, Osiris, and other divinely endowed figures.

[27]From the translation by Oscar Cullmann in Schneemelcher, *New Testament
Apocrypha*, rev. ed., vol. 1, p. 427.

[28]From the translation by Cullmann in Schneemelcher, *New Testament
Apocrypha*, rev. ed., p. 446.

[29]One aspect of the intention in the Infancy Gospel of Thomas to heighten the
supernatural qualities of Jesus—attributing to him occult knowledge—is
discussed in this chapter in connection with the Gnostic Gospels on
p. 258.

[30]Mentioned in Eusebius, *Ecclesiastical History* 1.9.3., Kirsopp Lake, in notes to
the Loeb edition (Cambridge, MA: Harvard University Press, 1957),
remarks that the Acts of Pilate were "introduced in the time of the great

persecution under Maximin" (i.e., Maximinus Daia, who bore the title of Caesar in the East from C.E. 305 to 312).

[31] Eusebius, *Ecclesiastical History* 9.5.1. The Acts of Pilate, with their anti-Christian polemic, were to be "exhibited openly for everyone to see in every place, both town and country, and . . . the primary teachers should give them to the children, instead of lessons, for study and commital to memory" (from the translation by H.J. Lawlor and J.E.L. Oulton, *The Ecclesiastical History and the Martyrs of Palestine* [London: Macmillan, 1927–1928; reprint, 1954]).

[32] A full account is given in Eusebius, *Concerning the Palestine Martyrs* 9.2–3 (from the translation by Lawlor and Oulton). Even the pagan populace was revolted by Maximinus' cruelty (9.9–12).

[33] Confirmation of the trial is given in Justin's *First Apology*, Chapter 35; corroboration of the miracles is implied in Chapter 48 (in *Fathers of the Church*, vol. 6 [New York: Christian Heritage, 1949]).

[34] See for example Felix Scheidweiler, "The Gospel of Nicodemus, Acts of Pilate, Descent into Hell," in Schneemelcher, *New Testament Apocrypha*, rev. ed., vol. 1, pp. 501–504, on whose analysis the argument set forth here depends.

[35] In *Four Other Gospels: Shadows on the Contours of the Canon* (Minneapolis: Winston Press, 1985), pp. 127–29.

[36] An older, still useful study of this question is offered in R.H. Lightfoot, *Locality and Doctrine in the Gospels* (New York: Harper Brothers, 1938). For Luke, Jerusalem is of prime symbolic significance, since it is from this center of the life and worship of the traditional covenant people that the world mission of the church is to begin (Luke 24:47), reaching out to the center of the civilized world, Rome (Acts 1:8; 28:11–31).

[37] From the translation by Cullmann in Schneemelcher, *New Testament Apocrypha*, rev. ed., vol. 1, p. 447.

[38] Dated to the middle of the second century by H.C. Puech, "Gnostic Gospels and Related Documents," in Schneemelcher, *New Testament Apocrypha*, vol. 1, p. 330. In the revised edition of *New Testament Apocrypha*, vol. 1, p. 287, D. Kirchner infers from the fact that this work shares some subject matter with New Testament Gospels and letters that it may have been written in the later first century C.E., but the second century date is in fact more plausible. See Puech, pp. 314–31.

[39] *New Testament Apocrypha*, rev. ed., vol. 1, p. 293.

[40] *New Testament Apocrypha*, rev. ed., vol. 1, p. 296.

[41] All quotations from the Gospel of Thomas are from *New Testament Apocrypha*, rev. ed., vol. 1, pp. 117–29.

[42] See A.F.J. Klijn, *The Acts of Thomas: Introduction, Text, Commentary* (New York: Humanities Press, 1962). The third-century dating is suggested on p. 26.

[43] In Chapter 39 the colt of an ass addresses Thomas in a manner reminiscent of Balaam's ass (Num. 22), but instead of offering reproof, the colt acclaims Thomas: "Twin of the Messiah, and apostle of the Most High, and sharer in the hidden word of the Life-giver, and receiver of the secret-mysteries of the Son of God" (Klijn, ibid., p. 85).

[44]The enumeration of the mysteries—up to twenty-four—is given in the Gnostic document Pistis Sophia, also from the early third century, which claims to be a report of Jesus' secret teaching during an eleven-year period after his resurrection. See H.C. Puech in Schneemelcher, *New Testament Apocrypha*, vol. 1, pp. 250–53. The text of Pistis Sophia is given in W.O. Till's revision of Carl Schmidt, *Koptisch-gnostische Schriften* [Coptic-gnostic writings], 2d ed. (Berlin: Akademie Verlag, 1954).

[45]In addition to Koester and Crossan who, as noted above, think that the Gospel of Thomas is based on sources which antedate the canonical Gospels, Marvin W. Meyer quotes with approval the statement of J.D. Crossan (in *The Historical Jesus: The Life of a Mediterranean Jewish Peasant* [San Francisco: HarperCollins, 1991] that Jesus was a "peasant Jewish Cynic" (in *The Gospel of Thomas: The Hidden Sayings of Jesus* [San Francisco: HarperCollins, 1992]). Meyer goes on to describe Cynics as "social critics and popular philosophers who lived a simple life and employed sharp, witty sayings in order to make people raise questions about their own lives" (17). It is revealing that in an epilogue to Meyer's work, Harold Bloom makes the same assessment of this gospel, adding that it is appropriate that the chief scholars to have discerned this are Americans, who share in the contemporary cultural inclination to radical individualism and iconoclasm toward tradition. *The Gospel of Thomas* does not engage in witty sayings, however, but in occult pronouncements which offer a radically dualistic view of the world, of a variety that has its explicit formulation in the Gnostic writings of the second and subsequent centuries. A recent balanced assessment of this evidence by Beate Blatz deduces that half the sayings have parallels in the synoptic Gospels, while many of them are Gnostic in content, and that the work was given its present form in mid-second-century eastern Syria (*New Testament Apocrypha*, rev. ed., vol. 1, pp. 112–13).

[46]*Oxyrhynchus Papyri*, vol. 4 (London: Egypt Exploration Fund, 1903), pp. 1–22; also in Grenfell and Hunt, *New Sayings of Jesus and Fragment of a Lost Gospel from Oxyrhynchus* (London: H. Frowde, 1904).

[47]*The Sayings of Jesus from Oxyrhynchus* (Cambridge: Cambridge University Press, 1920).

[48]*Unknown Sayings of Jesus*, 2d ed. (trans. R.H. Fuller; London: SPCK, 1964).

[49]J.A. Fitzmyer, "The Oxyrhynchus Logoi of Jesus and the Coptic Gospel According to Thomas," *Theological Studies* 20 (1959): 505–560.

[50]In contrast to Koester, Crossan, and others. Christopher Tuckett, in his study *Nag Hammadi and the Gospel Tradition* (Edinburgh: T.&T. Clark, 1986) concludes that there is "no firm evidence for the use of presynoptic sources (Q or otherwise) in these [Nag Hammadi] texts" (9), and the closest kinship of these documents is with the Gospel of Matthew. Although he withholds judgment as to whether this conclusion applies to the Gospel of Thomas also, it seems to be true of this writing as well.

[51]This saying is dependent on Luke 8:16, rather than on the more original parallel in Matthew 5:15, as Jeremias has shown (*The Parables of Jesus*, 6th ed. [trans. S.H. Hooke; New York: Scribner's, 1963], pp. 26–27). Luke's

version presupposes a house with a lighted vestibule, whereas Matthew faithfully portrays a one-room Palestinian house in which a single light can be seen throughout.

[52]See H.C. Kee, "'Becoming a Child' in the Gospel of Thomas," *Journal of Biblical Literature* 82 (1963): 307–14.

[53]"The 'Single One' in the Gospel of Thomas," *Journal of Biblical Literature* 81 (1962): 271–78.

[54]Kee, "'Becoming a Child' in the Gospel of Thomas." My interpretation of this text is simply dismissed rather than rationally refuted by H. Koester and J.M. Robinson in *Trajectories Through Early Christianity* (Philadelphia: Fortress Press, 1971), p. 174.

[55]So Jeremias, *The Parables of Jesus*, p. 224.

[56]Compare Logion 4: "Jesus said: The man old in days will not hesitate to ask a little child of seven days about the place *(topos)* of Life, and he will live."

[57]In the Acts of Thomas (Chapters 6 and 7) a hymn to the church (probably based on a Jewish hymn to Wisdom; see Klijn's commentary, *The Acts of Thomas*, p. 164) describes the Celestial Female, whose hands "proclaim the *place* of life" (lines 19–20), which is interpreted in the next line to mean heaven.

[58]This opinion about Marcion's single gospel was held by Adolf von Harnack in *Geschichte der altchristlichen Literatur* [The history of early Christian literature], vol. 1, part 1 (Leipzig: J.C. Hinrichs, 1893–1904), p. 195, and is simply assumed by Kümmel, *Introduction to the New Testament*, p. 486.

[59]This is the theory about Marcion's "gospel" advanced in F.C. Burkitt's treatment of Marcion in *Cambridge Ancient History*, vol. 12 (Cambridge: Cambridge University Press, 1939), pp. 452–55.

[60]Ibid., p. 453.

[61]See for example John Knox, *Marcion and the New Testament* (Chicago: University of Chicago Press, 1942).

[62]See for example Paul Kahle, *The Cairo Genizah* (Oxford: Oxford University Press, 1947), p. 279. Marcion is not included, however, in Adolf von Harnack's list of the three most important figures at Edessa in his *The Mission and Expansion of Christianity in the First Three Centuries*, rev. ed., vol. 2 (trans. and ed. James Moffatt; New York: Putnam's, 1908), pp. 292–300.

[63]A brief account of this discovery, with a translation of the fragment, is given by B.M. Metzger in *The Text of the New Testament*, pp. 90–91. Earlier, F.C. Burkitt had suggested (in *Cambridge Ancient History*, vol. 12, p. 494) that Tatian's original Diatessaron was in Latin; his chief argument apparently was that the oldest manuscripts of the Diatessaron are Latin versions, for example the Codex Fuldensis, prepared in the middle of the sixth century by Victor of Capua and based on an earlier harmony, which he correctly associated with Tatian. The codex found its way to Fulda, in Germany, apparently by way of England, whence it was taken back to the continent by Boniface or one of his fellow Saxon missionaries in the eighth century.

[64]Details can be found in Metzger, *The Text of the New Testament*, p. 91, esp. n. 1.

[65]H.W. Hogg in *The Ante-Nicene Fathers*, vol. 9 (New York: Christian Literature, 1896), pp. 35–138. Also the translation by J.H. Hill, *The Earliest Life of Christ* (Edinburgh: T. & T. Clark, 1894).

[66]Irenaeus, *Against Heresies* 1.28.1.

[67]See Metzger, *The Text of the New Testament*, p. 89.

[68]From the translation of Theodoret's *On Heresies* by Rendel Harris in his *Diatessaron of Tatian* (London: Clay & Sons, 1890), p. 13.

[69]See for example Origen, *Contra Celsum* 1.28 (from the edition by Henry Chadwick [Cambridge: Cambridge University Press, 1965]).

[70]Ibid., 1.40–41.

[71]Ibid., 1.42.

[72]See J.H. Charlesworth, "Tatian's Dependence upon Apocryphal Traditions," *Heythrop Journal* 15 (1974): 5–17.

[73]From Hill's translation in *The Earliest Life of Christ*.

[74]See for example Charlesworth, in "Tatian's Dependence upon Apocryphal Traditions."

[75]Paul Kahle, *The Cairo Genizah*, pp. 297–301.

[76]See for example B.M. Metzger, *Chapters in the History of New Testament Textual Criticism* (Grand Rapids, MI: Eerdmans, 1963), pp. 99–100.

[77]Kahle, *The Cairo Genizah*, p. 295.

[78]See Will Krogman, "Heliand, Tatian, und Thomasevangelium" [Heliand, Tatian, and the Gospel of Thomas], *Zeitschrift für die neutestamentliche Wissenschaft* [Journal for New Testament Study] 51 (1960): 255–68, in contrast to Gilles Quispel, "Some Remarks on the Gospel of Thomas," *New Testament Studies* 5 (1959): 276–90.

[79]See H.K. McArthur, *The Quest Through the Centuries* (Philadelphia: Fortress, 1966). On Augustine, see pp. 49–55; on Calvin, see pp. 97–99.

[80]A perceptive and comprehensive description of the rise of critical methods in New Testament study is that of W.G. Kümmel, *The New Testament: The History of the Investigation of Its Problems* (trans. S.M. Gilmour and H.C. Kee; New York: Abingdon, 1972). A valuable survey of the present state of critical methods, with basic bibliography, is *The New Testament in Its Literary Environment*, by David E. Aune (Philadelphia: Westminster Press, 1987).

[81]See my discussion of these methods and issues in *Christian Origins in Sociological Perspective* (Philadelphia: Westminster Press, 1980) and in *Knowing the Truth: A Sociological Approach to New Testament Interpretation* (Minneapolis: Fortress Press, 1989). New edition forthcoming from Trinity Press International, 1996.

Positive and Negative Results of the Search for Jesus in History

The most gratifying product of research is the achievement of spectacular new findings. Equally important, however—though often painful for the researcher—are the identification and acknowledgment of inappropriate methods and unattainable goals. This is as true of research in the field of Jesus in history as of intellectual inquiry in any other field.

Discovering Inappropriate Methods and Unattainable Goals

As this book demonstrates, it is inappropriate to seek to reconstruct the life of Jesus, tracing the development of his thought and his sense of mission, either by harmonizing the divergent gospel accounts or by choosing one gospel as a basic biographical framework and treating the others as supplements. Friedrich Daniel Ernst Schleiermacher (1768–1834) tried the second procedure using John; Heinrich Julius Holtzmann (1832–1910) using Mark; and Albert Schweitzer (1875–1965) using Matthew. All three men produced works that are remarkable in their own way but none of the results are wholly satisfactory accounts of the life of Jesus or of what was distinctive about his ministry. Attempts at this kind of inclusive reconstruction fail because each of the evangelists arranged the gospel material in sequences determined by the dogmatic aims and values of his community rather than by simple historical recollection or biographical interest. Since the sequence of events in Mark—demonstrably the oldest of the Gospels—unfolds as much by a dogma of apocalyptic determination

of history as by actual historical recollection, it would be method-
ologically unsound to adopt it or any of the later Gospels as an objec-
tively historical base for reconstructing the career of Jesus.

Some scholars, recognizing that they cannot achieve historical
certainty either by selecting one gospel as normative or by harmonizing the differences among the four, have turned to a reductionist
approach: They extract from the gospel tradition certain elements
that they believe can be proved authentic through the application of
a formula. Sometimes the formula is one of multiple attestation, rest-
ing on the assumption that an event or a saying reported in more than
one strand of the tradition—in Mark and Q, for example—is likely
to be authentic. This formula can be useful in evaluating the gospel
tradition, but only when it is employed in conjunction with methods
other than a purely literary separation of strands of tradition. Mark
and Q both include material that in its present form reflects the situation of the early church rather than providing objective information about Jesus, so the mere fact of dual attestation proves nothing
about the actual course of Jesus' life. The degree of probability that
we are dealing with authentic material is increased, however, by
employing the form-critical method, especially when it is correlated
with attention to the social setting of the gospel writer and his community, as has been undertaken in the analyses of the material offered
previously in Chapters 2 to 8.

Another formula of authenticity proposes a *via negativa:*
Whatever in the tradition can be explained as originating in the early
church or as taken over by the tradition from Judaism is to be
regarded as inauthentic.[1] This criterion is weak, however, because it
presupposes a more complete discontinuity between Jesus and
Judaism on the one hand and between Jesus and the early church on
the other than may actually have been the case.[2] Since the tradition
portrays Jesus as a critic speaking to Judaism from within, it would
be surprising if his teaching did not take over from Judaism a great
deal relatively unchanged. Similarly, although it must be acknowledged that the impact of the cross and the growth of the resurrection faith transformed Jesus' followers' understanding of him, it is not
necessary to assume that the early church simultaneously transformed
all facets of the message attributed to him or its recollection of events
in his public activity. One would expect, on the contrary, considerable carryover from the message and ministry of Jesus to that of the
early church. The changes that occurred were frequently modifications, not always innovations.

Another kind of formula that has been advanced requires the establishment of a formal thought structure to serve as a distinctive clue to the authentic words of Jesus. One of the axioms adopted by both the Jesus Seminar and the International Q Seminar, for example, is that the real Jesus spoke in wisdom sayings, similar to the wisdom traditions of Israel, as in Proverbs and later Jewish wisdom literature (Sir.; Wisd. of Sol.). The model contemporary to his own time to which he conformed, it is said, is that of the Cynic-Stoic itinerant philosophers, whose characteristic utterances are said to have been clever, timeless wisdom pronouncements. Thus Robert Funk has summarized the results of the Jesus Seminar: The historical Jesus will be "found in those fragments of tradition that bear the imprint of orality: short, provocative, memorable, oft-repeated phrases, sentences and stories."[3] Jesus spoke in parables and aphorisms, but the reports of his conflicts with the Pharisees and scribes are the product of the church in the post-70 period, after Jesus had become its supreme authority. None of the sayings of Jesus in relation to any of the miracles stories, as in Mark 5–6, are authentic, since "they are not particularly memorable, are not aphorisms or parables, and would not have circulated independently during the oral period. They cannot, therefore, be traced back to Jesus."[4] The story of Jesus' transfiguration is "a Christian fabrication," and all the sayings of Jesus given in Mark 9:33 to 10:12 are products of the early church.[5] All Jesus' statements concerning his mission ("I have come") and any references to an apocalyptic age to come are inauthentic, and so is all of the Lord's Prayer except the opening phrase, "Our Father."[6] The application of these principles in this scholarly group is erratic, however. For example, the absence of parallels to the sayings of Jesus in Luke 4 is taken as proof that they are not from Jesus, but the Parable of the Good Samaritan, the Lost Son, and the Lost Coin, which are also found only in Luke, are acclaimed as genuine.[7] There is one basic conceptual assumption: Jesus was nonapocalyptic. He conceived God's rule as all around him, but difficult to discern, and had a poetic sense in which present and future melted into each other. The more prosaic and apocalyptic view of Paul is what triumphed in the church, unfortunately, in Funk's view. Pronounced authentic are the major parables, which are said to be nonapocalyptic, and the sayings and parables of Jesus which speak of the present kingdom. All sayings and parables concerning the future are the invention of the early church.[8]

The criterion by which all apocalyptic references are dismissed as inauthentic is actually false on both logical and historical grounds.

Logically, it is simply assumed at the outset, and then the evidence is evaluated and conformed to this assumption. Historically, it ignores the fact that, as we have noted,[9] the Cynic-Stoic tradition which is appealed to as the model for the teaching of Jesus did not in fact consist solely of timeless wisdom pronouncements, but instead had a major concern for human moral accountability to the gods, envisioning a future judgment to be followed by a cosmic renewal and a new order. The details of the expectations differed from those of apocalyptic Judaism and the Jesus tradition, but precisely the same human issues were addressed in both and the solutions envisioned were formally remarkably similar.[10] In their evident desire to rid Jesus of what they regard as an embarrassing outlook on future judgment and cosmic renewal, they defy not only logic but also clear historical evidence.

It is true that the contrast between present difficulty and future deliverance is a characteristic of the teaching of Jesus throughout the gospel tradition, but both terms used (for example, the coming of the Son of Man "in the glory of his Father with the holy angels," Mark 8:38) and the syntax of Jesus' sentences ("Blessed are you that weep now, for you shall laugh," Luke 6:21) point unambiguously to an event in the chronological future of the world when, as we are told by Jesus' total eschatological message, the whole order of life will be transformed by God's direct action. Not all of Jesus' eschatological sayings refer to the present, as is true of Luke's (more original) version of the Lord's Prayer:[11] "Father, hallowed be your name. Your kingdom come" (11:2). But both Luke and Matthew's versions of the familiar prayer are clearly eschatological in outlook. On the other hand, some sayings of Jesus are eschatological only implicitly and contain no direct mention of the future, as when he declares, "If it is by the finger of God that I cast out demons, then the kingdom of God has come upon you" (Luke 11:20). Robinson's analysis is therefore inappropriate on two counts: (1) Not all the sayings of Jesus that are eschatological in intent contain direct references to present and future; and (2) whether explicit or implicit, the eschatological element is always focused on the chronological future, when the promised fulfillment will occur and the creation will be renewed. Furthermore, it is precisely in gospel sayings such as John 5:24, in which the temporal distinction (between this age and the age to come) has been replaced by a material contrast (between life apart from faith and life in faith), that we can be certain we are dealing with formulations of the early church and not with authentic sayings of

Jesus. At times the formal structure of contrast between present and future proves to be a mark of Jesus' teaching, but it is only one criterion among several and is not reliable when used apart from other critical methods.

Positive Results

Martin Kähler was correct in asserting that it is the biblical picture of Jesus as the Christ that has had the transforming impact on lives down through the history of the church. And Paul Tillich was justified in taking over this aspect of his teacher's theological view of the church's understanding of Jesus. However, this position ultimately deprives the church of the richness of interpretive diversity that is a proper part of its heritage: Failing to take with full theological seriousness the diverse pictures of Jesus represented in the biblical tradition, the analyst of the gospel tradition must either settle for a monochrome portrait, painted by conscious or unconscious harmonization of its diversities, or adopt one perspective—usually that of the Pauline kerygma—and force the gospel tradition to conform to that view of Jesus.

On the other hand, when modern serious students of the Gospels take into account the range of understandings of Jesus that critical study has shown to exist within the Jesus tradition as preserved in the New Testament and elsewhere in early Christian literature, the real diversity of interpretive structures for "Jesus in history" becomes evident. Understanding Jesus at various stages in the development of the gospel tradition provides insight into interpretations of him that have not been taken up by the mainstream of the church or that have been obscured by subsequent developments in christological formulations.

Essential to this kind of analysis is a method which builds on insights from sociology, and especially from sociology-of-knowledge, which recognizes that all human understanding and communication is shaped by the sociocultural world in which the individual lives and with which he or she shares perceptions, values, hopes, and fears. These understandings and points of view are simply taken for granted, often tacitly, but at times asserted, as is evident in contemporary clichés, such as "Y' know" and "You know what I mean."[12] The task of the historian is to analyze the gospel texts with the aim of discerning the basic view of the world, the assumptions about God,

Jesus, humanity, good and evil, and the divine purpose at work in the world. In Judaism of the first century, in the wider Greco-Roman world, and by extension among the early followers of Jesus, there was no single worldview which dominated. That diversity is reflected in all the documents from that period and must be taken into account if they are to be interpreted accurately and in an historically responsible way. The alternative is to impose current conceptual preferences on the evidence, as current interpreters continue to do when they select from the records those features which they find intellectually compatible with their own outlook.[13] Careful analysis of the Gospels, in light of the range of backgrounds from which they originated, can help one to understand the divergences within the evidence, but at the same time to discern the common features and the process of evolution through which this material has passed.

This mode of critical analysis can bring to light ways in which earlier understandings of Jesus were reformulated as a result of special interests already at work in the church before the tradition became fixed in the form of the canonical Gospels, including differentiation between older and later forms of the Jesus tradition. Although the older forms stand closer to the event of Jesus than do the later ones, there is no absolute guarantee that what is old is also authentic. Nevertheless, critics can extrapolate backward along the lines that they can trace in the development of the tradition and arrive at some general features that seem to have originated with Jesus of Nazareth. In some cases this process will be aided by converging lines of tradition. In other instances the distinctiveness of what is attributed to Jesus from what is known to have been taught by Judaism or by the early church will provide additional evidence. The fact that the church did not pick up on certain themes that remain embedded in the tradition serves as a clue that these undeveloped strands of the tradition may not be the creation of the church's faith but perhaps go back to Jesus. In that case they would have a right to consideration as more nearly authentic than those that the church exploited or modified for its own theological ends. For example, the coming Son of Man words, which do not accord well with either Mark's emphasis on the earthly Jesus as Son of Man or with Paul's failure to use the title are now widely thought by scholars to be authentic sayings of Jesus. And growing knowledge of the Jewish world of Jesus' day sheds new light on certain elements of the gospel tradition and heightens the probability of the authenticity of certain puzzling or little understood features. An instance of this is the correlation between the term (usually translated "rebuke") used for Jesus' performance of exorcisms and the eschatological expectations at Qumran.[14]

But what are the specific historical results from the critical assessment of the gospel tradition? Admittedly, we are dealing with probabilities, and the results are subject to modification in light of new insights. But a consistent picture does emerge.

Jesus appeared on the Palestinian scene as an itinerant teacher, probably self-taught, so that there was deep resentment of his authoritative manner among the official religious leadership of Palestine. He held his central mission to be the announcement of the imminent coming of God's Kingdom, and he regarded his extraordinary powers of healing and exorcism as evidence that the powers of the Kingdom were already breaking into the present situation. He sought to call together a band of followers who by repentance would prepare themselves for the impending event, and he therefore offered a severe critique of Israel and new criteria for acceptance within the membership of the covenant community. He interpreted the Law in a radical way that challenged the authority of its official interpreters.[15] The impetus for the redefinition of the people of God is likely to have come as a consequence of his associations with John the Baptist, although he parted company with John, probably on the issue of Jesus' conviction that the Kingdom was open to sinners and religious outcasts who truly repented. At the same time, Jesus refused to join with the political insurrectionist movements of his time, which sought to establish God's rule by their own militant initiative. Ironically, it was through the false charge that he was a political revolutionary that he was put to death by the Romans—a charge brought by the religious leaders whose authority his pronouncements seemed to threaten. His method of teaching was characterized as to content by eschatological pronouncement, and as to form by parable and reinterpretation of the Law, of the prophets, and of Jewish religious institutions. It is likely that he came to realize that the path he had set out on would lead to death, though we have no way of knowing when he came to this conclusion or whether he sought to force the issue. His metaphorical references to the "baptism" and the "cup" in Mark 10, and to the impossibility of drinking the cup until the coming of the Kingdom of God (Mark 14:25), suggest that he expected both death and ultimate vindication. Similarly, his reference to himself as "a glutton and a drunkard"— epithets that the early church would scarcely have invented!—imply vividly that, like the disobedient child whose parents ask to have him put to death (Deut. 21:18–20), the leaders of the community were going to execute him. But this is not to say he explicitly predicted his Passion and Resurrection, as the gospel tradition later reported. The tradition faithfully points to the genuineness of his anxiety in the face of death, even though it was starting to attribute to the earthly Jesus certain divine features, and even though the whole of the tradition was placed in a new framework of meaning by the resurrection faith.

What we are dealing with in the gospel tradition is not objective historical evidence that has become overlaid with the claims of Christian faith, but with evidence that in its entirety stems from the witness of faith at various stages of development, beginning with the original hearers of Jesus. Critical analysis of the tradition enables us to differentiate between earlier and later stages of the faith and provides us our best—indeed, almost our only—clues to the personal life that evoked that faith. Such study helps us to achieve a modest but significant goal: to discern how diverse were the ways in which the tradition about Jesus was appropriated in the period from the history of Jesus in his own time to the history of Jesus in the church and the modern world.

Suggestions for Further Reading

A useful survey of the Gospels and the evidence about Jesus is found in Graham N. Stanton, *The Gospels and Jesus* [Oxford Bible Series] (Oxford and New York: Oxford University Press, 1989). A fine nontechnical discussion of the historical issues relating to our knowledge of Jesus is *Jesus and the Constraints of History* by A.E. Harvey (London: Duckworth, 1982). Analysis of the New Testament material by the method of community identity is offered in my *Who Are the People of God? Early Christian Models of Community* (New Haven: Yale University Press, 1995). A nontechnical survey of the Roman, Jewish, and early Christian evidence for the historical Jesus is offered in my *What Can We Know About Jesus?* (Cambridge: Cambridge: Cambridge University Press, 1990).

Older studies of the historical Jesus question which continue to be valuable include Hugh Anderson, *Jesus and Christian Origins* (New York: Oxford University Press, 1964); Günther Bornkamm, *Jesus of Nazareth** (New York: Harper Brothers, 1961); and Geza Vermes,

Jesus the Jew (London: Collins, 1973). A readable survey of the historical evidence about Jesus accessible to nonspecialists, but reflecting current scholarly insights, including those of J.D. Crossan, R.W. Funk, B.L. Mack and the Jesus Seminar, is Marcus J. Borg, *Jesus: A New Vision: Spirit, Culture, and the Life of Discipleship** (San Francisco: Harper & Row, 1987).

*Available in a paperback edition.

NOTES

[1]Ernst Käsemann, "The Problem of the Historical Jesus," in his *Essays on New Testament Themes* (Naperville, IL: Allenson, 1964), p. 44. See Norman Perrin's discussion of criteria for authenticity of Jesus' sayings in *The New Testament: An Introduction*, 3d ed. (Fort Worth: Harcourt Brace, 1994).

[2]For appreciative comment on Käsemann's criterion, and for development of other possible criteria, see Norman Perrin, *Rediscovering the Teaching of Jesus* (New York: Harper & Row, 1976), pp. 39–43.

[3]Robert W. Funk, *The Five Gospels* (New York: Macmillan, 1993), p. 5.

[4]Ibid., pp. 62–69.

[5]Ibid., pp. 81–88.

[6]Ibid., pp. 137, 148–49, 342.

[7]Ibid., pp. 354–358.

[8]Ibid., p. 137.

[9]Pp. 78–79.

[10]James M. Robinson's earlier study of this theme in the Gospels ("The Formal Structure of Jesus' Message," in *Current Issues in New Testament Interpretation*, ed. William Klassen and M.F. Snyder [New York: Harper & Row, 1962]) came to a similarly unsatisfactory conclusion: that "the eschatological message of Jesus is directed to an eschatological understanding of existence in the present." Under the influence of R. Bultmann's existentialist interpretation of Jesus' message as primarily a call of the individual to decision, Robinson arbitrarily transformed not only the gospel evidence but even the technical term, *eschatology*, from its significance as analysis of the future of the cosmos to an understanding of the present of the individual.

[11]Matthew's version (Matt. 6:9–13), which came to be used down through the history of the church, seems to have been adapted along liturgical lines, at both the beginning ("Our Father, you are in heaven") and in the longer ending added in later manuscripts of Matthew ("for yours is the kingdom . . .").

[12]I have laid out the origins and implications of the historical method derived from sociology-of-knowledge in *Knowing the Truth: A Sociological Approach to New Testament Interpretation* (Minneapolis: Fortress Press, 1989). Second edition forthcoming in 1996 from Trinity Press International.

[13]Ironically, R.W. Funk warns in the opening section of *The Five Gospels* (p. 5) that "The last temptation is to create Jesus in our own image, to marshal the facts to support preconceived conviction." Yet this is precisely what are the results of the Jesus Seminar, in spite of the announced aim "To make empirical, factual evidence, evidence open to confirmation by independent, neutral observers—the controlling factor in historical judgments" (p. 34). In the face of this self-contradicting enterprise in the name of historical investigation, one can only hope that the conclusions reached by the few dozen members of the Jesus Seminar do not, as claimed (p. 35), represent the kind of scholarship "that has come to prevail in all the great universities of the world."

[14]See my discussion of exorcism terminology in "The Terminology of St. Mark's Exorcism Stories," *New Testament Studies* 14 (1968): 232–46; and more recently in *Medicine, Miracle and Magic in New Testament Times* (Cambridge: Cambridge University Press, 1986, 1990), pp. 24–25, 77–80.

[15]The dynamic theme of Jesus' critique of the dominant Jewish interpreters of the Law is explored in illuminating ways by J. Andrew Overman in *Matthew's Gospel and Formative Judaism: The Social World of the Matthean Community* (Minneapolis: Fortress Press, 1990); and by Anthony J. Saldarini in *Matthew's Christian-Jewish Community* (Chicago: University of Chicago Press, 1994).

A Classification System for the Synoptic Tradition

The nomenclature used by the originators of the form-critical method for classification of the gospel tradition (Rudolf Bultmann and Martin Dibelius) raised unintended and unnecessary difficulties for at least two reasons: (1) The terminology derived from classical literature conveys little meaning to the modern reader; and (2) the terms, or the translation of them, imply certain historical judgments that are inappropriate in what purports to be a formal classification system. Examples of the first type are "Apophthegms" and "Chriae"; examples of tendentious terms are "Tales" and "Myths." Perhaps some readers will find that the classification proposed here is subject to similar criticisms, but the terms employed are standard English. And they are used without prejudice to historicity.

More important, perhaps, is the fact that in literary analysis a sharp distinction is not possible between form and function. Some detractors of form-critical method have sought to show that the classification systems are not purely formal, as though that were a fatal flaw. But the use of form-critical method in the present work lays stress on a factor to which Bultmann and Dibelius gave little more than lip service: the social and cultural functions of the tradition. The vital questions to be asked are (1) What was the tradition as the evangelist found it in his sources? and then (2) What function did it serve in the community context where it was preserved? and finally, (3) What function has it been made to serve as reflected in the adaptation of the tradition?

In the following classificatory scheme no attempt is made to include all the synoptic material under one of the groupings; rather, a sufficiently wide range of material is provided to suggest the main categories and to illustrate them. In a few cases, examples are offered from noncanonical sources, such as the Oxyrynchus Papyri (Oxy.) and the Gnostic Gospel of Thomas.

Sayings Tradition

1. *Aphorisms*, or *Proverbial Sayings*

   Mark 4:9
   Thos. 24
   Matt. 13:43
   Luke 14:35b
   Mark 4:25 = Matt. 25:29; Luke 19:26
   Mark 9:35
   Mark 10:43 = Luke 22:26; Matt. 20:26
   Mark 10:15 = Luke 18:1; Matt. 18:3, (cf. John 3:5); Thos. 37, 46
   Matt. 10:39 = Luke 17:33; Matt. 16:25; Mark 8:35; Luke 9:24
       (John 12:25)
   Matt. 10:33 = Luke 12:9; Mark 8:38; Luke 9:26
   Matt. 10:26 = Luke 12:2; Mark 4:22; Luke 8:17; (1 Cor. 4:5?);
       Thos. 5; Oxy. 654
   Luke 17:20–21
   Luke 13:30–Mark 10:31; Matt. 19:30; 20:16

2. *Parables*

   Mark 4:1–8
   Mark 4:30–32
   Matt. 13:33
   Mark 4:26–29
   Matt. 13:47–48
   Matt. 18:12–13 = Luke 15:3–6
   Matt. 18:23–33
   Luke 10:29–37; 12:16–20; 14:15–23 = Matt. 22:1–10; Thos. 64

3. *Sayings Clusters*

   a. *Topical groupings*

      Matt. 5:13 = Luke 14:34–35 (Salt)
      Matt. 5:15–16 = Luke 11:33; Mark 4:21 (Light)
      Matt. 5:17–20 (Law)
      Mark 13:33–37 (Watchfulness)
      Mark 2:18–20 (Fasting)
      Mark 2:21–22 (Old and New)

Matt. 10:26–31 = Luke 12:2–7 (Freedom from Fear)
Matt. 10:37–38 = Luke 14:26–27 (Discipleship)
Matt. 11:7–19 = Luke 7:24–35 and 16:16 (John the Baptist)
Matt. 5:33–37 (Oaths)
Matt. 5:38–42 (cf. Luke 6:29–30) (Retaliation)
Luke 6:27–28, 32–36 = Matt. 5:43–48 (Love of Enemies)
Matt. 6:25–34; Luke 12:22–31 (Anxiety)
Matt. 7:1–5; Luke 6:37–38, 41–42 (Judging)
Matt. 19:1–12 = Mark 10:1–12 (cf. Matt. 5:34) (Marriage and Divorce)
Mark 4:10–12; 4:21–25 (Hidden and Revealed)
Mark 6:8–11 = Matt. 10:9–14; Luke 10:4–11 (Advice to Disciples)

b. *Formal groupings*

Matt. 5:3–12 = Luke 6:20–23 (Beatitudes)
Luke 6:24–26 (Woes)

(The parables of the Kingdom in Mark 4 = [Matt. 13] and the woes against the Pharisees in Mark 12:38–40 [= Matt. 23:1–36] exhibit a definite formal pattern and were probably preserved in the tradition in cluster form.)

Narrative Tradition

The terminology used for classifying the narrative tradition deserves some explanation:

Anecdote is used in the usual sense of a brief narrative, usually biographical, that reveals some unusual feature of the person described. The stories are short and lack biographical or chronological links with what is otherwise known of the person who is the subject of the anecdote.

Aphoristic narratives are brief accounts that culminate in a proverbial or pithy saying. The stories were probably not created as a vehicle for the saying, but they point up an issue to which the saying is a response.

Wonder stories are told to demonstrate the extraordinary powers of Jesus. They are often longer and provide more vivid detail than aphoristic narratives or anecdotes, including development of the situation along dramatic lines. On grounds other than form, the wonder stories of the synoptic tradition show the influence of the non-Christian miracle-story tradition, for example in the inclusion of thaumaturgic detail in the narratives of healing or exorcism (Mark 5:41; 7:34).

Legends are narratives which imply that a supernatural aura surrounds the central figure. The specific aim of a legend may be biographical or cultic. If biographical, it serves to amplify, illuminate, or enrich the christological significance of Jesus for the church, often closely correlating detail of the narrative with Old Testament predictions. If the aim is cultic, the narrative provides the background and therefore the authorization for the place of Jesus in the worship life of the Christian community. Thus baptism, the eucharist, and the christological interpretation of Scripture are all grounded in the ministry of Jesus by means of the cultic legends.

The *Passion narrative* is included here as a separate category of narrative, although with considerable reservation. There is good reason to question the older notion that the Passion story received a more nearly fixed form earlier than did the rest of the gospel tradition and that it served as the nucleus around which the rest of the tradition was later arranged. The Passion story itself does not appear to have been so unified as was once supposed by form critics, since Luke and Matthew felt free to introduce new material and to alter the substance of Mark's account, while John has a significantly different tradition. Mark's understanding of history and his community's interpretation of Scripture led him to modify the tradition about Jesus' trial and death to an extent that cannot now be determined with certainty but that must have been considerable. Furthermore, some scholars think that Luke had an independent passion narrative that he accommodated at some points to Mark's. John certainly had an independent tradition for his Passion story. But in at least one "gospel"—Q—there seems to have been no passion account at all. The probability is that as the Passion *kerygma* became dominant in the church's thinking, the Passion narrative was developed and expanded, partly on the basis of tradition units and partly on the basis of Christian reading of the Old Testament.

1. *Anecdotes*

    Mark 1:23–26 = Luke 4:33–35

Mark 1:29–31
Mark 2:1–4, 11–12
Mark 1:16–20 (cf. Luke 5:1–11)
Mark 1:40–44
Luke 7:18–23 = Matt. 11:2–6
Luke 19:1–10

2. *Aphoristic Narratives*

Mark 2:23–28
Mark 3:1–5
Mark 10:17–22
Mark 10:13–16

3. *Wonder Stories*

Mark 5:1–20
Mark 5:21–43
Mark 9:14–27
Mark 10:46–52
Luke 7:11–17

4. *Legends*

a. *Biographical legends*

Matt. 1:18–25 (Birth of Jesus)
Luke 2:1–20 (Birth of Jesus)
Luke 2:21–40 (Presentation in the Temple)
Mark 1:12–13; Matt. 4:1–11 (Temptation)
Mark 6:45–52 (Walking on the Water)
Mark 9:2–8 (Transfiguration)
Mark 10:35–45 (Baptism of Suffering)
Mark 14:12–16 (Preparation for the Passover)
Mark 14:34–42 (cf. Luke 22:43–44) (Prayer in
    Gethsemane)
Matt. 27:62–66 (Guard at the Tomb)
Matt. 28:2–4, 11–15 (Wonders Accompanying the
    Resurrection)
Luke 4:16–30 (Sermon and Rejection in Nazareth)
Luke 5:1–11 (Miraculous Catch of Fish)

b. *Cultic legends*

Mark 1:9–11 (cf. Matt. 3:14–15) (Baptism of Jesus)

Mark 6:30–44; Mark 8:1–10; John 6:1–13 (Eucharist)
Mark 14:22–25 (Lord's Supper)
Luke 24:13–35 (Christ's Presence in Word and Sacrament)

5. *Passion Narrative*

Mark 14:1–16:8 (= Matt. 26:1–28:10)
Luke 21:1–24:11
John 18:1–20:29

INDEX OF SUBJECTS

INDEX OF AUTHORS CITED